Information Communication Technologies for Human Services Education and Delivery:
Concepts and Cases

Jennifer Martin
RMIT, Australia

Linette Hawkins
RMIT, Australia

INFORMATION SCIENCE REFERENCE

Hershey · New York

Director of Editorial Content:	Kristin Klinger
Senior Managing Editor:	Jamie Snavely
Managing Editor:	Jeff Ash
Assistant Managing Editor:	Michael Brehm
Publishing Assistant:	Sean Woznicki
Typesetter:	Jeff Ash
Cover Design:	Lisa Tosheff
Printed at:	Yurchak Printing Inc.

Published in the United States of America by
    Information Science Reference (an imprint of IGI Global)
    701 E. Chocolate Avenue
    Hershey PA 17033
    Tel: 717-533-8845
    Fax: 717-533-8661
    E-mail: cust@igi-global.com
    Web site: http://www.igi-global.com/reference

Library of Congress Cataloging-in-Publication Data

Information communication technologies for human services education and delivery : concepts and cases / Jennifer Martin and Linette Hawkins, editors.
    p. cm.

Includes bibliographical references and index.
Summary: "This book covers main areas of education and practice of disciplines engaged in the human services, including policy, community work, community education, field education/ professional practicum, health promotion, individual and family work"--Provided by publisher.

ISBN 978-1-60566-735-5 (hardcover) -- ISBN 978-1-60566-736-2 (ebook) 1. Human services--Computer network resources. 2. Social service--Computer network resources. 3. Social service education--Computer network resources. I. Martin, Jennifer, 1959- II. Hawkins, Linette.
  HV29.2.I53 2010
  361.0068'3--dc22
                  2009007736

British Cataloguing in Publication Data
A Cataloguing in Publication record for this book is available from the British Library.

All work contributed to this book is new, previously-unpublished material. The views expressed in this book are those of the authors, but not necessarily of the publisher.

DEDICATION

To Lisa Harris in recognition of her commitment and innovation in online communities and social learning networks

Editorial Advisory Board

Table of Contents

Section 1
Information Communication Technologies and Human Services Education

Chapter 1
Jennifer Martin, RMIT University, Australia
Elspeth McKay, RMIT University, Australia
Linette Hawkins, RMIT University, Australia

Chapter 2
Christine Greenhow, University of Minnesota, USA
Beth Robelia, University of Minnesota, USA

Chapter 3
Lesley Cooper, Wilfrid Laurier University, Canada
Sally Burford, University of Canberra, Australia

Chapter 4
Belinda Johnson, RMIT University, Australia
Kathy Douglas, RMIT University, Australia

Chapter 5
Sandra Jones, RMIT University, Australia

Detailed Table of Contents

Section 1
Information Communication Technologies and Human Services Education

This section presents theories, methods and models for developing and applying information communication technology in human services education.

Chapter 1

    Jennifer Martin, RMIT University, Australia
    Elspeth McKay, RMIT University, Australia
    Linette Hawkins, RMIT University, Australia

This chapter explores technological developments in the human services and the educational requirements of a skilled labor force. It is argued that learner experiences can be enhanced by adopting a blended approach that includes face- to- face and online activities. Careful planning is required that matches desired learning experiences and learner characteristics with appropriate educational design and architectures. A case study highlights the complexity of applying these in practice, as well as the importance of community building in the online environment.

Chapter 2

    Christine Greenhow, University of Minnesota, USA
    Beth Robelia, University of Minnesota, USA

This chapter offers an introduction to online social network sites, summarizing their features, uses, demographics, and trends, and presents emerging research on their social and educational potential. An accompanying case study reveals how young adults might use online social network sites to further personal and educational goals. The chapter concludes with a discussion of how such sites might be employed by human services education students, practitioners and clients.

This chapter examines the concept of collaborative learning and its theoretical and practical foundations. The authors have trialed the use of various technologies in the human services and several case examples of online collaborative learning are provided. These case studies cover activities such as supervision and controversial issues in social work ethics. The chapter concludes with a discussion of the future directions and the challenges this poses for traditional classroom teaching.

Chapter 4

The focus of this chapter is on design options for asynchronous online role-plays that may assist students to integrate theory and practice and develop skills in reflexive practice. The design options discussed in this chapter adopt a "blended" learning approach where online learning is used to complement face-to-face learning. Five models of online role-plays are discussed and various learning and teaching strategies canvassed to assist those teaching in the human services area to adopt and adapt these design options to meet their curriculum objectives.

Chapter 5

This chapter explores how ICT can be used to create environments in which students engage in work-related learning opportunities through virtual situated learning environments. These VSLEs are created digitally as real-life learning opportunities. The chapter presents an example of a VSLE used to engage students in a related field of employment relations and outlines an example of how a virtual community centre may be used to develop employability skills for students in human services.

Chapter 6

This chapter reports on a qualitative research project designed to explore the significance of community for students studying online. Using three fundamentally different types of online learning environments as case studies, this research explored the relationship between the constructed online learning environment and the development of learning communities or what the author hasI have termed social learning support networks.

This chapter provides an insight into the use of information communication technology to create and sustain community. We are currently living in an electronic age where it is easier to travel the world and stay in touch with people who live away from our face-to-face environment without the need to leave home or to meet in a real life situation than ever before. The Web is becoming a place where we encounter others in ways to get our personal, social, and professional needs met. As a result of this growing phenomenon individuals are seeking to be a part of online communities of individuals who interact and associate with one another through the Web and the use of modern technology.

This chapter reviews the use of online technologies in post secondary education, the use of critical reflection as a pedagogical tool and social work field education, to contextualize the experience of the Dalhousie University School of Social Work's distance delivery field education course. Connections are developed amongst the online environment, adult education principles, and critical reflection on field education in social work, to craft an expanded message regarding transformative social work practice.

Chapter 9

Drawing upon the experience of students at one university in Australia who undertook international placements over a three year period, with particular attention to those engaged in group placements in Orissa, India, this chapter presents the different placement structures, the application of ICT and pedagogical factors requiring critical attention.

Section 2
Information Communications Technologies and Human Services Delivery

This section presents theories, methods and models for developing and applying information communication technology in human services practice.

Chapter 10

This chapter introduces a design process for developing useful information communication technologies for the human services. The stages involved in the design process are presented in this chapter and include: user and task analysis, persona and scenario development and the establishment of measurable usability goals. A case study illustrates the application of this design process to develop a Web enabled Electronic Work Requirement Awareness Program for people recovering from mental illness seeking employment.

This chapter aims to demonstrate the capabilities and practical applications of a case management software system for not-for-profit organizations- "Penelope". Penelope is a sophisticated piece of technology that can collect and analyze information on clients, services, human resources and outcomes. The requirements for effective use of case management software are discussed including technical, management and analytical skills combined with leadership and imagination.

This chapter analyses tools and techniques used to document human rights abuse. It outlines the opportunities and pitfalls associated with the use of information and communication technologies by human rights organizations, and it examines the importance of rigorous documentation to underpin human rights work. Tools developed to help grassroots organizations record usable and actionable information are contrasted with an initiative that actively involves citizens in the reporting of xenophobic attacks. The analysis shows that the tools and systems used to monitor human rights violations are essential to the effective implementation of human rights standards. It also shows, however, that new technologies can empower ordinary citizens to become directly involved in awareness building and debate about human rights abuse.

Chapter 13

Using electronic-Bario (e-Bario) project in the Kelabit Highlands of Sarawak in East Malaysia, this chapter explores how the introduction of information communication technologies (ICT) as developmental tools have been mediated and reconfigured by webs of social relations and the intricate interplay of social, political and cultural conditions specific to different social and technical settings. One crucial factor conditioning the effects of the project has been the Kelabit's own desire for, and expectations of, "development" and "progress." This is a quest which ties in closely with two fundamental Kelabit concepts: doo-ness and iyuk. As a result, the social and economic effects of ICT have unfolded through countless open-ended strategic and everyday decisions made by the Kelabit themselves, who actively consume, apply and make use of objects, ideas and services in the Highlands.

This chapter examines the contribution of information communication technology (ICT) to the operation of social and public policy. The governmentality analytic is introduced as a way in which to highlight how ICT is used by the state in governing populations. The chapter identifies four ways ICTs relate to social and public policy. First, social policy can be a response to ICT innovation and use. Second, ICT is used to implement and administer social policy. Third, ICT is used to develop and evaluate social policy. Fourth, the use of ICT can shape the very nature and substance of social policy. The chapter illustrates these theoretical and conceptual approaches by examining the extensive and innovative use of ICT in Australia's national income security agency, Centrelink

The aim of this chapter is to explore the utility of online knowledge sharing for the health and human services. Experiences in marketing are used as a basis for the development of three broad and interrelated theoretical concepts—the diffusion of innovations, viral marketing, and online word of mouth advertising—as well as several other influential factors to explain online knowledge sharing. Three major elements that stimulate online knowledge sharing are distilled from these theoretical perspectives including internal factors such as altruism, online social network size, and topic salience. This chapter uses these elements to propose a model of e-Mavenism which explains the cognitive processes that lead to online knowledge sharing behavior. Based on the e-Mavenism model, several strategies are suggested for online health promotion and community education.

Foreword

Information Communication Technology for Human Services Education and Delivery: Concepts and Cases is published at a time of exponential increases in the use of information communication technology in health and human services. It draws upon the expertise of authors from around the world, human services educators and practitioners developing and applying the latest technological advancements.

I began talking and writing about the Information Revolution nearly forty years ago. Back in 1999, Al Gore made the mistake of seeming to claim on a television interview – in a joking way – that he had invented the Internet. I don't want to fall into that trap and appear to claim that I invented the Information Revolution, but I can safely assert that I was the first Australian politician to talk about the information society, or post-industrialism.

In 1982 Oxford University Press published my book *Sleepers, Wake!: Technology and the Future of Work* which ran into four editions and twenty six impressions.

In *Sleepers, Wake!*, I ended my chapter 'The Information Explosion and its Threats', with a quotation from T. S. Eliot, part of a chorus from 'The Rock':

Where is the wisdom we have lost in knowledge?
Where is the knowledge we have lost in information?

I am intensely conscious of the hierarchy: data > information > knowledge > wisdom.

I thought, indeed hoped, that the Information Revolution would be profoundly liberating and would lead to an explosive increase in creativity and a vast improvement in what I call 'labour/time-use value'. I am still waiting.

Through Google and other powerful search engines we have instant access to what would have seemed like unimaginable richness to earlier generations – but I am not sure that the promise has been delivered.

Paradoxically, the age of the Information Revolution, which should have been an instrument of personal liberation and an explosion of creativity, has been characterized by domination of public policy by managerialism, replacement of 'the public good' by 'private benefit,' the decline of sustained critical debate on issues leading to gross oversimplification, the relentless 'dumbing down' of mass media, linked with the cult of celebrity, substance abuse and retreat into the realm of the personal, and the rise of fundamentalism and an assault on reason. The Knowledge Revolution ought to have been a countervailing force: in practice it has been the vector of change.

When writing *Sleepers, Wake!*, I worried about the implications of adopting economics as the dominant intellectual paradigm, and its impact on non-material values, as if nothing else mattered. Inevitably, as the public domain contracted, education, health and child care were regarded as commodities to be traded rather than elements of the public good, universities fell into the hands of accountants and auditors, research was judged by the potential for economic return and in the arts best sellers displaced the masterpiece. Language became deformed. Citizens, passengers, patients, patrons, audiences, taxpayers, even students, all became 'customers' or 'clients', as if the trading nexus was the most important defining element in life. Values were commercialized, all with a dollar equivalent. Essentially, the 'nation-state' was transformed into a 'market-state'.

I see this book as a very valuable instrument for improving quality of life, a countervailing force to 'dumbing down'.

The human services area inevitably depends upon human interaction for communicating and transmitting information in educational and workplace settings. This book explores innovative ways academics and practitioners have developed and applied ICT to enhance human services education and practice.

I applaud the outstanding efforts of the authors who have contributed to this seminal text. The diverse backgrounds of the contributors bring together global knowledge and understandings of the potential of ICT in the human services from a range of countries. They range from the use of ICT by indigenous communities in the Kelabit Highlands of Malaysian Borneo to the Australia's Commonwealth Government using ICT to manage its income security system. The range of topics covers all of the main areas of practice in the human services across rural, remote and urban areas; thus providing a comprehensive text for an international human services audience. The editors should be congratulated for sourcing these authors from around the world – no doubt with the assistance of ICT, the breadth and depth of the material and the manner in which it has been organized and presented.

This book provides relevant theoretical frameworks and the latest empirical research findings in information communication technology. It is written for professionals, educators and students who want to improve their understanding of the strategic role of ICT in improving the human services, with practical instruction on how to apply these technologies. The ideas presented are grounded in evidence based research and practice. All chapters have a theory and practice component with a case study demonstrating and discussing the technological applications to either human services education, or practice, or both. The reader not only learns about new technologies but is also equipped with knowledge of the processes and skills required to apply these.

The book is divided into the two main sections of education and practice. It concludes with a chapter on the future of ICT in the human services forecasting how human services' educators and practitioners might further utilize the potential of ICT.

The text will be valuable not only to human services professionals who want to improve their understanding of the potential and strategic role of ICT, but also to the many other workers and researchers in the field of ICT and human computer interaction from various disciplines. For an international readership this book contains many helpful ideas and strategies on how to develop and apply ICT in human services education and practice. It draws upon the successful experiences of experts in this field from around the world.

I hope that *Information Communication Technology for Human Services Education and Delivery: Concepts and Cases* will contribute to the development of a global workforce that ensures ICT is used to develop more equitable and accessible human services.

Barry Jones
AO, FAA, FAHA, FTSE, FASSA, FRSA, FRSV, FACE.
Professorial Fellow,
The University of Melbourne,
Australia

Barry Jones, *AO, FAA, FAHA, FTSE, FASSA, FRSA, FRSV, FACE is a Professorial Fellow, University of Melbourne. He was a Victorian State MP 1972-77; a Member of the House of Representatives 1977-98, Australian Minister for Science 1983-90, and represented Australia at UNESCO in Paris 1991-95. He is the only person to have been elected to all four of Australia's learned academies. His autobiography, A Thinking Reed, was published in 2006.*

Preface

Information Communication Technologies for Human Services Education and Delivery: Concepts and Cases covers main areas of education and practice of disciplines engaged in the human services. These include policy, community work, community education, field education/ professional practicum, health promotion, individual and family work, human rights advocacy, group work, multidisciplinary teamwork and program management and evaluation. Information communication technology has facilitated access to authors from around the world including Australia, Malaysia, the United Kingdom, India, the United States of America and Canada with backgrounds in social work, education and computer science.

The human services sector has been somewhat slow to embrace new technologies, particularly when compared with other areas such as marketing. Beginning ICT developments in the human services have focused primarily on basic functions to facilitate the collection and management of large quantities of data about clients by government bureaucracies. In social work education there was initial skepticism that interpersonal communication skills could be taught online due to the importance of critical reflection and relationships in social work practice. It is ironic that today the Internet is used primarily for interpersonal communication. Early developments in social work education saw ICT tools used for distance education courses for students who were unable to attend on-campus, primarily due to living in rural or remote locations and were not considered a viable option for those who could access an on-campus education. Human services educators and practitioners are now predominantly using ICT tools to augment existing practices rather than adopting one approach only. However they are proceeding with caution, and rightly so, to ensure that ICT tools are used to improve the quality of education and human services. In doing so it is necessary to be vigilant about the maintenance of professional practice standards and key ethical considerations, particularly respect for client confidentiality and responsible use of ICT tools. These exciting and innovative practices that are now occurring in human services education and practice are presented in this book.

Information Communication Technologies for Human Services Education and Delivery: Concepts and Cases is useful for students, educators and practitioners in the human services field who want to improve their understanding of different ICT tools and learn how to apply these. It is relevant for all disciplines in the human services including social work, psychology, legal studies, youth work, community work and welfare studies. It is also pertinent for other courses in the health field such as medicine, nursing and occupational therapy. The multidisciplinary nature of the book lends itself to all disciplines that work with people and want to use ICT tools to further develop and enhance professional skills and improve organizational processes. Instructional designers will gain insights into the range of activities conducted in the human services and how these might be best supported by ICT. The concepts and cases presented in this book are based on sound theoretical underpinnings and practice experiences.

This book is divided into two main sections. Section I focuses on ICT tools and human services education with Section II concentrating on ICT and human services delivery. The book concludes with an Afterword that endeavors to look into the future to anticipate ongoing developments and innovations in the use of ICT in human services education and practice.

SECTION 1: ICT AND HUMAN SERVICES EDUCATION

Approaches to the use of ICT in education are presented within the context of education for a multi-disciplinary human services workforce. A range of approaches are considered predominantly using a "blended approach" of ICT and face to face delivery. These include creating and sustaining community in a virtual environment to develop inter-professional skills. A focus of skill development is on reflective practices using online role-plays and group work principles and processes in virtual situated learning environments. Issues for professional practice cultures in the online environment are considered within a global context.

In Chapter 1 Jennifer Martin, Elspeth McKay and Linette Hawkins, from social work and Business Information Technology RMIT University in Australia, explore technological developments in the human services and the educational requirements of a skilled labor force. They argue that learner experiences can be enhanced by adopting a "blended approach" that includes face- to- face and online activities. The human computer interaction spiral is presented as an innovative approach that provides a model for integrating theory and practice for ICT design and application to the human services. A key message in this chapter is the importance of adopting an informed and reflective approach to the use of ICT that incorporates a variety of learning approaches and architectures. Ultimately student needs and the knowledge and skills required by the human services workforce will influence the most appropriate mediums to use.

Chapter 2, by Christine Greenhow and Beth Robelia from the University of Minnesota in the United States of America, combines knowledge and skills in education and science to explore the opportunities for educational and social benefits from social networking sites for human services education and practice. Insights are provided into the uses of social networking sites and how these can be used by human services education students, practitioners and clients to achieve personal and social goals of knowledge and skill development and networking. Social and emotional development can be supported by social networking sites as they provide spaces to express emotions, deepen friendships and demonstrate creativity. Self reflection and mutual self help can occur for those experiencing similar challenges. The authors demonstrate how private networks can be constructed to facilitate work with clients without exposing private information online.

In Chapter 3 Lesley Cooper from Wilfrid Laurier University in Canada and Sally Burford from the University of Canberra in Australia draw upon considerable experience in using collaborative online learning as a successful strategy for teaching social work. They demonstrate the application of group work concepts and techniques to promote collaborative learning in an online environment; particularly the concepts of group formation, stages of group development, and communication. A number of case illustrations are used from Cooper and Burford's practice experiences to demonstrate the creative application of ICT tools for social work education covering activities such as supervision and controversial issues involving professional ethical considerations.

The application of asynchronous online role-plays to develop communication skills is presented in Chapter 4 by Belinda Johnson and Kathy Douglas from RMIT University in Australia. They draw upon their experiences using online role plays to assist students developing skills in self reflection and the integration of theory and practice. A number of models and strategies for online role-plays, drawing upon the e-learning "conversational framework," developed by Dianne Laurillard (2002) are presented.

A case study demonstrates the use of Wikis and blogs in online role-plays to teach mediation. The authors argue that a blended approach to teaching and learning using face to face and online technologies provides for a superior learning experience resulting in human services practitioners who are better equipped for practice.

The use of online role-plays is examined further in Chapter 5 by Sandra Jones from RMIT University in Australia who demonstrates how virtual situated learning environments (VSLE) can assist with the development of skills for a multidisciplinary human services workforce. She demonstrates how VSLEs are created as "real world" authentic learning experiences to develop skills in multidisciplinary teamwork. This is achieved through participation in complex online role-play scenarios. VSLEs provide students with opportunities to experiment with different approaches and see the consequences of their actions. These online role-plays draw upon local and international experiences using a range of disciplines to reflect the reality of the workforce. A case study shows how a virtual community centre is used to develop employability skills for students in the human services.

Chapter 6, by Lisa Harris from RMIT University in Australia, examines design aspects of the e-learning environments to foster virtual social networks and student learning. She is particularly interested in the significance of community for students studying online and the social and cultural implications of new technologies. This chapter reports on a qualitative research project designed to explore the meaning of community for students studying online. Using three fundamentally different types of online learning environments as case studies, this research explores the relationship between the constructed online learning environment and the development of social learning support networks. This research is of particular significance for the design of online learning environments using social learning support networks to enhance knowledge and skill development in the human services.

David Colachico from Azusa Pacific University in California is also concerned with how to create and sustain community in a virtual world in Chapter 7 as he examines how virtual communities are formed and maintained. He explores different notions of community and how being a community member involves negotiating relationships that require commitment, mutual engagement and reciprocity; not unlike face to face relationships. A range of features are considered for developing, and participating in online communities, such as the centrality of motivation and the willingness of members to actively participate if the community is to be sustained. This chapter highlights the importance of a deep understanding of the issues that engage members and challenge the community with interactions based on the knowledge, expertise and preferences of its members. An emphasis is on the high level of care and attention required for the cultivation and support of online communities if they are to succeed.

The next two chapters are concerned with the use of ICT to support professional practice/field education in social work education and also highlight the importance of community for successful learning online.

In Chapter 8 Marion Brown reviews the use of online technologies in the national online field education seminar program of the Dalhousie University School of Social Work in Nova Scotia in Canada. The chapter explores how knowledge, skills, abilities, and attitudes of student practitioners are developed in this national online program. This includes consideration of critical reflection processes, the content in the field education courses, expanded contextual analysis and online seminars. A framework of critical success factors is presented highlighting the significance of social networks and sense of community. The importance of active engagement by both students and teachers is stressed, for the deep learning and critical reflection required of social work field education to occur.

Chapter 9, by Linette Hawkins from RMIT University in Australia and Supriya Patanayak from India, considers the increasing reliance upon ICT to support international field education placements. They share their experiences supporting social work students from Australia on international placements in India. ICT is acknowledged as an important tool for students on placement whether local or global, albeit ancillary to the core nature of field education comprising "real life" as distinct from "virtual" field practice. They consider the on-call/on-site supervisory presence as a critical component of field practicum.

The second section of this book examines the use of ICT tools in the delivery of human services with case studies provided to demonstrate the application of these.

The first chapter in this section, Chapter 10 by Jennifer Martin and Elspeth McKay from RMIT University in Australia, introduces a design process for developing useful information communication technologies for the human services. Central to successful design is an in-depth knowledge and understanding of user needs and requirements. The stages involved in the design process are presented in this chapter and include: user and task analysis, persona and scenario development and the establishment of measurable usability goals. A case study illustrates the application of this design process to develop a Web enabled electronic work requirement awareness program (e-WRAP) for people recovering from mental illness seeking employment. The authors urges social workers to use these new technologies to improve service provision and enhance quality of life without compromising ethical standards of practice; particularly in relation to client confidentiality, privacy and self-determination.

Chapter 11, by Lesley Cooper from Wilfrid Laurier University in Canada and Dana Fox and Diane Stanley-Horn from Athena Software in Canada, explores the practical applications of case management software for practitioners in health and social services.

These authors have collaborated to develop practical applications of case management software in practicum programs and in the human services. They use ICT tools to empower organizations through easing administrative burdens, facilitating the coordination, communication and supervision of service delivery and enhancing an organization's ability to demonstrate the benefits of those services to their clients, communities and funding bodies. Using "Penelope" case management software as an illustration the authors provide practical examples of the ways agencies can make the transition from using ICT tools for basic data collection to performance monitoring and demonstration of effectiveness.

In Chapter 12 John Lannon, a software designer/developer and human rights activist from the Senator George Mitchell Centre for Peace and Conflict Resolution at Leeds Metropolitan University in the United Kingdom, examines the role of ICT in human rights monitoring and advocacy. He analyses tools and techniques used to document human rights abuse and outlines the opportunities and pitfalls associated with the use of ICT tools by human rights organizations. He stresses the importance of rigorous documentation to underpin human rights work and argues that access to information enables human rights promotion through reflection and learning. While much of what is reported may never be used to build a case against the human rights offenders, it sets in motion processes that ultimately lead, through empowerment, to greater protection from abuse, persecution and oppression.

The author of Chapter 13, Poline Bala from the University Malaysia in Sarawak, explores the role of ICT tools for community development activities in rural Sarawak in Borneo. She looks specifically at the e-Bario project which she and a team of researchers initiated in the Kelabit Highlands of Sarawak in 1998, and examines social change connected to the use of ICT. She suggests that real-life situations can change the purpose of technologies, and the ways in which they are used may differ greatly from what was envisaged at the outset; what she refers to as the "social shaping of technologies." She supports this by demonstrating how the introduction of ICT as developmental tools have been mediated and reconfigured by the intricate interplay of social, political and cultural conditions specific to the Kelabit. These technologies have been partly integrated with, or subordinated by existing practices, internal values and socio-political arrangements in the Kelabit community.

Paul Henman from the University of Queensland in Australia, author of Chapter 14, has a professional background in both computer science and social science. In this chapter he examines how social policy can be used to develop, implement and evaluate social policy. At the same time social polices are developed in response to ICT innovation and use. A "governmentality framework" is used to illustrate how ICT can be understood as a mechanism for governing individuals and populations. The main message of this chapter is that ICT is central to the practice of contemporary politics and power in a manner that simultaneously alleviates and adds to social problems. The use of ICT in Australia's national income security agency, Centrelink is discussed to illustrate the main concepts presented.

In Chapter 15 Hyunjung Kim and Michael Stefanone, both from the Department of Communication at the State University of New York at Buffalo in the United States of America, explore online knowledge sharing for health promotion and community education. A model of "e-Mavenism" is presented to examine factors that influence online knowledge sharing. These include social network size and topic salience. They argue that people have a greater desire to share information with others online when they feel a sense of altruism or obligation to do so; expecting the message will be helpful to others. The authors recommend that human services educators and practitioners target weak tie online relationships for health promotion and community education activities.

The book concludes with an Afterword by Dennis Perry, who has pioneered the introduction of ICT information systems for state and federal governments in Australia. He provides a chronological overview of the use of ICT from a personal and political perspective. He looks at both old and new approaches and explores some of the ethical issues of security and privacy associated with the adoption of online technologies. He concludes that the challenges are many but that change is inevitable and perhaps may occur at a faster rate than we might have imagined.

Information Communication Technologies for Human Services Education and Delivery: Concepts and Cases is the first book of its kind offering a significant contribution to knowledge of the application of ICT tools in education and practice in the human services. All of the ICT tools currently available are presented with the application of these grounded in an extensive range of theories and practices. A multidisciplinary approach sees collaboration between authors with backgrounds in ICT, human services, education and management; with a number of authors qualified and experienced in more than one of these areas. Theories and practices from the human services include the disciplines of social science, psychology, social work, mental health and law. Those specific to ICT are; computer science, instructional design, information management, information systems, communication and science and engineering. The integration of knowledge from these diverse disciplines by authors from around the globe provides breadth and depth and makes for a comprehensive and authoritative text.

The concepts and models presented are consistent with Australian national indicators identified for "good teaching practice."

These include:

- Clear explanations by teaching staff;
- Helpful feedback on learning progress;
- Teaching staff motivate students to do their "best work";
- Teaching staff work hard to make the course interesting;
- Teaching staff make a real effort to understand the difficulties students may be experiencing with their learning;
- Teaching staff put a lot of time into providing feedback and commenting on student work (RMIT, 2009).

Care is needed to establish learning environments that foster a sense of community and provide clear instructions on roles and how to participate effectively. Active engagement by both staff and students, and adequate organizational support and infrastructure, are critical to support the effective application of ICT tools in both human services education and practice. The concepts and models presented in this book promote "best practices" in the human services with ICT tools used to assist with:

- Promoting social change;
- Problem solving;
- Empowerment and liberation;
- Enhancing well being (IFSW, 2000).

This book highlights the importance of adopting, or developing appropriate ICT tools to support the desired learning or practice experience to further the cause of social justice and human rights.

REFERENCES

IFSW. (2000). *International Federation of Social Workers (IFSW) – definition of social work*. Retrieved from http://www.ifsw.org/en/p38000208.html

RMIT. (2009). *RMIT – course experiences survey FAQ*. Retrieved from http://www.rmit.edu.au/ssc/ces/faq

Section 1
Information Communication Technologies and Human Services Education

Chapter 1
Educating a Multidisciplinary Human Services Workforce
Using a Blended Approach

Jennifer Martin
RMIT University, Australia

Elspeth McKay
RMIT University, Australia

Linette Hawkins
RMIT University, Australia

ABSTRACT

This chapter explores technological developments in the human services and the educational requirements of a skilled labor force. It is argued that learner experiences can be enhanced by adopting a blended approach that includes face- to- face and online activities. Careful planning is required that matches desired learning experiences and learner characteristics with appropriate educational design and architectures. The main views of learning discussed are absorption, behavioral and cognitive with consideration of the most appropriate learning architectures to support these. A case study highlights the complexity of applying these in practice, as well as the importance of community building in the online environment.

'Learning without thought is labour lost; thought without learning is perilous'.

Confucius (K'ung Fu tzu 551-479 BC), Chinese philosopher and reformer, *Analects, ch.15, v.38* in *Oxford Dictionary of Quotations* (2004, p.238:8).

INTRODUCTION

The human services industry in Australia employs 1,121,000 persons, approximately 10.9 per cent of the total workforce. Over the past five years employment in this industry has increased at rate of 3.9 per cent per annum, with the average age of workers 43 years (Australian Government, 2008). Certain

DOI: 10.4018/978-1-60566-735-5.ch001

characteristics distinguish the human services workforce from a number of other occupations. In the human services, workers are engaged in diverse roles and multiple functions with qualifications that range from short courses through to university degrees. The courses include: social work, psychology, aged care, disability, mental health, children's services, counseling, welfare studies, community work, human services and youth work. Employment is distributed widely across all levels of government, non government organizations, health, and social and community services fields. Several unions and diverse employment arrangements and awards have contributed to a blurring of disciplines and tension regarding professional identity and boundaries. A high gender imbalance (85 per cent female) together with increasing proportion of care related roles makes a disproportionate amount of fractional employment (part-time) another significant issue (Lonne, 2007). There are limited career paths for workers engaged in direct practice and wide salary disparities. Related to these are the difficulties of recruitment and retention in certain areas such as child protection and significant workforce mobility.

Human services have traditionally relied upon face-to-face interaction as a major form of communication and transmission of information in both educational and workplace settings. As in social work education, most human services courses give considerable attention to group learning and relationships (Shardlow & Horwath, 2000; Smith & Wingerson, 2006). This chapter explores the use of information communications technology (ICT) tools to educate the human services workforce. First, human services education is considered within the context of a multidisciplinary workforce and the varied needs of learners. This is followed by a discussion of the main approaches to teaching and learning and the architectures to support these. A case study illustrates the experiences of a human services worker engaged in continuing professional education. Future trends for educating

a multidisciplinary human services workforce are identified using a "blended approach" that includes face-to-face and online delivery as well as a variety of educational approaches and architectures to support these instructional/learning strategies.

EDUCATING A MULTIDISCIPLINARY HUMAN SERVICES WORKFORCE

In Australia the first social work program provided via distance education was developed by Monash University in response to pressure from the State Government to address a severe shortage of professional workers in rural Victoria. With the increased use of ICT tools for both on and off campus programs, the distinction between face-to-face learning and "distance education" became blurred. Moreover the distance education program initiated to meet the needs of rural workers soon attracted metropolitan students in need of, or attracted by its flexible delivery. In terms of levels of satisfaction and educational standards, Oullette (2006) found no significant difference in interview skill acquisition when comparing classroom based and online learning. In a further study by Siebert (2006) of a post graduate clinical social work skills course, the final results of online students were considered comparable to students in face-to-face classes. Using the virtual classroom of a graduate social policy course, Roberts-DeGennaro (2005) found that students enjoyed learning through the virtual classroom as much as traditional on-campus components the of course. Following their study of classroom and online field practicum seminars over a three year period Wolfson et al (2005) decided to offer the fourth year practicum seminar for social work students exclusively online.

Research on flexible learning in rural New South Wales in Australia found that human services were in a transitional period undergoing a rapid rate of change and growing complexities of job roles. This was reflected in a 'tension between the need to access training and the capacity of workers and organizations to embrace new technologies and ways of learning in a more flexible way' (Centre for Community Welfare Training for Adult learning in Australia (2004, p.27). This research found that in educating students for interpersonal contact, on which human services are traditionally based, the introduction of technology could be seen as displacing the significance of relationships in learning; the "virtual community" challenging the conventionally familiar meaning of community in human services education and practice. Rumble (2000, p.8) asserts that 'the use of new technologies will also favor innovations that create new roles, new social links, and new types of social behavior within a service context'. This service delivery context is multidisciplinary.

The human services workforce requires discipline specific knowledge and skills as well as the ability to work effectively in a multidisciplinary team context. The focus of formal education is primarily on the former. This is necessary for students to develop specific expertise yet it does not provide them with the knowledge and skills required to be an effective member of a multidisciplinary team. Education on teamwork is predominantly discipline specific. For instance social work students will learn from a social worker how to work effectively with those from other areas, relying upon social work texts to do so.

This narrow approach to learning and teaching needs to change to meet the complex requirements of the human services workforce. ICT tools provide a platform for students from different backgrounds to work together online to share ideas and collaborate. This may be through online simulation exercises or a sharing of resources (Anderson & Elloumi, 2004).

Combining the expertise across the human services with instructional designers poses major challenges. This necessitates careful planning by educators to structure meaningful and relevant learning experiences utilizing computerized information systems available. Tensions will necessarily exist due to different approaches to the same issue. Clarity is required concerning the roles and responsibilities of team members particularly leadership. In a multidisciplinary team the leader necessarily will be from an area that is not representative of all members. Other team members may become anxious that their particular discipline will become subordinate to that of the team leader. Effective leadership of the multidisciplinary team therefore requires a focus and commitment to the goals and tasks of the team in a manner that gives equal appreciation and consideration to all of the perspectives represented by the membership. When developing effective ICT tools the membership of the team is further diversified. Proactive development of effective communication, conflict management and prevention strategies are necessary for effective collaboration. Some guiding principles for effective multidisciplinary collaboration using ICT tools are:

- Tight project management to prevent functionality/scope creep (Schwalbe, 2004);
- A shared linguistic/cultural framework;
- A respectful, empathic and inquisitive attitude that continually navigates the knowledge acquisition process across all disciplines;
- Clear communication to all team members and in particular the instructional designer of: end product requirements, timeframe for completion of tasks, review processes and accountabilities;
- Acknowledgment of the complex nature of the ICT environment; and
- Effective communication strategies to encourage and promote knowledge sharing.

Often, the practice of instructional design is only referred to for justification of the selection of educational strategies or approaches adopted rather than being used as a starting point for the development of online courseware. This is fur-

Figure 1. Human-computer interaction (adapted from Preece 1994, p.16 and reproduced from McKay & Martin, 2007, p.322)

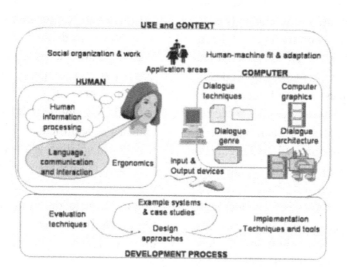

ther complicated by the highly visual nature of multimedia. In previous work (McKay & Martin, 2007) we have highlighted the complexity of the human computer interaction relationship. As detailed in Figure 1 all of these components need to be considered to successfully meet end-user requirements.

Ultimately successful multidisciplinary collaboration requires exceptionally good communication, analytic, problem solving and conflict resolution skills for optimum results.

CONTINUING PROFESSIONAL EDUCATION

Human service organizations in general employ a wide range of people with diverse skill levels across their provider network. The development of high level skills across the workforce is expensive and requires major investment (Richardson 2004). Traditionally, employers view training as an expensive solution that is implemented to fix problems. In the current climate of changing work practices, every time a new ICT learning tool enters the work-environment employers seem to

pour endless amounts of money into upgrading their employees' skill base. The dilemma of this continual investment in work-place training is the paucity of research on the actual impact of these emerging online training tools on institutional effectiveness.

Many of the e-Learning solutions that have been implemented recently have been poorly designed and inadequately tested. Often, paper-based training materials are simply loaded into a learning management system or electronic courseware shell without including adequate knowledge navigation or consideration for the principles of Instructional Design. Many e-Learning implementations fail to check whether learning actually occurs (as demonstrated by increased proficiency of the participants). In cases where checks are made, most attempts fail to use valid measures of the *changes* in proficiency (Anderson & Elloumi 2004). It is not surprising that current e-Learning solutions are poorly regarded by management and are often unused by employees, thereby making them ineffective and an expensive waste of limited online training resources. There is often no agreement amongst the various corporate stakeholders to take on ICT infrastructure resource ownership. Finding the right technological training

Figure 2. Online mentoring within an online human services course (McKay & Martin, 2007)

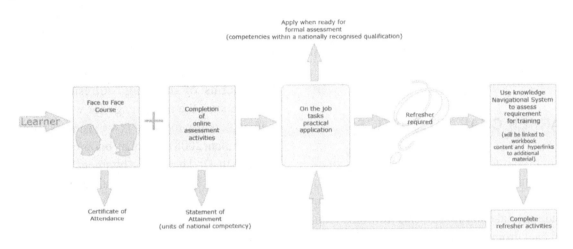

for the human services is further complicated in the government sector by the multi-disciplinary mix of expertise.

Usually a new employee or someone who is recently transferred to a new location will have an immediate need for learning specific processes. Typically training courses are scheduled at specific times during the year, forcing an employee to obtain one-on-one tuition or learn by trial and error in the meantime, neither of which is efficient for an organization. Conversely, an employee may be placed on a course to meet organizational mandates or to meet the selection criteria for a future position. Unless the new-skills learnt are immediately put into practice, key competencies achieved during this training are often forgotten. This results in an unsatisfactory training outcome for both the learner and the organization.

Often face-to-face training courses have difficulty catering for the individual needs of participants due to the training timeframe and volume of learning material. First time (novice) learners may become overwhelmed by technical details, the limitations of the formalized training timeframe and peer pressure as they endeavor to understand new ICT systems. More experienced staff, previously exposed to the learning content will easily become bored and frustrated by the presentation of simple concepts and repetition of familiar instructional content. Neither of these learner groups will have optimized learning outcomes for themselves or the organization.

In an ideal online training environment, once trainees have completed their online training modules they communicate directly with an online mentor or facilitator by sending them electronic versions of their newly created documentation (Martin et al, 2007; McKay, 2008). Depending upon the quality of the trainee's knowledge of the tasks, they either proceed to complete their training, or they return to relevant instructional modules to continue their instruction. This involves a blended approach using face-to-face and online delivery as illustrated in Figure 2.

Training materials are required for all employees and providers who have access to a government Intranet. In Australia this means that training in new procedures or legislative requirements can be distributed across the nation in a timely manner. In addition, continuous provision of training materials means that employees can access professional development when it is needed. Different learner pathways allow novice learners to go through the full learning program in a sequential (skill-building) order in their own time. More experienced learners can select relevant modules as refresher training to quickly obtain the specific knowledge they require. A key to the success of educational design is a sound knowledge of the characteristics and needs of user populations.

LEARNER CHARACTERISTICS

Learner characteristics include educational, cultural and socio-economic backgrounds. Most universities have access and equity programs that provide special entry for students from disadvantaged backgrounds. This may be due to a variety of reasons including financial hardship, disability or refugee status. All students are expected to have access to a computer to engage in their learning as well as complete necessary administrative tasks including enrolment online. Some newer housing estates on the urban fringe do not have Broadband Internet access and dial up connections can be costly and unreliable. The structuring of activities in real time is particularly important for these students with limited ICT access. It is not uncommon these days for lectures to be available for download onto I-Pods so that they can be listened to anywhere at anytime. Again there is an assumption that most students, particularly those from "Generation Y" will have ready access to this technology.

Increasingly in post-secondary education the main features of "the learner" are identified according to the main characteristics and perceived needs of Generation Y (1980 to 1994). This generation has witnessed increased capitalism and globalization alongside economic rationalization and a greater focus on the individual. They have grown up in a technologically rich society and are adept at using these new technologies to stimulate all of the senses, with instant text messages a preferred means of communication. Generation Y is seen as requiring increased flexibility due to the demands of balancing paid employment and education.

Generation X (1965-1979) witnessed the advent of early technology, high inflation and high unemployment. Like Generation Y they are comfortable with using ICT tools with a preference for e-mail, cell phones and electronic news.

In terms of on-going "refresher" training requirements the median age for workers in the human services industry is 43 years (Australian Government 2008) the "baby boomer" generation (1945-1964). The "baby boomers" grew up in the post World War II period that saw increased prosperity, as well as personal rebellion. They are typified as requiring clear explanations with questions answered. Preferred modes of communication using technology are e-mail, telephone and answer messages (Martin 2007; Staughton, 2006).

Generally arguments for increased use of technology in post secondary education are couched in terms of being "student-centered" and responsive to the needs of students, particularly the perception of Generation Y needing greater flexibility. This is also applied to other generations and population groups, particularly those living in rural and remote locations. These arguments can be quite persuasive, however academic standards and integrity can be at risk if they are not also factored into all decision making concerning increased use of ICT tools.

There are considerable fiscal savings for government and universities with increased online teaching and learning, administration and electronic library resources. Cost-shifting can occur as students spend more time on the Internet accessing online resources. However it is generally educational rather than economic rationalist arguments that are espoused when it comes to increased use of ICT tools in post secondary education.

The challenge for educators is to use the latest technologies to enrich learning experiences in ways that are responsive to the needs of students. While universities provide computer access it is important that students from disadvantaged backgrounds are not further disadvantaged in their

Figure 3. Human computer interaction spiral (Martin, McKay & Hawkins, 2006)

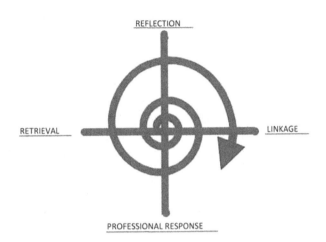

studies due to not having access to an adequate personal computer, the Internet and other technologies. An informed approach to educational design is required that integrates personal reflection, theory and practice.

KNOWLEDGE DEVELOPMENT: THE HUMAN COMPUTER INTERACTION SPIRAL

It can be difficult establishing meaningful links between theory and practice within a discipline with this becoming more complex when theoretical concepts from the disciplines of instructional design and education are also included. A key consideration is how to give theory operational meaning. Bogo and Vayda (1987) adapted the work of Kolb (1984) on experiential learning to social work education developing what they termed the "Integration of Theory and Practice Loop" (ITP Loop). As reported elsewhere (Martin, McKay & Hawkins, 2006) this model has been further developed into the "the Human Computer Interaction Spiral (HCI Spiral)" and applied more broadly to the multidisciplinary context of the human services. Another feature of this model is

the inclusion of "multidisciplinary" knowledge. The HCI Spiral is presented in Figure 3.

The application of the HCI spiral requires four steps. The factual elements of a situation are retrieved and reflected upon. This includes reflection on personal assumptions, attitudes and values as well as consideration of power relationships and possible discrimination according to; class, culture, ability, health, gender, age, spirituality and sexuality. This is followed by linkage with theory that can account for, or explain, the information retrieved and personal reflections. This in turn leads to the final step, an informed professional response. The cycle continues as new information is retrieved. The spiral is as an important element of the design with an upward spiral reflecting the progress achieved through design, re-design and continual improvement processes. However, the spiral may go up or down rapidly or slowly depending upon the responsiveness of the design team.

In applying this model to education, it is essential to differentiate between the type of learning and the technological means that bring forward an effective online instructional architecture to support it. This necessitates a close look at the type of learning activities that are required to prepare a learner to develop the desired knowledge and skills.

APPROACHES TO TEACHING AND LEARNING

The teaching style will necessarily influence the learner's experience and type and level of engagement with the course content. In education today an "active approach" to learning is generally preferred. It is argued in this chapter that there is much to be gained from using a variety of approaches that are carefully matched to learner requirements. For instance it may be appropriate to use a "didactic approach" when providing new content and a more active approach when translating this information into practice. This gives new meaning and depth to the term "blended learning"; the term generally used to describe education that combines face-to-face approaches with use of ICT tools. Blended learning is thus extended to include the combination of different approaches to learning and the instructional/learning architectures that support them. Accordingly, a blended approach to teaching and learning occurs on two levels by combining face-to-face delivery with ICT tools, and different approaches to learning with appropriate instructional/learning architectures.

In the following classification of approaches to teaching and learning by Clarke (2003), didactic approaches are typified in the passive absorption view of learning with more active approaches portrayed in the behavioral and cognitive views of learning.

The Absorption View of Learning requires clarity about the difference between learning and instruction. Learning in this view is about assimilating information, while instruction is about providing information to learners. Some call this a transmission-view of teaching (Mayer, 2001). Courses that rely on lectures or videotapes to transmit information generally reflect this view.

The Behavioral View of Learning was promoted in the first part of the 20th Century by behavioral psychology promoting a different view, considering learning to be based on the acquisition of mental associations. This view of learning is about correct responses to questions and instruction; providing small chunks of information followed by questions and corrective feedback. In the process of making many small correct responses, learners generally build large chains of new knowledge. The behavioral view is reflected in programmed instruction and many traditional Instructional Design approaches that emphasize bottom-up sequencing of instruction, short lessons, and frequent reinforcement in the form of feedback.

The Cognitive View of Learning has developed in the last part of the 20th Century, when learning was again re-conceptualized (McKay, 2008). This time the emphasis was on the active processes learners use to construct new knowledge. This construction requires an integration of new incoming information from the environment with existing knowledge in memory. In the cognitive view, learning is about active construction of new knowledge by interacting with new information, while instruction is about promoting the psychological processes that mediate that construction.

LEARNING ARCHITECTURES

Different learning architectures can be implemented to support the various types of learning experiences. Although the active construction of knowledge is commonly accepted today as the mechanism for learning that construction can be fostered through four diverse instructional environments (Clark, 2003). These are referred to as the "four instructional architectures": receptive, directive, guided discovery and exploratory. Table 1 illustrates the learning architectures best suited to each of the approaches to teaching and learning presented in this chapter.

Table 1. Teaching and learning approaches and instructional architectures

APPROACH	ARCHITECTURE
Absorption	Receptive
Behavioral	Directive
Cognitive	Guided Discovery
	Exploratory

Receptive architecture is characterized by an emphasis on providing information and reflects a transmission view-of-learning. The information may be in the form of words and pictures, both still and animated. A commonly used metaphor for the receptive architecture is that the learner is a sponge and the instructor pours out knowledge to be absorbed. In some forms of receptive instruction, such as lectures or video lessons, learners have minimal control over the pacing or sequencing of the training. In other situations such as text assignments, learners control the pace and can select the topics in the book of interest to them. Some examples of this architecture include a traditional (non-interactive) lecture, an instructional video, or a text assignment. Unfortunately, some online eLearning programs that are known as "page turners" lack interactivity. As such there is no corrective feedback given to the learner.

Directive architecture reflects a behavioral view of learning. The assumption is that learning occurs by a gradual building of skills; starting from the most basic and progressing to more advanced levels. The lessons should be presented in small chunks of knowledge, providing frequent opportunities for learners to respond to related questions. Immediate corrective feedback should be used to ensure that accurate associations are made. The goal is to minimize the aversive consequences of making errors which are believed to promote incorrect associations. Programmed instruction, popular in the 50's and 60's, is a prime example of directive architecture. Such lessons were presented in books originally; however, they soon migrated to a computerized delivery.

Guided Discovery architecture uses job-realistic problems to drive the learning process. Learners typically access various sources of data to resolve problems and have instructional support (sometimes called scaffolding) available to help them. Unlike the directive architecture, guided discovery offers learners opportunities to try alternatives, make mistakes, experience consequences of those mistakes, reflect on their results, and revise their approach. The aim of guided discovery is to promote construction of mental models by helping learners experience the results of decisions made in the context of solving realistic cases and problems. Guided discovery designs are based on inductive models of learning; that is, learning of concepts and principles from experience with specific cases and problems.

Exploratory architecture, also known as "open-ended learning", relies on a cognitive view of learning. Out of the four architectures identified by Clark (2003), exploratory architectures offer the most effective opportunities for providing high levels of "learner control." Architectures of this type are frequently used for online courseware. Instruction is designed to provide a rich set of instructional/learning resources that include: learning content, examples, demonstrations, and knowledge/skills building exercises that are complete with the means to navigate the materials.

Increasingly there is an emphasis on the need for educators to develop online communities to foster a sense of belonging and sharing of knowledge between students. This is an important component of online course development but does not replace the equally important task of adopting a teaching style that best suits the learner's needs and an appropriate architecture to support it. The following case study examines the use of ICT tools in a continuing professional development course according to; learner characteristics, community building, teaching and learning approaches and styles and architectures.

CASE STUDY: REFLECTIONS ON A CONTINUING PROFESSIONAL EDUCATION EXPERIENCE

Anna was an experienced worker and educator in the human services who enrolled in a teaching course for Continuing Professional Education to further develop her skills as an educator.

Learner characteristics: This course was offered at a postgraduate level and had been recommended to Anna by a friend and colleague who was also an experienced human services practitioner and educator. In terms of generational differences, Anna was a baby boomer and Mel was from Generation X, however their learning needs and proficiency with ICT were quite similar. Neither Anna nor Mel were particularly IT savvy but they did have sound basic computing skills and a desire to advance these. Both were competent with using Blackboard in blended course design using face-to-face and ICT tools. They particularly wanted to further develop these skills during the course. In terms of needing and wanting flexibility their situation was more akin with the characteristics assigned to Generation Y. This seemed to also apply to the other students enrolled in the course. Most worked full time as well as having family and other commitments. Even though Anna was very busy she was committed to undertaking the course and excited about new learning.

Community building: The student group was multidisciplinary comprising 15 students from the health and human services, sciences, ICT and creative arts. In the first class students intro-

duced themselves sharing, names, disciplinary backgrounds and what they hoped to achieve by undertaking the course. Tea and coffee making facilities and chocolate biscuits were provided and a room with a pleasant outlook. The teacher was engaging and Anna was feeling very positive about the course.

Anna had hoped to receive some printed information about the aims and objectives of the course but was assured by the teacher that these were available online. She went home and tried to access these on the Blackboard site set up for the course but found they were not there. Not overly concerned about this, Anna thought she would access these at a later date. However, by the end of the course these were still not available. Students' requests for hard copies were not responded to resulting in heated exchanges between the teacher and students. This situation highlights the importance of paper back up if ICT systems fail.

Teaching and learning approaches: The main approach used in the course was the "Cognitive View of Learning" although this was never discussed with the class. This surprised Anna as she had thought the teacher might take the opportunity to model different approaches to the class. This teaching method involved the construction of new knowledge through reading, discussion with other students and online role-plays. Every class involved student discussion groups and student presentations. While the cognitive approach generally includes instruction to promote the psychological processes that mediate the construction of knowledge this did not occur.

As each class was two hours Anna found the two hour small group discussions and lack of variation in the class format tiring and this did not motivate her to do her best work. In one small group discussion a class member made it apparent he did not want to listen to another member in the group and listened to his I-Pod for the entire class. When Anna tried to involve him in the discussion by asking his opinion, he said he was listening to a recording on his I-Pod and preferred not to be disturbed. It was only on the rare occasion that the teacher moved around the room and briefly listened to each group's conversation. At no point did she provide any input into these discussions or use any other learning approach for these face-to-face classes. Anna soon became frustrated by this. She was aware of the teacher's reputation for innovative teaching and her publications. Anna approached her and requested that she provide some input into the classes according to her areas of expertise. The following week the teacher brought some of her publications for the class to read and discuss. The teacher was solely utilizing a cognitive view of learning whereas Anna wanted an absorption or behavioral approach as well. Anna wanted clear explanations from the teacher and her questions answered.

Assessment activities included an online exercise that constituted 60 per cent of the marks for the course. This was a role-play exercise with students divided into small groups and allocated a role by the teacher. These roles included; teacher, local student, international student, discipline leader and Head of School. Each small group was assigned a particular issue to role-play over a two week period. Group members could communicate with each other as well as look at discussions within other groups. If they wanted to be in touch with the entire class they could do so on a general site. Blackboard functionality did not allow them to communicate directly between groups.

Anna had never done anything like this before and whilst slightly apprehensive thought it would be an interesting exercise. She accessed the site feeling quite pleased with how easily she found it and then started doing some postings in her assigned role. When no responses appeared she went off to do something else. Every now and then Anna would look in on the group discussion site and eventually found another student who had put up a posting introducing himself and detailing his hobbies and interests. Anna wondered if perhaps she should have done the same and if this was

appropriate netiquette for an online group such as this. People seemed to do postings on the site at random and rarely did a discussion develop.

On one occasion a group member took offence to some comments Anna made when "in role." Anna was embarrassed by this when it occurred to her that some people were role-playing and others were not. The assessment required five postings per student over the 10 day period and a summary posting on the general discussion board by a delegated group representative at the end of day 10. Some group members did not participate until one or two days before the exercise was to be completed – cramming their postings by making several in a row – often unrelated to other postings. Compiling the summary was difficult in terms of meaningful content and loyalty to group members.

The only online input from the teacher was a comment in response to the summary posting. While the teacher had taken care with developing a sense of community in the first face-to-face class this did not occur into, the online environment. Anna's experience demonstrates the importance of an active role by the teacher in the online environment to tend to all aspects of the role-play experience. This involves preparation, facilitation and moderation, de-briefing and continuous feedback.

Students were required to present the findings of these role-play discussions in class for a further percentage of their grade. These student presentations were video recorded by the teacher for purposes of student feedback. However these were not returned to students. Anna was surprised at what she considered to be the poor quality of some of these presentations. Many students used power point slides that contained far too much information and could not be read from a distance. One student stood with her back to the class while reading word for word off these slides. At no time did the teacher or other students offer any feedback on how to improve these presentations.

For this assessment exercise the teacher had adopted a behavioral approach, planning to give written corrective feedback, but unfortunately this never happened. Had the teacher blended the behavioral and cognitive approaches for this assessment task, peer and self assessments could have also been used to enrich the assessment feedback. It is difficult for teachers to avoid adopting a behavioral approach around assessment activities as there is an expectation that at least in assessment activities feedback will be provided. As this change in approach occurs the learning architecture also needs to be adapted.

Instructional/Learning Architectures: The learning architectures used by the teacher, "exploratory" and "guided discovery" matched the cognitive teaching approach adopted. However it was the minimalist application of these that was problematic. As mentioned earlier in this chapter exploratory architecture requires the teacher to provide a rich set of educational resources to support learning. These resources include; content, examples and demonstrations, and exercises to develop and build knowledge as well as instructions on how to navigate these. In Anna's course the only resources provided by the teacher were weekly readings. It seemed that it was assumed that the content was all in the readings and that learning would occur through reading and the sharing of students' views in small group discussions. The online role-play had potential for "guided discovery" with real life situations used to steer the learning process. However the lack of scaffolding for this exercise in terms of instructional support on how to engage and interact, limited its value.

FUTURE TRENDS

The human services workforce of the future is reliant upon useful and useable technologies. Educators must ensure that students are equipped with the latest knowledge in terms of their particu-

lar discipline and an ability to work effectively in multidisciplinary and online environments. A blended approach is required that mixes face-to-face and online mediums to enhance and enrich quality educational experiences as well as different learning approaches and architectures. Careful attention is required to develop a quality learning environment or community whether this be face-to-face or online with the same principles applying in both environments in terms of content, moderation and classroom etiquette. The teacher has a pivotal active role and voice online as a moderator and facilitator with this not dissimilar to what occurs in face-to-face teaching. The definition of "blended learning" provided in this chapter includes a second level order that not only combines online and face-to-face experiences but also blends a variety of teaching and learning approaches supported by the appropriate learning architectures and scaffolding.

Caution is required when pressure is applied to follow the latest trends or fashions in education that promote cognitive approaches and discard absorption and behavioral approaches as outdated or "behind the times." A reflective educator will use a range of theories, approaches and architectures to provide a quality learning experience that best meets most needs of learners and ultimately satisfies the educational requirements of the human services workforce. Appropriate organizational support and infrastructure is required for functionality and staff time for effective design and implementation. Attention to access and equity issues is needed so that some students are not disadvantaged in the process.

CONCLUSION

The human services workforce is complex and varied. Human services educators have traditionally relied on face-to-face interaction as the preferred means of communication. However, the distinction between face-to-face and distance learning has taken on new meaning in the human services since the advent of ICT. These days, learning environments that are considered as face-to-face educational programs now invariably adopt a blended approach and include an array of ICT tools to supplement or replace on-campus classes. Human services educators need to ensure that the "blended" learning experiences offered maintain and enhance the academic integrity of the discipline and meet the needs of the human services industry for both entry and refresher (continuing professional education) requirements. A considered approach to the use of ICT tools in human services is required; one that matches the planned learning experience with an appropriate learning design and instructional architecture. A key message in this chapter is the importance of adopting an informed approach to the use of ICT, using a variety of learning approaches and appropriate instructional architectures to support these. For instance, cognitive views of learning are well supported by guided discovery and exploratory architecture and seem well suited to human services education; particularly due to the emphasis on "learner control." However this can be well supplemented by absorption and behavioral approaches and architectures. Ultimately student needs and the knowledge and skills required by the human services workforce will determine the most appropriate approaches and architectures to use.

REFERENCES

Anderson, T., & Elloumi, F. (Eds.). (2004). *Theory and practice of online learning* (2nd ed.). Canada: Athabasca University.

Australian Government. (2008, December). *Employment outlook for health and community services*. Retrieved January 2, 2009, from http://www.skillsinfo.gov.au

Bogo, M., & Vayda, E. (1987). *The practice of field instruction in social work*. Toronto, Canada: University of Toronto Press.

Clark, R. C. (2003). *Expertise, learning, and instruction: Building expertise* (2nd ed.). MN, USA: International Society for Performance Improvement.

Kolb, D. (1984). *Experiential learning: Experience as the source of learning and development*. Upper Saddle River, NJ: Prentice Hall.

Lonne, R. (2007). Working together for health, community services and justice to shape local and global workforces. In *Proceedings of the RMIT University 2007 Partnerships for World Graduates Conference*, Melbourne, Australia.

Martin, J. (2007). *Conflict management and mediation*. Port Adelaide, Australia: Ginninderra Press.

Martin, J., McKay, E., & Hawkins, L. (2006). The human-computer interaction spiral. In *Proceedings of the 2006 Informing Science and IT Education Joint Conference*, Salford - Greater Manchester, UK (pp. 183-197).

Martin, J., McKay, E., Hawkins, L., & Murthy, V. (2007). Design-personae: Matching students' learning profiles in Web-based education. In E. McKay (Ed.), *Enhancing Learning through human computer interaction*. Hershey, PA: Idea Group Inc.

Mayer, R. E. (2001). *Multimedia learning*. New York: Cambridge Press.

McKay, E. (2008). *Human-dimensions of human-computer interaction: Balancing the HCI equation*. Amsterdam: IOS Press.

McKay, E., Axmann, M., Banjanin, N., & Howat, A. (2007). Towards Web-mediated learning reinforcement: Rewards for online mentoring through effective human-computer interaction. In V. Uskov (Ed.), *Proceedings of the 6th IASTED International Conference on Web-Based Education,* Chamonix, France (pp. 210-215). Retrieved January 2, 2009, from http://www.iasted.org/conferences/pastinfo-557.html

McKay, E., & Martin, J. (2007). Multidisciplinary collaboration to unravel expert knowledge. In M. Keppell, (Ed.), *Instructional design: Case studies in communities of practice.* Hershey, PA: Information Science Publishing.

Oullette, P. M. (2006). The acquisition of social work interviewing skills in a Web-based and classroom instructional environment: Results of a study. *Journal of Technology in Human Services, 24*(4), 53–75. doi:10.1300/J017v24n04_04

Richardson, S. (2004). *Employers' contribution to training, formal report.* National Centre for Vocational Education Research (NCVER).

Roberts-DeGennaro, M., & Clapp, J. (2005). Assessing the virtual classroom of a graduate social policy course. *Journal of Teaching in Social Work, 25*(1), 69–88. doi:10.1300/J067v25n01_05

Rumble, G. (2000). The globalisation of open and flexible learning: Considerations for planners and managers. *Online Journal of Distance Learning Administration, 3*(3). Retrieved January 2, 2009, from http://www.westga.edu/~distance/ojdla/fall33/rumble33.html

Schwalbe, K. (2006). *Information technology project management.* Canada: Thomson - Course Technology.

Shardlow, S. M., & Horwath, J. (2000). Empowering learners through open (distance) programmes: An evaluation of a practice teaching programme. *Social Work Education, 19*(2), 111–123. doi:10.1080/02615470050003502

Siebert, D. C., Siebert, C. F., & Spaulding-Givens, J. (2006). Teaching clinical social work skills primarily on line: An evaluation. *Journal of Social Work Education, 42*(2), 325–336.

SkillsInfo. (2007). *Health and community services employment outlook.* Retrieved January 2, 2009, from http://www.skillsinfo.gov.au/Industries/HealthCommunityServices

Smith, P. R., & Wingerson, N. W. (2006). Is the centrality of relationship in social work education at risk with IVT? *Journal of Technology in Human Services, 24*(2), 23–37. doi:10.1300/J017v24n02_02

Staughton, D. (2006). How to find and keep the best staff. In *Proceedings of the LIV Small Practice Conference.* Melbourne, Australia: Law Institute of Victoria.

Wolfson, G. K., Magnuson, C. W., & Marsom, G. (2005). Changing the nature of the discourse: Teaching field seminars online. *Journal of Social Work Education, 41*(2), 355–361.

Chapter 2

Educational and Social Benefits of Social Network Sites
Applications to Human Services Education and Practice

Christine Greenhow
University of Minnesota, USA

Beth Robelia
University of Minnesota, USA

ABSTRACT

Online social network sites present opportunities for human service educators, practitioners, and clients. Human services education students can collaborate through multimedia networks, sharing ideas and experiences. Human services professionals can leverage online networks to problem solve, socialize and develop common resources, and clients can use such networks to engage in self-reflection and get support from those facing similar challenges. This chapter offers an introduction to online social network sites, summarizing their features, uses, demographics, and trends, and presents emerging research on their social and educational potential. An accompanying case study reveals how young adults might use online social network sites to further personal and educational goals. The chapter concludes with a discussion of how such sites might be employed by human services education students, practitioners and clients.

'In education there should be no class distinction'.

Confucius (K'ung Fu tzu 551-479 BC), *Analects, ch.15, v.38* in *Oxford Dictionary of Quotations* (2004, p.238:8).

OPENING VIGNETTE

It is seven o'clock in the evening. Emilio has just finished dinner with his family and retreats to his bedroom to check in on the other social network in his life. Like the majority of U.S. online teens who are daily users of a social network site, logging twenty minutes to an hour or more, Emilio goes to MySpace.com and signs in. Once within

DOI: 10.4018/978-1-60566-735-5.ch002

his profile page — his entry point to this online international community—he notices that several things have changed among his "friends" in just the few hours since he last communicated with them. Looking at his list of "updates" he notices that Julia has joined the network. Alex has written in his blog about the challenges of college life. Jade has finished her midterm and thinks she did okay. Whitney has become a supporter of the Democratic president-elect, Barak Obama, and Jose has added four new photos of his new dorm room. Emilio accepts Julia as a friend so she can see his complete online profile. He comments, "Congratulations!" on Jade's update. He visits Alex's page to leave a comment about his blog entry on college life. He visits Whitney's profile to see what other people have said about her support for the U.S. president. He visits his own home page to read comments friends have left him about a video he created for a school project about sports casting, his career interest. Earlier, he had posted an unfinished essay for sociology in his blog so that friends could give feedback on what he had written. Using the instant messaging feature within the MySpace network, Emilio messages another classmate who appears to be online and asks for advice on a social work assignment. He stays logged into the MySpace system while he works on his homework, waiting for friends to respond to his requests and comments. Soon messages began to appear. One friend instant messages some feedback on the sociology essay. Another friend compliments him on the finished video, and another gives him advice on the psychology assignment. At nine o'clock, Emilio changes his MySpace mood setting to "tired" and signs out of the network. His work is finished. He looks forward to following up with his friends on the night's events when he meets them tomorrow, online or off.

INTRODUCTION

This opening vignette describes some of the many ways young people participate in online social network sites (SNSs). Emilio (a psuedonym) was a shy, soft-spoken eighteen year old who had a few close friends at university. Within MySpace (www.myspace.com), however, Emilio had a large network of friends, acquaintances, and contacts from within and outside his local community. His MySpace profile contained videos and photos he had created and posted to share. Often portrayed in the media as dangerous or distracting (Hass, 2006; Rowan, 2007), many young people are actually making important, positive connections through their use of online social network sites. They find emotional support, get help with school work, relax, socialize and flourish in using this outlet for their creativity.

The purpose of this chapter is to explore the social and educational benefits of online social network sites and the implications of social network site affordances for human services education and practice. The unique features of today's social network sites will be discussed in relation to other forms of virtual communities. The chapter will present theoretical foundations, application of social network site features to education and ways in which the competencies users demonstrate in social network sites can have educational benefits and enhance learners' experience. Moreover, a case study of one students' use of an online social network will be provided for tertiary social work students who seek to consider the potential application of this information communication technology for human services education and practice. This case study may also be useful for researchers in the field of information communication technology and human computer interaction in various disciplines who seek to describe and illuminate online social networking practices.

BACKGROUND

Adherents of social networking – including 70% of today's 15- to 34-year-olds – utilize their preferred social networking sites at all hours of the day and night to fulfill a roster of needs as diverse as the users themselves (February 2007, U.S. ComScore data, ages 15-34 at all locations).

Social Network Sites: A Unique Form of ICT

Since their introduction in the late 1990's, and rising to mainstream prominence with MySpace and LinkedIn in 2003, online social network sites have attracted millions of users. In the United States, a majority of online teens have created a personal profile on a social network site like MySpace or Facebook and visit their social network site daily or several times a day, devoting an average of 9 hours a week to the network (Lenhart & Madden, 2007; National School Boards Association, 2007).

According to boyd & Ellison (2007) an online social network site is a 'web-based service that allows individuals to (1) construct a public or semi-public profile within a bounded system, (2) articulate a list of other users with whom they share a connection, and (3) view and traverse their list of connections and those made by others within the system' (p. 1). What distinguishes social network sites from other forms of virtual communities is that they allow users to articulate and make visible their social networks, similar to allowing others to view your address book and interact with it online. In this way your connections potentially become the connections of your "friends." Boyd & Ellison (2007) suggest that these "friending" behaviors through social network sites can result in more and different types of connections between individuals that would not otherwise be made (Haythornthwaite, 2005). In addition to individuals, SNSs may include profiles of bands, companies, events, non-profit organizations or political parties (Childnet International, 2007).

Other terms such as "online social networking site," "networked social media" and just "social network" have been used to describe these Web 2.0 technologies. For our purposes, we will use the term online social network site (SNS) according to boyd and Ellison's (2007) definition.

A growing body of survey research suggests that youth's participation in online social network sites may cross gender, ethnicity, and income boundaries as teens once disconnected from the Internet (e.g., low-income African-American, Latino and other low-income students) now largely have access (College Access Marketing, 2008; Lenhart, Arafeh, Smith & Macgill, 2008). For instance, in our surveys with 600 urban high school students from low-income families in the upper Midwestern United States (i.e., median family income at or below US$25,000), we found that over 80% go online regularly from home and 77% have a profile on an online social network site. The majority use MySpace (65%) with Facebook (37%) being the second most popular site, and many students belong to more than one network (Greenhow, Walker & Kim, 2008).

Use of Social Networking Sites for Social and Educational Purposes

Social Networking Sites can serve a range of purposes, including helping users maintain existing friendships or forge new relationships based on shared professional interests, political views, a common language or shared racial, sexual, religious, or cultural identities. In studying U.S. Internet trends, Lenhart and Madden (2007) found that 91% of SNS users employed these sites to maintain relationships with existing friends with whom they frequently socialize, and 82%, to maintain connections to others with whom they do not socialize; 72% used these sites to make social plans.

Such relationship building can be accomplished through a range of SNS features that accommodate data-sharing in various forms (e.g., video, audio, text, photo, hyperlinks, etc.) and user-generated content. For instance, most sites allow users to share personal profiles, write comments, upload files, and select applications, although the extent to which sites incorporate new information and communication tools, such as mobile connectivity, blogging, and photo/video-sharing varies. Many SNSs offer condensed versions of their services for customers who want access via mobile handheld devices such as cell phones, which have become nearly ubiquitous among youth and adults of all ages (Lenhart, Madden, Macgill & Smith, 2007).

Some of the most common activities young people engage in are creating online profiles, visiting others profiles and leaving messages, viewing digital content, authoring content and sharing content created by a third party (Childnet International, 2007). Indeed, students engaged in SNSs are more likely to be content creators: posting or remixing digital images or video, creating or commenting in blogs, or maintaining a website (Lenhart & Madden, 2007). Interestingly, a recent survey involving over 2,000 nine- to 17-year old students, parents and school district leaders in the U.S., reported that much of students' online sharing in SNSs involves frequent exchange of private and public messages and comments, with education being a common topic of conversation —e.g., 60% of students surveyed reported using their SNS to talk about education topics and 50%, to talk specifically about schoolwork) (National School Boards Association, 2007). Outside of the United States, the Digizen Project of Childnet International is examining how SNSs can benefit young people in the United Kingdom and around the world. The Digizen site (http://www. digizen.org/) offers a framework for evaluating the appropriateness of SNSs for formal or informal learning. A downloadable evaluation chart considers a site's age restrictions, the presence of advertisements, collaboration tools, security options and data management restrictions. The site also outlines considerations for educators trying to integrate such sites, including privacy issues, cyberbullying prevention and legal issues.

Demographics of SNS Use

Typically thought of as a youth phenomenon, the demographics of SNS users are increasingly diverse. Today there are hundreds of online social network sites, the two most popular being MySpace and Facebook with about 115 million users each worldwide (Stone, 2008). Launched in 2004, MySpace generated more page views than Google or Yahoo and has broad appeal across all age ranges (Compete, 2008). More than half of MySpace users in the U.S. are under 35 years of age (77%), with young people 12 -17 years (29%), 18-34 years (44%) and the over 35 demographic representing a smaller (23%) but still significant proportion of users (Quantcast, 2008). About 300,000 new people sign up for MySpace every day. Its users span more than 20 international territories, including the United States, United Kingdom, Australia, Japan, France, Germany, Mexico, and Canada. In the U.S. one in four Americans is on MySpace and in the UK, it is as common to have a MySpace profile as it is to own a dog. Moreover, MySpace has a large presence within the entertainment industry. It maintains a dominant position as a media-sharing site (i.e., uploading music, videos, scanned artwork, photography, etc.), giving users the opportunity to interact with brands, bands, artists, actors, and other creative professionals as well as to self-express. Analysts expect to see more television and video networks integrate and work with MySpace (Owyang, 2008).

By comparison, Facebook also appeals to a broader demographic than simply teenagers. People ages 18-24 (34%) and 35-54 years of age (33%), constitute Facebook's two largest groups of users. Originally created to foster social networking among U.S. college students, Facebook is still a dominant presence on college campuses; however, more than half of Facebook users are outside of college, and its fastest growing demographic is 25 years of age and older (Owyang, 2008). Facebook has also expanded internationally, with the most active users residing in the U.S., Canada, the UK and Australia. Facebook's orientation overlaps with MySpace in that it maintains regional, profession-related, and school-related networks; however, Facebook is perhaps more strongly affiliated with collegiate and work-related networks than is MySpace and maintains 85 percent market share of 4-year U.S. universities.

Moreover, Facebook emphasizes its niche as a platform for independently generated applications. According to the company's analysts, 24,000 applications have been built on the Facebook platform and an estimated 140 new applications are added per day allowing users to increasingly customize the functionality of their network (See for more information: http://www.facebook.com/press/info.php?statistics). *Socialyze,* for instance, is an application Facebook users can add to their profiles (and invite friends to add) which enables them to analyze data, statistics and trends generated by their "friends" within the Facebook system. The application can be used as a game to get to know people better and strengthen social connections. Users can test their social knowledge and compete against friends to earn points and "climb the social ladder." *Books iRead* is a Facebook application that may be useful for educational or professional uses. It lets one share ratings of books and showcase a virtual bookshelf. Users can see what their colleagues or students are reading and read reviews of what others have read. Users can join a virtual bookclub, get book recommendations or meet new people who share the same reading interests. Facebook *translator* applications allow real-time translation of messages between users who speak different languages. The *Where I've Been* application allows users to post an interactive world map on their profile, showing those who visit their site, where they have been, lived and want to go. Visitors to a user's *Where I've Been* map can click on a country or city to get more information.

No overview of online social network sites would be complete without emphasizing the increasing proliferation and diversity of this emerging information and communications technology. A quick Google search reveals millions of hits for "online social network sites." Wikipedia lists over 130 on its list of "notable, well-known" sites (http://en.wikipedia.org/wiki/List_of_social_networking_websites) and reviews abound, such as this one from Top Ten Reviews (http://social-networking-websites-review.toptenreviews.com/), which strive to characterize and distinguish one site from another. Sites like Hi5.com, Friendster.com, Orkut and Bebo.com rank just below MySpace and Facebook in size and international presence (ComScore, 2008a). Bebo is especially popular in the U.K., Ireland and New Zealand while Orkut is popular in Brazil, Paraguay and India, and Cyworld is the site of choice among many young South Koreans (Wikipedia, 2008).

Furthermore, a growing number of SNSs are designed specifically to support education. EducatorCentral (http://www.takingitglobal.org/tiged/ec/) within TakingITGlobal (www.takingitglobal.org) supports teaching and learning (Childnet International, 2007). Ning (www.ning.com) is an increasingly popular SNS that allows people, schools, and companies, to build and design their own social Web sites tailored to their students, clients, friends, and employees. Within Ning.com there are a few SNSs that specifically address human services professionals. These include Social Work 2.0 (http://www.socialwork20.com/) and Social Work Advocates (http://socialworkadvocates.ning.com), which is a community of social workers who are passionate about advocating for vulnerable and oppressed populations. Other sites are just beginning such as Social and Human Services (http://sociallyhuman.ning.com) and Social Work Grad Students (http://socialworkgradstudents.ning.com/). In the UK, a relatively new SNS offered by the social work magazine *Community Care* (http://www.communitycare.co.uk/carespace/) features high quality podcasts of research seminars and educational products, which can be subscribed to within iTunes (http://www.iriss.ac.uk/audio). In addition, this SNS features an open access repository of human services related content called the Learning Exchange (http://www.iriss.ac.uk/openlx/).

There are also numerous networks for specific human services client populations. For instance, people addicted to alcohol and other drugs can identify treatment options and get peer support within SoberCircle (http://www.sobercircle.com/). Sobercircle blogs and chats offer a place for clients in recovery to voice their struggles with addiction and seek support from others. Separate forums for social service professionals allow those who counsel people recovering from addiction to connect and share ideas. PatientsLikeMe (http://www.patientslikeme.com/) allows people dealing with certain life altering neurological conditions such as multiple sclerosis or Parkinson's disease to share their experiences, find similar patients, and learn from the latest research. People with mood disorders (e.g., depression, bipolar disorder) are also supported within the site. The philosophy of open sharing within PatientsLikeMe allows people to discuss their treatment histories anonymously so others can benefit from information about successful approaches. Although we have been focusing on SNSs used primarily by teens and adults, there are also sites, such as ClubPenguin (http://www.clubpenguin.com/) and Imbee (http://imbee.com/) that are designed for and used by younger children, ages 8-14. These sites have stricter privacy controls and require a parent's email to sign up.

Finally, there is significant diversity in the SNS user population. A person's gender, race and ethnicity, and parental educational background, for instance, are all associated with SNS use. According to the Pew Internet and American Life studies in the United States, older girls ages 15-17 are more likely to have created an online profile on a social network site (70%), while only 57% of online boys have done so (Lenhart et al., 2007).

Hargittai (2007), in studying college students' differential adoption of online social network sites, found differences in the percentage of racial and ethnic groups that used four popular SNSs (Facebook, MySpace, Xanga and Friendster). Hispanics favored MySpace over Facebook and other sites. Students of Asian background favored Friendster and Xanga. Both African Americans and Caucasian students used MySpace and Facebook more than the other two sites in the study. Using parental education as a measure of family income, Hargattai (2007) also found that students with parents who had less than a high school diploma were significantly more likely to be on MySpace than Facebook. Students whose parents had a college degree where significantly more likely to use Facebook. However, it is important to note that this study was completed before Facebook opened its membership to everyone. Previously only those with a college email could use Facebook. Next we turn to the theoretical foundations underlying this chapter.

THEORETICAL FOUNDATIONS

Not surprisingly, given that people's use of online social network sites is a relatively recent phenomenon, much of the published research on the use of SNSs is still emerging. The handful of studies that exist stem mostly from communications, information science, anthropology, sociology, economics, political science, cultural studies, and computer science and are both conceptual and empirical in nature (boyd & Ellison, 2007). Very few studies explore the link between social network site use and education. For instance, Hewitt and Forte (2006) examined how college age students feel about having their professors on Facebook, and Mazer, Murphy & Simonds (2007) investigated how faculty presence on Facebook impacts student-educator relationships, but these studies do not deal directly with *students'* experiences in using online social network sites and how

SNS use may impact their *educational* experience, which is the focus of this chapter.

The theoretical foundations for this research stem from education, communication and sociology, specifically interpersonal ties theories from communication and sociology, constructivist frameworks for how people learn, and twenty-first century skills frameworks in education.

Meeting Interpersonal needs Online

Despite troubling public accounts of Internet-mediated communication as socially isolating and necessarily inferior to other modes of communication (Thurlow, 2006), a number of studies have argued that, in fact, communication via the Internet can help users develop, maintain, and extend social relationships, leading to a broader network of support when faced with important life decisions (Ellison, Steinfield, & Lampe, 2007; Kraut et al., 2002; Wellman, Haase, Witte, Hampton, 2001). Such findings are important for human services education if we consider that interventions which increase students' connections to their peers and community resources can lead to greater persistence and success in university programs (Zhao & Kuh, 2004; Tinto, 1998).

In examining interpersonal interactions within the context of a SNS and how SNSs may be supporting interpersonal needs, it is important to consider: the technological affordances of the environment; how users employ (or not) these and for what communicative purposes; and the conditions surrounding these interactions (e.g., computer and Internet access/context, frequency and duration of social network site use, nature of the relationship between SNS participants). This examination of the potential of social network sites to fulfill interpersonal needs, as illustrated in the case study that follows, is informed by recent studies on how social networks are created, maintained and negotiated through media (Donath & boyd, 2004; Gross & Acquisiti, 2005; Ellison, Steinfield & Lampe, 2007; Herring, 2004;

Wellman, Salaff, Dimitrova, Garton, Gulia, Hay-thornwaite, 1996).

Supporting Constructivist Pedagogy and How People Learn

Social Networking Sites are uniquely positioned to mesh with theories of adult pedagogy which stress that adults expect their experience and connections will be incorporated into their learning. Younger and older adults are entering university education classes with the expectation that they will be able to contribute to the discussion, giving feedback as well as receiving it. Students expect to critique each others' ideas and projects as well as contribute to class discussions blending their ideas and experiences with others to create learning. This atmosphere of constructivism is different from that of classrooms where students submit assignments to one person (their instructor) and receive feedback from that person. Multiple evaluations by peers, instructors, and others are quickly becoming the norm in the networked classroom. In synthesizing over a decade of educational and cognitive neuroscience research on how people learn, Bransford, Brown and Cocking (1999) developed guidelines for effective teaching that emphasizes learning with understanding. Effective instructors, they argue, help structure a complete learning environment that encompasses three focal points-- learner, knowledge and assessment--within a larger community or society (p. 120-130). High technology-using environments, such as those embodied by social network sites, may be conducive to both developing learning and innovative pedagogy because they typically feature "learners" informally sharing thoughts, emotions, and skills within a networked community where production, distribution, feedback and reciprocity are valued. Moreover, in developing and displaying a "public" profile and engaging in collaborative acts of production with others in the system, users may be demonstrating the kinds of knowledge construction and problem-solving activities frequently sought in twenty-first century instructional reform efforts.

Although there are various forms of educational constructivism, generally, constructivism is a theory of learning that views the nature of "knowledge" as created or formulated by the learner actively engaged in the process of making meaning (Fulton, 1999). Learners make or "construct" new meaning by taking what they already know and applying what is being learned to new situations. "Knowledge," rather than inherently meaningful, becomes meaningful through the learner's interpretation and application of what he or she knows in a community where knowledge is shared. Experience and individual differences, therefore, are important and respected, and situations that have direct relevance to the learner or applicability to life are those that provide the best opportunities for learning. In the constructivist model, the learner's background, expertise, and beliefs all affect the learning or knowledge that is assembled (Brown & Duguid, 2000). When applied to pedagogy, the constructivist view of learning supports a learner-centered instructional environment where learning and teaching are "facilitated" by the instructors rather than "transmitted" as in a traditional lecture-oriented teacher-centered classroom. Online social network site features may support such environments by enabling users to profile their individual differences and commonalities, communicate interests, ideas, and experiences in multimedia forms, negotiate learning goals, aggregate the wisdom of the group to co-construct solutions, and solicit and get feedback from multiple audiences.

21st Century Skills Frameworks

Ultimately, at all levels of education, from undergraduate to graduate programs, we want our students and clients to be trained in and proficient at using emerging digital tools and social media to ultimately enhance their career-related decision-making and performance. Therefore, this chapter considers how students, in using SNSs, are practicing the kinds of "21st century skills" that are increasingly emphasized in educational and workplace settings, but perhaps especially important in human services occupations. These include *creative thinking*: the ability to construct knowledge and develop innovative products and processes; *communication and collaboration*: the ability to communicate in multiple media and to work collaboratively to support individual learning or the learning of others; *research and information fluency*: the ability to locate, organize, evaluate and process data from a number of sources and present the results; and *problem-solving*: the ability to define problems and manage activities toward a range of solutions (International Society for Technology in Education, 2007; Partnership for 21st century Skills, 2008). Moreover, today's instructors are expected to develop and model these competencies as well as to facilitate their development in students (International Society for Technology in Education, 2008).

CASE STUDY CONTEXT

Drawing on these frameworks above, we undertook an exploratory qualitative study in the spring of 2008 to examine whether and how urban youth from low-income families in the upper Midwestern United States used the online social network site, MySpace.com, as part of their everyday lives and whether and how their MySpace use demonstrated educational and social benefits. This investigation is part of a larger three-year effort to profile these students' Internet technology access, use, and capacity. A total of 1200 students (17- and 18-years of age) were given paper surveys in the winter of 2007 (number of respondents=850) and again in the winter of 2008 (number of respondents=600). They were asked a series of questions about their location, frequency, duration, type of computer and Internet use, and their purpose for using various Web-based technologies. Focus groups were also conducted to triangulate survey data. Students who participated in this research were from thirteen urban high schools (56% female) and were all participating in an after-school program, Admission Possible, aimed at improving college access for low-income students. These students were from families whose incomes were at or below the county median income (at or below $25,000) (Greenhow, Walker, & Kim, 2008).

To investigate students' use of online social network sites, specifically, we conducted follow-up in-depth interviews, talk-alouds, and content analysis of MySpace profiles with a randomly selected sub-group of eleven students (all frequent MySpace users). The case study that follows draws from this larger research effort.

THE CASE OF THERESA SOMMERS

[You learn] different things about different people. . . . you get afforded different opportunities from the social network like with the [political] caucus invitation. I wouldn't have been able to go there; I wouldn't have known how to get there otherwise. (Theresa, age 21)

Theresa Sommers grinned as she talked about getting to know different sides to her "friends" within MySpace.com. She talked excitedly about friending the Democratic nominee for United States president, Barak Obama, and the opportunities to get involved in the 2008 presidential election that had come her way through her online social network. A young woman from a Chinese-American family, Theresa spoke animatedly of her plans to attend a university next year. In just a few short weeks, she would graduate from her large urban high school and transition to the next phase of her life.

Technology Background and Context for SNS Use

We met Theresa in the spring of 2008 when we interviewed MySpace-using teens in order to begin to understand whether and how online social networks might be utilized to support educational and social goals. Theresa was 18 years old and from a low-income family living in a Midwestern city. Like many of the students in our study, Theresa had access to high speed Internet at home. However, unlike others, she had her own laptop and did not have to share time on the Internet with siblings or parents. Theresa was a relatively experienced SNS user, having used MySpace for three years and Facebook.com for 1.5 years. Thus, she maintained two SNS accounts: her MySpace account, for its connections to high school friends, musicians, artists, politicians, and entertainment or school-related groups and her Facebook account as part of her journey toward college access and enrollment. In fact, she used Facebook to "network" with students currently enrolled in colleges she was considering, and she believed these online interactions had factored into her college decision. Theresa used her MySpace several times per week for about one hour, which was slightly less than the majority of students we interviewed who visited daily or every other day. However, her time on SNSs also varied depending on her workload and purposes; she used her SNSs most intensely in the time leading up to submitting her college application, wanting not only to network with current college students but to keep her contacts updated on her college search process.

Patterns and Purpose for SNS Use

As Theresa sat down in front of MySpace, she talked us through her most common activities and strategies when logging in. Like many online teens who prefer communicating through the multiple channels offered by SNSs rather than through older technologies such as email (Lenhart et al., 2007), Theresa used MySpace to make and maintain connections to friends, acquaintances, and potential "friends" within the system. Keeping up with "mail" communications within her MySpace account was, therefore, a top priority. Typically, she sorted through and responded to incoming messages and checked that older messages had been answered or deleted. Next, she moved on to review "friend requests," that is, other people within the MySpace system who wanted to be part of her "friend" network. She accepted the request of an old friend from middle school who had since moved away and that of an acquaintance who had graduated from her high school last year. She denied the request from a "random band" because she did not like the music playing on the band's MySpace page. Next, she skimmed the latest updates among her friends list (e.g., updated profile information, new connections among members, new photos posted to an online photo album, new blog entries on college life). Clicking on the most interesting updates, or on updates from those she had not visited in a while, took her to their individual profile pages. There she "commented people," posting her feedback to a friend's blog or picture or posting a message to a friend's page so that he knew she had stopped by. In travelling to the MySpace pages of people in her network, Theresa could also see who was connected to whom and decide who among her "friends' friends" she would like to get to know. Clicking on the photo of a person outside her network, instantly brought her to that contact's limited profile with the option to "add to friends." Clicking on this option would generate a "friend request" and send it to that person, asking him or her to accept Theresa as a new "friend, thereby, allowing her access to his or her complete profile and online address book.

Theresa also used her network to find multimedia resources and information. For instance, she was looking for a new photograph of herself for her profile homepage. She remarked that she had not changed her profile picture for some time yet valued the dynamic and continually updating nature of the MySpace world. Browsing for photos within her friends' online photo albums, where she had been tagged, enabled her to identify potentially useful images. She mentioned another incident where she had needed resources for a class project. Sending a bulletin or group message to the many friends in her network, she claimed, provided an easy way to gather valuable resources. When time allowed, she wrote poetry in her blog and composed updates on her college application process for those younger friends in her network she hoped to motivate and inspire.

When asked why she used SNSs such as MySpace, she explained how her purposes had shifted from purely social ones to more complex social and education-related purposes. Introduced to MySpace as a sophomore, she had logged in daily, spending an hour or more crafting an online persona through her profile page, searching for "cool" background layouts and changing the colors, design, music, and overall "look and feel" of her page. In many ways, she felt that she was participating in an online popularity contest to see who could have the most interesting-looking profile, the most number of "friends," and the most heavily visited site. As she eventually integrated MySpace into her everyday life, with its competing priorities and time constraints, her purpose for using the site became more authentic and personally meaningful. As a high school senior about to enroll in college, Theresa now says she uses MySpace primarily to strengthen and maintain relationships with people she has met online and offline, to obtain emotional support from her peers, to solicit help with school assignments, to report on school/college-related progress and accomplishments, and to express her creativity.

In this next section, we will discuss how these stated goals were manifested in Theresa's case, highlighting observed social and educational benefits of her participation in the MySpace network.

Developing Relationships and Meeting Interpersonal Needs

The young people in our study, like Theresa, used the capabilities of the online social network MySpace.com to develop and maintain various types of relationships. Contrary to the popular perception that SNS users falsify their identities making truthful relationships difficult, Theresa's profile illustrated her attempts to craft and present an authentic self within the online space. She posted an actual photograph of herself, listed her hometown and country, displayed a username that related to her first name only, truthfully reported her relationship status as single, provided her actual age and encouraged her "friends" to exchange messages with her: "Facebook or text me," now that she was entering college. However, she also took steps to protect her full identity from unwanted viewers, setting her MySpace profile to "private" and allowing only those within her approved network to see her full profile and contacts. Moreover, like the other students we interviewed, Theresa, talked about the advantages of freely expressing her thoughts, opinions, fears, and emotions through the multimedia channels SNSs afford but also noted her hesitancy to reveal too much personal information, such as her full name, address, and contact information, which could subject her to unwanted fraud or abuse.

Walking the line between self-expression and anonymity, Theresa's profile revealed that she used various MySpace features to maintain interpersonal connections with people she saw everyday as well as with those she rarely saw or had never met. Features such as the address book, asynchronous message system, online chat, bulletins, friend requests, event alerts, and automatically generated, aggregated lists of friend "updates" or "status and mood" reports allowed her to keep abreast of the lives of people in her network and grow it. In her view, MySpace was a virtual "hang out" where one could relax around other people (e.g., close friends, distant friends, acquaintances,

people she had never met) and keep the "line of communication open" without frequent and costly time and emotional investment:

I think it's a good way to keep in touch with people you may not have time to call or meet or even text them...it's kind of a "kick-back"...it's just kind of a way to relax and hang out and not necessarily having to worry about talking directly to a person but just kind of like keeping that line of communication open.

However, Theresa also noted that a core group of "friends" in her MySpace network were actually people she talked to and physically hung out with regularly. She felt that her connections to those people, especially, deepened with her use of MySpace because she was able to "see more sides to them" than she would have otherwise as they could now express themselves in audio, video, graphical, and text media. For instance, friends she never knew had political interests or artistic abilities were displaying these sides of themselves in MySpace. Friends who were not usually emotional in person were revealing emotions through emoticons, descriptive status updates, or online writing.

Maintaining this range of social connections from which to draw—e.g., "strong ties" as among family members and close friends and "weak ties" as among acquaintances, distant friends and potential contacts (Granovetter, 1973)— makes SNSs potentially advantageous to young people who are able to activate connections appropriate to their purposes when they need them. For instance, one "friend" in Theresa's network, a former classmate now at a distant university, activated his network to build an audience for his budding radio career. Using the "bulletin" feature in MySpace, he posted the following message titled "New Information," which asked his contacts to check out a new radio show:

I have a radio show entitled "Know it Al!" (a psuedonym for the real title). The information for that is on facebook. Also, if you search for "Know it Al!" on facebook there is a fan site that you can join and become a fan. Through that site I will be sending people updates and everything. So there are two things going on.... The radio show is on Thursdays from 2:30-3:30 and you can stream it online at [name of URL] . All you have to do is hit listen and even if you have a slow internet connection you can still get it. Trust me...

Theresa also used MySpace to initiate connections for career-building and inquiry purposes. For example, she was interested in photography as a potential career. Through MySpace she was able to view the work of professional photographers and exchange comments and questions with them about the field, including the kinds of training and skills that are needed. MySpace allows its users to join public forums and search within the network for people with particular skills like "professional photographers." Because it is a media-rich environment that lets users post their own content without requiring sophisticated technical expertise, experienced and novice artists can scan and upload or link to their work, asking others for advice and feedback. Such intergenerational and cross-disciplinary exchange might rarely happen in the "real world" but in the virtual world of SNSs, with its low costs to self-promotion and sharing, such interconnections are prevalent.

Similarly, Theresa used MySpace to become a resource for younger students, making visible her college search and application process. Posting personal updates where others could view them allowed her to model the process for students like her who were just beginning to think about choosing and applying to schools:

And I would even get questions [online] from different organizations I work with, like students in them, and they'll ask me like what's the process like? and what schools are you picking from? and

they seem like they're really into it because that's what they're looking forward to, and so I think I did it a lot more for them [posted that information on MySpace] than for my peers here in school that I work with. (129-133)

Mentoring younger students, something Theresa may not have had the time, inclination or opportunity to do face-to-face, was facilitated through this networked information space. As this example suggests, social digital technologies available on the Web, such as SNSs, may prove particularly useful in helping us address educational inequities. For instance, it is well known that students from low-income families do not graduate from high school, enroll in postsecondary education, or obtain undergraduate and graduate degrees at the same rate as their peers from more affluent families. Often these students lack the social and cultural capital available to students from college-educated and affluent families. Technologies, such as online social network sites, may help "level the playing field" by providing such students with rich, affordable access to supportive peers and adults from similar backgrounds who have succeeded.

Moreover, in providing a range of creative and communication tools without the physical social cues that can discourage self-expression face-to-face, SNSs offer young people an interactive outlet for their emotions, reflections, and experience. For instance, when writing in her MySpace blog, Theresa wrote about topics that were personally meaningful and emotional, "It's kind of me venting." She wrote for herself as well as for an audience, straddling the line between confession and meditation:

I know my friends will go on and read it. For the most part, I'm really up front with them, but then for some things that are kind of hard to say to people... with those things, they read it, and then they take it in their own way and they have time to digest it and then, react to it, like they [have] a little section where they can leave a comment (178-184).

Below, Theresa recalled how she was prompted to respond to a friend in need through MySpace, speculating that she probably would not have done so otherwise:

Like somebody will write me and tell me, "I'm going through this." And I wrote a poem for a friend because she and her boyfriend broke up, and that's just probably one thing I wouldn't have done [written the poem] if she hadn't written me about it on MySpace" (475 -478).

As these examples illustrate, SNSs facilitate semi-public sharing, as opposed to writing in a private journal, emailing, or posting in a public online community; feedback and encouragement from other members are aggregated, archived, and can be viewed over time within a sanctioned social circle. Such collective thoughts can provide a powerful source of support, motivation, and recognition for a job well done, even building on and extending relationships in the physical world. For example, in Theresa's case, one of her senior projects was to give a final in-class performance related to an issue she cared about. She felt that many of her peers gave fine performances and wanted to tell them so. Her strategy was to recognize her peers semi-publicly within MySpace: "I like to post it so that everybody can see it [my positive comments to a person]. Of course, you'll tell them face to face but I like to put it on MySpace just so everyone can know they did a good job. (591-596)"

In addition to cultivating and maintaining close and distant interpersonal connections for a range of purposes, young people may be using SNSs to demonstrate the 21st century competencies that educators value, including creativity, communication in multiple media, collaboration to support one's own or the learning of others, problem-solving, and research and information fluency. Examples

from Theresa's case illustrate how some of these competencies may be demonstrated.

Demonstrating 21st Century Competencies

Recent survey reports and preliminary descriptive research suggest that today's young people are using participatory media such as SNSs to practice and develop creative processes and innovative content (Lenhart et al., 2008; Lenhart et al., 2007; Perkel, 2008; Hull & Nelson, 2008; Coiro, Knobel, Lankshear & Leu, 2008). Copy/paste literacy practices where youth manipulate and "remix" code in the production of a MySpace profile are giving new meaning to our notions of "reading" and "writing" online (Perkel, 2008). Youth's digital stories, multi-medial compositions produced by layering text, music, and images, are engendering new, respected writing genres (Hull & Nelson, 2005). These are just some examples of how young people may be developing creative capacities and technical proficiency within SNSs which have implications for formal education. Theresa, for example, posted original photographs within her MySpace profile as a means of personal expression. She credits MySpace with motivating her to share this work with a wider audience:

I always liked to take photographs, and I had a bag full of like 15 disposable cameras that had not been developed. So MySpace got me to develop them and put them on MySpace. . . . I develop more pictures; I make more of an effort to get what I'm doing out to people just because it's an open space for people to observe.

In fact, she marveled at the positive effect SNSs had on her ability to represent herself, "I think [SNSs] have changed my communication skills in some ways because I don't necessarily have a problem [now] speaking my mind." We also saw evidence of this in the range of artifacts students posted within MySpace (e.g., videos they had created, photographs, graphically interesting backgrounds, music, song lyrics, links to other artifacts).

In addition to sharing photographs, Theresa shared her creative and school-related writing. Prior to joining MySpace, she felt others rarely read her work, but MySpace helped motivate such efforts by giving her multiple audiences for which to perform. The audience for her school writing was generally classmates while the audience for her creative writing and photography was a diverse group of people, such as artists she had come into contact with through MySpace and believed she would not have known otherwise. Theresa's sense was that people young and old enjoyed sharing their creativity in SNSs: "I know people that dance and sing and they have little videos on their profiles and I know some other poets and people who like to write and rap and do art and paint and take photographs and everything."

The interconnections and creative capabilities evident in SNSs like MySpace offer learners initiation into a Web-based "participatory culture" (Jenkins, 2006) with low barriers to artistic expression and civic engagement, strong support for creating and sharing one's digital productions, a sense of social connections to each another (or at least caring what other people think about what one has created), and a belief that contributions matter. Participatory culture is manifested as: *affiliations* such as "groups" or "forums" centered around people's background, interests, connections, and media; *creative self- or collective expressions* (e.g., video-making, mash-ups), and *circulations* (e.g., podcasting, blogging) (Jenkins, 2006, p. 1). Such opportunities potentially enrich learning by making it more personally meaningful, collaborative, and socially relevant.

Moreover, the self-assertiveness and confidence developed by "speaking my mind" to a select audience, often for purely social reasons, may encourage youth to turn to those networks for help in solving important problems or decisions. As 21st century educators, we value critical

thinking, reflective decision-making, and collaboration and seek to develop these competencies in today's learners to prepare them for tomorrow. In MySpace networks, youth may be developing their ability to solicit advice and feedback from others they trust in order to manage projects and explore solutions. This was evident in Theresa's case where she and her peers in a school program posted excerpts of their essays within MySpace so that the group could collaboratively determine how the essay should be structured. Theresa commented: "Everybody's always working on projects like this at the same time and so, we'll [post in MySpace]: 'How long did you take on your essay?' or 'How'd you begin in there? How'd you write it?' So then sometimes we'll share that and everybody kind of does it, at least in our SLC [small learning community]."

Beyond creative thinking, multimedia communication, and collaborative problem-solving skills, we as educators also want our students to develop research and information fluency for the 21st century. It is not enough to consult one source, such as a family member or book; in today's constantly shifting, global economy, learners need to be skilled in consulting multiple sources of information and people and synthesizing disparate bits of data, often in teams, to make well-informed, strategic decisions. Past research on students' online inquiry processes has documented students' difficulties in finding quality information online and discerning the truth or reliability of information they find (Kuiper, Volman & Terwel, 2005). "Social navigation" (Jonassen, 2000) within SNSs—as when a group of users with common interests help each other navigate the Web's complexities by sharing URLs, personal contacts, and aggregated resources —may help learners develop more nuanced research strategies and greater information fluency. The young people we interviewed told us they "tapped the network" to gather information on various topics, and this was evidenced in MySpace bulletin posts from individuals seeking information or responding to requests. In Theresa's case, she supplemented the information she found about different colleges from promotional materials, college Websites, college guides, and people in her local network with first-hand personal accounts from actual college students she had identified and contacted through Facebook:

It kind of was, like, I had a laundry list of schools I wanted to apply to. And so, I kind of narrowed it down based on my conversations on Facebook because the students on there, they feel more comfortable telling me what they think of the school . . . So they can kind of just share their honest interpretations and some schools, I got such great feedback and others, it's was just like, well, I know not to go there. (291-296)

Learning how to quickly mine different types of information from a diverse but bounded universe of social and professional contacts, as Theresa did, may help learners develop research and information fluency more effectively than relying on a single authority (e.g., the instructor) or peer group for guidance. Indeed, the new social Web is generating a particular brand of social network sites dedicated to making the Web more navigable and semantically organized. Social bookmarking and tagging sites (e.g., http://delicious.com/) allow their members to develop folksonomies. Folksonomies are collections of resources on varying topics such as educational research, cooking, video games, computer software, research on health conditions, tennis and other special interests. Anyone with a special interest can start tagging sites that relate to a topic and add them to an existing folksonomy or start one of their own. For instance, Citeulike.org is a site specifically oriented towards scholarly resources where groups can post articles related to the topic they are researching and other scholars can post articles to the same topic. These social bookmarks can be private, shared only among members of a particular social network (e.g.,

American Association of Internet Researchers) or they can be publicly available for anyone to use and contribute.

DISCUSSION AND RECOMMENDATIONS

The case of Theresa Sommers, and that of students like her who use online social networks for interpersonal relationships, school-related processes, college and career inquiry, leisure pursuits, community service, and 21st century skills development, offers several insights for human services education and practice.

SNSs in Human Services Education

First, in human services education, online social network sites might be integrated as a component in flexible learning and human service delivery within graduate school education, complementing the core practicum and other integrated learning components of university programs. Instructors seeking to implement learner-centered constructivist teaching strategies may benefit from layering an online social networking component over traditional in-class, online or hybrid course structures. For instance, it is well established that large enrollment classes and online or hybrid (partially online) courses which have high levels of peer-to-peer and instructor-student interactivity also tend to have higher student retention, satisfaction, and course completion. However, typical course management systems used to support or deliver such courses, such as Blackboard (http://www.blackboard.com/us/index.bbb), are designed more for content delivery controlled by a central administrator (instructor) than they are for ongoing, multi-channel communication, multimedia-sharing, and networking among course members. In addition, incorporating peer-to-peer interaction and group-building activities is time-intensive, costly, and usually not feasible where curriculum demands and staffing shortages favor direct instruction.

Supplementing human services courses with anytime/anywhere, freely available online social networking services may help work around these barriers, providing all course members with a cheap solution to help them monitor, learn from, and co-construct the group's experience. For example, *Social Work 2.0* (http://www.social-work20.com/) is an intergenerational SNS of current undergrad and graduate students, social work professionals (1-20 years in the field), non-profit leaders, researchers and others. Within this network, each member has an individual online profile page where he or she can list location, professional status, degree-granting institution, and areas of social work/interests. Online forums within this SNS such as "Speak" and "(ME)Career" reveal a wealth of career and job-seeking resources, experiences, and advice for social work students and early career professionals. In addition, each Social Work 2.0 member can share reflections in his or her blog, generate discussion questions, share resources, request contacts, invite new members, etc. When an online profile is changed, as when someone writes a new blog entry or uploads a video or shares a question, the change appears prominently on the community home page so all members can track each others' activities. For instructors who seek to foster reflective practitioners, group cohesion, and a supportive and caring community for their students, SNS environments may help facilitate this by motivating students' self-expression, public sharing, support and commentary as we saw in Theresa's case.

Moreover, information and communication tools such as SNSs offer a dynamically updating method of pooling users' collective wisdom, interests, and contacts. As Theresa's case suggests, when initiated into an online community where multi-media sharing is not only valued but promoted, students may be developing important habits, preferences and skills that prepare them

for the human service education workplace of the future. Theresa tapped her network to promote her creativity, solve problems, make life-altering decisions, augment her knowledge base, and pull others with varying levels and types of expertise into her network. Initiating students into these ways of thinking and using social digital technologies may help them develop the interpersonal skills and creative practices that are essential to cultivating an effective professional network of colleagues, service providers, and clients in the human services field. As future human services professionals, graduate students must develop proficiencies in: helping others obtain information and services, keeping and monitoring updated records, communicating clearly in varied formats to multiple audiences, collecting input/ideas/information from clients, establishing trust, and leading or facilitating team activities. Employing a customized SNS for similar tasks within a guided learning environment, such as a university course, may help students develop these proficiencies as part of their core practicum or work-integrated learning experience. However, SNSs may be most powerful as educational tools when the community students join goes beyond the limited experience base of a particular course or university program to encompass and expose students to the broader institutional, social, cultural, and political perspectives of a national or international network in their field.

SNSs as Tools for Human Services Practitioners

Second, human services practitioners might leverage SNSs to reflect on their work, tap peer-reviewed online continuing education, develop 21st century work practices, and grow their personal and professional networks, thereby improving their ability to develop, implement and maintain a comprehensive service plan. Similar to integrating these tools into human services education, practitioners in the field might utilize SNSs as outlets for personal reflection and creative expression. Keeping an online semi-private journal with SNS blogging tools, for instance, may motivate practitioners not only to vent and get support from friends or troubleshoot with colleagues but reflect on their practices over time. Within the Social Work Advocates and Community Care SNSs introduced earlier, human services practitioners use a range of online communication tools to reflect on their stance toward particular issues, to strategize how to advocate successfully, and to educate themselves (e.g., uploading educational videos, reports, relevant URLs, anecdotal evidence, etc.). SNSs that interface well with multi-functional handheld devices such as "smart" phones may be especially beneficial to travelling practitioners who need continuous, multi-channel, on-the-job access to their professional network. In addition, using SNSs to foster ongoing exchanges between students entering the field, current graduates, and experienced practitioners may do much to keep human services education programs relevant, to facilitate effective job placements, and to keep professionals current on research and evidence-based best practices.

Furthermore, Web-based SNSs, or some future version of them, may eventually help human service professionals engage in transformative inter-agency data-sharing, case planning and service coordination, which current proprietary knowledge managements systems and bureaucracies prevent (O'Looney, 2005). Various sectors, not just human services, are inquiring into how to harness emerging social technologies for organization- and job-changing impact. For instance, businesses are looking into how to tap their employees "social connections, institutional memories and special skills – knowledge that large, geographically dispersed companies often have a difficult time obtaining" by using social networking software to connect a company's employees into a single private Web forum (Stone, 2008, p. C2; Gratton, 2007). News media are increasingly tapping viewer participation in the

form of online comments and testimonials, independently produced videos, and citizen journalist blog entries to enhance the accuracy, power and spread of centrally produced stories (e.g., CNN's documentary *Black in America*).[1,2] And apparent in the U.S. 2008 presidential election campaign is a new style of "Netroots" politics: "open-sourced and inclusive, multi-racial and multicultural" where potential voters don't just consume campaign propaganda but help shape and distribute it via online meet-ups, blogs, videos and Internet social networks (Sheehy, 2008, p. 79) Small scale proof-of-concept projects between human services units may help move us closer to understanding how the field can similarly benefit from the range of affordances SNSs allow.

SNSs as Tools for Serving Clients

Third, practitioners may also consider identifying SNSs that fit the needs of particular clients and recommending how clients might use them to obtain support, learn healthy behaviors, mitigate stress, express their passions or career interests, and other potential uses as appropriate to an overall personal development plan. In Theresa's case, MySpace was a place to work out everyday personal, school, and career-related issues and identify or process emotions by blogging, writing poetry or finding a song that matched her mood. In SoberCircle, introduced earlier, clients can find support from others who understand how difficult recovery can be when struggling with emotional and relationship issues. Family and friends of those in recovery can also obtain support on SoberCircle. Clients and/or their families can explore treatment options as well as find a human services worker. Within PatientsLikeMe, members can find information on the latest treatments from those who are using them. Information is available on neurological disorders including: Multiple Sclerosis (MS), Amyotrophic Lateral Sclerosis(ALS), Parkinson's, Progressive Muscular Atrophy (PMA) and Devic's Neuromyelitis

Optica as well as other conditions. PatientsLikeMe also offers specific resources for people with mood disorders such as depression, anxiety, bipolar disorder, obsessive-complusive disorder (OCD) and post-traumatic stress disorder (PTSD). The site supports clients with immune conditions HIV/AIDS. Patients can volunteer to be in research studies or read about cutting edge treatments under development. The site is searchable by location, age, disease, treatment, or symptoms, making it easy for members to connect with each other and find relevant information. Privacy protections prevent using real names (patients use screen names) or contact information. Members have the option of posting photographs or diagrams with their condition, gender and age. Multiple communication channels encourage open sharing about new treatments, uncommon symptoms or overcoming everyday problems, and site features address a range of learning styles

In addition to potentially developing clients' basic technological competence, confidence, and 21st century skills, which are prerequisites for many jobs and education options, facilitating their use of social digital technologies, such as online social network sites, may provide them with a rich, multimedia toolkit through which to express their talents, interests and aspirations. Early research is beginning to discern how digital story creations, for example, serve social functions, especially for traditionally underserved, disengaged students (Hull & Nelson, 2005). Displaying different sides of oneself in a supportive peer-to-peer network may help forge beneficial social relationships around common interests and/or help human services professionals, if linked in to such profiles, better understand their clients' needs.

Gustavsson and MacEachron (2008), in examining the role of the Internet in foster care, suggest that where youth experience multiple placements and risk losing an accurate biography of their childhoods, email accounts that function as an electronic diary may be one solution. We suggest that agencies and human services professionals

might better serve such young people by not only helping them develop a secure digital repository —providing "a portable life biography and sense of self over time" —but also a portable, dynamic network of people and resources they take with them independent of place and time. An online support network can be available when a social services professional is not. Since many of these networked communities are international, members are online chatting and blogging at all hours of the day dealing with a variety of issues. Clients are likely to find someone who can empathize and offer support when other resources may be unavailable. In these ways, SNSs may complement or extend a client's overall treatment plan.

FUTURE TRENDS

As human service professionals utilize social networking technologies to forge individualized, constructivist learning experiences, work practices, and technology-integrated service or treatment approaches, new research opportunities will develop and best practices, evolve. People, both young and old, who understand how to use these online social networks for self expression, community-building and professional development, may have a decided advantage over those who do not. According to a survey by the U.S. National Association of Colleges and Employers published in March 2008, employers will not only use online social network sites to check profiles of potential hires, over 50% will use sites like Facebook (www.facebook.com) and LinkedIn (www.linkedin.com) to "network" with candidates. Recruiters and recruits in entertainment, business, higher education and other industries are beginning to capitalize on these social digital technologies to find new talent, make professional connections and promote their accomplishments (Rosenbloom, 2007). Moreover, technology executives predict an increasing proliferation of SNSs as online social networking moves away from restricting users to walled-off membership in a few sites toward a more open and flexible sharing between numerous niche communities (Stone, 2007; Helft & Stone, 2007). Thus, participation in such networks may increasingly become part of the educational and career development process for people of all ages, in all fields.

CONCLUSION

This chapter introduced the reader to online social network sites, summarizing their features, uses, demographics, and trends, and presenting emerging research on their social and educational potential through the case study of one young woman in transition. Exploring SNSs through a case study illustrated how they can be used to support young people's social and emotional development as they provide spaces to express emotions, deepen friendships and demonstrate creativity. The young woman in the case study developed 21st century skills working in the multimedia environment of her MySpace profile. She also utilized her connections for academic ends, getting help with homework as well as giving advice to younger students about the college application process. Other young people can use SNS's to similar advantage.

Social networking sites specifically for human service professionals and their clients were also discussed. Several sites where professionals can share resources, mentor others and find career information were listed. This chapter also listed SNSs that support clients such as SoberCircle and PatientsLikeMe. We also emphasized how private networks can be constructed to facilitate work with clients without exposing private information online. Finally, in our discussion and recommendations, we suggested how human services educators, students, professionals, and clients might take advantage of such information and communication technologies to advance their own development and the state of the field. Through

a greater accumulation of research and practice we look forward to building on the conversation started here.

REFERENCES

Boyd, D. M., & Ellison, N. B. (2007). Social network sites: Definition, history, and scholarship. *Journal of Computer-Mediated Communication, 13*(1), 11.

Bransford, J. D., Brown, A. L., & Cocking, R. R. (1999). *How people learn: Brain, mind, experience and school.* Washington, DC: Committee on Developments in the Science of Learning.

Brown, J. S., & Duguid, P. (1999). Learning- in theory and in practice. In *The social life of information* (pp. 117-147). Boston, MA: Harvard Business School Press.

Childnet International. (2007). *Young people and social networking services: A Childnet International research report.* Retrieved September 25, 2008, from http://www.digizen.org/socialnetworking

Coiro, J., Knobel, M., Lankshear, C., & Leu, D. (2008). Central issues in new literacies and new literacies research. In J. Coiro, M. Knobel, C. Lankshear, & D. Leu (Eds.), *Handbook of research on new literacies* (pp. 1-21). New York: Lawrence Erlbaum Associates.

College Access Marketing. (n.d.). *Achieving college access goals: The relevance of new media in reaching first-generation and low-income teens.* Retrieved September 30, 2008, from http://www.collegeaccessmarketing.org/campaignresourcecenter_ektid232.aspx

Compete. (2008, September 30). *Compete's top 10 sites ranked by: Page views.* Retrieved September 30, 2008, from http://lists.compete.com

ComScore. (2008, August 12). *Social networking explodes worldwide as sites increase their focus on cultural relevance.* Retrieved September 30, 2008, from http://www.comscore.com/ press/ release.asp?press=2396

Donath, J., & Boyd, D. (2004). Public displays of connection. *BT Technology Journal, 22*(4), 71–82. doi:10.1023/B:BTTJ.0000047585.06264.cc

Ellison, N., Steinfield, C., & Lampe, C. (2007). The benefits of Facebook "friends": Exploring the relationship between college students' use of online social networks and social capital. *Journal of Computer-Mediated Communication, 12*(3), article 1. Retrieved July 30, 2007, from http://jcmc.indiana.edu/vol12/issue4/ellison.html

Fulton, K. (1999). *How teachers' beliefs about teaching and learning are reflected in their use of technology: Case studies from urban middle schools.* Unpublished dissertation, University of Maryland. Retrieved from http://www.learn.umd.edu/fulton/

Granovetter, M. S. (1973). The strength of weak ties. *American Journal of Sociology, 78*(6), 1360–1380. doi:10.1086/225469

Gratton, L. (2007). *Hot spots: Why some teams, workplaces, and organizations buzz with energy – and others don't.* San Francisco, CA: Berrett-Koehler Publishers, Inc.

Greenhow, C., Walker, J. D., & Kim, S. (2008, March). *Millenial leaners and net-savvy teens?: Examining Internet use among low-income students.* Paper presented at the American Educational Research Association, New York, NY.

Gross, R., & Acquisti, A. (2005). Information revelation and privacy in online social networks. In [Alexandria, VA: ACM.]. *Proceedings of the WPES, 05,* 71–80.

Gustavsson, N., & MacEachron, A. (2008). Creating foster care youth biographies: A role for the Internet. *Journal of Technology in Human Services, 26*(1). doi:10.1300/J017v26n01_03

Hargittai, E. (2007). Whose space? Differences among users and non-users of social network sites. *Journal of Computer-Mediated Communication, 13*(1), article 14. Retrieved September 29, 2008, from http://jcmc.indiana.edu/vol13/issue1/hargittai.html

Hass, N. (2006, January 8). In your facebook.com. *New York Times.*

Haythornthwaite, C. (2005). Social networks and Internet connectivity effects. *Information Communication and Society, 8*(2), 125–147. doi:10.1080/13691180500146185

Helft, M., & Stone, B. (2007, October 31). Google and friends to gang up on facebook. *New York Times.*

Herring, S. C. (2004). Computer-mediated discourse analysis: An approach to researching online behavior. In S. A. Barab, R. Kling, & J. H. Gray (Eds.), *Designing for virtual communities in the service of learning* (pp. 338-376). New York: Cambridge University Press.

Hewitt, A., & Forte, A. (2006, November). *Crossing boundaries: Identity management student/faculty relationships on the Facebook.* Paper presented at the the Computer-supported Cooperative Work Conference, Banff, Alberta, Canada.

Hull, G., & Nelson, M. E. (2005). Locating the semiotic power of multimodality. *Written Communication, 22*(2), 224–262. doi:10.1177/0741088304274170

Hull, G. A., & Nelson, M. E. (2008, March). *Youth-designed social networking: Literacies, identities, and relationships at the intersection of online and offline experience.* Paper presented at the meeting of the American Educational Research Association, New York, NY.

International Society for Technology in Education. (2007). *The ISTE national educational technology standards (NETS-S) and performance indicators for students*. Retrieved September 26, 2008, from http://www.iste.org/Content/NavigationMenu/NETS/ForStudents/2007Standards/NETS_for_Students_2007_Standards.pdf

International Society for Technology in Education. (2008). *The ISTE national educational technology standards (NETS-T) and performance indicators for teachers.* Retrieved September 26, 2008, from http://www.iste.org/Content/NavigationMenu/NETS/ForTeachers/2008Standards/NETS_T_Standards_Final.pdf

Jenkins, H. (2006). *Confronting the challenges of participatory culture: Media education for the 21st century* [White paper for the MacArthur Foundation]. Retrieved July 1, 2008, from http://www.digitallearning.macfound.org

Jonassen, D. H. (2000). *Computers as mindtools: Engaging critical thinking* (2nd ed.). Columbus, OH: Merrill-Prentice Hall.

Kraut, R., Kiesler, S., Boneva, B., Cummings, J., Helgeson, V., & Crawford, A. (2002). Internet paradox revisited. *The Journal of Social Issues*, *58*(1), 49–74. doi:10.1111/1540-4560.00248

Kuiper, E., Volman, M., & Terwel, J. (2005). The Web as an information resource in k–12 education: Strategies for supporting students in searching and processing information. *Review of Educational Research*, *75*(3), 285–328. doi:10.3102/00346543075003285

Lenhart, A., Arafeh, S., Smith, A., & McGill, A. R. (2008, April). *Writing, technology, and teens.* Washington, DC: Pew Charitable Trusts. Retrieved September 29, 2008, from http://pewinternet.org/pdfs/PIP_Writing_Report_FINAL3.pdf

Lenhart, A., & Madden, M. (2007, January 3). *Pew Internet project data memo.* Washington, DC: Pew Charitable Trusts. Retrieved September 29, 2008, from http://www.pewinternet.org/pdfs/PIP_SNS_Data_Memo_Jan_2007.pdf

Lenhart, A., Madden, M., Macgill, A. R., & Smith, A. (2007, December 19). *Teens and social media.* Washington, DC: Pew Charitable Trusts.

Lewis, C., & Fabos, B. (2005). Instant messaging, literacies, and social identities. *Reading Research Quarterly, 40*(4), 470-501. Retrieved March 28, 2008, from http://www.reading.org/Library/Retrieve.cfm?D=10.1598/RRQ.40.4.5&F=RRQ-40-4-Lewis.pdf

Mazer, J. P., Murphy, R. E., & Simonds, C. J. (2007). I'll see you on "Facebook:" The effects of computer-mediated teacher self-disclosure on student motivation, affective learning, and classroom climate. *Communication Education*, *56*(1), 1–17. doi:10.1080/03634520601009710

National School Board Association. (2007, July). *Creating and connecting: Research and guidelines on social – and educational – networking.* Retrieved September 22, 2008, from http://www.nsba.org/SecondaryMenu/TLN/CreatingandConnecting.aspx

O'Looney, J. (2005). Social work and the new semantic information revolution. *Administration in Social Work, 29*(4), 5–34. doi:10.1300/J147v29n04_02

Owyang, J. (2008, January 9). Social network stats: Facebook, MySpace, reunion. Message posted to http://www.web-strategist.com/blog/2008/01/09/social-network-stats-facebook-myspace-reunion-jan-2008

Partnership for 21st Century Skills. (2008). *21st century skills, education & competitiveness: A resource and policy guide.* Retrieved September 30, 2008, from http://www.21stcenturyskills.org/documents/21st_century_skills_education_and_competitiveness_guide.pdf

Perkel, D. (2008). Copy and paste literacy? Literacy practices in the production of a MySpace profile. In K. Drotner, H. S. Jensen, & K. C. Schroeder (Eds.), *Informal learning and digital media: Constructions, contexts, consequences* (pp. 203-224). Newcastle, UK: Cambridge Scholars Press.

Quantcast. (2008, September 30). *MySpace.com*. Retrieved September 30, 2008, from http://www.quantcast.com/myspace.com

Rosenbloom, S. (2008, May 1). Status: Looking for work on facebook. *New York Times*.

Rowan, D. (2007, July 31). Log on and rediscover the generation gap. *The Times* (London).

Sheehy, G. (2008, August). Campaign Hillary: Behind closed doors. *Vanity Fair*, pp. 79-86.

Stone, B. (2007, March 3). Social networking's next phase. *New York Times*.

Stone, B. (2008, June 18). At social site, only the businesslike need apply. *New York Times*.

Thurlow, C. (2006). From statistical panic to moral panic: The metadiscursive construction and popular exaggeration of new media language in the print media. *Journal of Computer-Mediated Communication, 11*(3), article 1.

Tinto, V. (1998). Colleges as communities: Taking research on student persistence seriously. *Review of Higher Education, 21*(2), 167–177.

Wellman, B., Haase, A. Q., Witte, J., & Hampton, K. (2001, November). Does the Internet increase, decrease, or supplement social capital? Social networks, participation, and community commitment. *The American Behavioral Scientist, 45*(3), 436–456. doi:10.1177/00027640121957286

Wellman, B., Salaff, J., Dimitrova, D., Garton, L., Gulia, M., & Haythornthwaite, C. (1996). Computer networks as social networks: Collaborative work, telework, and virtual community. *Annual Review of Sociology, 22*, 213–238. doi:10.1146/annurev.soc.22.1.213

Wikipedia. (2008, October 1). *List of social networking websites*. Retrieved October 1, 2008, from http://en.wikipedia.org/wiki/List_of_social_networking_websites

Zhao, C., & Kuh, G. D. (2004). Added value: Learning communities and student engagement. *Research in Higher Education, 45*(2), 115–138. doi:10.1023/B:RIHE.0000015692.88534.de

Chapter 3
Collaborative Learning
Using Group Work Concepts for Online Teaching

Lesley Cooper
Wilfrid Laurier University, Canada

Sally Burford
University of Canberra, Australia

ABSTRACT

This chapter examines the concept of collaborative learning and its theoretical and practical foundations. Collaborative learning takes place in a structured social situation where a group of students work as a team to assist each other with learning tasks. The instructional strategies encourage student to student interactions. Drawing on group work skills, collaborative learning has been demonstrated to be effective in a variety of learning situations. Development of a variety of Internet technologies such as communication tools, emails, discussion forums, video and audio tools together with webcasting allow collaborative teaching strategies to be used creatively in online learning. The authors have trialed the use of various technologies in the human services and several case examples of online collaborative learning are provided. These case studies cover activities such as supervision and controversial issues in social work ethics. The chapter concludes with a discussion of the future directions and the challenges this poses for traditional classroom teaching.

'I entered the classroom with the conviction that it was crucial for me and every other student to be an active participant, not a passive consumer...education as the practice of freedom.... education that connects the will to know with the will to become. Learning is a place where paradise can be created'

bell hooks

DOI: 10.4018/978-1-60566-735-5.ch003

INTRODUCTION

Collaborative learning occurs when a group of students work as a team assisting each other with learning tasks. This form of learning began in classrooms and its effectiveness is that setting has been demonstrated. More recently, it is being used in the online environment. Education in social work and more generally in the human services requires an understanding of human relationships and a capacity to work successfully with other people. Collaborative learning, based on group work concepts is widely and successfully used in all social work education to enable student to student interaction to facilitate further learning. Some academics, however question whether online learning is a valuable framework for teaching the fundamental practice skills in the human services. The aim of this chapter is to explore the teaching of social work using the tools and technologies and the application of collaborative learning in an online environment. This chapter will encompass theoretical foundations, application of group work skills to teaching and ways in which collaborative learning is used for online learning. Case studies of collaborative online learning for tertiary social work students will be provided.

CONSTRUCTIVISM: THE THEORETICAL FOUNDATION

Collaborative learning is based on the tradition of constructivist epistemology. Simply, constructivism means that we learn through a process of experiencing and then reflecting on those experiences, a process which is often and best done with others. Through this process we create a different understanding of the world. As we encounter new experiences, we use our past experiences to understand and make sense of new information thus making new connections which are then organized into new forms of knowledge. With this new information, we can then discard knowledge that is no longer relevant.

Many educators have contributed to our understanding of the importance of constructivism in learning including Vygotsky (1978), Rogoff (1990), Lave and Wenger (1991), and Schon (1983, 1987). According to Vygotsky (1978), higher mental functions are enhanced when the more experienced or capable work with the less experienced or capable in social situations. This is referred to as the zone of proximal development.

In a similar way, Rogoff (1990) talked about the value of a cognitive apprenticeship in thinking and guided learning. The less experienced are guided by the more experienced in their thinking about complex problem solving. A parallel in human services is the responsibility taken by supervisors in the work place when they share their thinking about solving difficult cases with students and fellow workers. Lave and Wenger (1991) contributed to our understanding of learning by stressing the importance of context in the learning process. They referred to the concept of situated learning with Wenger (1998) elaborating the value of a community of practice (experienced workers) in the construction of new knowledge. They were particularly concerned with how workers developed their professional skills. In the area of professional teaching and learning, Schon (1983, 1987) also acknowledged the importance of social context. In our professional life, much learning whilst tacit does take place in a social context and through dialogue with others. We know through doing activities and we learn through a process of reflection on, and in action. The ramifications of constructivism are the importance of learning in a social context; the significance of more experienced others and peers in the learning process; and the value of real world issues as the focus for learning.

In summary, constructivism has been extensively researched as an educational principle that is well accepted as an approach to facilitating learning in today's educational institutions (Papert, 1991; Grabe and Grabe, 2001). This constructivist philosophy is particularly suited to social work education and has been widely used in the human services (Hanson and Sinclair, 2008).

DEFINING OF COLLABORATIVE LEARNING

Collaborative learning is not new. The Socratic Method, a process of questioning, inquiring and probing the views of others in a dialectical manner was an early form of collaborative learning used to explore ideas, positions and rational thinking. Dewey, a prominent educational philosopher writing in *Experience and Education* (1938) was critical of didactic, structured and traditional methods of education because they took little account of the human experience. He argued that learning should be part of everyday actions and everyday relationships. Within our community, many rural children who attended one teacher schools used collaborative processes for learning. Whilst the sole teacher worked with one small group of students other groups were given group activities as part of the classroom learning. The resurgence of collaborative learning emerged during the 1980s in the USA although Bruffee (1992, p.23) believed the idea was first developed in London together with movements towards democratization of education.

In this chapter, we have chosen the term collaborative learning as we prefer this to cooperative learning. Whilst there is debate in the literature about the differences between these two types of learning (Barkley, Cross & Major, 2005) both terms are often used interchangeably. Writers from both traditions draw on research from the other area. It appears that, in general, cooperative learning is regarded as learning that takes place in the classrooms of younger children whilst collaborative learning is more apparent in colleges and universities (Barkley, Cross & Major, 2005, p.7). In our mind, with our focus on higher education and the human services this distinction is artificial and, we prefer the term collaborative to cooperative learning. Despite the preference for a particular term, we will draw on the cooperative learning literature given the similarities, parallels and overlaps between the two terminologies.

Collaborative learning takes place in a structured social situation where a group of students work as a team to assist each other with learning tasks. The learning process is facilitated by a teacher using a range of instructional strategies derived from various theoretical perspectives. These instructional strategies encourage student to student interaction and allow the teacher to act as a guide for learning rather than as a sage who knows all answers. In these structured groups, learning becomes a process in which all participants collaborate to maximize their own learning and that of other students. When students work together, they create new knowledge by sharing ideas and experiences, evaluating ideas and concepts, and building or creating new ideas and ways of working from a professional area or discipline. Groups are able to achieve outcomes which an individual cannot achieve alone.

Collaborative learning does not always occur in traditional academic classrooms which may be both competitive and individualistic. In a traditional university classroom, the mode of teaching is through transmission of information from teacher to students. The teacher conducts the lecture and requires that students complete assignments independently. This is what Paulo Friere (1993) called the banking approach. In this model, students are passive and have little social interaction with the teacher. Not every classroom uses this approach but it is widely used for large lectures. Johnson, Johnson and Smith (1991b, p.3) compared the traditional teaching model with that of collaborative groups. Traditional teaching groups are characterized by a lack of interdependence and individual accountability, with homogeneous membership and one leader who is the teacher and direct specific classroom tasks. Traditional teaching groups ignore social skills and relationships, groups of students or group processing. In the collaborative classroom, there is positive interdependence between students but also individual accountability for group effort, deliberately encouraged heterogeneous membership and shared leadership between group members. The value of this to students is that individual strengths are valued and utilized and students can learn in a place where they feel safe. This is important for students who feel vulnerable in a more traditional classroom. The emphasis is on tasks to be completed but also on relationships between group members with learning of social skills and group processing being an important part of learning arrangements. The role of the teacher is to monitor and intervene in the groups as needed.

The relevance of group learning is immediately apparent to the human service workplace. With funding changes, many workplaces have flat organizational structures so that teams are self managing taking responsibility for a range of functions. For many years, government and industry have argued that group skills and the capacity to work in teams are fundamental skills for employment. This collaboration is necessary in areas such as social planning and community work, case management involving arranging services with other agencies, multidisciplinary teams in health care, and management of project work and research for policy. Students who come to the human services workplaces with group work and group processing skills and individual accountability for the group tasks are valued workers. They are able to talk, listen, take their turns as leader, problem solve and reflect on their activities.

EVIDENCE OF EFFECTIVENESS OF COLLABORATIVE LEARNING

Since these early beginnings, research into learning has shifted from a teacher centred transmission and acquisition model to one based on the co-construction of knowledge in a community of learners where learning is regarded as a social activity. In 2003, there were over 6000 references in ERIC to collaborative learning (Barkley, Cross & Major, 2005). A great deal of research into the effectiveness of collaborative learning has been done by David Johnson and Roger Johnson at the Centre for Cooperative Learning at the University of Minnesota. The Cooperative Learning Center is

a Research and Training Center focusing on how students should interact with each other as they learn and the skills needed to interact effectively.

Research on collaborative learning is extensive and the findings demonstrate the effectiveness of this strategy for learning. Johnson, Johnson and Smith (1991a) summarized research that compared the effects of cooperative, competitive and individualistic efforts on instructional outcomes. On the basis of their meta-analysis, they concluded that collaboration helps students to learn and that collaborative learning enables more positive interpersonal relationships and higher self esteem. Johnson, Johnson and Stanne (2000) did a further meta-analysis on the effectiveness of methods of collaborative learning used in schools. They found 164 separate studies and eight methods for enabling collaboration. All methods for developing collaborative learning were effective but the most successful of these was learning together, this being followed by academic controversy. Slavin, (1990) using a different methodological approach, compared cooperative learning groups with controls. He concluded that achievements with cooperative groups were significantly positive. They are most effective when they incorporate group goals and individual accountability.

COLLABORATIVE LEARNING AND GROUPWORK SKILLS

Joining Together: Group Theory and Group Skills (Johnson and Johnson, 2009) is a standard text book for students in group work and is written by one of the authors who pioneered collaborative learning. In their work, a group is regarded as a meeting where there is interpersonal interaction structured by roles, norms and stages of development, interdependence between participants, specific achievable goals, and more than two members. Group members are motivated to be part of that group to meet personal needs. These concepts form part of group work practice in human services, team work in organizations and teaching in higher education.

Teachers in higher education have a choice about how they structure student learning. It can be individualistic where students work alone and strive for personal success or a competitive situation where they battle against each other for good grades. The other possibility is to work collaboratively so students can achieve common goals (Johnson, Johnson, Holubec and Roy, 1984). Given the practice orientation of social work education, this collaborative goal is preferred. Collaborative learning groups are based on fundamental group work concepts. These concepts have been developed by Johnson, Johnson and Smith (1991) and include:

- positive interdependence
- face to face promotive interaction
- individual accountability
- social skills
- group processing

At the time these concepts were elaborated, the Internet was not widely used for teaching and face to face teaching was the norm. With the development of online learning face to face interactions in one physical location were not possible. With further development of the technology, webcasting became available so that students can see each other when communicating synchronistically. Johnson et al expanded and qualified the concept of face to face interaction with that of "promotive interaction." Accordingly group members provide each other with help and assistance and the exchange of resources within the group. Participants' process information quickly, providing feedback to improve performance and challenge the conclusions reached by group members. Within the group, advocacy for group goals will occur with all members influencing others to achieve these. Above all, the group

will act in trustworthy ways (Johnson, Johnson and Smith, 1991, p.7). It is these characteristics which are essential in the design of online learning.

Groups go through stages of development. In the 1960s, Tuckman outlined four group stages: forming, storming, norming and performing. Later he added adjourning (Smith, 2005). Although these stages are described in a linear manner, they are less clear cut in practice. In each of these stages, group members and leaders have particular tasks. This also applies to teachers running collaborative groups. Tuckman was writing about face to face interaction, but these stages also appear in online groups.

In the forming stage, participants are inclined to behave independently, get to know others in the group and test relationships. At the outset, teachers must be clear about the learning tasks and instructions and provide clear directions. In the storming stage, the real work of the group has begun. Students begin to polarize around issues. Conflict is apparent and the group interactions are often emotionally laden. Some members often resist the group dynamics. In this stage, the teacher notices that everyone has a different idea of the task or some may evade the work. Clarity about tasks remains important. By the time norming is reached the group members have developed trust and are acquainted with the learning requirements. Students participate and take responsibility for the activities. New standards for working together are likely to develop and new roles adopted. At this stage the teacher can stand back and watch carefully from the sidelines. The development of netiquette (see case study) is an important part of group formation and norming with netiquette standards assisting in managing difficult interactions. In the final stage the group works collaboratively with structural and procedural issues being resolved. The group makes the decisions.

In any group, there is differentiation in the roles people play. In formal groups, some members have designated roles and assigned tasks. In other groups,

Figure 1. Roles in the online learning environment

A group facilitator keeps the group on task and time ensuring that all the work is complete.
A recorder, acts like a secretary who keeps the records and pr epare the material completed by the group.
A summarize r condenses the main points in a discussion and encapsulates it in a clear statement .
An elaborator uses their understanding of theory and practice and makes links between these ideas.
A researcher/ investigator finds any resource or library material necessary to complete the task; and
A wildcard is the member who can slot into any of the above positions to enable the group to continue functioning (Millis and Cottell, 1998, p.53).

individuals take on roles because of a particular interest or skills. Associated with the role are expectations that a person will behave in a particular way. For example, a teacher and a student both have particular complementary roles and there are expectations of how both will behave. In learning groups, roles can develop informally or alternatively, roles can be assigned to group members. This has the advantage of creating positive interdependence and ensures that there are no "free riders" i.e. a situation where one person carries responsibility for the work. Some of the online roles are outlined in Figure 1. These group work concepts were used in the design of the case examples.

A *group facilitator* keeps the group on task and time ensuring that all the work is complete.

A *recorder*, acts like a secretary who keeps the records and prepare the material completed by the group.

A *summarizer* condenses the main points in a discussion and encapsulates it in a clear statement.

An *elaborator* uses their understanding of theory and practice and makes links between these ideas.

A *researcher/ investigator* finds any resource or library material necessary to complete the task; and

A *wildcard* is the member who can slot into any of the above positions to enable the group to continue functioning (Millis and Cottell, 1998, p.53).

INTERNET TECHNOLOGIES FOR COLLABORATIVE LEARNING

Internet technologies provide a global and accessible platform for knowledge creation and sharing as well as communication. Many of these technologies are generic communication tools such as email, weblogs, discussion forums and webcasts whilst others have been specially developed or customized for a particular collaborative learning activity.

Some technologies to support online collaborative learning require a funded project approach. A team effort, significant funding, the support of technical expertise and project management are all essential components of these endeavors. Gay et al. (1999) describe a technology that has been specifically crafted for online collaborative learning. The CoNote system is a web based document annotation system in which a document becomes the object of discussion. The document is drafted by an individual student and the shared annotations of group members provide ongoing feedback and improvement of the work. In this learning tool, the individually owned document provides a relatively fixed reference for discussion and co-creation of knowledge as opposed to shared authoring tools.

Naidu et al (2000) report on the development and application in the realm of political science of a collaborative role-play simulation technology using Internet protocols. A student assumes a particular role in the "world" that has a particular goal or mission associated with it. Learning takes place as the student acquires the skill and knowledge necessary to achieve their goal. Their scenario or simulated real life has all the complexity and richness of the real world. Web based conferencing takes place between the participants in the scenario. The simulation continues in the conference areas designated as news agencies such as BBC or CNN and students interact via different document types such as memos, draft articles and news, which vary depending on their roles. This impressive collaborative framework for learning immerses the student in a scenario where they must learn in consultation with others in their "world." Students are at the centre of the learning process and the emphasis is on an interdependent collective. This rich and purposeful compilation of Internet technologies for collaborative learning is not the norm however.

More often generic Internet technologies are involved in group learning and a learning strategy is built around them. Generic technologies such as email, discussion forums, chat rooms, weblogs, wikis, webcasting and podcasting systems are readily available to tertiary teachers and are often incorporated in online learning management systems - that may be either of a proprietary nature e.g. WebCT, Blackboard or open source systems e.g. Moodle or Sakai.

Email and discussion forums need no introduction to readers in the 21st century. These extensively used communication tools have the advantages of asynchronicity and provide a permanent record of "conversation." A chat room provides the benefits and chat of synchronous communication and must be carefully incorporated into a learning environment to overcome the chaotic communication of too many textual "voices" at once.

The discussion forum or bulletin board is the most widely adopted and successful Internet communication tool in collaborative learning to date. The literature provides a plethora of examples of collaborative learning strategies using the discussion forum (McLoughin, 2000; Cooper, 2001; Curtis & Lawson, 2001; Treleaven, 2003). Its success is based on openness and ease of use. Any number of discussion "spaces" can be created to cater for full class interaction or smaller group activities. The discussion forum does not require learners to participate at a particular time or place making it a very adaptable and flexible tool in the lives of learners and their teachers.

Textual Internet technologies complemented by audio and video and learning are often enriched by varied forms of presentation. Webcasting technology enables audio or video files to be hosted and accessed by multiple Internet users. Streaming technology allows large amounts of data to be continuously downloaded whilst being viewed. Viewing the video or audio file begins before the whole multimedia file has been transmitted. Podcasting now provides the added benefit that audio/video files can be downloaded to an individual's own media storage and playing device for future replay.

The term Web 2.0 is used to describe significant and recent shifts in using the web. O'Reilly (2005) describes Web 2.0 as having an "architecture of participation." Web 2.0 is based on social software where users generate content rather than simply consume it; in so doing they give spontaneous shape to the organisation of information. The web takes more of a peer-to-peer shape than its previous top-down, authorised presentation of information.

A participatory mode of informing and communicating using the web has evolved – users not only read what is on the web but are also given a chance to be co-creators of web information. It might therefore be said that the focus of the web is changing, from an informing to a conversational platform. Some of the particular web-based tools that enable this to occur are blogs, wikis and social categorisation sites. We will now investigate these particular tools.

Weblogs are a more recent online communication tool and are defined as much by the way the tool is used as by the technology itself. Weblog entries are characterised by natural and spontaneous voice, frequent updates and a lack of formality; entries are made in the web-based log in chronological order. Weblog technology is a simple browser-based authoring tool that removes any technical barrier to participation.

A weblog is, traditionally, a "log" on the web – a diary-style site in which the author - a weblogger, or "blogger"- links to other web pages he/she finds interesting. It is traditional for old entries to fall to the bottom as newer ones are added. Comments on each weblog posting provide the collaborative aspect of this tool.

A wiki is a web page/site that can be viewed and changed by visitors to the site using only their browser technology. 'A wiki, from the Hawaiian term for "quick", is an ongoing, ever-evolving, organised compilation of information' (Lee, 2006). A site maintains a history of all the changes made to it, and an older version can be restored if need be. The community of interest surrounding a wiki tends to keep the content of a site valid and respectable.

Wikis differ from weblogs in that:

- they have a collective rather than an individual voice
- they are structured by topic rather than chronologically

- changes to content take place organically – it is open to editing and evolution
- there is an element of trust in wiki use – while abuse is quite possible, the value and use of wikis is created by a watchful collective.

It is important to note that the use of wikis is different to traditional publishing, for example Wikipedia is a successful knowledge sharing phenomena but is not an authoritative traditional encyclopaedia and should not be viewed as such. The uses of wikis continue to emerge, but they clearly offer a collaborative potential and a new way of constructing and sharing knowledge repositories on the web.

Social tagging (also called social bookmarking) sites have an initial role in the organisation of web-based information and resources for an individual – they provide a tool for personal management of resources and knowledge. Because of their emphasis on openness (users names are public and any user can view the information organisation of another) they are an excellent tool for sharing resources. Likeminded people or communities of interest will collect resources that can be easily accessed by others. With a significant number of users focusing on a sphere of interest, a pattern will emerge – a folksonomy. This becomes a means of discovering new information using the organisation systems of others whose interests are similar. Resources can be discovered by tags or by individuals.

Key features of social tagging include the following:

- special web software/sites exist that enable a specific web resource, identified by its URL, to be tagged or labelled by the person who values it
- individual tagging of resources. The user of the resource assigns a keyword(s) to the resource in order to create categories

of information. The users' concepts and words are used rather than a formal, authorative vocabulary

- information is organised in a social environment; the outcomes are open and shared
- as the tagging of an object reaches a critical mass, common language and tags enable findability and sharing of resources.

The opportunities for using web 2.0 for collaborative learning are manifold and will be discussed later in the chapter.

In this chapter, we used WebCT with its associated emails and discussion boards to design the collaborative learning examples that follow. Students used this platform to write about their practice, to do role plays of various kinds, to debate and defend ideas and to construct new understandings. With webcasting and the opportunity for students to work face to face, the examples in the section below can be expanded and learning deepened.

CASE EXAMPLES

The case examples that follow illustrate concepts of constructivism, collaborative learning principles and knowledge of online technology. These programs have been used in the education of social workers for practice in the human services.

Netiquette

Students in the human services practice and learn in groups. The ability to form and operate within a group context has become an essential skill in our "networked" world. Forming a group is never easy requiring effort, thought and clear communication from all members to be effective. In online classes that entail online discussion, it is helpful to discuss netiquette, to provide parameters

for social behavior in electronic communication. Students are asked to discuss in their groups ways in which they would like to be treated and to identify things they find intimidating or upsetting. Students' views can be expressed on the bulletin board with the instructor responsible for collating the information and using these guidelines as the basis for online communication. This exercise can be done online or in class.

Online Group Supervision with Assigned and Rotating Roles

Supervision is an important learning strategy for students and workers in the human services. Supervision courses are generally part of graduate education programs and are provided to practitioners with professional experience who want to extend their theoretical understandings and practical experiences.

There are two broad approaches to supervision. One is an individualistic approach where the supervisor and the student work in a dyad. The other is a group approach where students or peers work with a more experienced practitioner to provide the learning experience. These group approaches are most frequently based on collaborative relationships and use the expertise, strengths and capacities of group members to achieve learning outcomes.

In the example that follows, the supervision course was taught as part of a MSW course called "social work practice education," a topic for experienced students. It was a face to face intensive but the assessment was done as an online group supervision exercise over several following weeks. The aim of the course was to provide students with an opportunity to learn about group supervision with a focus on peer to peer collaboration and shared leadership and offering the opportunity to develop their personal practice theories of supervision. Many of these graduate students had already been supervisors using a dyadic approach. The technology used for this program was WebCT with the discussion forum and email being the main features utilized by students. Students were in small groups of no more than seven.

Each student was asked to provide a small vignette of 50 words which could be discussed in an online environment. It was suggested that students use an example that a worker or beginning student may bring to a supervision session. One vignette was discussed every two weeks with the discussion being lead by the graduate student who had presented the vignette. Graduate students were asked not to bring material that was overly complex as the focus was on learning about collaborative supervisory skills. All material brought to class contained no identifying information to respect the privacy of clients or individuals within their example. Students were then assigned to roles that group members take in supervision, including coordinator/facilitator, presenter, integrator of theory and practice, critic, compromiser, summarizer, and wild card.

On the discussion board, students were then asked to describe their allocated role, the characteristics of this role and examples of questions a person in this role might take. As students were rotating through various roles, the role descriptions were made available for the next students to see. In preparing this material, students were encouraged to use and make reference to group work literature. When a student completed discussing a practice example using a particular role, they provided their reflection on this role and added additional comments to assist the next student allocated that role. In this way, students reflected on their experience and developed practice theory about using particular roles developed. This provided the basis of formative assessment with the lecturer providing comments and questions.

Preparation for Online Learning

The importance of respectful relationships in the online environment was discussed in the intensive class prior to beginning the first online session with a set of agreed conventions developed by consensus. Whilst respectful relationships are always important in learning, they are more important when the focus is on supervision. Supervision is a process where professional competencies and performance are the focus of discussion. Students whose professional performance is the subject of discussions, are sensitive to the supervisory relationship and the way information is communicated. Students used the concepts discussed in face to face classes on the supervisory relationship to build agreed goals and specify desired and undesirable behaviors. When consensus was reached, this information was posted.

Students also attended a preliminary face to face teaching session in a teaching laboratory to familiarize themselves with WebCT including use of the bulletin boards, online chats and emails. The lecturer wanted to ensure that no time was lost due to trial and error learning creating disruptions to the group processes. Students used this meeting to make their general online introductions to each other and establish working relationships. Although students occupied the same classroom when completing this task there was little face to face discussion.

Outcomes

There was no formal evaluation of this course although students did provide comments on their learning and the process. The lecturer also provided comments to students throughout the program.

Students were very positive about their learning experience. As one vignette was discussed every two weeks, students found they needed to connect to WebCT and discuss the vignette on a day to day basis. During the course, one student was unable to access WebCT because of a computer virus which meant an absence of many days from the class. The failure of one member to participate in group activities had a big impact on group functioning particularly given the allocation of roles. Here the member holding the wild card could step in and take over the missing member's role to ensure maintenance of cohesion.

The most important role was that of coordinator. The importance of this role in maintaining group functioning was initially underestimated by both students and the lecturer. All students took a turn in this role. Throughout the functioning of the group, the skills of the coordinator improved with active learning from the prior experiences of students who proceeded them in this role. In the initial session, the student with the role of facilitator was reminded to take the initiative. Checking the web and being on time became an important student learning task.

Although there was no formal evaluation, the lecturer was pleased with the learning experience. There was a high degree of trust between the students within the online environment and it is assumed that this developed in the intensive that preceded the online work. Students were provided with an opportunity to make the transition from the safety and security of the face to face environment to online work by having the first session in a computer laboratory. Anxieties were eased allowing students to focus on their tasks.

The students participated in a collaborative learning group and demonstrated the features of positive interdependence, individual accountability, shared leadership, and responsibility for each other. Throughout the group supervision, students stayed on task and learnt the importance of social skills. If this course was to be repeated, the lecturer would have fewer vignettes with discussion taking place over several weeks. This would allow for more thoughtful conceptualization of roles, greater reflection on the process and the elaboration of practice theory for group supervision.

Controversial Issues

The aim of this course was to introduce students to the ethics and values underpinning professional practice and to enable students to reflect on the way in which their personal beliefs and values constrain and influence practice decisions. Collaborative learning was achieved through an online assessment where students discussed controversial ethical issues. These controversial issues were written as "ought statements" that indicated how social workers *should* behave in their professional practice. In reflecting on these debates, students were expected to take account of their responsibility to clients, their employing agency, self and profession.

Students in groups of six to ten were allocated a controversial issue on social work ethics for discussion. They were required to research their allocated topic using on-line electronic library resources and in 500 words post a commentary to the bulletin board. The first bulletin board had particular requirements. Students were required to:

- Justify the controversial issue as stated (even if they disagreed with the statement - many so doing)
- Examine practice implications of the controversial issue
- Identify a claimant (or stakeholder) and then determine what the person would want you, as a professional, to do about that issue and
- Specify the social worker's professional obligations to that person.

The discussion topics included whether:

1. Clients who express racist attitudes about other people in counseling sessions should be challenged by social workers.
2. Social workers should report all ethical infringements by colleagues to their professional ethics committee.

3. Touching clients should always be avoided in social work practice
4. Sexual intimacies with current and former clients should be prohibited.
5. Religious issues should not be discussed in work with clients
6. Social workers should not disclose identifying information when discussing clients with supervisors unless the client has consented to the disclosure of confidential information or there is a compelling need for such disclosure.

As part of this process students were asked to use collaborative concepts and complete several activities: research the allocated topic using reading material and electronic journals; post the commentary to the discussion group and give your posting a title. In this commentary include:

1. A justification of the ought statement
2. Examination of the practice implications of the ought statements
3. Identification of one claimant in the ought statement (e.g. client, agency, supervisor, professional association, family member)
4. Determination of what that claimant would prefer you to do in this situation
5. Your professional obligations to that claimant.

After reading the original comments posted by other students in your group, provide at least two questions, and comments on, and responses to student postings presented on the bulletin board. Take into account the netiquette exercise and ways to assist other students.

Reflect on the online discussion including the comments of your peers and submit your written paper.

Students were required to justify the "ought statement" irrespective of their personal or professional views. This was very difficult for some students as they did not agree with either

a part or the whole of the statement. It was here that the collaborative efforts of all students with their questions, responses and postings enabled co-learners to see the statement from different viewpoints.

In a class prior to the online discussions, students were given a series of questions to challenge themselves and support others as part of assistance with the learning task. For example, when thinking about the "ought statement," students could question whether the "ought statement" applied to every practice situation as a matter of principle or only to particular groups. They were asked to think of any exceptions to their statement and consider occasions when the statement would be always justified or never justified. Finally, students were asked if and how the statement might be qualified.

As students had diverse experiences prior to attending university and during their placement experiences, they were able to see these statements in a variety of different contexts and use this to explore the validity of the contention. Students used these diverse experiences to talk about stakeholders and claimants thus adding to the richness of the learning.

The final part of this process was a reflection paper. In this first posting students were asked to justify a stated position. In this reflection paper students were able to outline their personal position on the paper including where and how they developed these views. They were asked if and how their views had changed over the course of the assignment and whether other students challenged and changed their views. It was in and through this process that the benefits of students working together on the one task became evident. The perspective of each student and their representation of different stakeholders enabled perspective taking and the differentiation of the views of others (Johnson, Johnson, Holubec and Roy, 1984).

Students clearly indicated that they started the discussion with uncompromising attitudes toward the topic but through the process of reading and responding to the views of other students, their views changed significantly. These changed views were more sophisticated and noted exceptions and qualifications to the statement. The benefits of the online learning examining controversial issues came through student feedback (Cooper 2001).

THE FUTURE

The impact of the Internet on our working lives is significant and we must develop competencies in the use of the online environment for communication, knowledge sharing and teamwork. The 21st century also brings the challenge of continual learning and workplace change. Providing tertiary human services students the experience of learning collaboratively using communication technologies is preparing them for a lifetime in a workplace where ability to learn, adaptation to change and effective participation in global communication technologies are a critical set of skills.

An ability to learn throughout life is now of greater benefit than any body of domain knowledge that we may possess at any one time. Changes in careers and the nature of work are now commonplace throughout a person's life. It is increasingly likely that people will work longer and in a variety of guises than at any time in the past. Some of the most desirable skills in the workplace are interpersonal. The ability to communicate and maintain productive relationships with colleagues and to work in teams and across communities is central to an effective learning organization. Imbuing students with the ability to learn in collaborative situations is central to lifelong learning.

We work and live in a society that increasingly demands an ability to learn, communicate and relate to others in an online environment. This requires an ability to find and synthesize digital information, integrate it into decision making processes and to effectively connect and work with people within and across organizational boundaries. Teamwork in virtual communities using online tools is a valued skill. The Internet is ubiquitous and competencies and discernment in using it effectively are essential.

Collaborative learning online has, to date, been largely enabled by the communication tools that are encompassed in enterprise learning management systems (LMS). Educational institutions invest significantly in these online course systems and individual teachers have been restricted in their choice of online communication tool to those that are offered within the LMS. Over the last fifteen years, LMS technology has provided a platform for significant innovation in teaching online, especially in the use of the discussion forum. But being sizeable and tightly integrated "whole of organization" systems, LMS lack the agility to quickly integrate the new and innovative tools of the Internet.

The increasing uptake, availability and prominence of Web 2.0 technologies is now offering collaborative learning new tools with great promise. There is a new agility, open access and choice in the lightweight suite of tools of Web 2.0. Many Web 2.0 technologies are freeware and are easy to establish and use. With increasing frequency, a collaborative learning exercise takes place outside the enterprise systems of the educational institution and utilizes the Web 2.0 tools of the open web.

We have trialed the use of wikis for knowledge building and sharing class activities with Masters' students studying in fully online mode. Students were required to collectively build a repository of knowledge in a specific knowledge domain by co-authoring the web pages of a wiki. All students had full access to shape the content and structure of the web space – they were required for assessment purposes to write a reflective article on their experience of this social media and to identify any problems or prejudices that this activity presented to them. Social tagging activities have also been explored by the authors where the class selected and tagged web resources in a particular domain. The class resources were "aggregated" by predetermining one tag for all members of the class. We predict that the future of collaborative learning in an online environment will be rich in the use of the agile tools of Web 2.0.

With the introduction of new technologies, there will be increasing use of participatory pedagogical approaches. Fountain (2005) points out that as Web 2.0 tools such as wikis are used for collaborative learning activities in universities; they will in turn unsettle and challenge traditional pedagogical practices and norms. Wikis are spaces of shared, unfinished and unacknowledged authorship and 'are based on a principle of non-exclusive authority' (Fountain, 2005). Contrast this to the traditional power structures around knowledge and strongly owned authorship that is found in universities. The future will reveal the interplay of these issues.

CONCLUSION

Collaborative online learning is a successful strategy for teaching social work. It draws on constructivist learning principles and findings from educational researchers at the Centre for Cooperative Learning at the University of Minnesota. These researchers found that collaborative learning provides effective learning and teaching strategies that can be used in many different educational environments. Collaborative learning draws on group work principles especially concepts of group formation, stages of group development, and communication within groups. This form of learning is particularly beneficial for social work education in the online environment. The introduction of web based technologies has allowed this effective educational strategy to be used in the online environment with effective results. This chapter provides examples of how collaborative learning has been used in social work education

at the undergraduate and graduate level. With the introduction of newer technologies, it is expected that participatory strategies will increase and unsettle the traditional teaching practices in professional education.

REFERENCES

Barkley, E. F., Cross, K. P., & Major, C. H. (2005). *Collaborative learning techniques: A handbook for college faculty*. San Francisco: Jossey Bass.

Bruffee, K. A. (1992). Collaborative learning and the "Conversation of Mankind." In A. S. Goodsell, M. R. Maher, & V. Tinto (Eds.), *Collaborative learning: A sourcebook for higher education*. University Park, PA: National Centre on Postsecondary Teaching.

Cooper, L. (2001). Teaching controversial issues on-line. *New Technology in the Human Services, 13*(3-4), 11–21.

Curtis, D., & Lawson, M. (2001). Exploring collaborative online learning. *Journal of Asynchronous Learning Networks, 5*(1), 22–34.

Dewey, J. (1938). *Experience and education*. New York: Collier.

Fountain, R. (2005). *Wiki pedagogy. Dossiers pratiques, profetic*. Retrieved October 13, 2008, from http://www.profetic.org/dossiers/dossier_imprimer.php3?id_rubrique=110

Freire, P. (1993). *Pedagogy of the oppressed*. New York: Continuum.

Gay, G., Sturgill, A., & Martin, W. (1999). Document-centered peer collaborations: An exploration of the educational uses of networked communication technologies. *Journal of Computer-Mediated Communication, 4*(3). Retrieved October 13, 2008, from http://jcmc.indiana.edu/vol4/issue3/gay.html

Grabe, M., & Grabe, C. (Eds.). (2001). *Integrating technology for meaningful learning* (3rd ed.). Boston, MA: Houghton Mifflin.

Hanson, J. M., & Sinclair, K. E. (2008). Social constructivist teaching methods in Australian universities - reported uptake and perceived learning effects: A survey of lecturers. *Higher Education Research & Development, 27*(3), 169–186. doi:10.1080/07294360802183754

Johnson, D. W., & Johnson, F. P. (2009). *Joining together: Group theory and group skills.* Upper Saddle River, NJ: Pearson.

Johnson, D. W., Johnson, R. J., & Stanne, M. B. (2000). Cooperative learning methods: A meta-analysis. Retrieved October 13, 2008 from http://www.co-operation.org/pages/cl-methods.html

Johnson, D. W., Johnson, R. T., & Smith, K. (1991a). *Cooperative learning: Increasing college faculty instructional productivity* (ASHE-ERIC Higher Education Report No. 4). Washington, DC: The George Washington University, School of Education and Human Development.

Johnson, D. W., Johnson, R. T., & Smith, K. A. (1991b). *Active learning: Cooperation in the classroom.* Edina, MN: Interaction Book Company.

Lave, J., & Wenger, E. (1991). *Situated learning: Legitimate peripheral participation.* Cambridge, UK: Cambridge University Press.

Lee, E. (2005). The wonderful world of Wikis. *Contra Costa Times.* Retrieved October 13, 2008, from http://www.accessmylibrary.com/coms2/summary_0286-31685346_ITM

McLoughlin, C., & Luca, J. (2000). Cognitive engagement and higher order thinking through computer conferencing: We know why but do we know how? In A. Herrmann & M. M. Kulski (Eds.), *Flexible futures in tertiary teaching, Proceedings of the 9th Annual Teaching Learning Forum,* Perth, Curtin University of Technology. Retrieved October 13, 2008, from http://lsn.curtin.edu.au/tlf/tlf2000/mcloughlin.html

Millis, B. J., & Cottell, P. G., Jr. (1998). *Cooperative learning for higher education faculty.* Phoenix, AZ: The Oryx Press.

Naidu, S., Ip, A., & Linser, R. (2000). Dynamic goal-based role-play simulation on the Web: A case study. *Educational Technology & Society, 3*(3), Retrieved October 13, 2008, from http://www.ifets.info/journals/3_3/b05.html

O'Reilly, T. (2005). *What is Web2.0: Design patterns and business models for the next generation of software.* Retrieved October 13, 2008, from http://oreillynet.com/lpt/a/6228

Papert, S., & Harel, I. (1991). *Constructionism.* Norwood, NJ: Ablex Publishing Corporation.

Rogoff, B. (1990). *Apprenticeship in thinking: Cognitive development in social context.* New York: Oxford University Press.

Schon, D. (1983). *The reflective practitioner: How professionals think in action.* New York: Basic Books.

Schon, D. (1987). *Educating the reflective practitioner: Toward a new design for teaching and learning in the professions.* San Francisco: Jossey-Bass.

Slavin, R. E. (1990). *Cooperative learning: Theory, research and practice.* Boston, MA: Allyn & Bacon.

Smith, M. K. (2005). Bruce W. Tuckman - forming, storming, norming and performing in groups. *The encyclopaedia of informal education.* Retrieved October 13, 2008, from http://www.infed.org/thinkers/tuckman.htm

Treleaven, L. (2003). Evaluating a communicative model for Web mediated collaborative learning and design. *Australian Journal of Educational Technology, 19*(1), 100–117.

Vygotsky, L. S. (1978). *Mind and society: The development of higher psychological processes.* Cambridge, MA: Harvard University Press.

Wenger, E. (1998). *Communities of practice: Learning, meaning, and identity.* Cambridge, UK: Cambridge University Press.

Chapter 4
Asynchronous Online Role-Plays Using a Blended Learning Design
Integrating Theory and Practice

Belinda Johnson
RMIT University, Australia

Kathy Douglas
RMIT University, Australia

ABSTRACT

The use of online role-plays has grown in university education as an increasing number of teachers in a variety of discipline areas utilise role-play simulations in the online environment. The focus of this chapter is on design options for asynchronous online role-plays that may assist students to integrate theory and practice and develop skills in reflexive practice. The design options discussed in this chapter adopt a "blended" learning approach where online learning is used to complement face-to-face learning. Five models of online role-plays are discussed and various learning and teaching strategies canvassed to assist those teaching in the human services area to adopt and adapt these design options to meet their curriculum objectives.

'When you teach, you learn '.

Helen Suzman, United Nations Human Rights Award recipient in Zuckerman, A. *Wisdom* (2008, p.176).

DOI: 10.4018/978-1-60566-735-5.ch004

INTRODUCTION

The aim of this chapter is to describe and discuss e-learning approaches in the area of online role-plays to provide teachers in the human services area with a range of choices in designing online activities that promote reflexive practice. Online role-plays can contribute to the development of reflexive practice skills for those working or preparing to work in the human services field. These role-plays can allow "active learning" (Ramsden, 2003) opportunities where role-players can integrate theory and practice in an online environment. Reflexive practice skills are integral to working in human services (Taylor & White, 2000) and are commonly taught in social work and similar human services programs. Reflexive practice occurs when a student or practitioner not only evaluates practice experiences as a way of developing better skills and practice, but also by questioning the theory behind these actions and in light of this experience develops a more contextually relevant approach (Fook, 2002; Taylor & White, 2000). In our discussion the learning and teaching focus is on design elements in online, asynchronous – that is, not in real time – role-plays.

The e-learning theory and design options discussed in this chapter have been trialled in the discipline area of mediation where students engage with theory and practice dealing with the third party facilitation of conflict (Douglas, 2007a; Douglas, 2007b). The online role-plays that have been trialled have largely mirrored face-to-face role-plays traditionally conducted in the university classroom. Our design asks students to integrate theory, through the required reading and online discussion of selected articles, with practice, that is the interventions played out in the online role-play. The online environment provides students with more leisure to consult relevant theory prior to acting in a role-play (Wills & McDougall, 2008) and thus arguably allows students to make more considered choices regarding an appropriate intervention than is available in a face-to-face role-play (Douglas, 2007a). The online role-play options discussed in this chapter differ somewhat from more open-ended problem solving simulations (see for example McLaughlan & Kirkpatrick, 2008) as they are focussed on the development of professional interactions with service users through such processes as interviewing, counselling or facilitation.

This chapter has four main objectives. First, as background the usefulness of online role-plays in integrating theory and practice is considered. A particular focus is on the way that the online environment can slow down interaction and enable students to engage in more critical thought and reflection, offering opportunities for learning about reflexive practice skills. Second, we consider e-learning theory and practice to assist in designing online role-plays and in particular consider a design that blends online role-plays with face-to-face role-plays. The development of role-play simulations as an interactive option in e-learning is also discussed and the work of Diana Laurillard (2002) is canvassed to provide a theoretical framework for the e-learning design models discussed in this chapter. Third, five design models are presented each with a different approach to online asynchronous role-plays with the benefits and limitations of each of these models discussed. This is followed by the identification of some learning and teaching strategies that may be adopted in developing online role-play activities. Through these e-learning design models and strategies we hope to enable other teachers to design their own customised online role-play activity that develops interactive practice skills and a reflexive capacity. Finally, a case study of the use of such a model in teaching the discipline area of mediation as one example of the use of this blended design is presented.

ROLE-PLAYS AND REFLEXIVE PRACTICE

Role-plays in teaching human services professions are used to develop a range of interpersonal skills such as in interviewing, counselling and facilitation. Role-plays provide students with authentic learning experiences (Herrington & Herrington, 2006) whereby the scenarios they are role-playing mirror those they may face in their future professional roles. Scenarios can be drawn from practice and may be accessed through dialogue with those in the field (Bennett, Harper & Hedberg, 2002). Role-plays allow students from a range of disciplines to engage with their imagination and "play" with a variety of interventions and approaches, incorporating storytelling in their learning (Dracup, 2008). In this way students are able to rehearse scenarios from professional practice within a supported learning environment. In social work education role-plays can be used to develop reflexive practice. This kind of practice is an approach that sees theory as informing practice decisions and practice experience in turn enabling social workers to adapt theory (Fook, 2002). Reflexive practice requires the assumptions in the context of practice to be questioned. These include assumptions being made about service users and their issues as well as those made about the role of the social worker. Through reflexive practice practitioners become aware of the impact they may have on the service user and the service user's interpretation of this experience. The complexity and context specific nature of social work makes reflexive practice essential for good practice (Taylor & White, 2000). This is a key concern in social work and human services education more generally (Dominelli, 2004; Fook, 2002; Allan, Pease & Briskman, 2003), and a graduate capability aspired to in many social work programs (Taylor & White, 2000).

A capacity for reflexive practice enables theory to be adapted to better meet the context of practice, particularly given that work in the human services can be highly contextualised. A social worker may be working in an area that is predominantly legal, medical, or economic and within discourses based on psychology, social structures, or consumer rights (Healy, 2005). This diversity means that social workers need to be familiar with a range of theoretical approaches as one approach is unlikely to be appropriate in all practice contexts.

Bagshaw (2006) emphasises the importance for social workers to engage in reflexive practice

that acknowledges the connection between language and power. Drawing upon feminist post-structuralist theory Bagshaw highlights the ways that power, knowledge and language construct gendered identities. For example, Bagshaw points to the absence of a commonly understood term to describe "domestic violence" prior the 1980's. The lack of a generally accepted term led to the experiences of many women and children being largely ignored in human services and in society more broadly. Bagshaw stresses the importance of social workers considering the language that they use in practice and the need to avoid essentializing language to describe service users and their experiences. Essentializing language can impede good social work practice by narrowly defining service users' experiences rather than allowing service users to define their own experiences. Bagshaw argues that social workers need to be aware of their own presence and use of language in their practice, and the impact this has on how service users are interpreted. Bagshaw (2006, p.8) describes this practice as "self-reflexive practice" whereby practitioners are required to:

- acknowledge power dynamics in relationships;
- use empowerment strategies;
- challenge dominant discourses;
- ensure marginalised stories are validated; and
- value "the transformative power of the process" rather than focus on the outcome.

Arguably, the online environment offers the opportunity for social work, and other human services students, to develop reflexive practice through online role-plays. Online learning offers the opportunity to combine practice skills with theory. This is because the online environment slows the pace of a role-play and allows students to consult and reflect upon theory prior to acting in the role-play. The usefulness of online role-plays lies in the opportunity for students to interact in authentic scenarios as a novice professional in an e-learning environment (Bird, 2001). In contrast face-to-face role-plays tend to be fast paced and provide little opportunity for reflection. Face-to-face role-plays generally create their own momentum beyond the control of the student. Not only does this restrict students' capacity to think about how they are applying theory during the process, it has also been found to be a stressful experience for some students (Day, 1977). Importantly, we do not suggest that face-to-face role-plays should be abandoned. A combination of role-play experiences provides the optimum opportunity for engagement with reflexive practice. Through the e-learning approach of blended learning students can experience *both* online and face-to-face role-plays to develop reflexive skills. The design options outlined in this chapter utilise a blended learning framework (Graham, 2006). Blended learning is an approach to e-learning that combines online and face-to-face modes of delivery to achieve optimum results in learning. This approach is gaining momentum in university education (Graham, 2005). In our design online role-plays dealing with professional interventions can be blended with face-to-face classroom role-plays aimed at developing professional skills. The design aims to utilise online role-plays to assist students to understand relevant theory and to use face-to-face role-plays to assist students to understand relevant human services practice skills. In this chapter we provide detail of a number of design models for university teachers to choose from and combine these models with recent learning and teaching strategies such as the use of wikis and blogs. The design elements identified in this chapter are suited to university education but may also be used in short course training that adopts an e-learning approach.

BLENDED LEARNING

There are a number of options available in e-learning, such as for example the virtual classroom, use of multimedia in the online environment, CD ROM packages and electronic discussion boards (Laurillard 2002). More recently e-learning has included electronic interactive software such as wikis, web-pages that can be edited by various users of the interface (Robertson, 2008) and blogs, author "diary" web pages (Tekinarslan, 2008) as methods of communication. One option in e-learning is blended learning which is now being acknowledged as one of the more successful ways to utilise the online environment.

Blended learning is the term used to describe the combination of multiple learning modes in teaching and mainly refers to the integration of online with face-to-face learning environments (Graham, 2006). Although face-to-face is still the dominant teaching mode in higher education there has been a steady growth in the use of e-learning including blended learning (Owston, Garrison & Cook, 2006). Online options range from the minimal use of the online environment, primarily for the displaying of text material or information distribution, through to entire courses being offered in online mode (Laurillard, 2002). Potential benefits of using online learning methods are both practical and pedagogical (Graham, 2006). Practical advantages include overcoming geographical limitations and the time restraints of classes that allow increased access to education for students in remote areas or with mobility issues, as well as being an instant and cost effective way for the institution to distribute materials to students. Pedagogical advantages come from perceiving online as an entirely different learning environment that requires both students and teachers to approach learning in a new way. Key to this is that online allows, and arguably requires, an extended thinking process to occur before students engage with others (Garrison & Vaughan, 2008). Whereas the face-to-face environment is spontaneous, fast paced, highly social and interactive, the online environment slows down the interaction between students giving them more time to think before they participate, and more time to reflect regarding interactions before they participate again.

In blended learning the online environment is not a simple replacement for components previously covered in the face-to-face environment as transferring an activity to online fundamentally changes the activity. Instead, blended learning is a new approach to designing learning and teaching that utilises the benefits of each mode to produce an enhanced learning experience for students (Garrison & Vaughan, 2008). In order for this to happen the alignment between modes of delivery and the learning objectives needs to be well thought through. It has been found that blended learning courses develop a greater sense of community among students than face-to-face or online modes alone. Importantly, it has also been found that a sense of community is seen by students as connected to greater learning. Studies have also shown that students engaging in a blended learning course found that their experience in one of the modes increased their confidence in the other, creating reciprocity between the two (Garrison & Vaughan, 2008). Relationships between students, as well as between students and teachers were found to benefit from this reciprocity. The face-to-face classroom situation naturally develops the social component of learning as students are constantly engaged with each other and their teacher. This is an ideal environment for developing a community of inquiry where students feel connected through their shared learning experience. Blended learning of face-to-face and online modes does not simply expand the educational experience to offer two streams of learning outcomes. Rather, it is a cohesive model that works towards one set of learning outcomes. What students experience in one of the modes is then brought into the other in an interactive and developing cycle (Garrison & Vaughan, 2008).

One example of blended learning in the human services field is the use of discussion boards in combination with social work field placements. Maidment (2006), whilst warning against a reliance on computer mediated learning, reports upon efforts to provide online discussion boards for students on social work placements. She discusses the benefits of discursive opportunities for students whilst engaged in work-integrated learning and points to the opportunities for greater student reflection provided by these discussion boards. According to Maidment (2006):

...online asynchronistic discussion can be used to promote collaborative, reflective, inclusive and meaningful learning during the practicum. In this context, the asynchronistic discussion involves students accessing an online notice board where they write questions, ideas and their responses to other student postings in an ongoing way throughout the semester (p.49).

In this design the experience of field education practice was blended with the opportunity for students to debrief online about their placement experiences. These postings dealt with practice issues that arose in their agencies, with students reflecting online about their reactions to these issues and at times seeking guidance from peers and their teacher.

The online component of blended learning has been found to be particularly useful when students are learning how to apply theory and develop critical thinking. One blended learning evaluation conducted at the Southern Maine Technical College in the United States concluded that whereas functional knowledge was best achieved in a face-to-face environment, addressing conceptual knowledge online encouraged students to become more active learners and led to greater retention of conceptual information (Ross & Gage, 2006). Both students and teachers in a blended learning evaluation in Canada identified that the use of online encouraged greater levels of critical thinking, a learning objective of the course evaluated (Owston, Garrison & Cook, 2006). It seems that a more self-reliant environment online meant that students sought to actively solve theoretical problems rather than turning firstly to the teacher as they may in a face-to-face classroom environment.

One social work course taught almost entirely online was evaluated for its effectiveness in teaching clinical skills. Students in the online course reported achieving the same level of skill development as those in a comparable face-to-face course (Siebert, Siebert & Spaulding-Givens, 2006). Interestingly, it was found that role-plays were the one component of the course difficult to transfer entirely to the online environment. In the course the students were asked to conduct real time role-plays with another student on a discussion board. Students found this to be problematic due to the absence of non-verbal cues and body language. A second round of role-plays was then played out, the only component of the course not conducted online, with students engaging in a face-to-face role-play with a practitioner at a local agency. In the student responses to the course many students reported that the worst aspect of the course was not having face-to-face contact to practise their developing skills. This evaluation indicates two important opportunities for the design elements discussed in this chapter: first, that the online environment can successfully be utilised to teach social work skills albeit with the limitation that students valued face-to-face interactions for the development of practice skills. Second, that online role-plays should not be considered as a replacement for face-to-face role-plays, but should be used in combination with this approach. In the next section of this chapter we provide more detail regarding the use of online role-plays in university education.

ONLINE ROLE-PLAYS

Online role-plays have been used for some time in e-learning and provide the opportunity for active learning that incorporates collaborative problem solving (McLaughlan & Kirkpatrick, 2008). For example, Vincent and Shepherd (1998) describe an innovation in online role-plays that provide students with the opportunity to play characters in

conflict in Middle Eastern politics. This role-play incorporated email and teleconferences and required students to negotiate complex international relations issues. Wills and McDougall (2008) identify a key distinguishing feature of online learning through role-plays as the opportunity for 'students to interact with each other via the computer rather than the traditional simulation in which students interact with a computer model' (Wills & McDougall, 2008, p 762). The impact of new online teaching and learning tools on teacher workload also needs to be considered as this is often the hidden cost of innovative online learning and teaching (Spector, 2005). One possible option in e-learning is the use of role-play simulations. A role-play simulation 'combines the attributes of both simulations and role-plays where participants adopt a functional role or persona within a simulated environment or scenario' (McLaughlan & Kirkpatrick, 2008, p. 311).

The use of such simulations is not widespread in tertiary teaching but this learning and teaching strategy has been successfully utilised in politics, economics, psychology, engineering, history and education (Wills & McDougall, 2008). Sophisticated software (Fablusi, 2007) is available through the Internet to assist in designing online role-plays including the opportunity to provide for multiple characters, a scenario, a chat room, an updating newsletter and a debriefing room. Participants can add to their character profile to build their own personal qualities in their character. Email or the use of university systems, such as the Blackboard Learning Management System, can also be utilized to play out an online role-play. The end of the role-play may be a solution to a problem, exploration of an issue, the creation of something or it may be an agreement through a negotiation exercise (Jones, 2007; Spencer & Hardy, 2008; Wills & McDougall, 2008).

Role-play simulations can be designed to require complex decision making that incorporates accommodation of diverse and competing perspectives (McLaughlan & Kirkpatrick, 2008).

They can be used in conjunction with authentic learning environments to provide students with the opportunity to develop "real world" skills (Jones, 2006; 2007). For example, in the context of human services practice there is growing use of the online environment such as in online human services counselling (Chechele & Stofle, 2003; Goss & Anthony, 2003). This type of development makes online training even more relevant to the authentic learning experience of human services students.

Some role-plays can be played out anonymously which may have benefits for participation in that players are not inhibited (Bell, 2001). However, there is a need to carefully monitor online behaviour in anonymous contexts (Chester & Gwynne, 1998) due to the possibilities of anti-social behaviour. There may be designs where combinations of the use of technology and face-to-face role-plays are utilised. For example, Dracup (2008) reports on a blended learning approach where character information and background is electronically distributed to students prior to role-plays in a face-to-face environment. This approach highlighted the benefits of students engaging in storytelling through role-plays. Online role-plays can also be used in field practicum settings to provide assessable tasks that provide the opportunity for interaction and reflective dialogue with other students and field tutors (Ogivlie & Douglas, 2007). Role-playing online can be used to assist students to develop ethical practice in contexts such as public relations (Demetrious, 2007).

In a survey of assessment used in the online environment Byrnes and Ellis (2006) found that online role-plays formed only a small part of the assessment for university subjects. This may be due to the extensive time usually required to set up online role-plays and the fact that these are mostly customised to particular learning disciplines and contexts (Wills & McDougall, 2008). However, even given the length of time setting up a role-play of this nature there are unique benefits including the slower pace of the environment which can enable students to give more time to the application of a particular theoretical approach (Douglas, 2007a; Wills & McDougall, 2008). Limitations of role-plays online relate to the lack of visual cues (Spencer & Hardy, 2008) but students can be briefed regarding the need to provide visual cues through symbols. Potentially students could use such symbols as a sad face to replicate non-verbal and body language responses. Students unfamiliar with technology may also need to be briefed how best to use technology and the possibility of the technology breaking down (Douglas, 2007b; Spencer & Hardy, 2008).

LAURILLARD'S "CONVERSATIONAL FRAMEWORK"

A theorist who provides a framework for teaching in the online environment is Diana Laurillard (2002). Her work has been widely used in online learning and teaching and we have applied her approach when developing a range of online role-play models and strategies. According to Laurillard it is rhetoric, dialogue with a student, which is the key to learning generally and in particular in the online environment. There is no certainty that utilising dialogue will ensure learning in the online context, but it is a principled approach that gives us the best opportunity to give rise to learning. Interaction is important to this approach. Students and teacher are involved in the dialogue and the process is a partnership in learning. To achieve this kind of dialogue Laurillard offers a "conversational framework" of four parts. These parts are described as: discursive, adaptive, interactive and reflective (Laurillard, 2002). By utilising Laurillard's conversational framework we ensure that there is a structured approach to online role-plays. As indicated earlier in this chapter other role-play simulation designs tend to be more open-ended in their organisation (see for example McLaughlan & Kirkpatrick, 2008, p. 301). We have chosen a structured learning and teaching design to allow students to engage in a staged approach to reading relevant theoretical literature and applying this theory to professional interventions in the online role-play. Notably, students engaging in online role-plays of the kind that we advocate will also have engaged in face-to-face role-plays. The learning that is achieved through online interaction will draw from these face-to-face experiences due to the blending of the two approaches. The conversational framework is incorporated in the following manner in the design:

Discursive: To begin the learning and teaching design the students are given readings that the teacher identifies as relevant to developing reflexive practice. After reading the material, which may be posted to university learning portals such as the Blackboard Learning Management System, students can be asked to post responses to set questions to a discussion board. Students and teacher then have the opportunity to interact through a description and re-description of relevant theories. Where necessary the teacher can adjust descriptions of theory to be more meaningful to students and to promote an understanding of relevant concepts, such as for instance the importance of language in reflexive practice.

Adaptive: The online role-play scenario is then posted to the website and is devised in light of the task goal of learning about reflexive practice. In combination with the teacher students can have input in relation to the goal of learning about reflexive practice through dialogue on the discussion board. The scenario of the online role-play is aimed at providing the opportunity for students to test competing notions of practice. The role-play storyline can be adapted to highlight issues that were identified by students as requiring further reflection and description on the discussion board. The facts of the role-play common to all participants, together with the objectives of the learning task, can then be posted to the discussion board.

Interactive: Students and teacher engage with the role-play. This might mean that students interview, counsel or facilitate conflict with a service user. Students have the opportunity to consult relevant literature before deciding upon an intervention and playing out this choice in the online environment. The dynamic of the online role-play changes with the actions of the role-players and there is intrinsic feedback given in the role-play by the role-players when choices are made regarding professional interventions. The online interactions between role-players mean that there is meaningful exchange during the role-play.

Reflective: After the online role-play students and the teacher have the opportunity to debrief about the role-play in a threaded discussion. This is an important part of the design as reflection enhances learning and allows students to make further connections between the relevant theory and the interactions of the online role-play. If appropriate the students can further reflect regarding the online role-play in an assessable journal entry.

These four elements of the conversational framework provide the opportunity for "deep" rather than surface learning (Ramsden, 2003) that incorporates both theory and skill development in the online environment. Through reflection and experimentation, a number of different models of online role-plays have been identified that can assist with teaching theoretical concerns (Douglas 2007b). These various models can be applied to the human services context and each provide differing benefits. We now outline these models and suggest potential advantages and disadvantages of each approach.

MODELS FOR ONLINE ROLEPLAYS

We have identified five kinds of models as being useful in the online environment utilising Laurillard's conversational framework. These are:

1. Traditional role-play online;
2. Fishbowl with a demonstrated role-play online;

3. Interactive fishbowl role-play online;
4. Comparative role-play online; and
5. Fishbowl role-play online with a reference group.

Importantly, each model incorporates a discursive element where student and teacher can have dialogue relating to theory through an online discussion board. As indicated in the framework outlined above following the discussion online the scenario of the role-play can be adapted by the teacher to meet the needs and understandings of the particular student group. Intrinsic feedback is then given as role-players interact in the online role-play. With this part of the design we have identified a range of models that can be applied to the teaching of reflexive practices for the human services sector.

Model 1: Traditional Role-Play Online

Transferring a traditional face-to-face role-play to the online environment is a simple way to utilise this learning and teaching strategy, however as noted earlier in this chapter placing activities online necessarily change those activities (Garrison & Vaughan, 2008). After discussing relevant readings online the teacher can electronically provide an authentic role-play scenario that might be encountered in social work practice. For example, the scenario may deal with a social worker interviewing a service user. Students can be given emailed detail of the background information of the roles in the role-play. All the students in the class can be allocated the role of either social worker or service user and can conduct an initial interview online as it might take place in the workplace. Student service users can recount their scripts online while the student social worker attempts to combine theory and practice skills to engage in reflexive practice. As we have indicated online role-plays allow students the opportunity to consult relevant literature prior to action in the online environment. Students can consider

relevant theory and relate the theory to possible interventions in the interview without juggling the momentum of a face-to-face role-play experience. As the role-play is played out intrinsic feedback is provided by role-players. This feedback ensures the active learning of participants as in role service users respond to the various interventions and skill sets used by the in role social workers. At the completion of the role-play students have the opportunity to reflect upon their experience in the form of an assessed journal. Importantly, students can comment upon the online environment as part of their reflection and compare and contrast this kind of role-play to the experience of the class face-to-face role-plays. In this way students can be asked to reflect upon the blended nature of their learning.

Of the five models presented here, this approach is the one that is closest to a simple transferral of a face-to-face dyadic role-play to the online environment. The advantages of this model lie in the active participation of all students in a class and the opportunity for the slowing of the role-play and the resultant extra thinking time for the student. However, the objectives of this learning and teaching approach can be frustrated by tardy role-players who are either late in responding to the asynchronous electronic communications or who do not respond at all. The impact of tardy role-players on the success of simulations was recently discussed in the results of an online negotiation role-play carried out between students of Macquarie University and the University of Tasmania (Spencer & Hardy, 2008). The teachers of the negotiation classes at the two universities noted the frustration of students who participated promptly in the online negotiation with those who failed to respond electronically in a timely manner. Thus the disadvantage of this kind of approach is the potential for lengthy gaps in time between electronic responses and the role-play taking a substantial amount of time to complete (Spencer & Hardy, 2008). This drawback can be circumvented by the requirement of strict time limits for the completion of parts of the role-play. However, some students may still not respond in the designated times and thus hamper the completion of the role-play.

Model 2: Fishbowl: Demonstrated Role-Play Online

In this version of the online role-play two students are selected to take the roles of social worker and service user and the role-play is played out electronically, viewed by the rest of the class online. The observing students have the opportunity, in a separate threaded discussion, to suggest and critique intervention choices made by the in role social worker. As in the first model this role-play experience is preceded by an online theory discussion. Students can contribute comments on either a particular intervention, or on the general approach being taken by the student in the role of the social worker. In this discussion the teacher can engage in Laurillard's (2002) discursive framework through describing and re-describing relevant theory to assist students in understanding interventions that would promote reflexive practice. A disadvantage of this approach, in contrast to model one, is that only a limited number of students are actively engaged in the role-play. There is however, some level of active engagement for the rest of the class as students are engaged in the concurrent, critiquing process. A recent study by Roberts (2007) has found that it is not the quantity of interaction online that is important but the quality of interaction provided in a role-play. Thus arguably observation may have merit in promoting student learning where combined with students offering critique of interventions in a linked discussion board.

Model 3: Interactive Fishbowl Role-Play Online

The interactive fishbowl role-play is similar to the demonstration role-play, except that all students

(or alternatively those who self-select) participate in the actual role-play by jumping in and out of the roles of social worker and service users. If student numbers are large in a class then a number of interactive fishbowls can operate at the same time. A concurrent separate discussion board for allows those students not in role to comment upon the role-play. As in all the models outlined here this discussion is informed by the readings on reflexive practice discussed prior to the role-play commencing. During the role-play students move from a critiquing role in one discussion thread to actively participating in the role-play in the other thread. The teacher moderates the changing of roles by students, and can email students who require extra coaching in the theory or interventions. The teacher can also, where appropriate, jump into role herself to model "best practice" in reflexive practice.

The advantage of this model is that many students can actively participate in the role-play scenario, and move between critique and action. The modelling of "best practice" by the teacher allows students to understand reflexive practice in this area. A disadvantage of this model is that it can be time intensive for the teacher who moderates role changes, the discussion board, on occasion jumps into role and also conducts private coaching. This approach to the online role-play is described in more detail later in this chapter as a case study dealing with learning regarding discipline area of mediation theory and practice, which includes facilitation skills.

Model 4: Comparative Role-Play Online

In the comparative role-play online groups of students are asked to take part in two different versions of a online role-play that is demonstrated to the rest of the class through the Blackboard Learning Management System. Each role-play starts with the same brief scenario and service user details. The difference between the role-plays comes from the in role social workers using two separate theoretical approaches to inform their engagement with the service user. For example, the first role-play could use an approach that is not reflexive, failing to critique societal discourses and their own history in the engagement with the client. The second role-play could use a reflexive approach to engaging with the service user. For example, by utilising the reflexive practice suggestions made by Bagshaw (2006), outlined earlier in this chapter, role-players could practice interventions such as acknowledging power dynamics in relationships; using empowerment strategies; challenging dominant discourses; ensuring marginalised stories are validated; and valuing the transformative power of the process rather than focusing on the outcome.

A benefit of all role-plays conducted online, which this model takes advantage of, is that an instant and complete written record of the entire interaction is generated. Once the respective role-plays have reached completion the two transcripts can be used for students to carry out an assessment of the two approaches through comparing them with each other. They can identify the different outcomes that each approach achieves and draw out the benefits and disadvantages of each of the theories. Students can also consider which contexts might be more appropriate for each theory to be utilised. This comparison can be carried out online or in the face-to-face environment.

This model may help students make informed decision about different theoretical approaches. A disadvantage of this approach is the significant amount of time that must be devoted to playing out the online role-play according to the various theories of practice. A strategy to minimise the time expended on this learning and teaching option is to play this online role-play out as an online demonstration or interactive fishbowl role-play.

Model 5: Fishbowl Role-Play Online with a Reference Group

In this model the role-play has two fixed players in the roles of social worker and service user. Once again a discussion precedes the role-play based upon readings on reflexive practice. The difference in this model is that the discussion thread, which is used for the concurrent critique of the role-play, includes not only students but also industry representatives (Douglas & Ogilvie, 2007) to act as a reference group for the in role social worker. This reference group can make suggestions regarding reflexive practice interventions as the role-play progresses. The industry representatives can provide authentic feedback and critique garnered from their practice experience as social workers. For example, industry representatives can inform the in role social worker of interventions they have used as part of their reflexive practice. The disadvantage of this model is the effort required to recruit industry representatives, however university teachers may already have these contacts from their ongoing engagement with relevant industry.

ONLINE STRATEGIES COMMON TO ALL MODELS – "MIX AND MATCH" FOR THE BEST FIT FOR STUDENTS

Careful planning is necessary regarding online simulations in order to ensure that learning objectives are achieved. The teacher must be skilled in educational facilitation to manage issues that may arise during the course of the simulation (McLaughlan & Kirkpatrick, 2008). Further learning and teaching issues that we have identified as important to consider when designing online role-plays can be arranged into three broad categories. These are:

(i)   the type of online tools that are utilised;

(ii)   the degree to which the activity is blended with face-to-face learning; and

(iii) the way that the activity is put into action.

Online Tools

There are a number of relatively new software options that may enhance e-learning design that are now widely used in the world-wide-web (Robertson, 2008). Wikis and blogs in particular have great potential as e-learning tools in online role-plays as they require the construction of knowledge by students rather than students passively being presented with content (Robertson, 2008). The constructivist approach to learning and teaching posits that knowledge is constructed by students based upon what it is that they are doing rather than what it is that they are being told (Biggs & Tang, 2007). We now provide definitions of these online tools, how they may be used to assist with online role-plays and also canvass a number of important design issues:

Wiki

A wiki' - which means "quick" in Hawaiian (Fountain, 2005) - is a shared online site where published documents can be added to or amended by anyone who has access to the site. Wikis are designed to be simple to use and are ideal for collaborative tasks. Arguably, the most famous example is "wikipedia" the free online encyclopaedia which anyone with Internet access can amend (Wikipedia: 2008). The premise in wikis is that there is a range of sources of expert knowledge and that anyone can participate and contribute (Fountain, 2005). However, the problem that arises from this approach is that the information contained in a wiki is not necessarily reliable. For example, the *Wikipedia* site contains a warning to users that new material may contain misinformation despite the site having a constant checking system in place (Wikipedia: 2008). Another problem with wikis is that another person's

contribution can be amended or deleted without consent (Fountain, 2005). Wikis could be useful in online role-play activities in several ways: first, after the initial student discussion online regarding reflexive practice and the theoretical approaches to be used in the role-play, a wiki could be used by an online discussion group to develop a shared understanding of the theory. Second, wikis could be used to develop both the characters and scenarios that are the starting point of the role-play. This would help to develop a shared understanding among students of the relevant issues, characters and situation. Third, a wiki could be used after completion of the role-play to summarise the students' understandings of critical issues brought up in the discussion thread.

Blog

A "blog"- shortened from the term "web log"- is a simple online publishing tool that allows diary-type entries to be published online in chronologically reversed order without the author needing to have complex computing skills. Along with wikis, blogs are a popular social networking tool in the broader online environment. They are most often used for keeping journals that are intended to be read by others (Tekinarslan, 2008). The use of blogs in higher education is growing, and studies have shown that students find blog journals easy and convenient to maintain. One concern raised by students is where Internet access becomes an issue, frustrating the writing of the blog (Tekinarslan, 2008). It is an important therefore to ensure students have access to the required technology and are not disadvantaged due to issues of the affordability of the software or hardware used in blogs. In recent evaluations of e-learning options blogs have been found to work effectively for reflective tasks in higher education (Bouldin, Holmes & Fortenberry, 2006). They can replace an offline reflective journal and arguably offer improved learning opportunities through their accessibility to other students engaged in the same online tasks. Access by others online means that they can be designed to allow peers or mentors to make comments on a student's entries. Blogs can be used in online role-play activities as a means for students to reflect on the role-play experience following completion of the role-play.

Pod-Casting

A pod-cast is an oral piece that is broadcast online but is able to be accessed at any time. Commonly used by radio programs, pod-casting also offers opportunities for online role-plays. The use of audio online can increase the authenticity of a service user character and literally give them a voice (West, 2008). A recorded account of a service user character talking about their life circumstances could be used as a basis for a role-play scenario. Some pod-casts include visual material. For example, after listening (and possibly viewing) a pod-cast for initial background information students could work together to develop the character and scenario on a wiki in preparation for the role-play.

Blending the Task

The degree to which the role-play activity is run between the online and face-to-face environments is a strategy to be decided when designing the activity. As noted earlier in this chapter, the online role-play is not intended to replace face-to-face teaching, but rather offers learning opportunities through combining the two learning modes. Blending options include:

(i)   online learning in tandem with weekly face-to-face classes;
(ii)   online learning in between two intensive periods of a course; and
(iii) online learning after an intensive.

The first option allows for the blending of the two modes of learning on a weekly basis. Students

attending weekly classes can discuss the on-line role-play in class and canvass any difficulties that are occurring online. McLaughlan and Kirkpatrick (2008), developers of the role-play environmental simulation entitled eSim, have raised concerns relating to the difficulties of assisting students to develop practice skills from the online experience. To address this concern in our design face-to-face class time can be used to build understandings of reflexive practice through dialogue concerning insights developed online. McLaughlan and Kirkpatrick (2008, p 307) note that the skills set that students bring to the role-play simulation may not be sufficient to engage fully with the online tasks in a design. In the context of this chapter's focus upon reflexive practice skills such as interviewing, counselling and facilitation, we argue that these skills can be built up in the face-to-face classes. After mastering such skills in face-to-face role-plays students can then transfer these skills to the online environment. McLaughlan and Kirkpatrick (2008, p 308) also note that in their experience it is sometimes problematic to build relationships between students online and that a lack of student relationships can negatively impact upon a simulation. The blending of the two modes can deal with this issue by building student relationships in the classroom so that these relationships can be drawn upon in the online environment. Due to the time spent on online interactions through the role-play a reduction in face-to-face class time is desirable.

In the second approach a substantive amount of a course can be taught by day-long classes for example for three to six days. Where this approach is adopted the online component may begin after the first two or three days of the intensive mode and continue for the rest of the teaching period. The advantages of this approach are that theoretical issues can be canvassed and assessed in the online environment and the focus of the face-to-face classes can be largely upon skills development. In the later part of the intensive mode classes students can refer back to the online role-play and thus allow for the greater blending of the two approaches. This is made easier by the fact that the online role-play is in written format and can generate an instant transcript. Additionally, other learning activities can be based on these transcripts, for example groups can analyse each other's role-plays. Transcripts of the role-plays can also be used as teaching tools for future groups of students if permission is received from the students who generated them.

The final option of undertaking the online fishbowl role-play after an intensive class provides students with an opportunity for engaging with theoretical issues after completing skills focussed face-to-face classes. This approach does not allow for the opportunity for the students to refer to the online role-play in class discussion. However, the students can discuss the experiences of the face-to-face class activities in their discussion board threads.

Online role-plays generate their own unique set of learning and teaching considerations. The number of role-plays utilised and the number of students involved will depend upon the model used, which in turn is based upon the needs and strengths of a particular group. In the online environment it is possible for multiple role-plays to run concurrently. The number of students involved in each role-play can also vary. Where a traditional approach to the online role-play is taken and students each take one specified role, a greater number of students are engaged in the role-play itself for a sustained period of time. Alternatively, an interactive fishbowl role-play approach can be used where a large number of students jump in and out of role. The choice of approach is important as this will impact upon teacher workload. The interactive fishbowl role-play may mean increased work for the teacher as role moderation is required and on occasion the demonstration of best practice.

Putting the Activity into Action'

It is also important for online role-plays to have a sense of authenticity to them so that students are able to imagine that they are involved in a genuine scenario. Utilisation of industry representatives, to assist in the design of the role-plays, is an option to consider in order to ensure the authenticity of the role-play storylines. On occasion some student groups will benefit from seeing how other groups' role-plays are played out. If a number of online role-play groups are run concurrently it may be helpful to students to have the opportunity to view each others role-plays. Additionally, groups could develop scenarios for other groups, exchanging role-plays and then playing out the scenario online with the option of viewing each other's efforts.

Strategies can be combined to create the most appropriate model to meet the learning needs of a specific group of students. When designing an online role-play several factors should be taken into consideration when selecting strategies. One crucial pedagogical concern is the standard that the student group already has reached in their reflexive practice skills. A group that is just beginning to learn about reflexive practice may benefit from a demonstration fishbowl online or an interactive fish bowl online where best practice is modelled by the teacher. A more experienced group may benefit from a comparative role-play online that leads to a critical comparison of different theories, or a possibly a role-play online with a reference group which adds the expertise of industry to the online discussion board. Other factors that need to be considered are more practical. A group with good access to and comfort with online technology is well suited to incorporating wikis into the activity to develop scenarios and characters before a role-play or to summarise a theoretical approach, and may enjoy the opportunity provided in using blogs for individual reflection following the role-play experience. A group with less access to or familiarity with the online environment may find these tools increase stress and create technological barriers to the learning activity. To assist teachers we now provide a case study to illustrate some of the design choices available through a discussion of the use of an online role-play in the discipline area of mediation.

CASE STUDY: INTERACTIVE FISHBOWL ROLE-PLAY ONLINE

The following example demonstrates how some of the ideas outlined in this chapter were applied to teaching the use of gender theory and power imbalances in the discipline area of mediation. This subject area has been taught over a number of years to a range of students including the disciplines of legal studies, social work, psychology and youth work. In this course students learn about the nature of conflict and of the process of mediation and also develop a number of practice skills, including facilitation skills. This area of understanding is of particular interest to social workers as they are one of the main professional groups acting as mediators (Martin, 2000). It is important that social workers understand gender concerns and power imbalances in mediation to ensure reflexive practice as mediators (Martin & Douglas, 2007). We now outline the design of an interactive fishbowl role-play online, dealing with gender, power and mediation.

In the interactive fishbowl role-play online model students jump in and out of the roles of mediator and the parties involved in the dispute. Other roles can also be included in the online role-play such as lawyers, experts and support people. This learning design was engaged with by students concurrently with weekly face-to-face classes. This blended model meant that students had already learnt a number of skills, including facilitation and understood the steps in the process of mediation through the experience of face-to-face role-plays undertaken in class. The aim of the online role-play was to allow students to integrate theory and practice

in the online environment. Some discussion of theory had occurred in the face-to-face role-plays, but the focus in class had been on skills development. The learning online was referred to and discussed in weekly classes and the online role-play was played out over six weeks. There were twenty seven students in the class and only one fishbowl was run with one concurrent discussion thread.

Discursive: Students were provided with readings that discussed gender, power and mediation practice. They then had the opportunity to interact with the teacher and each other through an online discussion forum using the Blackboard Learning Management System. The teacher posed questions to students, such as "Can women come to the mediation table and negotiate equally?" Students then posted responses to this question to the discussion board. The teacher reflected back to students the descriptions they gave in the discussion group. Where necessary, the teacher adjusted descriptions of the theory relating to gender and power to be more meaningful to students and to develop their understandings of the relevant concepts. The discussion allowed students to debate and summarise concepts in the readings relating to gender, power and mediation. The discussion developed from the differing perspectives that students articulated regarding the relevant issues and the different interventions possible to engage with power issues.

Adaptive: The scenario of the online role-play was set up with the aim of raising concerns regarding gender, power and mediation. The aim was to canvass a number of methods of dealing with power in a reflexive manner by the mediator. Students had learnt of different models and interventions to deal with power through reading the set readings and the ensuing online discussion conducted on the discussion board. The particulars of the scenario of the online mediation was crafted by the teacher and the role-play storyline was adapted to highlight issues that were identified as requiring further reflection by students, such as imbalances of access to knowledge and resources or approaches to deal with verbal aggression. The scenario of the role-play, which related to a domestic building dispute between a single mother and a builder, was posted to the discussion board and dialogue was provided relating to the opening statements of the mediator and the parties. The single mother, who had few resources was attempting to convince the builder of the need to repair the foundations of her house where there had been significant cracking. Students were then invited to participate by posting as one of the roles in the scenario with the teacher moderating the roles taken by students. Email was used to volunteer and confirm roles. Concurrently with the playing out of the mediation role-play students were invited to interact regarding the choices made by the role-players in the mediation in a separate thread.

Interactive: Students and teacher acted in the task environment to achieve the task goal of coming to some sort of conclusion in the online mediation. The dynamic of the online role-play changed with the actions of the students. On occasion, the teacher took the role of mediator to model best practice in relation to interventions to deal with power concerns. Intrinsic feedback was provided to the students through the reactions to mediator interventions by the parities. For example, when the builder was verbally aggressive to the single mother and called her a "stupid woman" who didn't understand building the mediator intervened by naming the abuse and reiterating the ground rules relating to appropriate interaction in the mediation. Students suggested options in the concurrent threaded discussion such as having a private session to speak with the builder about his behaviour and the asking of open ended questions to assist the builder to understand gender issues in mediation. Other students suggested strategies to assist the female party to feel more empowered, such as the mediator helping the woman to understand societal forces impacting upon the story of the mediation and by enlisting

the support of an expert to assist with knowledge disparity. Students spoke of power circulating in the mediation and the need for the mediator to be reflexive about her own power. Students playing the mediator took up some of the suggestions in the threaded discussion and the role-play unfolded with a variety of interventions trialled. The responses to mediator strategies meant that there was meaningful change in the role-play as a result of the mediator's actions. Role-players responded to mediator interventions and these responses were also commented upon in the concurrent discussion thread. A number of students volunteered to role-play and other students were content to be part of the discussion group and contribute in this manner alone.

Reflective: After the role-play was brought to a close by the teacher both students and teacher debriefed about the role-play in the concurrent threaded discussion. Students were directed to reflect upon intrinsic feedback derived from mediator interventions and role-play reactions in this reflection online. Following the debriefing students were asked to reflect further on the experience in a journal entry. This component of the task was assessed. In the journal students linked the experience on the online fishbowl to descriptions of practice. The journal gave students the opportunity to reflect in a self-paced manner and they could also comment upon the learning experience in the online environment.

CONCLUSION

E-Learning has grown in use in university education across the full range of academic disciplines. There is a need to provide more flexibility in the delivery of higher education due to competing pressures of education, work and family on the lives of students. This need for more flexible delivery in higher education is likely to increase the use of online learning as the online environment offers opportunities for flexibility without compromising standards. However, there needs to be widespread familiarity with relevant software, theories and models before higher education can take full advantage of the e-learning potential. This growth of online technology in higher education has arguably opened up a host of opportunities for innovative approaches for teaching in human services. Even a minimal usage of online technology provides a convenient way to make information and materials available to students thereby overcoming restrictions of geographic location or scheduled office hours and class times. With students today having grown up with interactive technology an online environment can be a very familiar one for them to use in acquiring knowledge, much more so than the traditional face-to-face lecture format which is arguably becoming increasingly outdated. Online role-plays in a blended learning environment have the potential to assist human services students to integrate theory and practice and develop into reflexive practitioners. Blended learning offers the opportunity for engaging with both face-to-face and online options in role-plays to better prepare human services students for practice.

REFERENCES

Allan, J., Pease, B., & Briskman, L. (Eds.). (2003). *Critical social work: An introduction to theories and practice*. Crows Nest NSW: Allen & Unwin.

Bagshaw, D. (2006). Language, power and gendered identities: The reflexive social worker. *Women in Welfare Education, 8*, 1–11.

Bell, M. (2001). A case study of an online role-play for academic staff. In G. Kennedy, M. Keppell, C. McNaught, & T. Petrovic (Eds.), *Meeting at the Crossroads, Proceedings of the 18th Ascilite* (pp. 63-72). Retrieved September 9, 2008, from http://www.ascilite.org.au/conferences/melbourne01/pdf/papers/bellm.pdf

Bennett, S., Harper, B., & Hedberg, J. (2002). Designing real life cases to support authentic design activities. *Australian Journal of Educational Technology, 18*(1), 1–12.

Biggs, J., & Tang, C. (2007). *Teaching for quality learning at university*. Berkshire, England: McGraw Hill.

Bird, L. (2001). Virtual Learning in the workplace: The power of 'communities of practice.' In G. Kennedy, M. Keppell, C. McNaught, & T. Petrovic (Eds.), *Meeting at the Crossroads, Proceedings of the 18th ASCILITE* (pp. 93-100). Retrieved September 9, 2008, from http://www.ascilite.org.au/conferences/melbourne01/pdf/papers/birdl.pdf

Bouldin, A. S., Holmes, E. R., & Fortenberry, M. L. (2006). "Blogging" about course concepts: Using technology for reflective journaling in a communications class. *American Journal of Pharmaceutical Education, 70*(4), L1 (8 pages).

Byrnes, R., & Ellis, A. (2006). The prevalence and characteristics of online assessment in Australian universities. *Australasian Journal of Educational Technology, 22*(1), 104–125.

Chechele, P. J., & Stofle, G. (2003). Individual therapy online via email and Internet relay chat. In S. Goss & K. Anthony (Eds.), *Technology in counselling and psychotherapy: A practitioner's guide* (pp. 39-58). Basingstoke, NY: Palgrave Macmillan.

Chester, A., & Gwynne, G. (1998). Online teaching: Encouraging collaboration through anonymity. *Journal of Computer Mediated Communication, 4*(2). Retrieved July 11, 2007, from http://jcmc.indiana.edu/vol4/issue2/chester.html

Day, P. R. (1977). *Methods of learning communication skills*. Oxford, UK: Pergamon Press.

Demetrious, K. (2007). Playing a critical role: Experiential learning resources and analytical media studies in higher education. In *ICT: Providing choices for learners and learning, Proceedings of the ASCILITE*. Retrieved September 9, 2008, from http://www.ascilite.org.au/conferences/singapore07/procs/demetrious.pdf

Dominelli, L. (2004). *Social work: Theory and practice for a changing profession*. Cambridge, UK: Polity Press.

Douglas, K. (2007a). E-learning as a way to reflexive practice: Online mediation role-plays. *International Journal of Education, 13*, 73–80.

Douglas, K. (2007b). Mediator accreditation: Using online role-plays to teach theoretical issues. *Australasian Dispute Resolution Journal, 18*, 92–100.

Douglas, K., & Ogilvie, A. (2007). Online role-plays, virtual placements and work integrated learning: Exploring the example of mediation communities of practice. In *Proceedings of the Partnerships for World Graduates Conference*.

Dracup, M. (2008). Role-play in blended learning: A case study exploring the impact of story and other elements. *Australasian Journal of Educational Technology, 24*(3), 294–310.

Fablusi. (2004). *The online role-play simulation platform*. Retrieved July 25, 2007, from http://www.fablusi.com/

Fook, J. (2002). *Social work: Critical theory and practice*. London: Sage.

Fountain, R. (2005). *Wiki pedagogy. Dossiers technopedagogiques*. Retrieved September 9, 2008, from http://www.profetic.org/dossiers/dossier_imprimer.php3?id_rubrique=110

Garrison, D. R., & Vaughan, N. D. (2008). *Blended learning in higher education: Framework, principles, and guidelines*. San Francisco: John Wiley & Sons.

Goss, S., & Anthony, K. (2003a). Introduction. In S. Goss & K. Anthony (Eds.), *Technology in counselling and psychotherapy: A practitioner's guide* (pp. 1-12). Basingstoke, NY: Palgrave Macmillan.

Graham, C. R. (2006). Blended learning system: Definition, current trends, and future directions. In C. J. Bonk & C. R. Graham (Eds.), *Handbook of blended learning: Global perspectives, local designs* (pp. 3-21). San Francisco: Pfeiffer.

Healy, K. (2005). *Social work theories in context: Creating frameworks for practice*. New York: Palgrave Macmillan.

Herrington, A., & Herrington, J. (Eds.). (2006). *Authentic learning environments in higher education*. Hershey, PA: Information Science Publications.

Jones, S. (2006). Using IT to augment authentic learning environments. In A. Herrington & J. Herrington (Eds.), *Authentic learning environments* in higher education (pp 172-181). USA: Information Science Publishing.

Jones, S. (2007). Adding value to online role-plays: Virtual situated learning environments. In *ICT: Providing choices for learners and learning, Proceedings of the ASCILITE*. Retrieved September 9, 2008, from http://www.ascilite.org.au/conferences/singapore07/procs/jones-s.pdf.

Laurillard, D. (2002). *Rethinking university teaching: A framework for the effective use of learning technologies* (2nd ed.). London: Routledge / Falmer.

Maidment, J. (2006). Using online delivery to support students during practicum placements. *Australian Social Work, 59*, 47–55. doi:10.1080/03124070500449770

Martin, J. (2000). Social workers as mediators. *Australian Social Work, 53*, 33–39. doi:10.1080/03124070008415219

Martin, J., & Douglas, K. (2007). Social work and family dispute resolution. *Australian Social Work, 60*, 295–307. doi:10.1080/03124070701519660

McLaughlan, R., & Kirkpatrick, D. (2008). Online role-based learning designs for teaching complex decision making. In L. Lockyer, S. Bennett, S. Agostinho, & B. Harper (Eds.), *Handbook of research on learning design and learning objects: Issues, applications and technologies.* Hershey, PA: Information Science Reference.

Ogilvie, A., & Douglas, K. (2007). Online role-plays and the virtual placement: Aiding reflection in work integrated learning. In *ICT: Providing choices for learners and learning, Proceedings of the ASCILITE.* Retrieved September 9, 2008, from http://www.ascilite.org.au/conferences/singapore07/procs/ogilvie.pdf

Owston, R., Garrison, D., & Cook, K. (2006). Blended learning at Canadian universities. In C. Bonk & C. Graham (Eds.), *The handbook of blended learning: Global perspectives, local designs* (pp. 338-349). San Francisco: Pfeiffer.

Ramsden, P. (2003), *Learning to teach in higher education* (2nd ed.). London: Routledge.

Roberts, A. (2007). Beyond a participation focus. In *ICT: Providing choices for learners and learning, Proceedings of the ASCILITE.* Retrieved September 9, 2008, from http://www.ascilite.org.au/conferences/singapore07/procs/roberts.pdf

Robertson, I. (2008). Learners' attitudes to Wiki technology in problem based, blended learning for vocational teacher education. *Australasian Journal of Educational Technology, 24*(4), 425–441.

Ross, B., & Gage, K. (2006). Global perspectives on blended learning. In C. Bonk & C. Graham (Eds.), *The handbook of blended learning: Global perspectives, local designs* (pp. 155-167). San Francisco: Pfeiffer.

Siebert, D. C., Siebert, C. F., & Spaulding-Givens, J. (2006). Teaching clinical social work skills primarily online: An evaluation. *Journal of Social Work Education, 42*(2), 325–337.

Spector, J. M. (2005). Time demands in online instruction. *Distance Education, 26*(1), 5–27. doi:10.1080/01587910500081251

Spencer, D., & Hardy, S. (2008). Deal or no deal: Teaching on-line negotiation to law students. *QUT Law and Justice Journal, 8*(1), 93–117.

Taylor, C., & White, S. (2000). *Practising reflexivity in health and welfare.* Buckingham, UK: Open University Press.

Tekinarslan, E. (2008). Blogs: A qualitative investigation into an instructor and undergraduate students' experiences. *Australasian Journal of Educational Technology, 24*(4), 402–412.

Vincent, A., & Shepherd, J. (1998). Experiences in teaching Middle East politics via Internet-based role-play simulations. *Journal of Interactive Media in Education, 98*(11), 1–35.

West, J. (2008). Authentic voices: Utilising audio and video within an online virtual community. *Social Work Education, 27*(6), 665–670. doi:10.1080/02615470802201762

Wikipedia: About. (2008, August 30). *Wikipedia, the free encyclopedia.* Retrieved September, 8, 2008, from http://en.wikipedia.org/wiki/Wikipedia:About

Wills, S., & McDougall, A. (2008). Reusability of online role-play as learning objects or learning designs. In L. Lockyer, S. Bennett, S. Agostinho, & B. Harper (Eds.), *Handbook of Research on learning design and learning objects: Issues, applications and technologies.* Hershey, PA: Information Science Reference.

Chapter 5
Virtual Situated Learning Environments
Developing Inter-Professional Skills for Human Services

Sandra Jones
RMIT University, Australia

ABSTRACT

This chapter explores how ICT can be used to create environments in which students engage in work-related learning opportunities through virtual situated learning environments. These VSLEs are created digitally as real-life learning opportunities. Situating students of human services in these environments presents the opportunity for learning opportunities that are authentic, apply adult learning principles and are learner centred. They enable participants to develop inter-professional skills by presenting scenarios that require inter-professional engagement in a safe and secure environment in which participants can experiment with different approaches to problem-solutions. They provide a safe-fail environment in which students can experiment with different approaches and see the consequences of not working appropriately without negatively affecting real clients. The chapter presents an example of a VSLE used to engage students in a related field of employment relations and outlines an example of how a virtual community centre may be used to develop employability skills for students in human services.

Any genuine teaching will result, if successful, in someone's knowing how to bring about a better condition of things than existed earlier. -- John Dewey

INTRODUCTION

A report on employability skills to the Australian Business, Industry and Higher Education

Collaboration Council (Precision Consultancy 2007, p.1) states that graduates need to apply "a broad range of employability skills learnt in many contexts and through a range of experiences". Employability skills for Australian industry were identified in a 2002 Government Report (DEST 2002) as communication, teamwork, problem-solving, innovation, planning and organising, self-management, life-long learning and technology. While identifying these skills as necessary,

DOI: 10.4018/978-1-60566-735-5.ch005

the learning approach required to develop these skills is less clear.

One field of thinking is that while these skills are generic, the context in which they are learnt is different. Becher (1994) uses the term "academic tribes" to describe disciplinary differences that, he claims, result in four intellectual cultures each with its own approach to learning and teaching. Using the work of writers, Biglan (1973) and Kolb (1981), he links disciplinary perspectives to subject matter research that he argues will affect both teaching and learning. He identifies, first, the natural sciences as underpinned by an emphasis on hard, pure subject matter and requiring abstract reflective enquiry. Second, humanities and social sciences relating more to soft pure subject matter and concrete reflective enquiry. Third, science-based professions as using hard, applied subject matter and abstract active enquiry and social professions as soft applied subject matter and concrete active enquiry.

Others, notably Trigwell et al (1999), Meyer and Vermunt (2000) and Prosser et al (2003) argue that these disciplinary differences, if not factored into educational design, can create dissonance in student learning.

While recognising the potential differences between disciplines in attempting to graduate students with appropriate employability skills, the task is complicated further in areas where there is need for professions to work at the intersection of a number of disciplines to present a holistic solution to complex problems. This creates the need to design learning environments that cater to a variety of learning styles associated with a broad range of disciplines.

Arising from the Report of the World Health Organisation (1998) that advocated teamwork across disciplines through inter-professional learning, there has been a growth in government pressure on universities to deliver learning opportunities that are designed to develop inter-professional skills. Starting in the United Kingdom health care industry, the spread of interest in inter-professional

learning approaches in Australia is evidenced by the establishment of a Discipline-Based Initiatives grant scheme by the then Carrick Institute (now Australian Learning and Teaching Council) in 2007. This DBI aimed to 'encourage greater sharing of quality practice and learning within and across disciplinary communities' with one of the principles adopted being to 'foster creative interdisciplinary engagement' (Carrick Institute 2007). Examples of learning initiatives for inter-professional education presented at the first DBI forum on trans, multi and inter-disciplinary learning and teaching curriculum design covered a broad spectrum of disciplines with the Health and related Sciences (Biotechnology, Community) prominent.

In a recent publication devoted to the implications of the increasing focus on inter-disciplinarity for higher education teaching and learning, Davies and Devlin (2007, p.3) identify three main types of learning. The first is multi-disciplinarity, which they define as the co-existence of a number of disciplines. The second is cross-disciplinarity, described as the investigation of a topic from outside a particular field of study with no co-operation from within the field of study concerned. The third is inter-disciplinarity in which the subtleties of the nature of academic disciplines is recognised. The latter, in turn, can occur by students undertaking an elective subject on general topic eg women's studies from a variety of disciplines, or pluri-disciplinarity, where two or more disciplines combine their expertise to jointly address an area of common concern. For example a complex issue, such as obesity management, requires an integrated approach from behavioural scientists, molecular biologists and mathematicians (Aboelela et al 2007).

The implications of the move to inter-professional education, and the underlying complexities involved in identifying what is actually meant by the term inter-professional, results in significant pedagogical issues for universities about methods of education delivery and the learning environment provided for students. The creation of appropriate learning environments that cater for disciplinary differences while at the same time encourage the development of generic employability skills required to operate in an inter-disciplinary future workplace, is challenging for all parties - academics, industry representatives and students.

This chapter discusses how an innovative development of ICT to create virtual situated learning environments, accessible to students in the online learning environment, can be used to engage students in inter-professional human services learning opportunities to develop generic employability skills.

VIRTUAL WORLDS FOR INTER-PROFESSIONAL SKILL DEVELOPMENT

It is acknowledged that in order for students to develop the knowledge and skills required to function effectively in the highly ambiguous technologically sophisticated knowledge era, there is need for students to be provided with learning opportunities that go beyond simply content delivery. Biggs (2005, p.90) states:

when the basic bodies of knowledge and knowledge relating to professional practice, are changing as rapidly as they are, it no longer makes sense to teach students all those things they will need to know in their professional careers....Students should be taught how to learn, how to seek new information, how to utilze it and evaluate its importance, how to solve novel, non-textbook, professional problems.

Expert practitioners such as Brown Collins and Duguid (1989, p.2), have long argued that, given that change requires multiple intertwining forces of content, context and community, what is needed are learning environments that immerse students in real situations that provide a "sym-

biotic relationship between knowledge and the situation in which it is produced". These learning environments need to create opportunities for students to both experience real world complexity and ambiguity and to experiment with alternate responses to addressing these. Stein (1998) states that learning should be seen as a social process in which students are presented with opportunities to think, perceive, problem solve, and interact. Kolb's (1984) description of experiential learning and Schon's (1983) action-based-reflective learning process, both demonstrate this concept.

While acknowledging the need for such "real-world" learning opportunities that can be provided through work-related and work-integrated learning, it is also important to recognise that students need to be provided with opportunities to envisage the future world of work. Vince (1998) identified the need to acknowledge that real-world learning engagement often limits knowledge development to individual retrospective reflection on past and present experience that may fail to recognise current and future complexity. This is particularly so when a more holistic approach to work in which traditional separation of disciplines and professions, is envisaged. Human Services is an example of such an inter-professional approach. However, while acknowledging this, neither traditional face-to-face learning environments nor work-places into which students may be placed to develop practical experience, are currently designed to provide learning experiences to develop such inter-professional skills.

The view presented in this chapter is that ICT, if designed effectively, can provide opportunities to create interactive learning environments that, while modelling real world activities, present students with the opportunity to develop skills for inter-professional work.

In the early 1990s proponents of innovative ICT use described how computers could be used to provide students with a simulated environment in which to interact. Gerrard (2001) explained how the third generation of technology enables communication between students that eradicates the disadvantage of "social distance" by enabling students to share ideas, knowledge, and experience. Laurillard (1994, p.20) described ICT as providing opportunities to 'simulate the real world and to link students to various audio and visual databases'. Reeves (1993) argued that a well-designed multi-media environment can be used to provide a wealth of learning support activities through the design of situated learning environments. More recently Reeves, Herrington and Oliver 2002, p.565) claimed that the digital environment provides opportunities for the development of authentic learning environments by enabling learners to:

move freely around the resources provided rather than move in a linear fashion that may not ape the complexities of real life. Problems presented to students can use the full capacities of the technology to present situations and scenario's in video clips, texts links and images to give meaning and purpose to the students' endeavours, and to provide motivation to complete.

Digital advances are creating ever-expanding opportunities for student engagement in learning activities in the ICT environment that are in accord with the so-called Computer literate or "C" generation identified hunger for interactive experiences. Virtual education is defined as:

instruction in a learning environment where teacher and student are separated by time or space, and the teacher provides course content through course management applications, multimedia resources, the Internet, videoconferencing... Students receive the content and communicate with the teacher via the same technologies (Kurbel, 2001, p.133).

One of the most recent advances has been the use of ICT to create "virtual worlds." "Second Life", developed by Linden Research Inc, is a semi-structured Internet-based virtual world in which users (*called Residents*) can interact with each other through motional "*Avatars.*" The ability of Second Life to enable text-based communication through local chat and global 'instant messaging' has developed the potential for universities to create virtual classrooms as communities of practice and situated constructivist learning environments. One of the first virtual universities established was the privately funded Virtual Global University (VGU) (http://en.wikipedia.org/wiki/Virtual_Global_University). The VGU was founded in 2001 by 17 Professors of Business Infomatics for 14 different universities in Germany, Austria and Switzerland. A UNESCO Report stated that the emergence of the virtual university is being seen as a 'potentially powerful complement or competitor to the traditional campus-based offer of higher education' (D'Antoni & Mugridge 2004, p.1).

While such digital environments initially seem to provide an appropriate learning environment for students of human services to engage in inter-professional learning opportunities, there are many issues that need to be considered before such digital innovations can be used effectively for educational purposes. These include issues such as how to ensure that the digital environment is used as an enabler rather than a determiner of how teaching and learning should take place and how to develop a pedagogy for e-learning that benefits from instructional design. There are technology issues such as what delivery platforms and quality assurance mechanisms are appropriate. Finally, there are questions related to whether law and policies have been established at institutional, national and international levels (D'Antoni & Mugridge 2004). These issues have recently been exacerbated by instances of virtual universities that have had to close because of unethical and dangerous actions by some student "avatars" to others.

The use of ICT to create Virtual Situated Learning Environments provides an alternative way to engage students in realistic learning opportunities for inter-professional skills development in safe environments. For example, virtual hospitals, schools and communities are being created to engage students in real-world problems and dilemmas that require students working together inter-professionally to provide holistic solutions.

VIRTUAL SITUATED LEARNING ENVIRONMENTS (VSLES)

VSLEs are virtual environments that students access through the university ICT system. They can be linked to any course (subject) and to learning platforms such as Blackboard and WebCT. VSLEs are created as work-places, community-spaces or public and private organisations. In providing the situated environment in which students can engage in real-life problem solving, they add a realistic work environment dimension to learning. As the VSLE is provided behind the university ICT environment, students are protected from exposure to potential predators engaging in adverse and illegal behaviour. In addition inappropriate behaviour between students can be blocked by the academic.

In providing a common environment in which students can normalise their experience and explore how they might need to act and what skills they may need to use in handling real world-or-work challenges in a protected and controlled digital "safe-fail" learning environment, students can experiment to explore the implications of both good and bad practice. In so doing the VSLE provides the opportunity for students to experience working at the intersection of the professions such as in the human service arena. This is particularly important in professions in which sensitivity is required when dealing with people in vulnerable situations.

When designing a VSLE and scenarios appropriate for student engagement in inter-professional activities associated with the VSLE a number of factors need to be considered. First, it is important to decide if ICT is the best medium for engagement of students in inter-professional activities. This requires consideration of a number of factors:

1. Is the task under analysis able to be explored using a written form of communication?
2. Do both students and academics have easy access to regular connections to the Internet?
3. Are students mature enough to handle learning from any issues that may arise from the scenario and aware of the appropriate protocols for online social networking?
4. Do the scenarios created for online student engagement contain sufficient complexity and differences of opinion to spark debate between the stakeholders?
5. Are any privacy issues contravened for the students or for real-world characters that may be modelled in a role play or problem-solving activity?

Second, what factors need to be included in the VSLE to give it a "real-world" character with sufficient information provided to enable students to realistically engage in inter-professional learning despite the virtual environment. Table 1 presents a summary of the issues that need to be considered when identifying factors to be included in designing a VSLE. This includes consideration of the:

Environment: Is the environment for the VSLE realistically situated locally, nationally or globally in order for it to have meaning to the participants? Does it have the potential to adjust from one environment to another? If so, does it present opportunities to engage participant-learners from different disciplines and cultures?

Profession: What professions are likely to be involved in scenarios associated with this organisation? Is the VSLE designed with this in mind?

External relations: Are external relations, between people engaged in this enterprise and others from similar of dissimilar organisations,

Table 1. Designing a VSLE

	INFORMATION	CHOICES
1	Environment	Local, national or global
2	Disciplines involved	Common or dissimilar "tribes"
2	External Relations	Government/Regulators Competitors/Clients
3	History	Significant events and/or peopleChanges over time
4	Structure	Industry sector, Ownership
5	Culture	Traditions, politics, ethics, values
6	Decision-making process	Management-Leadership
7	Work Organisation	Work flow, value, measurement
8	Resources	People, resources, money, materials

important? For example what government rules apply and how will this affect the approach taken by the enterprise? Do competitors exists and is this important? Is this a not-for-profit organisation and will it be affected by for-profit actions? What is the source of the clients/customers for this organisation?

History: What historical knowledge is necessary for students to engage in realistic learning activities in this organisation? Does this include significant events and particular periods of change that affect how activities are organised?

Structure and culture: What is the influence of structural and cultural factors on this organisation? Are there tacit factors such as traditions, political, ethical and social and value factors that are important in this context?

Decision-making and work organisation: How are decisions made in this organisation? What work organisation and processes exist that are important for identifying the service being provided?

Resources: What resources would realistically be available for people within the organisation, including people, finance and materials?

Third, what form of ICT activity is most appropriate for the employability skills sought to be developed? Participant-learners can engage in role-plays, negotiations and problem-based learning, simulations and group discussion

through WIKIs and Blogs using a range of scenarios taken from real-world practice. Figure 1 presents a matrix that enables consideration of the skills to be developed mapped against the type of on-line activity in which participant-learners can engage.

Fourth, how students are engaged in the online activity will depend on the form of interdisciplinary engagement that is the focus of the learning. Students as participant-learners may engage in specified or assumed behavioural types, personalities, characters, situations or roles and may test theory in practice or develop new theory. For example role-play involves participants acting out scenarios. Crookwell et al (1987, p.155) describe role-play as a "social or human activity in which participants "take on" or "act out" specific "roles" often within a predefined social framework or context. Discussion Boards, Wikis and Blogs provide opportunities for students to explore a range of approaches to problem solving from different disciplinary perspectives to both develop an understanding of multiple worldviews (paradigms) as well as to explore new approaches to problem solving by combining a number of disciplinary perspectives. Students as participant-learners may engage in these activities as an individual, a member of a team or a participant in a Community of Practice of Interest. Students

Figure 1. Inter-disciplinary employability skills

	Teamwork	Problem solving	Innovation	Communicate	Planning and Organising	Self Manage
Problem-based learning						
On-line Role play						
Simulation						
WIKI, Blog,						

as participant-learners may be either identifiable to other participants or they may engage in the ICT activities anonymously. Finally, students as participant-learners may self select their particular engagement in the ICT activity, or be appointed by the academic. Each of these choices will be influenced by the inter-professional activity being modelled. Figure 2 provides a model of these decisions.

The VSLE can be used in either a full or part (blended) on-line learning environment. When designing the learning environment it is necessary to recognise the importance of providing opportunities for students to debrief as a group as well as individually. This enhances the development of reflection by students on the skills they have developed, and enables them to become disassociated from the reality of the role-play or simulation in which they have been engaged.

Finally, the use of VSLEs can be used to more effectively constructively align learning aims, ICT activities and assessment, with the assessment combining peer, self and expert review. This enables new types of formative assessments to be designed with new forms of industry participation in assessment encouraged. For example industry

representatives can both assist with assessment from a "real-world" perspective while at the same time, be provided with the opportunity to reflect upon their own disciplinary practice and to explore the challenge of inter-professional practice. This adds a further element of realism to the learning environment. Table 2 presents an example of such a potential constructive alignment against employability skills.

Examples of how VSLEs have been used to engage students in activities that are real world and that exist at the intersection of disciplines are presented in the second half of this chapter.

DESIGN OF VSLE AND SCENARIOS FOR USE IN AN INTER-PROFESSIONAL BUSINESS CONTEXT

I have used VSLEs to engage students of Employment Relations and Negotiations in real-world learning challenges (Jones 2005; Jones & Richardson 2002). Using the categorisation introduced earlier human services lies both within the sciences and social sciences, while Employment Relations

Figure 2. Types of participant-learner engagement

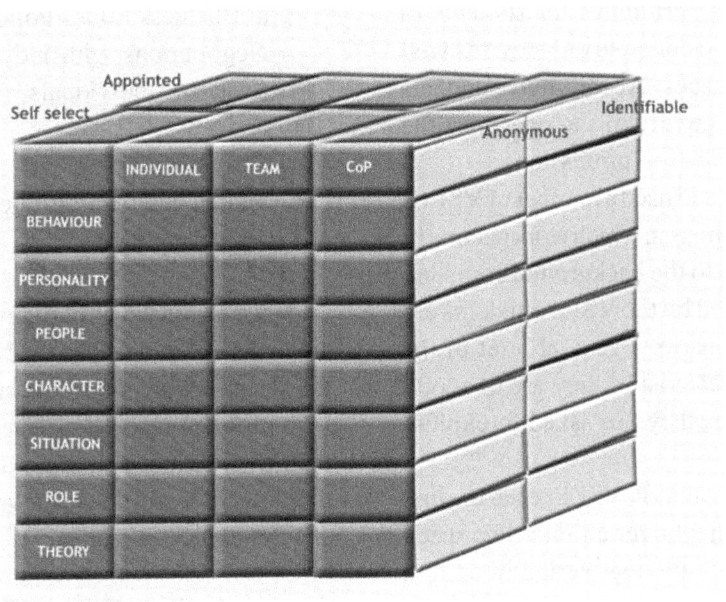

Table 2. Constructive alignment of learning outcomes, aims, activities and assessment

Learning Outcome	Learning Aim Demonstrate ability to	Learning Activity	Assessment Ability To
Communicate	Participate effectively in group discussion	WIKI BLOG	Explain ideas & concepts; Logically present information
	Present information	Role play	Demonstrate awareness of others feelings & beliefs
	Use information from a range of sources		Interpret resources appropriately; Structure contribution coherently
Teamwork	Work together effectively a team for a range of situations	Preparation final group decision Peer review	Identify similarities and differences of team work in online and F2F environment; Contribute effectively to the team
Problem solving skills	Problem solve	On-line presentation to external partner	Develop argument logically; Analysis and description of the problem
Innovation	Use initiative and enterprise to develop innovations	Innovative approaches for feedback of solution	Identify strategies for establishing and maintaining effective working relationships
Planning and organizing	Operate effectively in a work environment	Contribute to on-line Report	Describe methods to improve knowledge and awareness of work environments, particularly the virtual workplace
Self-management	Develop and demonstrate self-management skills	Contribute personal reflections on activity	Plan and organise contribution to meet timelines and deadlines in on-line environment; Reflect on and identify development needs
Life-long learning	Develop and demonstrate learning skills	Self assessment	Identify personal strengths and weaknesses
Technology	Demonstrate ability to apply ICT skills to suit different purposes	All ICT activities	Enter information on-line in an appropriate format using appropriate conventions

lies within the humanities. However, the VSLE is able to provide opportunities for students to both soft and hard and concrete reflective as well as abstract active issues. Accordingly students require professionals with skills to operate at the intersection of a number of professions.

I have developed and used a number of VSLEs designed as organisations in which work occurs. In all cases, in addition to the background company environment provided by the VSLE, students are provided with a Scenario, a general brief of the issue, Roles or characteristics they are to adopt, and various Theories they are asked to explore in practice.

While using the common VSLE, each on-line learning activity is held over an intensive week period (in some cases a longer period of up to a month) followed as close as possible by a face-to-face de-briefing sessions. In all cases, assessment of the skills developed by students includes a combination of lecturer assessment of knowledge and skills demonstrated against theories; peer assessment; self reflection through journals and group reflection through group journals.

An Australian Owned, Globally Located Manufacturing Company (Renovators Dream)

The first VSLE is designed as a manufacturing organisation (Renovators Dream Pty Ltd) in which each participant-learner is identified as either a process worker, a manager, or a representative of a specialist department. Learners are presented with an outline of the company: what it produces, strategic plan and vision; cost structure and organisational structure.

Scenarios of inter-professional challenges in which learners engage have included the following:

- Effects of globalisation and offshore outsourcing on issues of social justice, production efficiency and employee voice;

- Development and implementation of global Business Ethics Policy;
- Negotiations with individuals and collectives of individuals (including unions); and
- Development of strategies to network knowledge sharing between professions and disciplines.

Activities in which participant-learners engage are designed to develop their abilities to analyse the scenario and contribute suggestions to assist with problem resolution. They then reflect upon their own actions and those of others in terms of the "lessons learnt" from the various contributions and the agreed outcome.

An Australian-Based Restaurant Complex (Delicate Dining)

The second VSLE is designed as a restaurant chain with a number of (locally based) outlets in which each participant-learner is either a manager/lessee or employee in a particular outlet (chef, kitchen hand, waiting staff, bar staff). Learners are presented with an outline of the company including strategic plan and vision and cost structure.

Scenarios of inter-professional challenges in which learners engage have included negotiations of:

- Pay and conditions of employment (including relative rates of pay between roles);
- Negotiation of resolutions of occupational health and safety issues;
- Identification of legal and ethical employment issues; and
- Resolution of individual disputes between participant roles.

Activities in which participant-learners engage are designed to develop their abilities to analyse the effectiveness of different negotiation theories, styles and tactics used in resolving disputes. These include inter-disciplinary disputes and reflection on personal and group preferred behavioural styles.

A Publicly-Owned, Internationally Located, Complex Hotel and Restaurant Organisation (Fibco)

The third VSLE is designed as a global hotel and restaurant chain which originated in France as a private company, was floated on the stock exchange as a public company and bought out by an American company. It has expanded into Asia and developed a complex supply-chain from production of raw food inputs to the transportation of products. Each participant-learner is either a local or expatriate manager, an employee in a hotel or restaurant, raw food producer or engaged in transportation.

Scenarios of inter-professional challenges in which learners engage have included:

- Development of knowledge strategies, including social networks, to link the organisation and numerous discipline-based personnel;
- Exploration of disciplinary and inter-disciplinary frames through which the organisation is viewed; and
- Design of professional development programs to link the cross-cultural and cross-disciplinary workforce.

Activities in which participant-learners engage are designed to develop participant-learners abilities to analyse different styles of leadership and management required for inter-disciplinary cross-cultural engagement and reflect on personal behavioural styles.

In summary, activities and scenarios in which participant-learners engage cover a broad gamut of factors that engages them in identifying salient issues of changing work in a complex environment, framing judgements and making decisions,

identification of value judgements made by organisations and employees, developing research skills, and using reflection to develop strategies (Jones, 2007a; Jones 2007b; Jones 2007cJones & McCann 2005; 2004). Students engage in on-line role play, on-line negotiations and on-line group discussions according to a variety of scenarios, designed as ill-defined, open-ended and complex tasks. Issues that form the basis of student interactions relate to employment issues such as wage payments, training, equity, sexual harassment, diversity policies and practices, occupational health and safety as well as general business issues such as developing risk management procedures and takeover strategies.

STUDENT ENGAGEMENT IN VSLE

In each case the level and intensity of student engagement in, and feedback on, their participation in the activities has been positive, indeed more positive than expected. There has been ample evidence of employability skills developed by students. Even in this asynchronous environment students exhibited improved "communication" skills, particularly in developing appropriate protocols for communicating in the online environment and the effects on relationships when these are followed. "Team-work skills" developed significantly over the period of on-line group engagement. This was particularly evident in international students who reflected that the on-line environment provided them with the time to develop their thinking and perfect the English level in their written contributions and analyse the contribution of other team members that assisted them to develop new levels of confidence to contribute to discussion. "Problem-solving" skills developed with students often referencing earlier written discussions to find "innovative" solutions by combining ideas from earlier discussions that, in the face-to-face environment, may have been lost. "Planning and organising" skills developed as students' organised time for research activities to accord with the progress of on-line discussions. This was particularly noticeable for students located in different time zones who had to organise when to make their on-line contributions. Students stated that they had to improve their "self-manage" skills to organise their time and their research. Students also exhibited greater awareness of the potential use (and limitations) of "technology" as a tool for social networking and communication, and lastly, many identified the contribution their involvement had made to them realising both the availability and value of "life-long learning."

Student feedback has also provided positive evidence of the value of active engagement in these on-line learning activities for developing skills to operate in the inter-professional arena. In one example participants engaged in an on-line role play as managers of various departments about how a defined budget provided by the Government was to be shared between various departments (research and development, production and human resources). In the initial online discussion attention focussed on competition to wrest funds away from the other discipline. For example, one initial comment was "*I do not believe that valuable R&D government grant money should be used to fund such an initiative….this is not really a research program but an educational program –so why fund it from an R&D grant'*. However, over time more innovative inter-disciplinary solutions were proposed. For example the same person quoted above suggested '*I think we need to come to some sort of arrangement whereby our R&D department can continue working towards their goal, and we are also able to deliver this training in order to contribute towards that goal'*. This eventually resulted in an innovative solution to approach an outside body to provide extra funding so that both the proposed training program could be implemented and R&D could continue through the suggestion that '*surely we can get a strategic partnership set up whereby we can together fund*

this project so that we and the industry can benefit from this work'. In other examples, "norms" of behaviour that have become ingrained in disciplinary practice have been identified. For example, feedback from one participant-learner included the comment '*I was able to see the contradictory views of my colleagues and their justification of them. This led me to further understand the ethical codes which they adhered to'*.

POTENTIAL OF VSLES FOR HUMAN SERVICES: VIRTUAL COMMUNITY CENTRE

The experiences identified in the examples above suggest that there is potential for similar on-line learning experiences to develop inter-professional skills for the Human Services. Indeed the author is currently developing a VSLE of a Community Centre. Table 3 identifies the elements of the Virtual Community Centre using the factors, identified earlier in Table 1, to consider when designing a VSLE to give it a "real-world" character.

The Virtual Community Centre is in a new suburb on the boundary of several existing suburbs. It is located close to a rail line and has been designed to take advantage of natural resource in an attempt to leave as small an environmental "footprint" as possible. It is to be run by a joint Board that has both Community and private organisation representatives from the service providers within the Centre. It provides a range of community services for the local community including health (both traditional and alternative), a range of human services for all ages and needs and legal services (legal aid and private legal support) to support local community members. In addition it has a large (privately run) Leisure and Sports complex with a gymnasium and swimming pool. A number of shops and cafes are leased to for-profit owners.

The Virtual Community Centre operates under a range of local, state and national government

Table 3. Community Centre

	INFORMATION	Community Centre
1	Environment	Locally-based in a new suburb at the boundaries of existing suburban network Located close to a rail-line
2	Disciplines involved	Health services Human services – counselling, aged care, youth Sports services Legal services Management of Centre
2	External Relations	Government/Regulators Local community is mixed culturally, ethnically and age-wise
3	History	Aim is to create a community centre to bring diverse groups together
4	Structure	Local government plus private businesses operate within centre
5	Culture	Opportunity to create a new set of values and culture
6	Decision-making process	Mix government and private Centre Management to be employed
7	Work Organisation	Each service is creating appropriate work organisation with new employees
8	Resources	Decisions as to employment levels of resources needed to be decided

regulations governing individual and community services. The local Council requires the Community Centre to operate with the aim of bringing the culturally diverse community together and creating a new set of value and culture for the new suburb.

The Community Centre is operating with limited capacity at present, chiefly through the provision of children's services, counselling services and legal aid representatives. An external company has been appointed to operate the Sports and Leisure Centre. The Board has recently appointed a large Not-for-Profit organisation to manage the Virtual Centre.

The VSLE is accessible across the university as both a means of engaging students in typical activities involved in providing the range of discipline-related services and to explore inter-professional engagement. This will require students to operate at the intersection of a number of professionals, across and beyond human services.

The first Scenario designed for student engagement in this Virtual Community Centre involves discussion and negotiation between the

existing human and legal services personnel and the organisation contracted to run the sports and leisure complex to develop and market a proposal for a *Healthy Life-Style Management Strategy* for members of the community that is culturally sensitive. This is a real-world challenge that does require a holistic approach to inter-professional engagement. It includes social work, youth work, aged care, community and health care services. In addition the example identifies the potential for this VSLE to also involve students from outside human services to include legal aid, sport management, advertising, marketing, public relations (as an example).

Figure 3 identifies the constructive alignment designed to engage students in activities around this scenario. The employability skills chosen for demonstration in this example include communication, teamwork, problem-solving, innovation and self management. The ICT based activities chosen include WIKIs and BLOGs for open discussion board, on-line role-play and simulation for problem-solving and negotiations between differing discipline views, e-journals

Figure 3. Human services: Developing a healthy lifestyle management strategy

EMPLOYABILITY SKILLS	VSLE COMMUNITY CENTRE –	ACTIVITY	ASSESSMENT
Communication	Social work, youth work welfare, community art Medical; Health	WIKI Blog	Critical analysis in written contributions
Teamwork		WIKI Blog	Contribution of individual to team
Problem solving	Legal	On-line role-play Simulation	Theory demonstrated in activity
Self-management	Sport Management	Personal reflections in e-journal	Reflection paper
	Advertising, Marketing, Public Relations		

for reflection of self and team learning and simulations.

The assessment is designed to test the development of employability skills identified through written contributions and reflections and ability of the team to agree on a holistic plan for a healthy life-style.

In summary, the Virtual Community Centre, offered as a VSLE, provides a common place for students from a variety of human services professions to explore skills needed at the intersection of practice. This is done in a realistic setting in which there are a number of alternate needs from a variety of service providers. The on-line environment creates the opportunity for a common "language" to be developed as students use the written word to identify commonalities and differences in their approaches. The fact that discussions, negotiations and role-play responses are recorded in a written form enables students to "revisit" these to both reflect upon challenges and to explore continuous improvements in approach. The use of written communication means that different disciplinary approaches can be explored over

time and modifications made as innovative approaches are explored.

CONCLUSION

When designing learning environments for the human services, it is important to combine learning opportunities that mix both pure and applied approaches to developing subject matter and abstract and reflective learning techniques. Human services exist at the junction of many disciplines and thus it is important that students are provided learning opportunities that not only develop their employability skills in specific subject areas, but are also presented with learning opportunities to develop their inter-professional skills. This chapter has argued that ICT, through its use in supporting VSLEs designed to provide a common context for students, combined with ICT social networks tools that enable on-line role-play, simulations and discussion activities, provide a learning context in which students of human services can develop these skills. The outline of a possible approach to linking learning activities in the on-line environment with the development of employability skills through a VSLE of a Virtual Community Centre is presented to demonstrate this.

REFERENCES

Aboelela, S., Larson, E., Bakken, S., Carrasquillo, O., Formicola, A., & Glied, S. (2007). Defining interdisciplinary research: Conclusions from a critical review of the literature. *Health . Research and Educational Trust, 42*(1), 329–346.

Becher, T. (1981). Towards a definition of disciplinary clusters. *Studies in Higher Education, 6*(2), 109–122. doi:10.1080/03075078112331379362

Biggs, J. (2005). *Teaching for quality learning at university.* Buckingham, UK: SRHE and Open University Press.

Biglan, A. (1973). The characteristics of subject matter in different scientific areas. *The Journal of Applied Psychology, 57,* 195–203. doi:10.1037/h0034701

Brown, J. S., Collins, A., & Duguid, P. (1989). Situated cognition and the culture of learning. *Educational Researcher, 18*(1), 32-42. Retrieved November 11, 2001 from http://www.astc.org/resource/educator/situat.htm

Carrick Institute. (2007). *Discipline-based initiatives scheme.* Retrieved from http://www.carrick-institute.edu.au/carrick/go/home/dpi/pid/82

D'Antoni, S., & Mugridge, I. (2004). *Virtual universities and transnational education, UNESCO Forum Report, 2007.* Retrieved July 12, 2007, from http://www.unesco.org/iiep/virtualuniversity/forumfiche

Davis, M., & Devlin, M. (2007). *Interdisciplinary higher education: Implications for teaching and learning.* Australia: CSHE centre for study in higher education, University of Melbourne. Melbourne

Department of Education, Science and Training and Australian National Training Authority. (2002). *Employability skills for the future, Commonwealth Department of Education, Science and Training.* Retrieved June 23, 2008 from http://www.dest.gov.au/archive/ty/publications/employability_skills/final_report.pdf

Gerrard, C. (2001). Promoting excellence in distance education – a TQM led approach. In K. Ho & M. Donnelly (Eds.), *Integrated Management – Proceedings of the 6th International Conference on ISO 9000 and TQM* (pp. 578-583).

Jones, S. (2005). Using IT to augment authentic learning environments. In A. Herrington & J. Herrington (Eds.), *Authentic learning environments in higher education* (pp. 172-181). Hershey, PA: Information Science Publications.

Jones, S. (2007). Adding value to on-line role-plays: Virtual situated learning environments'. In *Proceedings of the Annual ASCILITE Conference,* Singapore.

Jones, S., & McCann, J. (2004). Virtual situated learning environments-the business education model for developing countries in a knowledge era. In *Business education and emerging market economies* (pp. 201-216). Amsterdam: Kluwer.

Jones, S., & McCann, J. (2005). Authentic situated learning environments-the flexible learning alternative for peripatetic managers in a global world of flexible workplaces. *Journal of Workplace Learning –E-Learning at the Workplace, 17*(5/6), 359-369.

Jones, S., & Richardson, J. (2002). Designing an IT-augmented student-centred learning environment. In A. Goody, J. Herrington, & M. Northcote (Eds.), *Quality conversations: Research and development in higher education* (p. 25).

Kolb, D. (1984). *Experiential learning.* Englewood Cliffs, NJ: Prentice-Hall.

Kurbel, K. (2001). Virtuality on the students' and on the teachers' sides: A multimedia and Internet based international master program. In ECEF Berlin GmbH (Eds.), *Proceedings of the 7th International Conference on Technology Supported Learning and Training* (pp. 133-136). Berlin Germany: Online Educa.

Laurillard, D. M. (1994). Multimedia and the changing experience of the learner. In *Proceedings of the Asia Pacific Information Technology in Training and Education Conference and Exhibition* (pp.19-25). Brisbane, CA: Apitite

Linden Labs. (2007). Retrieved January 12, from http://secondlife.com/whatis

Meyer, J., & Vermunt, J. (2000). Dissonant study orchestrations in higher education manifestations and effects. *Higher Education*, 15.

Prosser, M., Ramsden, P., Trigwell, K., & Waterhouse, F. (2003). Dissonance in experience of teaching and its relations to the quality of student learning. *Studies in Higher Education, 28*(1), 37–48. doi:10.1080/03075070309299

Reeves, T. (1993). Evaluating interactive multimedia. In D. Gayeski (Ed.), *Multimedia for learning: Development, application, evaluation* (pp. 97-112). Englewood Cliffs, NJ: Educational Technology Publications.

Reeves, T., Herrington, J., & Oliver, R. (2002). Authentic activities and online learning. In A. Goody, J. Herrington, & M. Northcote (Eds.), *Quality Conversations: Research and Development in Higher Education.*

Schon, D. (1983). *The reflective practitioner.* San Francisco: Jossey-Bass.

Stein, D. (1998). *Situated learning in adult education. ERIC Digest No 195.* Washington, DC: Office of Educational Research and Improvement (ED). (ERIC Document Reproduction Service No. ED418250)

Trigwell, K., Prosser, M., & Waterhouse, F. (1999). Relations between teachers' approaches to teaching and students' approaches to learning. *Higher Education, 37*, 57–70. doi:10.1023/A:1003548313194

Vince, R. (1998). Behind and beyond Kolb's learning cycle. *Journal of Management Education, 22*(3), 304–319. doi:10.1177/105256299802200304

World Health Organisation. (1998). *Learning together to work together for health.* Geneva, Switzerland: World Health Organisation.

Chapter 6
Electronic Classroom, Electronic Community
Designing eLearning Environments to foster Virtual Social Networks and Student Learning

Lisa Harris
RMIT University, Australia

ABSTRACT

The capacity for online learning environments to provide good quality learning experiences for students has been the focus of speculation and debate in the higher education sector from the late 1990s to the present day. In this area, "quality" has become synonymous with engaging students in a learning community. This chapter reports on a qualitative research project designed to explore the significance of community for students studying online. Using three fundamentally different types of online learning environments as case studies, this research explored the relationship between the constructed online learning environment and the development of learning communities or what the author has termed social learning support networks (SLSN). Exploring the common themes to emerge from these three case studies, this research provides new evidence of the benefit of community for students studying online and argues that future online learning environments should be shaped by five key principles designed to foster a sense of social connection between students.

'I pay the schoolmaster, but 'tis the schoolboys that educate my son'. -- Ralph Waldo Emerson (1803-1882)

INTRODUCTION

Many Australian universities grapple with both interpreting and responding to student engagement data (Coates 2006) and working through the effective use of online learning environments. Creating learning communities or a sense of belonging for students has emerged in the Australian higher education literature as a key goal for those interested in improving the student experience (Coates 2005; McInnis et al 2000). At the same time, many universities are coming to terms with the failure of their

DOI: 10.4018/978-1-60566-735-5.ch006

investments in eLearning to generate the new revenue streams forecast in the late 1990s, (Zemsky and Massy 2004; Reynoldson and Vibert 2005). This has required them to focus on developing sustainable eLearning policies that try to reconcile the demands of professional development for staff with increasing student demands for courses that are flexibly delivered (Minshull 2004). This chapter reports on research into the significance of community for students studying online and what role the constructed online environment can play in the development of community for students. This is particularly relevant for social work and human service students studying online because much of their education is predicated on the development of good interpersonal communication skills. The use of poorly designed online learning environments for the delivery of social work and human services study programs may well hinder the development of these interpersonal communication skills.

This research is significant because it provides a new way of thinking about "community" for students by showing the importance of community and how it works in both on-campus and online learning environments. But more importantly, it provides a new way of thinking about community that shifts our understanding away from a nebulous, ill-defined idea - to a practical, student-centred idea of community defined as Social Learning Support Networks (SLSN). The research findings indicate that the constructed online environment can facilitate the development of SLSN's for courses delivered fully online if it provides students with what Burbules (2000) calls, a *place* to inhabit. While the evidence for this second finding came from students who were effectively distance learners, it is likely that the elements of the online environment that supported their development of SLSN's are also relevant for the online environment we provide for on-campus students. In this chapter I draw together the common themes from three case studies and detail the significance of this research for future developments of eLearning in higher education by providing five significant challenges to the current design of Course Management Systems (CMS).

THE THREE CASE STUDIES

This research used a multiple-case study approach to explore three different online environments. The first case used a rudimentary web page with email communication and discussion boards. The second, a purpose built Virtual Social Space operating within a Course Management System (WebCT). The third, a text based virtual campus operating in a MOO environment (Multi user dimensions-Object-Oriented).

The first case study took a group of undergraduate social science students who were studying a single course online as part of a three-year on-campus program offered by the School of Social Science and Planning, RMIT University Melbourne, Australia. The online environment in which these students were studying was primitive using only a web page and email, and provided little or no opportunity for the participating students to develop a sense of connection with each other. Students' interactions were teacher driven and focused on course content and assessment activities. The students interviewed in this case were asked to explore their experiences of developing connections with other students both on campus and in the online learning environment they were studying in.

The second case study was a Masters in Information Technology Management program offered from Sheffield University, England. The academics responsible for this program decided to develop a Virtual Social Space (VSS) to act as an umbrella social space running across courses and throughout the program. The VSS provided discussion boards for social interaction, an area for student profiles and program information. Students in this program already displayed a high level of non-content related social discussions within the discussion boards provided in each course module. It was expected that students would use the VSS to further develop these social relationships. However, to the surprise of all concerned, after initial use of this environment, few students returned and no ongoing social contact occurred via the site.

The third case study was a group of students studying an undergraduate, context curriculum course offered by the School of Psychology, RMIT University, Melbourne, Australia. These context curriculum courses are offered to students from other faculties in order to provide them with an extra-discipline experience. As such, the students are from a wide variety of faculties and disciplines and are generally not known to each other. This course, *Personal Identity and Community in Cyberspace,* operated within a text based virtual environment of a Multi user dimensions-Object-Oriented (MOO). This environment provided students with a virtual environment that attempted to replicate a campus. A MOO is a real time, three-dimensional, text based virtual environment that provides users with both a sense of location and a sense of identity. A MOO replicates the real world by having separate spaces (rooms, buildings, etc) in which conversations and interactions can occur privately. A user literally moves between rooms and encounters others as they walk through the spaces. Creating the spatial distinctions between rooms is very important because it parallels aspects of the real world, for example when people in a room are talking, people in an adjacent room cannot see them or hear them unless they come into the room. One can choose to join someone in another room by either being transferred to the space (via a @join command) or you can choose to walk through the various gardens, corridors and stairways until you get to the room - bumping into others on the way. As Clodius (1994) suggests, the MOO creates a sense of place through location 'The sense of "being" somewhere is reinforced by the illusion of moving through spaces - one types

"north", the description of the room changes, the objects in the room are different, and different options exist' (para. 24). A virtual campus, the RMIT Tokyo Building was developed in the saMOOrai MOO. This MOO provided a virtual representation of Tokyo and surrounding countryside.

Data was gathered from each of these cases using a variety of methods including in-depth interviews, qualitative surveys and 13 weeks of ethnographic observations in the MOO. Over 50 students participated across the three cases. Data was analysed and key themes developed using the qualitative software computer program NVivo.

KEY THEMES

There are four major themes to emerge from the three cases and each influenced a student's capacity or willingness to develop community. They are:

- *Community,* in the form of Social Learning Support Networks, was identified as a critical factor in supporting student's learning in each case.
- *Work-life-study balance* - Students choosing to study online usually have significant demands outside of their study including family, work, recreational and social commitments. The development of Social Learning Support Networks had to be integrated into their life as a student.
- *Modelling behaviour* - Understanding how to *be* online for students was a result of their interactions with others and the environment. University staff played a key role in establishing the culture of how to *be* online.
- *Physical/virtual environment* - turning space into place. The physical and virtual environments played a significant role in providing students with the opportunity to

connect with each other and develop Social Learning Support Networks.

In exploring the significance of community for students, these factors emerged as core to understanding the value of community from a student's perspective. This research points to the value of stepping outside the electronic classroom and recognising that for many students, developing support networks is as much about what happens between them as it is about what the teacher either does or designs into the electronic classroom.

SOCIAL LEARNING SUPPORT NETWORKS

–Arranged marriages vs. having mates: being pushed rather than pulled into connecting with each other.

Stage one of the research explored definitions of community, trying to get to the heart of why the concept of "community" has been so important in the online learning literature. Interestingly, through the process of research, I have come to understand something fundamentally problematic about the way we theorise "community", and therefore how we try to operationalize it. For the most part in the literature and in many student engagement policy documents (Conrad, 2002; Palloff & Pratt, 2001; Tinto, 2000; The University of Melbourne Teaching and Learning Plan 2006), the term "community" is used in a very "objective" way. It is generally referring to something we should create for the students or that the students should have or be engaged in – because we know it will be good for them! In the interviews for the first case, students from the RMIT University undergraduate social science course often responded to the idea that they needed to be part of a community with a question. Typical of this, one student looked at me rather quizzically when I asked him if he

felt part of a community at university. He paused and tentatively responded *'You mean like, have I got any friends!'*(Harris 2007, p. 209). I suspect community has become something we either do *to* people or it is represented as some utopian dream. This binary either results in people wanting to avoid it or else never feeling like they are quite part of it. It is worth exploring this binary because it shapes student's notions of what it means to be part of a community.

When we are "doing" community "to" people it is often represented by a deficit model, as if the people we want to be part of community suffer a lack of capacity (Frank and Smith 2006), that is there is a problem, and a bit of "community" will fix it. Typical scenarios go something like this. It is said that there has been a "break down" in community when young people in an area are rioting; community development workers are employed to improve 'troubled' housing estates, or people 'with problems' (for example drug users, the mentally ill or young people at risk of suicide) require support. In this deficit model, being someone who "needs" community equals being someone who has a problem or worse, is lonely. A student from the second case, reflecting on the Virtual Social Space (VSS), comments as if he is an outsider on a space he desperately does not want to be associated with:

The VSS as a social space is akin to sitting alone in a bar with no atmosphere drinking diet Tango and, just before you leave, jot a cryptic message to say that you have been there on a post it note and stick it on the fruit machine. (a bit sad really) (Harris, 2007, p. 216)

There is nothing in his reflections that might hold the slightest hope that he could get something positive out of such a space. Sticking the post-it note on the fruit machine is the desperate act of a lonely person – but it is not what he did or wanted to do. Everything about his reflection points to a resistance about the very idea of the space. Conrad (2002) suggests the desire to engage students in learning communities can result in teachers designing activities where "learners are pushed, not pulled, into a community framework, somewhat like an arranged marriage" and that doing this often results in "conscious restraint on the parts of learners in contributing to community" (p.4). Students from all three cases confirmed Conrad's point, with only two students from the first case mentioning that one of the ways they made connections with fellow students was through collaborative activities in an on-campus class. I am sure, that at some level this is not an accurate reflection, and that all the students, at some point, developed connections with other students via their engagement in class. The interesting thing however is that the students did not own those connections as their own. The connections they owned were those they made in spaces outside of the classroom. Importantly, for many students with quite established networks, they still did not identify as part of a community when the term was used without further explanation or clarification.

I suspect this was possibly because when students hear the term community they overlay a concept of community that represents some long-past utopian dream that has been important to the history of the social sciences (Toennies 1963). This dream is a representation of community that is outside of most peoples lived experience (Bauman 2001). Contemporary students are all too familiar with idealised stories of political campus life in the 1960s and 1970s – told by academics in their fifties who drift nostalgically back to the days of student activism, free love, drug use, no fees and seemingly no consequences for not passing your exams! It is unclear if this was ever an accurate representation of the student community life. Utopian ideals rarely are accurate. There is little wonder that students today do not identify their experience of university life as "feeling part of a community" if this is the kind of image of community that they are thinking about. Several students

from across the three cases, at some point in our preliminary discussions regarding participating in this research, talked about their experience of university life as not being as good as X – "X" being what I call the X factor. For one student the X factor was her husband's university experience 20 years ago, for another it was a mate at a sandstone university. For another it was a friend studying in the U.S. and for another it was a student in the same school but in a different program. It may well be that these friends and relatives did have a better experience of university community life, but it is also possible, as Bauman (2001) argues, that the ideal of community is seemly never within our grasp. Student's resistance to identifying with the term community had a profound effect on this research. During the initial call for participants for the first case, a number of students commented that when they heard that the research was about community, they did not respond because they felt they did not know anything about community. It was from this point on I started to talk about the research in terms of understanding the connections students made with each other.

When community was put in these more subjective, practical and concrete terms it became a question. That question pointed to issues like – *what support do I get from my connection with fellow students, or what support do I give to someone I study with?* Students had no problem identifying the value this type of connection provided for their studies and why they would attempt, where possible, to create these connections. In each case students identified an understanding of how a social network of associations with peers might be of practical benefit. They provided their own examples of these types of relationships working within their lives. They could spell out how these relationships developed and existed. They could also detail how these relationships supported their learning, and they could say how these relationships were active inside and outside of the classroom. Students did not always talk about these connections in terms of strong friendships. For some they were more like "acquaintance-ships" that could be reliably called upon for assistance. These relationships represented an individual student's network of support that existed outside of the constructed learning space and often extended beyond the duration of a single course. I define these as Social Learning Support Networks (SLSN) partially to distinguish them from both the intensity of a "friendship", with its sense of longevity and intimacy, as well as from the less reliable concept of an "acquaintance", with its sense of transience and lack of obligation to assist another.

The use of the term "Social" in SLSN, denotes these relationships as connections that exist outside of the designed learning space but are also social in that they are defined by people coming together (as opposed to learning support resources students might find on a university web site for example). And importantly, SLSN includes the term "Learning" because this dimension was critical for students. Students valued SLSN's and put energy into creating and maintaining connections with others over time because they understood the importance of these connections during times of study stress, and importantly, that these personal networks actually assisted them in achieving their learning objectives. This was important for undergraduate students, but postgraduate students especially made the point that the choice to study was a choice to redirect resources - time, money and personal energy, from some other aspect of their lives.

WORK-LIFE-STUDY BALANCE

- I work hard and late, I have studies to do and somewhere fit in a social life. This schedule does not leave time to engage in VSS-ing (Sheffield student from 2nd case)

Students participating in this research clearly identified that juggling their study with other parts of their lives was stressful and affected the way they developed connections with each other. This research makes it clear how study is just one part of a multifaceted identity for students. While the depth of this feeling was very strong for the postgraduate students from Sheffield, the undergraduate students from the first case also confirmed that most students who choose to study online, do so in order to be able to fit their studies in with other parts of their life. Palloff and Pratt (2003) characterise the virtual student as someone who "tends to be older, working, and involved with family activities and the community" adding that "The convenience factor is what draws these students to the online environment, because it allows them the time for other equally important aspects of their lives" (p.113). The students in this research certainly reflected Palloff and Pratt's profile of an online student. For the students in the first two cases, nothing in their constructed online environment facilitated their engagement with one another in the same way as the physical campus did for on-campus students, or the way the MOO did for students in the third case.

In the third case I did not explicitly set out to explore this work/life/study balance. However, students often commented in their daily interactions in the MOO on the pressures of fitting everything in. Interestingly, some students from the third case were able to integrate the time they spent in the MOO with their work life. Some worked in jobs that allowed them to have the MOO running in a background window on their computer. They organised for a pop-up message to hit their screen if someone else logged into the MOO and would click over to the MOO window and say "hello" to whoever had logged in. Spender (1995) and Turkle (1997) have pointed to multitasking as an emerging capability linked to the use of technology like windows-based computers, both in the practice of having multiple applications open on a computer as well as in terms of people's capacity to effectively be engaged in a number of different tasks at one time. This, in effect, allowed them to be in two places at once. These students tended to be the more active participants in the MOO in general but their behaviour also had the unintended consequences of making them available to offer support to fellow students in a "just in time" manner. In the MOO, the timeliness of this support facilitated the development of SLSN's and balanced out the study pressures associated with managing work, home life and study.

Students in the MOO started to establish patterns of online behaviour that colleagues could rely on for support *when* they needed it. These patterns included various practices: some students usually logged into the MOO and hung around the night before an assignment was due; certain students logged on at about 8pm most nights; and one or two students could usually be found in the MOO during the day. These patterns of behaviour and the synchronous nature of the MOO supported students in integrating their study period with other aspects of their lives in two ways. Firstly, the quality of the SLSN's they had developed with each other and the culture of the online environment meant they could confidently seek support from each other. Secondly, the knowledge of their colleague's availability in the MOO allowed students to seek support at common times of study stress. The students in the MOO developed SLSN's that were integrated into their lives as students but existed outside of the defined learning activities in their course.

The students from the first two case studies believed these connections were important but said they did not have either the time or the desire for contributing to a contrived online community. While wanting and valuing the connections between students that resulted in the development of learning support networks, the capacity to build these connections needed to be integrated into their learning processes and/or the learning environment, and modelled by those familiar with the space. In effect, as the literature on community

development has suggested (Campfens 1997; Ife 1995), someone needed to take a leadership role in the online environment and model the type of behaviour that could then set the groundwork for students to develop SLSN's.

MODELLING BEHAVIOUR

It was significant that the students in case study one, from the RMIT Social Science program, talked about not knowing how to *be* in the online environment. Knowing how to *be* online is a mixture of both being familiar with the environment, and feeling a sense of presence from others in the space. For many students in this first case, there was uncertainty at a number of levels. They were uncertain about how formal they should be. There was a need for them to both familiarise themselves with the online medium, while at the same time, to understand the permanence of text in online spaces like discussion boards. They looked for clues from other students and from the teaching staff about how much of their personal life they should bring into the online environment, and how "academic" they should be in their contributions. In effect, the entire online environment represented an online classroom space in which their every comment remained permanently on show (for the life of the course). Students from all three cases talked about feeling nervous when going online to make contributions and waiting for others to have their say first, so they could follow their lead. This level of anxiety certainly had an effect on student's willingness to engage online.

However, there was some evidence from the students in case study one that teaching staff could reduce some of this anxiety by modelling the type of behaviour expected in the environment. A tutor from one version of the course started to model a very relaxed style of engagement with students. He did this by commenting in the discussion forums about his personal life and bringing his offline experiences into the discussions. Some of his students said this helped by reducing their sense of anxiety about contributing to the discussions and it provides evidence confirming the importance of teaching staff modelling the type of interactions and engagement they want from their students (Salmon 2001). Most of these students had very little experience in the online classroom and for many there was no sense of how to *be*. They had not developed an online voice or sense of identity in this environment.

The design of the Virtual Social Space that the students in the Sheffield University course encountered tried to reduce their anxiety by having the social environment completely separate from the prescribed learning environment. The Virtual Social Space was built in a separate online environment altogether. The project was designed to allow students to own this space through their management of it. However, knowing how to *be* and achieving a sense of social presence, a sense that the space was a lived place - was not modelled by anyone. Not only was this an unfamiliar environment for students, but activity in the space was not being driven or modelled by teaching staff. There were no course related learning activities in the space and it was not integrated into the students' online learning environment. The experiences of students from the first and second case studies confirms Salmon's (2001) arguments for the modelling of behaviour by teaching staff in what she defines as the "online socialization" stage of an online course (pp. 28-30). Salmon (2001) argues 'When participants feel "at home" with the online culture, and reasonably comfortable with the technology, they move on to contributing' (p. 29). There was little evidence in either the first or second case study of the online environment supporting students to feel "at home" and, as such, there was little online interaction between students that could be defined as social.

This was in contrast with the environment created within the MOO where students learnt how to *be* via their initial interactions with teaching and technical staff, and then through their daily

interactions with each other. They developed the confidence and capacity to develop an online voice and a sense of identity. This environment brought together the elements lacking in the other two cases. Namely, the teaching and technical staff modelled the type of behaviour that encouraged casual, friendly, informal contact, and students inhabited the space in a way that ensured that it became a lived space, a place where a student knew they could go to catch up with another student.

This type of casual, just-in-time type of engagement was important in the development of SLSN's because it offered students a "place" they could drop into "without prejudice." Although students were required to log into the MOO for three group conferences, online behaviour outside of these conferences was not monitored or moderated (Salmon, 2001) by teaching staff at any other time. As such this meant that in logging into the MOO they were not publicly committed in their intent. This is similar to when a student comes onto campus. They may be intending to go to the library, they might be going to class, they might be meeting up with friends, they might be attending a counselling service or they might not have a clear intent – they are just coming onto campus as part of their life as a student. In a sense, the MOO provided a similar environment to this. Students could check who was logged on before logging in and some just logged on and went straight to one of the study orientated spaces (galleries or seminar rooms) to complete a task. Others just hung out in their dorm rooms while others wandered around the MOO space, exploring student's contributions to the notice boards or heading off on a virtual train to explore the MOO's virtual representation of Tokyo. Regardless, a MOO etiquette was established that ensured students always greeted each other on entry to the MOO. Teaching and technical staff spent a number of hours each day during the first two weeks of semester in the MOO, and students quickly recognised they could call on staff for assistance with technical issues and questions related to the course. Students developed clear communication processes that allowed them to ask for help in a casual way because of the behavioural etiquette established in the first few weeks. Evidence of the effectiveness of this modelled behaviour started to appear early in the course when some students started to organise to meet at arranged times so they could help each other with technical aspects of operating in the MOO. The MOO was both a familiar and foreign environment for most students. Although spaces had familiar labels, students had to gain technical skills as well as work through their relationships with each other to complete content related tasks. The modelling of behaviour initially by teaching and technical staff, and later between the students, not only reinforced a constructivist approach, it created the opportunity for informal "chat" which became one of the factors for people "getting to know each other" and the development of SLSN's. The environment supported them in this because of the patterns of engagement they had developed with each other.

PHYSICAL/VIRTUAL ENVIRONMENTS: PURPOSEFULLY TURNING SPACE INTO PLACE

The most significant theme to emerge from this research is the relationship between the environment and the development of Social Learning Support Networks. While the literature reviewed for this research related the development of community for students with the learning activities designed by teaching staff, there was no evidence in the literature of the need to understand the relationship between student's engagement with each other outside of the formal learning activities and the vital role the environment played in supporting the development of these relationships. This requires a more holistic understanding of the *environment* to include not just the activities designed in classrooms, nor just the constructed physical or virtual environment students study in, but to understand

how students move and engage with each other in those areas not defined as classrooms.

For all three cases, students illustrated the significance of SLSN's and the effect the environment they encountered had on them developing connections with each other. Although students from the first case did not engage socially with each other online, they clearly illustrated how the physical campus environment supported the incidental contact between them that provided the foundations for the development of their SLSN's. Students from the second case went to great effort to ensure they spent social time with most of their colleagues around the on-campus workshop days held each semester, specifically because they understood the value of developing supportive relationships with others; and yet they did not use the virtual space provided online to facilitate these social connections. However, the most compelling evidence for the importance of the relationship between the constructed online environment and the development of SLSN's comes from the third case.

The MOO environment provided students who had no other opportunity to engage with each other, with the capacity to develop SLSN's. This is because the constructed environment of the MOO contained the key elements students required to transform an online space into a lived place - a place they could inhabit by creating things, engage in defined learning activities, play in, and importantly, a place students went to for support in times of study stress.

The idea that the design of the online environment can facilitate the development of community is certainly not new, nor is the idea that people will strive to create support networks using whatever means at their disposal. In 1993, Rheingold argued this in his seminal book *Virtual Community: Homesteading on the Electronic Frontier*:

My direct observation of online behaviour around the world over the last ten years have led me to conclude that whenever computer mediated communication technology becomes available to people anywhere, they inevitably build virtual communities with it, just as micro-organisms inevitably create colonies (Rheingold 1993, p. 6).

This research provides evidence to support the work of those interested in the development of online communities in an educational context and who recognise that the design of the online environment has a relationship to the sustainability of the connections students make with each other. Unlike most Course Management System based online learning environments, the MOO provided the type of environment that supported students' engagement with each other for a few simple reasons. As well as providing an environment that contained the defined learning activities and specified learning spaces (classrooms), it also provided a campus-like environment based on concepts that were familiar to students. This environment provided the capacity for synchronous contact that was not monitored (and therefore represented private space) and the students had the capacity to create objects that enabled them to extend a sense of social presence and their own personality into the MOO. These factors, together with the modelling of a "relaxed and supportive" behavioural etiquette or culture in the MOO by teaching and technical staff, ensured students made sustainable connections with each other that supported their learning.

The behaviour of the students in the MOO confirms the work of Prasolova-Forland and Divitini (2002). They have argued for the use of appropriate spatial metaphors to inform the design of online learning environments. Their work recognises the vital interplay of the spatial arrangements and incidental contact in the development of connections for learners in a way that was confirmed by the students in case study one when they talked about "bumping" into each other, and by the behaviour of students I observed in the MOO. According to Prasolova-Forland and Divitini (2002):

Communication plays a key role in keeping a community alive. Particularly important is the communication that is triggered by casual encounters. This communication is reported to be essential for knowledge sharing and strengthening the ties among community members. The communication is dependent on spatial arrangements, e.g. proximity of desks in a laboratory and attendance in the same classroom. A student that is not physically present in the "territory" of the community cannot take part in this communication. (pp. 259 - 260).

Importantly, Prasolova-Forland and Divitini discuss the implications of using different metaphors in the design and labelling of online environments. They make the distinction between labels that describe real spaces verses those that describe the intended purpose of the space. Key to their argument is the idea that the use of appropriate design metaphors, such as buildings and campuses, creates online environments that are familiar to students. The authors suggest this is in contrast to metaphors that describe the intended purpose of the space (i.e. a discussion board in a Blackboard or WebCT unit) which they suggest focuses 'on the information itself, not the person behind it', arguing that in these environments there is a need 'to strengthen the social aspect in such a system' (Prasolova-Forland and Divitini 2002, p. 262). Focusing on the person behind the information exchange requires an engagement with the environment using a more holistic understanding of the whole online space. It requires a shift in focus, moving beyond the electronic "classroom" to effectively include a student-centred view of a student's online life.

Focusing on a student feeling comfortable in a learning environment requires them to know how to *be* in that environment. This is reflected in Wilson's (1995) work when he talks about the outcome of learning not as "knowing that, know how" or knowing "names for knowledge" but rather as feeling like "we know our way around" in a subject. In advocating for the use of the term "learning environment", Wilson (1995) argues that the use of the metaphor "classroom" invariably starts the conversation from a teacher-led, teacher-centred perspective, as opposed to a learning environment that situates the learner and their experiences in the foreground. The MOO represented starting from this learning environment perspective. It required all involved to negotiate their relationship with both the constructed online environment and each other. In negotiating this relationship by authoring their own identity and social presence, the MOO, as an environment conformed to both Burbule's (2000) understanding of the conditions that mediate the existence of community and Goodyear's (2002) understanding of the learners' need to configure their own "learnplaces." In both these formulations, the learners have licence to act and the capacity to author their own spaces. The construction of the MOO represented this fluidity and the relationship between elements of the online environment and people's behaviour. Students knew how to *be*, and how to use of the environment to develop SLSN's because the environment felt familiar. They could create things and shape their own environment, while others were present in the MOO in ways that facilitated greater engagement. For example students created objects to carry around, authored their own identity via a text-based descriptor of themselves, decorated their own dorm rooms and developed objects for a virtual gallery.

IMPLICATIONS FROM THIS PROJECT FOR FUTURE RESEARCH AND THE DEVELOPMENT OF ELEARNING ENVIRONMENTS

The plague of academic research historically has been its failure to inform practice (Robinson, 1998). Whether research in teaching and learning has been misunderstood, refuted, or simply ignored, the result at the dawn of the new millennium is a mismatch between what we know and what we do. (Brown and Johnson-Shull 2000)

Reflecting on Brown and Johnson-Shull's lament on the failure of academic research to inform practice, it is a little daunting to speculate on the place of a piece of research such as this – one that uses the experiences of students to explore the three distinct fields of "online learning", "community" and "learning environment design" – and to argue for its capacity to inform a new approach to the development of online learning environments. And yet that is precisely the implications of this research. It provides a grounded understanding of the significance of community in the form of Social Learning Support Networks for student learning, and demonstrates that the design of the online learning environment plays a significant role in providing students with an opportunity to build connections and relationships with each other.

Is it right to suggest that all future online learning environments should look something like the MOO used in the third case? The answer to this is simply, no. The development of online learning environments and the use of the Internet in higher education is a rapidly evolving field - as is the technical capability of students - with teaching staff in most fields often lagging somewhat behind, but improving nevertheless. Certainly, we have some examples of graphics-based virtual online educational spaces (such as tappedin.org for K-12 teacher's professional development and projects in SecondLife – a virtual world which will be discussed in detail later). It is fair to suggest these virtual worlds have not really influenced CMS design to date. It is reasonable to argue that this is because the resource issues these environments create, both in terms of the need for broadband Internet access for students, and the technical capacities of teaching staff required to build learning environments in them, are still too great. The MOO was a text-based environment and was very accessible using a dial-up connection and was easy to develop for staff. Further research will be required to understand the changing capacity of the environment and the capacities of those who learn and teach in them. However, a project such as this, that has focused on the human elements of relationship building, our sense of place, and our capacity to know how to be in an environment, has a great deal to offer the field of eLearning particularly when it relates to the education of social work and human services student. The contributions from the students in these three case studies to our understanding of "community" certainly has much to contribute to those engaged in designing tomorrow's eLearning environments. In particular, for the next generation of course management systems, which are the mainstay of most university's commitment to online learning and the typical online environment encountered by social work and human services students.

The individual practice of teachers will always shape the student's learning experience, however, teachers work within the constraints of the learning environments provided in both the on-campus and online worlds. Just as on-campus teaching staff will attempt to move the desks in a room to reshape the learning activity into a more collaborative approach, or struggle to work interactively in large lecture theatres, the vast majority of teaching staff who venture into the online environment use the Course Management System provided by their institution. The findings from this research are a challenge to the designers of CMS to break out of the old paradigm of providing separate electronic classrooms - into creating rich online learning environments. These online learning environments will not only be rich in the various teaching tools educators like to use, but will also be rich in the sense that they take into account the way in which students engage with each other outside the classroom. The following five principles represent challenges from this research for future developers of enterprise-wide online learning environments. These principles bring together the various findings from this research and translate them into core design elements critical for improving the development of SLSN's:

- *Getting together outside the electronic classroom.* Tinto's (2000) research into the benefits of on-campus learning communities found, amongst other things, that members of learning communities developed their own self-supporting groups, they spent more time together outside of the classroom, and did so in ways students reported as supportive. The students' experiences from this research certainly support Tinto's work, but more importantly, their behavior in the MOO is a challenge to us to think outside of the classroom and to provide students with space to inhabit and make their own.

- *Learning environments need to be integrated into the social environment, not the other way round.* To date the development of online learning environments has been split between CMS and content. Effectively, the CMS has shaped the pedagogical approach used by most educators. However, students from these case studies owned and valued the SLSN's they developed outside of the formal learning environment. For students in the MOO and for those in on-campus courses, the learning environment is situated *within* the broader social environment they encountered.

- *Performance anxiety in a text based classroom: students need a space to bounce ideas off each other in their own time.* The provision of "classroom" only type online spaces limits the opportunities for student to engage with each other and heightens the performance anxiety associated with a written medium. The MOO case study clearly demonstrated that students would take their learning processes outside of the "classrooms" provided and into the halls, dorms and cafes of their virtual university campus or other online sites. These interactions outside the formal learning environment provided them with a safe space to explore their learning with peers.

- *Student identity and social presence: deciding what color shirt to wear that day!* The provision of social spaces with the capacity for extended social presence by a student has both a sense of time and location. The capacity to author their identity and leave their mark on a virtual space transforms it into a *place* that students choose to inhabit.
- *Bumping into each other.* Lastly, the provision of real time (synchronous) opportunities for contact supported the incidental sharing of information between students, which proved to be important in the development of trust relationships and the building of Social Learning Support Networks.

Although the ideas of integrating working environments into social spaces and the importance of incidental, or what is often termed "chance encounters", is discussed in non-learning orientated online work environments [as detailed in the literature on Teleworking, Computer Supported Co-Operative Work and Collaborative Virtual Environments - see Avon (2001), McGrath and Prinz (2001), Buscher et al (2001), Sonnenwald et al (2001) and Wellman et al (1996)], these five design principles provide a radical departure from the dominant eLearning environments found in most universities. It requires us to reassess both how students use online environments and how we conceptualise the boundaries of the online environments we provide for students. The understanding of human interaction and the development of SLSN's from this research contributes to four emerging areas of research and thinking on eLearning, namely: understanding the learning principles designed in successful online computer games; the growth of identity based online communities related to university student life; the development of student portals by many universities; and the use of virtual environments (such as SecondLife) in higher education. While there are certainly commercial drivers involved with some of these projects (facebook.com for example), arguably their success or failure relates to their capacity to start from a student-centred approach and to understand what happens for students as they engage with the online environment.

It is clear that the success of online gaming environments in teaching complex concepts and context related knowledge to players is of interest to the academic community. Authors such as James Gee have started to explore these issues in publications such as *What video games have to teach us about learning and literacy* (2004). At the same time, authors such as Chen (2006) and others have started to explore the value of immersive and non-immersive virtual reality learning environments. Others are exploring Massively Multiplayer Online Games (MMOGs) to understand the education and engagement principles within them (Young et al 2006). Certainly, the remarkable growth of Facebook. com (a website designed for university students to create their own profile) relies on students wanting to make connections with each other and creating a web presence for themselves. In April 2006, Facebook.com reportedly had over seven million users and was worth more than $1.30 Billion US (Kushner 2006). By 2007 the site had grown exponentially, with a reported seventeen million users (Robbins 2007a). The acceptance by students of sites like Facebook, has caused some authors to challenge educators to abandon their university CMS altogether and use social networking sites (such as Facebook) to deliver their courses:

Getting tired of the Learning Management System on your campus? Ever look to see how infrequently your students actually log in to see their assignments etc? Let me tell you, it's pretty darn infrequently. So why not create a course site on a social network where they already live? (Robbins 2007b, para. 1)

Trying to understand where students of the future will "live" online will be significant in the medium-to-long term as we move towards a more integrated idea of online life. However, the more short-term areas of interest, likely to directly effect the development of CMS, is the work being done by many universities in developing student portals, and the use of online environments such as SecondLife by more and more educators.

Many Australian universities have developed student portals in an attempt to provide 'more complete, holistic online environments for students and staff by converging a number of technologies' (Kennedy et al 2002, p. 24). A student portal attempts to provide an electronic entry point for students from which all the online services a student will use are available. This password protected environment includes everything from library access, to the course management system, student administration and student supports – usually with some capacity for students to provide some identity information about themselves which fellow students can access. While there has been the development of portals designed to improve student literacy skills (Hiscock and Marriott 2003), and other portals designed to improve critical aspects of the student's experience, such as transition (Nelson et al 2005), more universities are now looking towards portals as a way of providing a seamless administrative, communication and learning environment for students. While there is evidence of extensive use of these facilities (with sites like My.monash reporting 95% of students accessing the portal on a weekly basis (Kennedy et al 2002), there is little evidence appearing in the literature on the capacity of these environments to support the development of community for students in the form of SLSN's. This may be because this type of research is underway but just not reported yet or, more worryingly, that there are assumptions that the high usage of these environments will automatically translate to students developing communities. While most Australian universities work on their student portals, many

educators, particularly in the US, Europe and UK are starting to explore virtual environments such as SecondLife.

SecondLife, developed in 2003 by the Linden Corporation, is evolving into a rich virtual world capable of sustaining its own economy and developing its own culture. The use of SecondLife for education has been supported by the Linden Corporation but has, until recently, been characterised mainly by individual academics venturing into the environment to teach individual courses (Kirriemuir 2007). The SecondLife environment has similar characteristics to that of the MOO used in this research and, as such, it should provide students with similar opportunities to develop SLSN's. Many higher education institutions are starting to commit resources into SecondLife, develop their own islands, replicate their campuses and run courses "in-world" - a term used to describe being logged in to a virtual world. These institutions have included universities such as Harvard University, New York University, Stanford University (SimTeach 2007) and Oxford University (Kirriemuir 2007). There is also significant research occurring in SecondLife with a view to understanding how the environment might be used in higher education. Kirriemuir (2007) details several projects including: work by Krotoski exploring social network; work by Childs on the learners' experience; work from the University of Portsmouth examining the strengths and weaknesses of virtual environments; and work by Imperial College London comparing two groups of students' experiences – one completing a module SecondLife and the other in WebCT. Recent research is also making the links between educators experience in MOO environments and what implication this might have for the use of SecondLife for tertiary education (Mazar and Nolan 2008)

Certainly many of the institutions building campuses within SecondLife are including the type of social spaces in which students are likely to "bump" into each other, and there is some evidence of 'students commenting on the confidence given them by the environment and how this has helped them as learners' (Kirriemuir, 2007, p. 22). However, there is no evidence of any universities choosing to move from their Course Management Systems fully into SecondLife. This is not unreasonable given that the high-level computer graphics and bandwidth requirements for SecondLife will continue to pose a barrier for many universities outside of the U.S., both for content development and student access. While academic staff can learn the SecondLife programming language and create the learning environments relevant to their course, this requires a significant commitment on the part of the academic and is likely to remain another barrier to the broad adoption of this environment without significant institutional support.

In a sense this is the "tough" question for universities. Build their own integrated online environment including administrative function, learning spaces (both virtual-immersive and CMS like), library resources and social environments - providing them with clear risk management of issues such as copyright and branding. Or choose a third-party environment, not just a third-party application such as BlackBoard run on their own servers, but a whole environment – which will inextricably link their online presence with the branding of the third-party provider and provide all the future-proofing issues universities have face when deciding to move from one CMS to another. While the findings from this research do not provide any clear direction on this question, the five design principles outlined will play an important part in the success of any future online learning environment's capacity to foster a sense of social connection for students.

CONCLUSION

While there is still significant debate about the quality of online learning in universities, it is clear that eLearning and the use of the online environment to support students in their studies will continue to be a dominant factor in university life – including for social work and human services students. While the last decade has seen the almost universal adoption of Course Management Systems by universities, the decades to come are likely to see new developments in online learning environments that will attempt to integrate the student's zeal for products like Facebook, with the richness of virtual environments such as SecondLife, while still proving the security and risk management associated with CMS. The findings from this research will contribute to this new environment.

This qualitative research project used three case studies to explore tertiary students' thoughts and expectations about community in the online environment. Evidence from the first case study suggested there was a need to explore the relationship between the constructed online learning environment and the development of learning communities or what I have termed Social Learning Support Networks. To explore this issue further, the project was expanded and subsequent cases were chosen that included fundamentally different types of online learning environments.

This research had two significant results. Firstly, students not only confirmed popular educational theories on the value of learning communities, but also described how this form of social connection might practically benefit their learning. Secondly, this research found that certain forms of synchronous online environments provided enhanced opportunities for students to form social connections that supported their learning.

These results have provided new evidence of the benefit of social connection, or what many term "community", for students studying online and have been translated into five key design principles. I have argued that future online learning environments should be shaped by these five key design principles to foster a greater sense of social connection between students and to aid in the development of Social Learning Support

Networks. Emerson understood the overriding power and currency of the connections students make with each other and the subsequent shaping of their learning experiences. I think it is fair to say, that over a hundred years later, we are still working through how we translate the power of what "schoolboys" (and schoolgirls) have relied on for centuries – "having a mate to call on!" - into a vibrant, sustainable university eLearning environment. This research, while important for all students, is of particular significance for the design of online learning environments social work and human services students encounter. These students are often required to work on the development of interpersonal communication skills as part of their professional development and clearly an online environment, which fosters the development of Social Learning Support Networks, also provides them with the opportunity to develop these skills.

REFERENCES

Bauman, Z. (2001). *Community: Seeking safety in an insecure world.* Cambridge, UK: Polity Press.

Brown, G., & Johnson-Shull, L. (2000). Teaching online: Now we're talking. *The Technology Source.*

Burbules, N. C. (2000). Does the Internet constitute a global educational community. In N. C. Burbules & C. A. Torres (Eds.), *Globalization and education: Critical perspectives* (pp. 323-355). New York: Routledge.

Buscher, M., O'Brien, J., Rodden, T., & Trevor, J. (2001). "He's behind you": The experience of presence in shared virtual environments. In E. F. Churchill, D. N. Snowdon, & A. J. Munro (Eds.), *Collaborative virtual environments: Digital places and spaces for interaction* (pp. 77-98). London: Springer.

Campfens, H. (1997). International review of community development: Theory and practice. In H. Campfens (Ed.), *Community development around the world: Practice, theory, research, training.* Toronto, Canada: University of Toronto Press.

Chen, C. J. (2006). The design, development and evaluation of a virtual reality based learning environment. *Australasian Journal of Educational Technology, 22*(1), 39–63.

Clodius, J. (1994). *Concepts of space and place in a virtual community.* Retrieved August 2, 2003, from http://dragonmud.org/people/jen/space.html

Coates, H. (2005). The value of student engagement for higher education quality assurance. *Quality in Higher Education, 11*(1), 25–36. doi:10.1080/13538320500074915

Coates, H. (2006). *Excellent measures precede measures of excellence.* Paper presented at the Australian Universities Quality Forum, Perth, Australia.

Conrad, D. (2002). Deep in the hearts of learners: Insights into the nature of online community. *Journal of Distance Education, 17*(1).

Frank, F., & Smith, A. (2006). *Community development and partnerships: A handbook for building community partnerships.* Bentley, Western Australia: Curtin University of Technology.

Gee, J. P. (2004). *What video games have to teach us about learning and literacy.* New York: Palgrave MacMillian.

Goodyear, P. (2002). Psychological foundations for networked learning. In C. Steeples & C. Jones (Eds.), *Networked learning: Perspectives and issues* (pp. 49-75). London: Springer.

Harris, L. (2007). *Electronic classroom, electronic community: Virtual social networks and student learning.* Unpublished doctoral dissertation, RMIT University, Melbourne.

Hiscock, J., & Marriott, P. (2003). A happy partnership: Using an information portal to integrate information literacy skills into an undergraduate foundation course. *Australian Academic and Research Libraries, 34*(1), 32–41.

Huxor, A. (2001). The role of the personal in social workspaces: Reflections on working in Alpha world. In E. F. Churchill, D. N., & A. J. Munro (Eds.), *Collaborative virtual environments: Digital places and spaces for interaction* (pp. 282-296). London: Springer.

Ife, J. (1995). *Community development: Creating community alternatives - vision analysis and practice.* Melbourne, Australia: Longman Publishing Group.

Kennedy, D. M., Webster, L., Benson, R., James, D., & Bailey, N. (2002). My.Monash: Supporting students and staff in teaching, learning and administration. *Australian Journal of Educational Technology, 18*(1), 24–39.

Kirriemuir, J. (2007). *An update of the July "snapshot" of UK higher and further education developments in second life*

Kushner, D. (2006). Meet the boy wonder behind facebook.com, the hottest Web site the Internet. *Rolling Stone.*

Mazar, R., & Nolan, J. (2008). Hacking say and reviving Eliza: Lessons from virtual environments. *Innovate, 5*(2).

McGrath, A., & Prinz, W. (2001). All that is solid melts into software. In E. F. Churchill, D. N. Snowdon, & A. J. Munro (Eds.), *Collaborative virtual environments: Digital places and spaces for interaction* (pp. 99-114). London: Springer.

McInnis, C., James, R., & Hartley, R. (2000). *Trends in the first year experience in Australian universities* (No. DETYA No. 6546.HERC00A). Melbourne: Department of Education, Training and Youth Affairs.

Minshull, G. (2004). *Vles: Beyond the fringe and into the mainstream.* Retrieved June 28, 2006, from http://ferl.becta.org.uk/content_files/ferl/pages/news_events/events/Online_events/VLEs%20 -%20into%20the%20mainstream.pdf

Nelson, K., Kift, S., & Harper, W. (2005). *'First portal in a storm': A virtual space for transition students.* Paper presented at the Balance, fidelity, mobility: maintaining the momentum? Proceedings of the 22nd ASCILITE conference, Brisbane, CA, USA.

Palloff, R. M., & Pratt, K. (2001). *Lessons from the cyberspace classroom: The realities of online teaching.* San Francisco: Jossey-Bass Inc.

Palloff, R. M., & Pratt, K. (2003). *The virtual student: A profile and guide to working with online learners.* San Francisco: Jossey-Bass Inc.

Prasolova-Forland, E., & Divitini, M. (2002, September 9-12). *Supporting learning communities with collaborative virtual environments: Different spatial metaphors.* Paper presented at the IEEE International Conference on Advanced Learning Technologies (ICALT 2002), Kazan, Russia.

Reynoldson, C., & Vibert, C. (2005). *Creating value in ict-enabled business education.* Paper presented at the Frontiers of e-Business Research 2005, Tampere, Finland.

Rheingold, H. (1993). *The virtual community: Homesteading on the electronic frontier.* New York: Addison-Wesley.

Robbins, S. (2007a). *Roll your own lms with Facebook.* Retrieved October 15, 2007, from http://ubernoggin.com/archives/75

Robbins, S. (2007b). *Sarnoff, Metcalf, and Reed: The secrets to social network growth.* Retrieved October 15, 2007, from http://ubernoggin.com/archives/102

Salmon, G. (2001). *E-moderating: The key to teaching and learning online*. London: Kogan Page.

SimTeach. (2007). *Institutions and organisisations in Second Life*. Retrieved September 18, 2007, from http://www.simteach.com/wiki/index.php?title=Institutions_and_Organizations_in_SL

Sonnenwald, D. H., Bergquist, R. E., Maglaughlin, K. L., Kupstas-Soo, E., & Whitton, M. C. (2001). Designing to support collaborative scientific research across distances: The nanoManipulator environment. In E. F. Churchill, D. N. Snowdon, & A. J. Munro (Eds.), *Collaborative virtual environments: Digital places and spaces for interaction* (pp. 202-224). London: Springer.

Spender, D. (1995). *Nattering on the Net: Women, power, and cyberspace*. Melbourne: Spinifex.

The University of Melbourne. (2006). *The University of Melbourne teaching and learning plan 2006*. Retrieved July 18, 2006, from http://www.unimelb.edu.au/publications/docs/2006learn_teach.pdf

Tinto, V. (2000). Learning better together: The impact of learning communities on student success in higher education. *Journal of Institutional Research, 9*(1), 48–53.

Toennies, F. (1963). *Community and association (gemeinschaft to gesellschaft)*. New York: Harper & Row.

Turkle, S. (1997). *Life on the screen: Identity in the age of the Internet*. London: Phoenix.

Wellman, B., Salaff, J., Dimitrova, D., Garton, L., Gulia, M., & Haythornthwaite, C. (1996). Computer networks as social networks: Collaborative work, telework, and virtual community. *Annual Review of Sociology, 22*, 213–238. doi:10.1146/annurev.soc.22.1.213

Wilson, B. G. (1995). Metaphors for instruction: Why we talk about learning environments. *Educational Technology, 35*(5), 25–30.

Young, M., Schrader, P. G., & Zheng, D. (2006). Mmogs as learning environments: An ecological journey into Quest Atlantis and The Sims Online. *Innovate, 2*(4).

Zemsky, R., & Massy, W. F. (2004). *Thwarted innovation: What happened to e-learning and why*. West Chester, PA: The Learning Alliance.

Chapter 7
Creating and Sustaining Community in a Virtual Environment

David P. Colachico
Azusa Pacific University, USA

ABSTRACT

We are currently living in an electronic age where it is easier to travel the world, stay in touch with people who live away from our face-to-face environment without the need to leave home or to meet in a real life situation than ever before. The Web is becoming a place where we encounter others in ways to get our personal, social, and professional needs met. As a result of this growing phenomenon individuals are seeking to be a part of online communities of individuals who interact and associate with one another through the Web and the use of modern technology. This chapter will provide an insight into the use of information communication technology to create and sustain community.

'Technology.... the knack of so arranging the world that we need not experience it'. -- Max Frisch, (1911-91), Swiss novelist and dramatist in Oxford Dictionary of Quotations (2004, p.335:1).

INTRODUCTION

How is a web-based community different from one in a face-to-face environment? Both are the same in the way they involve the member of that community and the way one interacts with another member of the community. In brief, a virtual community is simply a community that happens to exist online, rather than in a classroom or other venue where individuals come together. I first realized the power of online instruction in 1999 when volunteers were sought to develop online courses and to teach them at the university where I am employed. For most instructors, the first few years were very basic and addressed the learning of content materials. The online courses included studying vocabulary, memorizing terms, and completing assignments in a private setting, usually alone at one's computer. As time went on, it was realized that students enrolled in the courses were not getting the

DOI: 10.4018/978-1-60566-735-5.ch007

opportunity to interact with classmates and some students could not survive without this. My own courses which I taught in the Special Education credential/masters program evolved to include this interaction both in synchronous and asynchronous settings. After seven years of teaching online I have developed my courses to the point where my classes are becoming very interactive. This was in part the result of creating assignments where the students were required to work together. This was also the result of the scheduling of my time for all of us to dialogue with one another with more active participation on my part as a community member in the class, using this to model and direct students to follow my example.

This chapter will help the person who is a community builder online to identify the dynamics and method of establishing successful web communities. It also addresses the key issues that web-based communities face and ways to design opportunities for interaction among the members of that community. The roles, rituals and events that bring people together into a group inside a virtual environment and make them into an online community are examined.

BACKGROUND

Virtual communities, or online communities, are used when individuals within a personal or professional group choose to interact with each other via the Internet. It does not necessarily mean that there is a strong bond among the members as is the case with a face-to-face group. Interaction in a virtual community takes place through email, chat rooms, synchronous learning sessions, etc. An email distribution list may have hundreds of members and the communication which takes place may be merely informational (questions and answers are posted), but members may remain relative strangers and the membership turnover rate could be high. This is in line with the liberal use of the term "community."

It is useful to examine definitions of what a learning community is meant to be. According to Chang (2003) a learning community is 'a group that shares ideas and information with all members of the community'. It is also a place where spontaneous learning and active knowledge construction takes place by the individual learners within the community. Chang continues to define this community as 'a virtual social organization of learners who share knowledge and experiences, exchange information as well as collaboratively solve problems in the pursuit of a common learning objective or interest' (p.28).

Thomas Sergiovanni (1993) defines community as 'a collection of individuals who are bonded together by natural will and who are binded to a set of shared ideas and ideals' (p.xvi). The members of the community have sought membership into this particular group. Communities don't happen randomly but are systematically organized and expanded.

It is not easy trying to create a virtual community of people in an online format unless it is planned and opportunities for interaction are specifically built into the online program. A person who is "surfing" the Internet for information but not dialoging with someone else is not a member of a community in the truest sense. The stage has to be set for community to develop. It is possible in an online environment to involve others and to heighten one's awareness of learning strategies, abilities and preferences. The planning of such opportunities must be specific in an online environment but should be deliberately designed as an integral part of an online program. Today more and more opportunities are being developed through distance learning or computer-assisted instruction where individuals can come together in a virtual setting to interact with one another and build a relationship in this setting. More opportunities are being designed through web technologies such as Facebook or MySpace for people to join a social community where frequent interaction occurs online and is reinforced offline.

MySpace and Facebook are similar because they are web-based social sites and function alike. These social communities are a current form of an interactive site that is popular with young people. Many users in these sites are teenagers or young adults who prefer this form of communication over emails or similar forms of postings that older people prefer.

Virtual communities essentially establish parallel realities and extensions of the social environment that allow individuals to interact on the web. To be active in a community there must be some knowledge and competence in the focus area around which the community interacts. A person must be willing to interact and learn from others as well as being prepared to share knowledge and experiences (Sherer, Shea, & Kristensen, 2003, p. 185).

Many colleges and universities as well as a variety of employers are exploring ways to offer training through online, web-based technology. This creates a challenge that is unique to those wishing to take advantage of these opportunities. How can a person communicate and interact with someone else online and how can they together create the type of community that enriches each other's experience?

Virtual community groups are popular because they make greater participation possible in remote locations. They also allow people with learning difficulties who may otherwise shy away from face-to-face contact to be able to interact with a diverse population on a variety of subjects (Tullar & Kaiser, 2000, p. 408).

All communities, whether face-to-face or in a virtual setting, need places for the members to meet. This may be the office lunchroom, or the neighborhood coffee shop, the local bookstore—places where you see groups coming together. There are similar opportunities on the web such as being part of a mailing list, being in a chat room, interacting in a web site, or a combination of these places. Over time these groups of people get to know each other better, and to feel comfortable interacting with each other in online settings.

Learning communities that are formed on the web are done so as a reaction to needing mutual support as well as the need for shared values, goals and resources. Learning communities provide an environment for one to learn in an atmosphere of sharing, collaboration, trust, support and respect for diversity (Chang, 2003, p.28).

Online communities have been a part of the Internet since its beginning. There have been a number of communities established such as the use of newsgroups, listservs, and virtual worlds. However, in an online community the members depend on each other to achieve the outcomes established in that controlled environment (Lock, 2002, p. 397). People join the various communities to meet specific needs which that group can accomplish for them. They may not remain in a group forever, but may be a part of that group whilst their needs are being satisfied. They will then move on to another group that will address alternate needs and feelings.

CURRENT ISSUES FOR ONLINE COMMUNITIES

In today's society many colleges, universities, and businesses are being transformed by the convergence of two powerful forces—the need for lifelong learning and the technology revolution of the Internet. As the body of knowledge grows at unprecedented speeds in many areas, people no longer consider their education to be complete once they are graduated from a college (Bento & Bento, 2000, p.603). Ongoing continuing practice is important in order to remain marketable; individuals need to be renewing their skills and keeping current in all areas of their professions. Web developers and instructors need to plan for this continuation of learning to occur. A person's learning basis of knowledge can be expanded via a web-based course or community. Learners can complement one another and share their knowledge and opinions by means of a community designed with a specific topic or purpose in mind.

One of the greatest benefits of a web-designed community of learners is that all course materials are available to the members at all times. If students travel away from home they can keep up with the coursework or activity in the community setting that is occurring. Materials can be accessed anywhere and students can be involved in a discussion or dialogue with colleagues in the community as long as the Internet is available. Location does not matter when content and information sharing occurs via the Internet.

Isolation is a common problem for many individuals. By "isolation" I do not mean being alone or being left alone. I mean being in a location that is set geographically away from the mainstream of a city, or a cultural group where travel is difficult to be a part of that location. It may seem paradoxical that a technology that makes one sit alone in front of a display screen can meet the need for community. However, this is true in today's society. There are many locations worldwide that do not allow for participants to interact in a face-to-face setting and therefore must resort to a virtual environment to meet this need. A virtual or online community allows people to respond to the feeling of 'hunger for community that has followed the disintegration of traditional communities around the world' (Di Petta, 1998, p.55).

So how can a person who is isolated from the rest of the community feel a part of this-group of learners? In on-line discussion groups, for example, we meet new people and confront new ideas. We share particular interests or ideas with like-minded individuals who share similar interests. Being a part of this type of experience gives a feeling like coming home. A virtual community can make one feel as personal and real as a physical neighborhood can. A community member can be active and participate with others often and begin to feel closer than if they were in a face-to-face setting. People from all over the globe can get to know one another and learn from one another in

a way that would not have been possible as little as twenty-five years ago.

There are concerns with membership in a virtual community. Being in a virtual environment is not free from problems, from difficulties with either the technology or with the interactions with other members of the group. Being a viable member of a community takes time, commitment, and a willingness to work with others. Being in a virtual community is a voluntary and participatory process. People within a community expect others to be active and participatory. A community is enriched only when others are willing to cooperate and interact with peers inside that environment.

In a face-to-face setting we are often concerned with who chooses or is chosen to participate. In an online community we more often choose those with whom we want to interact. If you become a member of a group where you are reinforced for your skill and knowledge, you will return time and time again. You will converse with others and build a relationship around the online program that is being used (Hill, 2005). To state this simply an online community and online interactions involve people who connect with one another over time and through space using the Internet as the primary medium. Online communities can form or function around anything such as talking about summer plans, vacations, pets, and work. Online communities organize around political action, introduce each other to would-be spouses and together create new concepts.

A community is not an entity or a product. Instead, it is a process which is fluid in nature (Lock, 2002, p.395). A community evolves and requires a highly interactive, loosely structured organization with relations based on personal interactions. It is a supportive environment where the members are accommodated and empowered. It is also a place that is responsive to the members' actions and interactions. How the members relate to one another and how the participants are kept engaged all influence the evolution of the community. The growth and longevity of the community is based on how well the needs of the members continue to be met. Each member of the community needs to be fostered and nurtured by the other members of the community. It is through this constant and meaningful interaction that the community comes to life and is sustained.

Communities are complex entities. It is not simply a matter of applying a number of rules for a community to survive. Rather, it is an effort to support the natural development of relationships among the members (Schwier, 2001). If the members of the community do not feel they are trusted or feel comfortable they might not return to the community. This will not contribute to the development of others within that community. Participants need a safe environment in which to be active and be interactive with one another.

Community building and strengthening takes time and not all members will feel the same sense of community within the same period of involvement. The newest members of a community will traditionally spend a great deal of time getting acquainted with the virtual environment and how to manipulate the program design where the community will be involved. The veteran member will traditionally spend more time working to establish a feeling of community among the members in a particular setting and does not need to learn to manipulate the technology.

There is a process for community development whether one is a new or a veteran member of the community. Brown (2001) identified three levels of community development. The first is where the members get acquainted with one another or make friends within the community. This is where the participants find others with similar backgrounds, feelings, or ideas. The second level is one of community acceptance. Here the members create an affiliation with others in the group as a result of frequent interactions and discussions. The final stage is one that is called *camaraderie*. When people reach this level they have had long-term relationships with others in the group bonding over topics for discussion areas. Communication

has occurred often enough that the members have gotten to know one another in ways that mirror the interactions that would occur in a face-to-face setting.

Therefore, one needs to realize that a virtual community has some drawbacks. Being active in this environment takes time. New members of a community may take time adjusting to the new forms of tasks and activities. The abundance of information found on the Internet and within a community setting can be a barrier for some learners as well as some instructors. Too often students in a community tend to be polite and nice to each other. Comments usually tend to be opinion rather than supportive in nature. The lack of visual cues and physical presence can be a deterrent to those who need this type of stimulation to be sustained in a learning setting.

Among the challenges that community members face in a virtual environment is trying to create and guide an interactive session within an educational setting. If the members are to learn from one another, the learning needs to be active and engaged with experiences. Effective learning leads to change, development, and a desire to continue to grow (Alexander, 2003). Learning is sustained by the stimulation and encouragement of the other members of the community.

With the onset of new technologies come the challenge and the joy of creating an interactive learning environment for the members of the community. In addition, the participation of the members in the community reduces the feelings of isolation and improves their abilities to communicate despite geographic restrictions.

Questions remain concerning whether or not a virtual environment can serve as a venue for increasing relationships between its members in urban, rural and international settings. Other reasons for a person to become involved in a virtual community may be due to one's busy schedule—work hours do not allow one to take classes or to interact when others are available—or family life may be too hectic to be able to leave home to enter a face-to-face community setting. Dialogue, staff development, discussion groups, etc. can extend boundaries and reach into the more geographically isolated areas. Connections among the members of an online community can take place anywhere, anytime as long as the Internet is accessible. The key to an online community group working successfully is in the balance between synchronous and asynchronous interactions between those who use the online learning community. Geographic boundaries do not play a role in this interaction working successfully; it is the members who make it work.

Technology's potential for instruction and learning can pose numerous challenges to the members of an established community. Despite its potential for innovative teaching and learning practices, technology also contributes to an unfortunate division between the information-rich and the information-poor. The information-poor are often minorities, low-income, or children in single-parent homes. This group also includes those who may wish to interact with others or may wish to gain further education but cannot do so because of geographic isolation (Ho & Burniske, 2005). It is a hardship to have to travel to a location where these technologies are available. Therefore, being active in a community is not always possible and this can compound an individual's feeling of isolation.

The advancements in technologies have recently begun to transcend the boundaries of time and space and to create online learning communities for interactions with others around the world. While one does not need to be physically near another member of the same community, it is critical to be alert and active in the community so that the boundaries of distance and information levels are not obvious.

DESIGNING A VIRTUAL COMMUNITY

Being an active and effective member of a virtual community requires not only the proper equipment but also careful consideration and planning on behalf of all those involved. This includes the designer of the community. There is an extra workload imposed on both the member and the designer if both are to be active in this setting. The members have to be willing to take an active responsibility because, no matter how much effort one exerts in this setting, it will not be beneficial unless they actually spend time interacting with one another. The designer needs to also be interactive if they wish others to feel that they are not using this community without any guidance or support. The leader in the group (whether or not it is the designer) should guide the members in establishing the direction of the discussions and the goals that the members want from this group.

People rely on the members of the community for a number of reasons and in all areas of their lives. Communities are defined in many ways—by geographic region, by demographics, by topics, or by interests. The community may evolve over time and change as the core members' interests change. As a community grows subcommunities may emerge as people find themselves in different categories. The designer of the original community needs to be prepared for this to happen. This may happen unexpectedly and the community membership can either increase or decrease according to the interests of its members. One needs to realize that the make-up of the community is an ever-changing presence defined by the members involved. This includes the resources available to them. Resources does not always mean the Internet, or newspapers, etc. In this environment it can mean the knowledge of those in the community. As the members grow and learn, the information shared (i.e., the resources) changes. This can cause the memberships' interests to change and therefore the membership to change.

When one goes to the theatre to see a play it is easy to recognize the actors by the way they are dressed. It may be easy to recognize the other members of that theatre community by the roles they play—ticket taker, concession stand worker, etc. Every virtual community is a performance of sorts. We should be able to recognize the members of the community by how they interact with the people they meet and we can figure out who to turn to in times of need or for help. If we look carefully enough we can find the visual identifiers in each member's public profile.(Kim, 2000) However, all of these players are interconnected under the umbrella of the organization, in this case the theatre. This is the same in any online or face-to-face community. We become interconnected as we continue to be active in the community.

It is important to consider the type of feedback and interactions members of a community want to validate their participation in the virtual community. Curtis (2004) conducted a study where he sought to supplement threaded discussion with social interactions to better support meaningful learning and allow students to make knowledge their own. He discovered that many members of the community wanted individual responses to questions sent via emails to avoid showcasing their ignorance on a topic in front of their peers. Members wanted the opportunity to get to know each other especially when new members joined the group. As the group begins to solidify the members share experiences or activities. When the veterans of the group interacted, they wanted to have time to make conversation.

Interactions and guidance as mentioned above can extend face-to-face interactions or physical communities to virtual communities and strengthen the membership of such a group. They also work to lessen the space and time constraints. As the members become more familiar with one another they extend the opportunity to create international "families" of learners where participants work on shared interests at their own convenience. This creates a community where

its members "engage in idle conversation" in a supportive environment in which members feel comfortable enough to publicly share and express their ideas within a collaborative context.

Collaboration is another factor that needs to be fostered in an online setting. Collaboration is defined by Lock (2002, p. 398) as 'a process that involves interaction amongst individuals in a learning situation'. This type of learning asserts that knowledge is constructed through social interaction. Where better to find social interaction but in a virtual community of interest? Participants in a collaborative setting, even a virtual one, need to have opportunities to shape the style and degree of their participation within the group. It is possible that the participants will perform multiple roles within the community. Depending on the needs of the members, the participants may interact as discussion moderators, and at other times as discussion participants.

The members of the virtual community need to be aware of the pedagogical framework of the community. Participants need to be open and willing to reframe their roles within the community.

An effective community requires its members to be active, to use teamwork, and to be interdependent. They also need to understand that the community is the basis of authority (Lock, 2002, p. 399). No one within the community works independently from the others. It does take time for the members to shift into an active learning environment where everyone is responding to the needs of the others within the group. There needs to be a fostering of the network of social relationships and a promoting of leadership and collaborative learning. The collaborative nature of a learning community helps to foster the overall learning process.

Communities need a gathering place. Similar to that of a face-to-face setting, those in a virtual community need a "place" where they can meet others and carry on a dialogue or engage in an instructional session. In the virtual environment, this usually means a listserv, or a chat room, a bulletin board, a Web site, or any combination of these. These are places where the community member receives informative emails (listserv) about a particular topic of interest; a place where members gather synchronously (chat room) and have an ongoing dialogue—all participating at the same time; a place where ideas are posted (bulletin boards) for the members of the community to leave comments or ask questions; or a site on the Internet (Web) where there is a interactive component attached to it for contacting the designer/creator of the site and receiving a response back. All these contribute the life of a community and being active within that environment. Each of these areas mirrors what could be occurring in a face-to-face setting but have been adapted to a virtual environment.

When the community is ongoing and its members are active there is a need to sustain the life of the community and to meet the needs of its participants. Special consideration must be given to how the community can be nurtured within the virtual environment. It is important to work to expand communication and to facilitate greater interaction among the members. Members need to be able to articulate and to accept a shared vision, goals, and aspirations of the community. They need to know the purpose of the community being in existence and they need to know how this purpose is influenced by the group members.

When the community is ongoing its members need to be able to articulate and apply the necessary knowledge, skills, and attributes that facilitate the development of the members and the evolution of the community itself. The members of the community need to be prepared to support the other members so that a climate is fostered for collaboration and interaction. Lock (2002, p.1) raises three questions to consider for sustaining a community:

1. Who is responsible for promoting and nurturing the longevity of the community?

2. What is required of the community members to sustain the community? and

3. What is required to create a history and sense of connection with those involved in the community in the past, present and future?

The sustainability of the community requires the development of a philosophy of community that embraces both continuity and change. It requires the engagement of all involved—leaders, instructors, participants, and spectators. It may well be these individuals who take the current community to new levels expanding upon the original vision of the community when it was first designed.

To be an effective community the members and the leaders must accept such characteristics as 'ownership, social interaction, group identity, individual identity, participation and knowledge construction' (Misanchik & Anderson, 2000, p.146). Administrators of the technology, instructional designers, and the online participants in the community play key roles in the building of relationships in the community setting. The fostering of these relationships is what helps to solidify the feeling of community in this environment. It is the informed interactions of the members and leaders of a community that influence and foster the vitality and resiliency of the online community.

Intentional learning and participation involves an awareness of one's abilities, preferences, and understanding or lack thereof of the dialogue within a community setting. It is important to nurture this type of interaction in a community in order for its members to gain a sense of worth and growth. This is based on the premise that learners can gain more knowledge with the help of the proper tools and guides than they would if they were working alone. In a virtual environment, the members are the guides and influence each others' ability to be active, on target, and learn.

In an virtual environment there needs to be consideration of the diversity of knowledge and skills among the members (McGrath, 2003). Diversity can be defined in a number of ways. In most areas it is defined as the quality of being diverse or different. These differences may include: geographical location, physical and, intellectual ability as well as age, gender, class, ethnicity and culture, spiritual beliefs and sexuality. In a virtual environment these issues of diversity are not a factor in one's active participation in the community's success. Those who might otherwise be considered as being "different" are not seen this way when interacting with others via technology unless they are willing to announce these differences. It is however the diverse make-up of the community that actually enriches the experiences of all members. Participants are resources to one another and this should be seen as a way of developing the knowledge of the members so that the entire community can benefit. All virtual community members have varied backgrounds and experiences to share and the ability to educate one another with new information or skills.

It is common that as a community develops that the members become more interdependent. They want responses to questions. They want to contribute to the increase of knowledge for the other members. They begin to feel responsible to one another and to the group and grow in mutual respect and in their identity as part of the group. All the members play a critical role in the community as models for the others within the community. As stated by Roland Barth (2001), 'Teachers and students go hand in hand as learners—or they don't go at all' (p.23). I feel this applies to the developers/designers of a virtual community as well as its members. Everyone participating in this setting must go hand in hand to support and nourish each other or the community cannot be sustained and its purpose is lost.

PARTICIPATING AND BELONGING IN A VIRTUAL COMMUNITY

Strong feelings of community increase the flow of information among all members of a virtual environment. The availability of support, commitment to goals, cooperation, and satisfaction grow along with group efforts. Members benefit from community membership by experiencing a greater sense of well being and having a larger set of willing individuals to call upon to answer questions or to offer support (Rovai, 2001). This will decrease the feelings of isolation, distraction, and social status amongst those who are communicating online. Virtual communities must move away from imparting feelings of isolation and move toward generating greater feelings of community and personal attention.

To create a true sense of "belonging" a community must convey a strong sense that members matter to one another and to the group. Essential requirements for a Virtual Community are:

1. A shared faith that members' needs will be met through the commitment to spend time together. A feeling that the community can be trusted.
2. A belief that there are shared values and a mutual benefit that comes from the membership within the community itself.
3. Shared emotional connection in time and space within the virtual environment.

This results in a virtual community where members are actively engaged and willing to contribute through having established a sense of purpose, belonging and acceptance.

Many virtual communities exist as a result of the designer/developer having an interest in a particular topic or area of investigation. The membership expands as others discover this site and join the community to enrich their own learning. Friendships develop and grow as a result of this union around a central topic. A thriving community continually creates and improves the system being used and the format of the discussion tool and site. The thriving community enables its members to carry out all the functions of life which includes areas such as studying a specific topic, reading and discussing what others are also doing or writing to colleagues. These can be developed to each individual's highest potential. Participation of the members is critical for the success of the community. This becomes a conceptual tool for understanding the learning in community and for members to engage in learning. Without active participation learning would not happen. Participation becomes the framework around which the community is built, no matter what the content or subject. What does participation look like in a virtual community?

Participation means:

1. Engagement with others and generating the ideas around which discussion will be formed or will be continued;
2. Members will create their own meanings to dialogue issues and will take actions based on the context of the topics being discussed;
3. Shared ownership in the discussion and topic;
4. Everyone who is in the community knows something about the topic and can contribute to the evolution of the dialogue;
5. Honoring the contributions of the others in the community; and
6. Everyone will be involved in defining and resolving issues that may arise.

Ultimately participation needs to be nurtured by all who have membership in a given community. If this is done effectively and with careful consideration of the others in the group, this can reduce the distance between the status markers and the geographic barriers of members. With active participation the members own the ideas and actions of the community.

Active communication is a key component of community because the dialogue people use brings them closer together through a set of shared understandings. Without good communication the members cannot develop the connections and closeness that can move the members from being task oriented to being community oriented. It can be the role of the community leader or even that of all its members to engage themselves and others in active communication. This can be done through the posting of questions for the members to respond to or the clarification of others' postings as well as being able to direct others through a given topic and to a conclusion.

With all this in mind, one needs to realize that a community is not categorized or described only as a set of representatives but is expanded to include the cultural and geographic backgrounds of the members. Community becomes a process where its members want to participate individually as well as collectively for diverse purposes such as establishing policy and practice around a particular area of interest.

FUTURE TRENDS

Putting a new concept into practice is a challenge. Creating an active and effective virtual environment is difficult. Many of the earlier online communities got off to a rocky start. The earlier online communities depended on e-mail and hand-held devices. We are moving quickly through a technology age that no longer binds us to the basic areas of technology where community members can interact. Despite its newness and perhaps because of it, connecting to peers through Facebook, MySpace and other online social networks has become the norm for today's society around the globe. These are considered to be social networks. It is predicted that more than 85 percent of the students at college campuses who have Facebook accounts use this as their primary way of being connected to the members of this virtual community (Eberhardt, 2007). Even before entering college it is not uncommon for people to have a Facebook account and already identify with a particular community through this network. This is not the only way to connect with a community. There are numerous similar venues available in today's world. Evolution of these types of social communities is swift and these may become passé in the not-too-distant future.

Discussion Boards are a typical community-expanding tools used in online education. These provide online synchronous "conference rooms" where people can enter and dialogue with others who are already in this room. There may be a moderator who connects those who may wish to dialogue on a particular topic and they may steer the topic in a particular direction if that is the desire of the members. A Learning Activity Bulletin is a tool that provides a location where a leader can post an activity such as a class assignment from a teacher or a problem-based issue that need individual attention. Group members can then go into this area and complete an assignment or offer an opinion or a solution to a problem.

Online learning environments are becoming the norm in higher education. There are well-known and used sites such as BlackBoard, eCollege, that are widely accepted on college campuses for the delivery of on-line courses. These learning sites are viewed as a way of providing increased access to professional development opportunities for faculty and students alike. Current technology is making it possible to build virtual town halls as venues for professional association and development. In these communities geography, culture, or personal preferences do not pose themselves as a limitation nor, a defining condition, of the professional community.

We need to realize that a community of learners working together can create an online environment that will work for and not against its members. Virtual environments, if used effectively, can promote a sense of belonging that crosses national and international boundaries. Collaborative work is required to develop appropriate models of community and skills that enable the members to ac-

tively participate and develop personally through involvement in these new environments.

CONCLUSION

This chapter has attempted to define the term "community" within a virtual environment by examining how communities are formed and maintained. Community is a negotiated, intimate relationship that requires commitment and mutual engagement. Interaction must be based on the knowledge and experiences of the members who can provide each other with a practical and effective model for working together to define and shape their futures. These virtual communities reduce the feeling of personal and professional isolation and enhance the ability to improve in one's practice despite geographic limitations. Interactions can take place anywhere, anytime as long as Web access is available. Everyone who has participated in an online community knows that this takes time away from family, leisure activities, and day-to-day routine of one's life. The members of an online community must be motivated and willing to take an active role if the community is to be sustained. Social web sites are not useful unless the members spend time using it. They must cultivate and support each other. Successful communities require daily attention from the members. They require deep understanding of the issues that engage the members and challenge the community.

REFERENCES

Alexander, G. C. (2003). Reaching out to rural schools: University-practitioner linkage through the Internet. *Journal of Technology and Teacher Education, 11*(2), 321–330.

Barth, R. (2001). *Learning by heart*. San Francisco: Jossey-Bass.

Bento, R. F., & Bento, A. M. (2000). Using the Web to extend and support classroom learning. *College Student Journal, 34*(4), 603–608.

Brown, R. E. (2001). The process of community-building in distance learning classes. *Journal of Asynchronous Learning Networks, 5*(2).

Chang, C.-C. (2003). Towards a distributed Web-based learning community. *Innovations in Education and Teaching International, 40*(1), 27–42. doi:10.1080/1355800032000038831

Curtis, R. (2004). Analyzing students' conversations in chat room. *College Teaching, 52*(4), 143–148. doi:10.3200/CTCH.52.4.143-149

Di Petta, T. (1998). Community on-line: New professional environments for higher education. *New Directions for Teaching and Learning*, (76): 53–66. doi:10.1002/tl.7604

Eberhardt, D. M. (2007). Facing up to Facebook. *About Campus, 12*(4), 18–26. doi:10.1002/abc.219

Hill, C. R. (2005). Everything i need to know i learned online. *Library Journal, 130*(3).

Ho, C. P., & Burniske, R. W. (2005). The evolution of a hybrid classroom: Introducing online learning to educators in American Samoa. *TechTrends: Linking Research & Practice to Improve Learning, 49*(1), 24–29.

Kim, A. J. (2000). *Community building on the Web*. Berkeley, CA: Peachpit Press.

Lock, J. V. (2002). Laying the groundwork for the development of learning communities within online courses. *Quarterly Review of Distance Education, 3*(4), 395–408.

McGrath, D. (2003). Developing a community of learners. *Learning & Leading with Technology, 30*(7), 43–45.

Misanchik, M., & Anderson, T. (2000). Building community in an online learning environment: Communication, cooperation and collaboration. Retrieved from http://www.mtsu.edu/-itconf/proceed01/19.html

Rovai, A. P. (2001). Building classroom community at a distance: A case study. *Educational Technology Research and Development, 49*(4), 33–48. doi:10.1007/BF02504946

Schwier, R. A. (2001). Catalysts, emphases, and elements of virtual learning communities: Implications for research and practice. *The Quarterly Review of Distance Education, 2*(1), 5–18.

Sergiovanni, T. J. (1993). *Building community in schools*. San Francisco: Jossey-Bass.

Sherer, P. D., Shea, T. P., & Kristensen, E. (2003). Online communities of practice: A catalyst for faculty development. *Innovative Higher Education, 27*(3), 183–194. doi:10.1023/A:1022355226924

Tullar, W. L., & Kaiser, P. R. (2000). The effect of process training on process and outcomes in virtual groups. *Journal of Business Communication, 37*(4), 408–427. doi:10.1177/002194360003700404

Chapter 8
Building Professional Practice Education Cultures in the Online Environment

Marion Brown
Dalhousie University, Canada

ABSTRACT

The gradual introduction of Internet-based delivery methods into higher education has broadened technology usage and led to reflection on the pedagogical implications for social work education taught online, with considerations for content, design and delivery. This chapter reviews the use of online technologies in post secondary education, the use of critical reflection as a pedagogical tool, and social work field education, to contextualize the experience of the Dalhousie University School of Social Work's distance delivery field education course. In the experience of Dalhousie University School of Social Work, the knowledge, skills, abilities, and attitudes of its student practitioners have been enhanced through the use of online integrative seminar case analysis and critical reflection facilitated via distance delivery. This chapter develops the connections among the online environment, adult education principles, and critical reflection on field education in social work, to craft an expanded message regarding transformative social work practice.

'Education is what survives when what has been learned has been forgotten'. -- B.F. Skinner (1904-90), American psychologist quoted in New Scientist 21 May 1964 in Oxford Dictionary of Quotations (2004, p.739:11).

INTRODUCTION

Over the last 20 years computer assisted technologies for online learning have become integrated within social work education programs internationally (Stocks & Freddolino, 2000). While largely an-

DOI: 10.4018/978-1-60566-735-5.ch008

ecdotal, some faculty and administrators among Schools of Social Work have voiced concern that social work education may not be particularly suited to online delivery, given long-standing assumptions regarding face to face relationships as the basis of interaction, knowledge translation, modeling and evaluation (Siegel, Jennings, Conklin, Napoletano, 1998). Although recognizing these pedagogical concerns, the School of Social Work at Dalhousie University, in Halifax, Nova Scotia, Canada, had an existing commitment to advancing post secondary education in communities marginalized by the socio-economic and racialized barriers of this region, and thus began delivering decentralized programs throughout the Maritime Provinces in the 1980s. As technologies have been refined, our means for delivery have focused on Internet technology, and we now offer national graduate and undergraduate level social work degrees, both fully accredited by the Canadian Association of Social Work Education.

This chapter begins with a review of the use of computer assisted technologies in post secondary education generally and social work specifically, with an emphasis on the literature regarding how students are considered to best learn within an Internet-based design. The specific social work curriculum under consideration is the field education course, required for both graduate and undergraduate social work degrees nationally and internationally. Next, the chapter draws on the rich literature of adult education and experiential learning to lay the foundation for a focus on critical reflection as the central content and process for learning in field education. With its commitment to generate knowledge both "empirically and self reflectively, in a process of interaction, in order to analyze, resist and change constructed power relations, structures and ways of thinking" (Fook, 1999, p.202), critical reflection is taken up here as a tool for transformative social work practice. The chapter concludes with examples and experiences from Dalhousie of how the online medium can interact with the message of critical reflection on

the field placement experience to advance social work education for practice.

THE MEDIUM: THE ONLINE ENVIRONMENT

Online learning is at the cusp of educational innovation, in its accessibility and flexibility as well as technological advances, to address a range of learning styles and needs. Particularly at the post secondary level, student demand for computers and Internet based approaches to education has reached unprecedented volume, with highly refined tools and methods forming the measure for the satisfaction of their experiences (Aminzade & Pescosolida, 1999; Grauerholz, McKenzie & Romeo, 1999; Green & Dorn, 1999). Accessibility and utility are fundamental to a student population that is mobile, migrant and mature in its expectations that educational institutions will deliver products and processes consistent with the rapidly advancing telecommunications market. Moreover, in the current climate of education as commodity, and students as consumers, optimal flexibility and opportunity for choice are considered basic terms of engagement as students survey the offerings of universities and colleges (Calhoun, 1999; Soley, 1999).

Incorporating electronic media in social work education has been a practice for almost two decades, originating in part to address education and training needs in rural and remote areas (Stocks & Freddolino, 2000). The limitations of providing only on site, classroom-based, synchronized learning was clearly recognized as privileging students with the resources and means to travel to larger centres for their learning. In addition, patterns of out-migration were a concern to rural communities, which saw their former residents, now professionals, not returning to provide a range of helping services back at home. Social work programs therefore began to incorporate the methods of teleconferencing, audio and videotapes, interactive television, satellite transmission, and video teleconferencing in clustered sites as means through which to connect students and faculty located in geographically separate sites. Today, the Internet offers unparalleled opportunity, speed, and capacity for the exchange of learning material for undergraduate, graduate and professional development learning. The Internet has become the basis for computer assisted learning and the preferred option among students. The appeal reflects several features. As Chalmers & Keown (2006) suggest,

There are three main factors that determine [the Internet's] value: mixed media dissemination of material at high speed and volume, synchronous transmission to all members of a group or class independent of location, and the facility to respond to collective interests in both the original and subsequent contributions of the group (p. 145).

Universities and colleges today cannot but be influenced by the free-market based ideology which emphasizes accountability to the consumer for a product "well made" (Soley, 1999). The corollary for educational programs is reflected in the development of accreditation standards and bodies, which establish and then measure for benchmarks in curriculum planning and implementation, quality of instruction, operating policies, physical space requirements and support structures required to ensure quality program delivery (Canadian Association of Schools of Social Work Standards of Accreditation, 2007). The inclusion of computer assisted learning technologies into social work education has been met with scepticism, uncertainty and resistance by some, and enthusiasm, optimism and fascination by others (Siegel et. al., 1998). On the one hand there is concern that the preparation of student learners in social work must rest on face to face instruction, communication, teaching and evaluation, in order to uphold the credibility of social work education and the profession. On the other hand, there is an emphasis on the imperative to offer social work education more broadly than

diverse geographic representation can withstand with on site instruction only. Moreover, as the focus of this chapter argues, there are unique pedagogical benefits available through online education. Nonetheless, in accordance with the current context and climate of accountability and "outcome measurement", it behoves the proponents of online, Internet based education to offer systematic evaluation of its methods.

Systematic evaluation begins with developing a means to classify and categorize the efficacy and experiences of online learning; a framework through which the design and delivery of programs can be filtered and assessed. In the literature on online learning, also referred to as e-learning, such a framework is borrowed from the world of business management, where, in the 1980s, researchers sought to understand why some organizations are more successful than others. The concept and language of *critical success factors* was developed to isolate and define the things that must be done correctly if a company is to be successful (Freund, 1988, cited in Selim, 2005). Adapted to the computer assisted learning sector, critical success factors are the ingredients for productive and positive online learning experiences and their inter-relation (McPherson & Nunes, 2008; Selim, 2005). These are the small number of measurable and controllable requirements necessary for an educational program to be successful when delivered online. Selim (2005) makes the argument that while there is much written regarding Internet-based learning, scant attention has been paid to delineating and studying what quantifiable components are required to provide educational institutions with the feedback regarding the efficacy of their programs; essentially, a set of accreditation standards for online learning.

The literature regarding the evaluation of online learning seems divided into two distinct categories. There are those studies that evaluate primarily for administrative considerations such as copyright issues, delivery platform, technological innovation and technical skill of instructor (for example, Pace, 2000, cited in Selim, 2005). Volery & Lord (2000) similarly defined critical success factors as sophistication of technology, instructor approach and the existing technological comfort of the student, in their assessment of online learning. However, other researchers have centred pedagogy and student experience as categories for consideration, with studies increasingly examining the collaborative social network developed between students and faculty and the resulting sense of community that can be developed online. For example, Benigno & Trentin (2000) developed a framework for evaluating the efficacy of online learning which included measuring for the criteria of student-to-student interaction, meaningful support and the quality of the learning environment. Similarly, Soong, Chan, Chua & Loh (2001) include the social, collaborative components of online learning when they list as indicators of success the "human factors" of mindset of faculty and students and level of collaboration within the class; these are in addition to technological competency and perceived infrastructure for technology-based learning. Carswell, Thomas, Petra, Price & Richards (2000), in a comprehensive study of the student experience at Open University, a fully online university in the UK, found that the central anchor for the student experience of online learning rested on responsiveness and interactivity among students and faculty. The research of Stocks & Freddolino (2000) concurs that interactivity, which includes feedback and opportunities for discussion, enhances learning outcomes.

Conrad (2005) explored the perceptions and experiences of learners' sense of community by using both quantitative and qualitative methods. Using a longitudinal design, she questioned students before they commenced online learning (thus tapping into their pre-conceptions), throughout their online engagement, and afterward, for reflections on their experiences. The study reports that students initially did not conceive of the uses of an online community and that they were focussed on their technological concerns at the onset of the course. However, these gave way to what Conrad refers to as "affective" considerations, as students increasingly emphasized their relationships, interactions, and familiarity with each other. According to Conrad:

Learners appeared to have shifted from considering community in its external dimensions as an entity defined by temporarily, action and space to a more intuitively understood, relationship-based construct (p.6).

The idea of "community" is taken up by several studies into the online learning environment according to the terms "community of practice, "community of inquiry" and "learning community." The concept of "community of practice" is identified by Lave & Wenger (1991) as a process through which to examine how adults learn together through their social processes, as opposed to overtly educational initiatives. Chalmers & Keown (2006) locate the community of practice concept within the broader framework of the "dialogue community" approach in education. In direct contrast to the "banking" concept of education (Freire, 1972), the notion of communities of practice emphasizes that knowledge is constructed through the examination of personal and collective values, attitudes and beliefs through a shared social process.

Although in its pure form, communities of practice are self organizing systems and not housed in formal educational institutions, there are valuable insights that can be gleaned from this model and taken into the online post secondary setting. For example, while not exactly a self-organizing system of informal learning, status as online students in universities and colleges implies a degree of competence and capability in the subject area, thus differentiating from other populations of people. Second, and capturing the discursive possibilities of a learning community, students interact with and learn from each other by sharing perspectives, completing common projects, and assisting each other along the learning journey. Through these engagements, the seeds of community can be seen to be planted. As more and more experiences, questions, challenges, problems and solutions are shared, a collective identity as a community can build.

An example of how the concept of communities of learning can be applied to the online learning environment is found in the research emphasis and findings of Cho, Gay, Davidson & Ingraffea (2007). Cho et. al (2007) sought to research the specific conditions which foster optimal communication and interactivity. In so doing, they studied links between communication styles, social networks and learning performance in online courses, concluding that "learning is a social and collective outcome achieved through seamless conversations, shared practices and networks of social connections" (p. 310). As does the concept of communities of practice, these researchers seek to distinguish their finding from the empty vessel/banking approach to education, wherein instructors are considered to make "knowledge deposits" into the minds of passive students. This approach underscores the epistemology, shared by the communities of practice concept, that knowledge is co-constructed through iterative processes of experience, reflection, sharing, and experimenting within a social setting. They conclude that social networks created and maintained online act as unique conduits for developing and transferring resources and knowledge.

Online instruction and learning built upon this constructivist epistemology suggests that the principles of adult education and of experiential learning are well met via methods and means of online learning. First, adult education principles of learner autonomy, responsibility, and reflection merge with the practical considerations of online delivery, wherein learners can exercise choice regarding when, where and how long to engage with the content material (Bourn & Bootle, 2005). Moreover, Jarvis (1995) reports greater efficacy

in the learning of adults when teaching methods allow for learners to adjust pacing and completion of learning tasks. Second, nested within the core tenets of adult education are the experiential learning principles articulated by Kolb (1984) and Merizow (1991). Building upon John Dewey's foundation that "all education comes about through experience" (1938, p. 25), Kolb (1984) developed a model which articulates that personal transformation occurs when perspectives are influenced through exposure to new experiences, reflection upon the these, and abstraction of the experiences taken forward into new situations. This is the cycle engaged in by social work students as they experience their field education placements, and the online field education seminar medium provides the conceptual and temporal space through which they can reflect, abstract and experiment for deep learning.

THE CONTEXT: THE DALHOUSIE UNIVERSITY SCHOOL OF SOCIAL WORK

The Dalhousie University School of Social Work (SSW) has an extended history of commitment to social justice principles through social work education. First, the Dalhousie SSW has long been a vanguard for inclusion of marginalized populations and communities, expressed through affirmative action admissions policies, Indigenous-centred research agendas, community engagement and progressive scholarship. This commitment is borne of recognition of the history of colonization and racism white European settlers brought to Nova Scotia beginning in the 1600s. For example, the Mi'kmaq Nation, living since the earliest of days on the land now known as Nova Scotia, have been systematically subjugated by force, by law, and by 'the reach of imperialism into our heads' (Tuhiwai-Smith, 1999, p.23). This domination has resulted in the widespread obliteration of Mi'kmaq culture, language, heritage, with devastating effects felt throughout the generations and still apparent today (Paul, 2006). Indigenous-centred social work services designed to support the reclamation of Mi'kmaq ways of being and ameliorating the damages of colonialism have been one means for sovereignty identified by local elders.

Beckoned by the moral imperative to increase the number of Mi'kmaq social workers working in Mi'kmaq communities and social work agencies, and having offered decentralized programs on Cape Breton Island, Prince Edward Island, and New Brunswick, in 1984 forty Cape Breton Mi'kmaq students enrolled in a Bachelor of Social Work offering that combined campus and decentralized delivery. Over the years since that time, students in our campus programs continued to request accessible and flexible program options to meet their learning needs, changing demographics, and long-term social work practice goals. On the basis of an ideological commitment to inclusion, diversity and accessibility, plus expertise in delivery methods and commitment to following through on responsiveness to students, incorporating distance delivery methods to the undergraduate and graduate curricula was a logical advance.

As a result, the School of Social Work at Dalhousie University launched national Bachelor and Master of Social Work programs in 2001, both fully accredited by the Canadian Association of Schools of Social Work (now called the Canadian Association of Social Work Education). Both degree programs are offered on a part-time basis for study, in recognition of the prevailing student demographic of full-time employment. The platform WebCT was used at the launch of the programs, with the latest version of WebCT subsumed under Blackboard Learning Systems. Since 2001, seven cohorts of BSW and MSW students have been admitted, with four cohorts graduated since 2004. Students live in their home communities across the nation, from the far west of Victoria, British Columbia to the northern tip of Newfoundland to the rural north of Nunavut. The life experiences and exposure to the social work

field of students range broadly, from entry level introduction to the profession for most Bachelor students, to the return of seasoned professionals for their graduate qualifications.

At Dalhousie, both undergraduate and graduate social work programs have a field education course which includes a social services agency-based placement and participation in a concurrent bi-weekly seminar. Field education is regulated by the Canadian Association of Social Work Education Standards of Accreditation (2007) which state that the objectives of field education are "the development...and the preparation of a professionally reflective, self-evaluating, knowledgeable and developing social worker" (CASWE Standards of Accreditation, 2008, p. 9). Further, at Dalhousie, all curriculum, policies and procedures related to field education are governed by the Bachelor of Social Work and Master of Social Work Committees, respectively.

Field Education is a significant anchor in social work education. It is the sole course which is completed principally within a social service agency, whether in direct practice, policy development, research and/or community mobilization, and as such it offers unique opportunities for the integration of theory and practice. Students are embedded in rich ideological, political, ethical and theoretical discussions and complex practice situations, which provide the focus for continuous critical reflection and self assessment required for the ongoing development of the effective social worker. Within the field courses, students occupy an inimitable position among academic structures, agencies, communities, and practitioners, to analyze the realities of practice and their personal frameworks for practice within the profession.

At the School of Social Work, field education is pivotal to the mission statement to "educate students and collaborate with others to advance change within the social work profession, social institutions and the broader society" (Dalhousie School of Social Work's vision, mission and guiding principles can be found at www.dal.ca/

socialwork). Our web of partnerships within Nova Scotia and across Canada enables a wide range of placement settings according to the learning needs and goals of our students. Further, as a school committed to social transformation, students in their field placements are primary agents through which the ideologies, analyses and practices of critical, anti-oppressive practice are taken from the academy into the community. In so doing, our social work students are in the position to influence the prevailing discourses across the profession and practicum contexts, expanding and enacting the messages of social change.

Social work students at both the undergraduate and graduate levels of study undertake a field education course. Second year Bachelor of Social Work students have one field education course that runs for 550 hours. Of these, twenty-four hours are allotted to participation in the online seminars, with the remainder taken up in the placement agency. Master of Social Work students have one field education course of 450 hours, 30 hours of which include participation in the seminar, with the balance occurring in the placement agency. The seminar is comprised of a small group of 10-14 students who attend concurrently with completion of their agency placement hours. A faculty person facilitates the seminars, coordinates regular visits to the agencies and is responsible for evaluation of the field course. The faculty person is the primary school liaison for the student. The Agency Field Instructor, who is the supervisor in the field agency, provides onsite supervision and instruction while the student is in the agency based placement.

The online field education seminar which accompanies the field placement provides the opportunity for group discussion of issues, challenges, provocations and learning encountered by students in the field agencies. In this setting students reflect on and debrief their experiences in their placements and seek to integrate their academic learning with their practice experiences. The structure and format is largely student led,

with the faculty person prompting questions and facilitating discussion regarding the translation of social work theory, knowledge and skills into the practice setting. This seminar is often experienced by the students to be a central site for the articulation of their evolving framework for practice, the constellation of ideology, theory, ethics, insights and skills that are honed throughout their degree and carried forward after their graduation. Having a specified space to pause for thought and consider the integration of their academic education with the practice based education is integral to the delivery of field education at Dalhousie SSW and a foundational component of the student experience. In keeping with the experiential learning cycle of Kolb, it is in the seminar that students have the peer support and facilitation to abstract from their concrete experiences and consider alternatives, new ideas and insights as they continue on in their placements. Being in a peer environment can stimulate greater depths of this reflection, as many minds can perhaps more likely tease out various and diverging perspectives on one situation. Sharing and contrasting direct practice skills, analysing complex circumstances of people's lives and extending the possibilities for advocacy on behalf of our clients are all enhanced when several minds are engaged.

Technological tools used to facilitate and enhance the social networks within the online courses at Dalhousie University's School of Social Work draw largely on asynchronistic discussion boards and private email functions. In addition, the voice board feature allows for recorded messages, which can appeal to an auditory learning style as well as provide an alternate means for engagement, beyond the written text. Synchronistic text based chat (in the style of Instant Messaging) and voice-over Internet protocol (voice based chat) are options for students and faculty seeking to interact with a sense of proximity and immediacy. Finally, the "live classroom" option, which supports real time synchronistic video learning, is available for the online seminar, offering an option closest to the onsite classroom experience. There are also personal profile pages developed by and for students and faculty and the capacity for streamed media, both audio and video.

Our distance delivery programs are national in scope, therefore students can benefit from analysing the diverse ideological and political contexts that are reflected across geographical regions. Given that social work practice is constructed according to ideological and political contexts as much as professional knowledge and skills (Healy, 2005), particular regional politics and ideologies are implicated in direct practice approaches. As the social work profession responds to global labour mobility, honing one's skills in contextual analysis is yet another priority for social work education. In our distance education delivery, the online field education seminar facilitates experiential learning and reflection about the micro, mezzo and macro dynamics of social work practice in the local contexts of students, between provincial jurisdictions, and according to the regional disparities of policy and initiatives on the national stage.

For these reasons, the online seminar corresponds well to our school's focus on critical reflection as a cornerstone of progressive, effective practice. The online environment offers space and time to first, consider one's experiences in retrospect, outside of the actual occurrence of events and second, to articulate the insights and conceptualizations that emerge. Social workers regularly tell of the fast pace of their work, the minimal time afforded to supervision and the lack of structured opportunity to reflect on practice. The realities of shrinking human and financial resources, organizational changes and ethical pressures experienced by ever more complex service situations are felt directly by students while in their placements. The online seminar for social work students offers a reprieve from these often competing and contradictory demands. Indeed, the online seminar offers a model which can be taken into long term future

practice, given its use of asynchronous activity in a self-directed design.

THE MESSAGE: CRITICAL REFLECTION ON THE FIELD PRACTICUM EXPERIENCE

Field education courses, comprised of an agency-based practicum and the online seminar, are a central component of social work education and a direct expression of the experiential education tenet of "learning by doing" (Kolb, 1984). This is often the opportunity that students have been looking forward to since their first day enrolled in the program; finally, a chance to try out all the theoretical formulations, skills, and procedures studied at length. The student placement in a community agency immerses the adult learner in a myriad of experiences and draws on the full extent of preparedness, both academic and practical. The online field education seminar facilitates conscientious reflection on the broad scope of experience in the interests of developing and enhancing conceptualizations of social issues, socio-political analysis, self awareness, practice skills, and understanding of ethics in action. Dalhousie's orientation to field education understands that adult learners come with previous experiences and insights, drawing upon these to strengthen the linkages among social work education, social work practice and personal professional development.

As experiential learning is nested within the principles of adult education, the concept of critical reflection is further embedded within experiential learning. While there are divergent definitions circling the terms "reflection", "reflexivity" and "critical reflection" (see D'Cruz, Millingham & Menendez, 2005 for a thorough review of the literature), some coherence can be found in the work of Fook (2002), Hick (2004) and Ife, Healy, Spratt & Solomon (2004). These works provide foundation for this chapter's exploration of critical reflection, particularly as they relate to the practice education experience and the online seminar. In this conceptual framework critical reflection is informed by the traditions of reflective practice, reflexivity, postmodernism and deconstruction, and critical social theory. Each of these components is discussed below.

Reflective practice borrows from the work of Argyris & Schon (1974), building upon the premise of "reflection on action." In this process, the event of note is in the past, and the social work student uses the incident to consider, more deeply than is possible in the moment, the uses of formal theory, the complexities of the situation, and the personal reactions that were engaged. This process is considered useful in honing practice theories that are responsive to context and therefore dynamic. Given the concern that formal theory sometimes becomes irrelevant or at least somewhat distanced from practice situations, the processes of reflective practice allow for analysis of the inconsistencies that are experienced when theories are applied.

Reflexivity refers to the ability and practice of a social worker or social work student to locate her/himself in the picture of what is happening, in order to analyze how one's own self influences the social work act. In other words, this self-critical approach includes understanding how one's relationship to power is implicated in one's social work practice. Power here is considered in accordance with the Foucauldian conceptualization: a component of individual agency, available to all through social performances as well as through social locations and social structures. This use of reflexivity aligns with the critical social science research traditions as well, in seeking to make transparent the ways in which we in social work can be complicit in oppressive relations of power, undermining the very emancipatory actions to which we aspire.

This analysis of power calls on postmodern influences, as the invoking of Foucault suggests. The postmodern turn on knowledge creation supports a call for social work theory that is rooted in practice wisdom and the subjective, interpre-

tive knowing stance. Here we see a rejection of the traditional tendency to value objectivity and distance, privileging the academic to the practice base of theory broadly, and in social work as well. Deconstructing claims to truth and veracity takes centre stage here, from an epistemological vantage point that seeks to honour the subjugated voice of the front line social worker.

Finally, the consciousness provided by critical social theory is that social structures, policies, laws and codes of conduct play a significant and concrete role in people's lives. Notwithstanding an analysis of power that understands the discursive, tacit movement of influence, intention, performance and positioning, the emphasis on critical social theory makes clear that the effects of racism, poverty, misogyny, heterosexism and classism, to name only a few, are experienced as real and as true (Mullaly, 2007). Social workers need to have an analysis of these structural oppressions.

The process of critical reflection is one means through which to deconstruct the personal challenges to the political realities of the social work field, present in every practice encounter. Critical reflection provides a means through which to unpack both personal and social assumptions, examining their relationships to material and discursive power; it is a means through which to 'look both inwards and outwards to recognize connections with social and cultural understandings' (Fook, 2002, p.2). When we expose to scrutiny relationships of domination and oppression, which are structurally rooted and personally experienced, we may indeed be engaged in transforming the social structures that perpetuate inequity and injustice.

Clearly, this practice framework is ideologically positioned. It demands different criteria for the evaluation of theory and practice than that promoted by positivist epistemologies: it refutes the priority, even the capacity, of the worker to stand objectively outside of her own experiences when assessing the lives of others. It denies that workers can "bracket" the assumptions and biases always at play in our work, and instead *goes looking* for their influence on our choices. It does not shy away from the questions of how social work perpetuates the power differentials experienced by our clients seeking services. This practice framework asks us to grapple with the tensions inherent in conceiving of power as available to everyone, even as we see structures all around us that reinforce the opposite. It does not allow formal theories to disengage from these complexities: formal theory is interrogated according to the above-defined lenses of reflection, reflexivity, postmodern conceptions of power and truth, and analysis of material inequities. Formal theory left untouched by these processes is considered limited because it stands outside both social context and personal engagement by the worker. In contrast, the practice framework informed by critical reflection asserts that theory is only relevant when it is accountable to these challenges.

In this conceptualization, then, theory is rooted in practice experiences, personal assumptions and political contexts. Theory is that dynamic body of ever-accumulating knowledge constructed by the practitioner, with all layers of context, self and client/client system inextricably intertwined. This conceptualization, with its ideology and epistemology made clear, frames theory *as practice*. This integration of "knowing' and 'doing", as legitimized theory development, is the precise focus of the online field education seminar. The online field education seminars provide a forum within which students reflect on their experiences in the field placement, critique the political, cultural, and social contexts within which people and communities function, analyse the implications of discursive and material practices of power, and deconstruct their own thinking.

THE RELATIONSHIP: HOW THE MEDIUM AND THE MESSAGE INTERACT

Online integrative seminars for the social work field placements in the Bachelor of Social Work and Master of Social Work degree programs at Dalhousie University's School of Social Work have emerged as a transformational site for critical reflection among social work student practitioners. The seminars bring together student practitioners from across the country in multiple jurisdictions, practicing in a breadth of social work settings, to deconstruct the socio-political contexts of their experiences, make connections between the personal, the social and the political. In so doing they develop "skills of divergence…[the idea of] opening ourselves up to the ideas of others, especially when these people provide a new angle of vision" (Mezirow, 1999: 369). Students can compare and contrast the social, political and ideological perspectives and realities in their fields of practice and dissect how these impact the development of their practice knowledges, assessment, intervention and evaluation skills, research agendas, and policy analyses. Exposure to and engagement in dialogue and critique of cross-regional parameters, multiple jurisdictions of social work practice, and diverse venues for social work activity results in expanded contextual analysis, with plentiful examples of "the realities of social work practice" ready for examination. Deborah from Prince Edward Island spoke of this exchange:

Sometimes I can forget about the different pressures other social workers are experiencing. It can get easy to just pay attention to our provincial laws and the resources we have here. It was fascinating to hear about the new child welfare changes in Alberta, because we just had an inquiry here after a child died in care and everyone is waiting to see what changes will come our way. Now I will have something to compare to.

Josyl from Northern British Columbia said,

Because so many of the distance students are already practicing in the social work field, the wealth of practical experience available to me is far superior to what I might expect on campus.... It has broadened my knowledge of social work in this country.... The bonus in online work is staying current with practice issues across Canada

Expanded contextual analysis available through the broadened community of learners available online merges with the imperatives of critical reflection, which includes the deconstruction of structurally embedded and personally experienced oppression. Facilitation by faculty anchors the processes of critical reflection, notably hinged on looking from the inside out and from the outside in, in review of social and cultural understandings of clienthood, social justice, agency and ethical practice.

The role of faculty in adhering to the tenets of critical reflection is central to the project of advancing deep integration of personal assumptions, context and practice challenges. Reading the literature on critical social work broadly, and critical reflection specifically, can be helpful to prepare for this role. Forming a support network among faculty using this pedagogical process is an important means through which to continue to hone one's skills in the questioning pivotal to reflection, reflexivity and analysis of material and discursive power within the group. Further, modelling the unpacking of assumptions can validate the legitimacy of this approach. Toward this end, faculty members are encouraged to present their own practice situations and identify their assumptions, values, beliefs, and understandings at play. Rochelle, a student from Alberta, commented on this practice by the faculty person facilitating the seminar:

She always asked great questions as we were trying to make sense of our experiences. She also talked (wrote) about her own experiences as a social worker and wasn't afraid to say she made mistakes and didn't have the answers. One time she talked about her own family member and his right to 'live at risk' and that she found it really hard compared to how she handled that kind of thing with clients. It was refreshing to see a prof do that.

Faculty are also instrumental in establishing an atmosphere wherein exploration and examination of assumptions, biases, issues and actions can occur with due respect to the sensitivity and vulnerability of all involved. Here is an excerpt from a posting I made to the class in my role as faculty for the online seminar:

In much of our daily interactions, and in this online seminar as well, it can be easy to discuss issues and suggest actions without thinking about our assumptions. How does this happen? Well, all around us are the encouragements to leave the status quo as is; society seeks to maintain itself at its least critical. Yet in social work we know that assumptions often serve to disadvantage particular individuals and groups in society. We analyze the dominant discourses that perpetuate discrimination and oppression. Our role is to be aware that disagreements, conflicts and opposing perspectives might be the result of differences in hidden assumptions about the issue being addressed. In this seminar we have a great opportunity to parallel critical social work practice, by surfacing and identifying our assumptions about the issues we raise here, so that discussion and analysis can be formed on common understandings. While I know that we need to feel safe in order to take a risk, remember that with every risky step forward, we create a little more safety....and on it grows.

As this excerpt suggests, the pedagogical congruencies between the online medium and the processes of critical reflection are significant. Students in the online seminar assert that asynchronous engagement allows for ample deliberation on experiences in placement, scenarios shared by colleagues and provocations offered in the class, and that this pacing encourages diligent contemplation and careful analysis prior to response. Tasha, from Alberta, said,

I tend to be a listener, taking time to process and integrate new information into my practice. I liked taking the time to consider and process my own feelings and reactions without pressure to respond immediately. I contributed to the dialogue when I felt that I had new information to add and appreciated doing so on my own time and initiative.

As noted by Tasha, online learning responds to a wide variety of learning styles. The student who learns best by reading ("listening") and responding right away can do so; the person who learns more effectively by reading ("listening") and pondering at greater length and collecting her thoughts before scripting a response is also honoured. In contrast, on site classrooms tend to privilege the extroverted, spontaneous learner, leaving fewer options, or little later chance, for the student whose learning is not compatible with this format.

In addition, students report that text-based responses require greater conceptualization and articulation of their reflections than do spoken responses. Together, these conditions foster layered and nuanced debate and discussion within the seminar setting, creating an enriched learning community. Jeremy, from Ontario, said,

Each posting is like a mini-assignment! Which bugged me at first, but then I realized I had this great opportunity every time I go to respond, to really think about what I was saying, and take the time to word it just right.

Yasmin, from Newfoundland, concurred:

There is no way I will post something that is not good – I mean, not my best work. It's kind of like the written word lasts longer than the spoken word, you know? So I am going to take my time and post something I can be proud of, not just today, but next year.

In the online environment faculty have the opportunity to read each posting, an experience distinct from the campus based settings, where they might circulating during small group discussion time, often missing much of the discussion and debate among students while doing so. One faculty member who teaches both online and on site commented,

My course evaluations from on site teaching regularly include student frustration that I do not spend my time evenly among all the small groups. I simply cannot spread myself across several simultaneous discussions, yet I regret not getting to hear all the students weigh in on the material, particularly the students who are quiet in the larger group. But online, I can take my time, reading the transcripts of the small groups, preparing questions or reflections that are considered, not rushed, and have more meaningful engagement with each small group than I ever could with my on site class.

In addition to participation in the online group dialogue, faculty can follow up via email with students regarding the content or process of the seminar. The literature supports that these two functions of online communication between student and faculty – discussion boards and email – are experienced as less intimidating and threatening than traditional face to face communication. It is both preferred by students and experienced as more effective (Kitsantas & Chow, 2007).

The critical success factors discussed above prioritize consistent and authentic engagement between faculty and students. The work of Cho et. al. (2007) underscores the lesson that attention to social networks is integral to the performance and efficacy of online learning. They note that, "it is not enough to implement new instructional technologies or collaborations, but an appropriate social infrastructure, i.e. social networks and practice that support desired interactions between participants, should also be in place" (pp. 322-323). Their work suggests that a strong social network has a tangible impact on individual performance in learning online. Several other studies bear out this assertion (Conrad, 2005; Guilar & Loring, 2008). This has indeed been the experience at the Dalhousie School of Social Work.

The ingredients of expanded contextual analysis, critical reflection, and enriched learning atmosphere combine within the social networking and interactivity features of the online medium to create a new message, one that offers a seamless interface of practice and education that is critical and progressive. This community of simultaneous learners and practitioners promises transformation of self, structure and social work.

FUTURE TRENDS

The beacon of online learning is bright and it is beckoning educators to experience a manner of being learner centered that corresponds with the adult education principles of post secondary learning. Online learning has capacities what were unheard of 20 years ago, in its ability to reach across the globe to unite collectives of students invested in their academic studies and preparations for practice. The future lies in understanding the importance of developing the social alongside the scholarly; maintaining the "high touch" alongside the "high tech." Guilar & Loring (2008) uphold the particular care and attention required to build an online community, and while they note the development of engaging content and cost containment as requiring attention, they reserve a particularly passionate emphasis for the commitment to caring and to dialogue that must be evident among

faculty, students, staff and administrators. In the learning environment, faculty who act as models in content, in comportment and in the experience of feeling valued, can nurture a community of respectful engagement. This direction forward mirrors that of much scholarship on higher education: that attention to process over concentration on content is the means through which meaningful learning occurs. The online learning environment requires the same diligence in this regard as does on site, campus based education. The early days saw heavy emphasis on the technological tools as the foundation for online learning and the transmission of content as the key to translation of knowledge. Yet the scholarly study of online learning has caught up, and it informs us of the need to attend to social networking, developing community, the value of connection and building relationships of meaning. Therein lies the future of online learning and all its successes.

CONCLUSION

This chapter has reviewed the emergence and incorporation of computer assisted technologies in post secondary education generally and at the Dalhousie University School of Social Work in particular. The framework of critical success factors was examined for its utility in providing feedback on program design and delivery. In particular, the critical success factors related to social networks, reliant on the engagement student learners and faculty, were highlighted, given their relevance to the deep learning sought via critical reflection for social work education. Critical reflection was presented as offering both content and process for learning in social work field education in the online environment. Utilizing the critical reflection process and content in the field education courses, together with the expanded contextual analysis available through the distance learning format and the enhanced learning environment available through the online seminar, students have the opportunity to transform their experiences of social work education and practice.

REFERENCES

Aminzade, R., & Pescosolido, B. A. (1999). Introduction to the changing landscape of higher education. In B. A. Pescosolido & R. Aminzade (Eds.), *The social worlds of higher education: Handbook for teaching in a new century* (pp. 6-8). Thousand Oaks, CA: Pine Forge Press.

Argyris, C., & Schon, D. (1974). *Theory in practice*. San Francisco, CA: Jossey-Bass.

Benigno, V., & Trentin, G. (2000). The evaluation of online courses. *Journal of Computer Assisted Learning, 16*, 259–270. doi:10.1046/j.1365-2729.2000.00137.x

Bourn, D., & Bootle, K. (2005). Evaluation of a distance learning, post graduate advanced award in social work programme for child and family social work supervisors and mentors. *Social Work Education, 24*(3), 343–362. doi:10.1080/02615470500050644

Calhoun, C. (1999). The changing character of college: Institutional transformation in American higher education. In B. A. Pescosolido & R. Aminzade (Eds.), *The social worlds of higher education: Handbook for teaching in a new century* (pp. 9-31). Thousand Oaks, CA: Pine Forge Press.

Canadian Association of Schools of Social Work Standards of Accreditation. (2008). *CASWE-ACFTS*. Retrieved September 1, 2008, from http://www.cassw-acess.ca/

Carswell, L., Thomas, P., Petra, M., Price, B., & Richards, M. (2000). Distance education via the internet: The student experience. *British Journal of Educational Technology, 31*(1), 29–46. doi:10.1111/1467-8535.00133

Chalmers, L., & Keown, P. (2006). Communities of practice and professional development. *International Journal of Lifelong Education, 25*(2), 139–156. doi:10.1080/02601370500510793

Cho, H., Gay, G., Davidson, B., & Ingraffea, A. (2007). Social networks, communication styles and learning performance in a CSCL community. *Computers & Education, 49*, 309–329. doi:10.1016/j.compedu.2005.07.003

Conrad, D. (2005). Building and maintaining community in cohort-based online learning. *Journal of Distance Education, 20*(1), 1–20.

D'Cruz, H., Gillingham, P., & Menendez, S. (2005). Reflexivity, its meanings and relevance for social work: A critical review of the literature. *British Journal of Social Work, 37*, 73–90. doi:10.1093/bjsw/bcl001

Fook, J. (1999). Critical reflexivity in education and practice. In B. Pease & J. Fook (Eds.), *Transforming social work*. St. Leonards, AU: Allen & Unwin.

Fook, J. (2002). *Critical social work practice*. Thousand Oaks, CA: Sage Publications.

Freire, P. (1972). *Pedagogy of the oppressed*. New York: The Seabury Press.

Grauerholz, E., McKenzie, B., & Romeo, M. (1999). Beyond these walls: Teaching within and outside the expanded classroom – boundaries in the 21st century. In B. A. Pescosolido & R. Aminzade (Eds.), *The social worlds of higher education: Handbook for teaching in a new century* (pp. 582-600). Thousand Oaks, CA: Pine Forge Press.

Green, C. S., & Dorn, D. S. (1999). The changing classroom: The meaning of shifts in higher education for teaching and learning. In B. A. Pescosolido & R. Aminzade (Eds.), *The social worlds of higher education: Handbook for teaching in a new century* (pp. 59-83). Thousand Oaks, CA: Pine Forge Press.

Guilar, J. D., & Loring, A. (2008). Dialogue and community in online learning: Lessons from Royal Roads University. *Journal of Distance Education, 22*(3), 19–40.

Healy, K. (2005). *Social work theories in context.* London: Palgrave MacMillan.

Hick, S. (2004). Reconceptualizing critical social work. In S. Hick, J. Fook, & R. Pozzuto (Eds.), *Social work: A critical turn* (pp. 39-51). Toronto, Ont.: Thompson Educational Publishing.

Ife, J., Healy, K., Spratt, T., & Solomon, B. (2004). Current understandings of critical social work. In S. Hick, J. Fook, & R. Pozzuto (Eds.), *Social work: A critical turn* (pp. 3-23). Toronto, Ont.: Thompson Educational Publishing.

Jarvis, P. (1995). *Adult and continuing education: Theory and practice.* London, UK: Routledge.

Kitsantas, A., & Chow, A. (2007). College students' perceived threat and preference for seeking help in traditional distributed and distance learning environments. *Computers & Education, 48,* 383–395. doi:10.1016/j.compedu.2005.01.008

Kolb, D. (1984). *Experiential learning: Experience as a source of learning and development.* London: Prentice Hall.

Lam, C. M., Wong, H., & Leung, T. T. F. (2005). An unfinished reflexive journey: Social work students' reflections on their placement experiences. *British Journal of Social Work, 37,* 91–105. doi:10.1093/bjsw/bcl320

Lave, J., & Wenger, E. (1991). *Situated learning: Legitimate peripheral participation.* Cambridge, UK: Cambridge University Press.

Mazzolini, M., & Maddison, S. (2007). When to jump in: The role of instructors in online discussion forums. *Computers & Education, 49,* 193–213. doi:10.1016/j.compedu.2005.06.011

McPherson, M. A., & Nunes, J. M. (2008). Critical issues for e-learning delivery: What may seem obvious is not always put into practice. *Journal of Computer Assisted Learning, 24,* 433–445. doi:10.1111/j.1365-2729.2008.00281.x

Mezirow, J. (1991). *Transformational dimensions of adult learning.* San Francisco: Josey-Bass.

Mullaly, B. (2007). *The new structural social work.* Toronto, Ont: Oxford University Press.

Paul, D. (2006). *We were not the savages* (3rd ed.). Halifax, Canada: Fernwood Publishing.

Selim, H. M. (2007). Critical success factors for e-learning acceptance: Confirmatory factor models. *Computers & Education, 49,* 396–413. doi:10.1016/j.compedu.2005.09.004

Siegel, E., Jennings, J. G., Conklin, J., & Napoletano Flynn, S. A. (1998). Distance learning in social work education: Results and implications of a national survey. *Journal of Social Work Education, 34*(1), 71–80.

Soley, L. C. (1999). Underneath the ivy and the social costs of corporate ties. In B. A. Pescosolido & R. Aminzade (Eds.), *The social worlds of higher education: Handbook for teaching in a new century* (pp. 318-327). Thousand Oaks, CA: Pine Forge Press.

Soong, B. M. H., Chan, H. C., Chua, B. C., & Loh, K. F. (2001). Critical success factors for on-line course resources. *Computers & Education, 36*(2), 101–120. doi:10.1016/S0360-1315(00)00044-0

Stocks, J. T., & Freddolino, P. P. (2000). Enhancing computer-mediated teaching through interactivity: The second iteration of a World Wide Web-based graduate social work course. *Research on Social Work Practice, 10*(4), 505–518.

Tuhiwai-Smith, L. *Decolonizing methodologies.* (1999). Dunedin, NZ: University of Otago Press.

Volery, T., & Lord, D. (2000). Critical success factors in online education. *International Journal of Educational Management, 14*(5), 216–223. doi:10.1108/09513540010344731

Chapter 9
Virtual Communication for Field Education Placements in a Global Context

Linette Hawkins
RMIT University, Australia

Supriya Pattanayak
State Representative (Orissa), Department for International Development India (British High Commission)[1]

ABSTRACT

Increasing reliance upon information communication technology is one of the major factors in the current student profile which challenges the traditional concept of professional field education. In Australia the involvement of a growing minority of students in international field education highlights the value of communication via different technological methods. Drawing upon the experience of students at one university in Australia who undertook international placements over a three year period, with particular attention to those engaged in group placements in Orissa, India, this chapter presents the different placement structures and the application of ICT and pedagogical factors requiring critical attention. Another longer term field education challenge has been the increasing demand for human service field placements in an environment of decreasing resources. A common electronic data base, developed by the schools of social work, in one state in Australia presents an approach aimed at promoting co-operation in a competitive situation.

'Learning is a treasure that will follow its owner everywhere'. -- Chinese proverb

INTRODUCTION

Our journey towards sustainable models for international field experience was initially coincidental.

The steep learning curve of students and staff during the past several years has led to policy based on established processes for social work students seeking overseas placements together with a realization that this development has been an incremental process.

The partnership between a tertiary institution in India from which Supriya Pattanayak operates,

DOI: 10.4018/978-1-60566-735-5.ch009

and RMIT University in Australia where Linette Hawkins is a field education coordinator has facilitated a blending of western social work curriculum with significant learning experience in rural areas in Orissa.

Pattanayak's involvement in lecturing, liaison, and international placement coordination at Deakin University in Victoria (Australia) and transference of these roles as coordinator, supervisor and liaison officer to her home state Orissa provides the bridge required by undergraduate students from Australia.

During the early years of the past decade ad hoc responses to individual students seeking overseas placements in countries to which they were attracted resulted on occasions, in critical situations and questionable standards relating to issues such as student accountability, liaison, relationship between international experience and curriculum. Overshadowing all these factors has been the satisfactory, or otherwise, means of communication amongst all parties. This has led us to focus on the development of two of the four models outlined below and recognition of the essential complementary role of ICT for international placements.

CONTEXT OF FIELD EDUCATION

No agreed upon concept regarding "international social work" has been identified in recent literature. The re-emerging possibility 'for social work to play a role in international social work and social development' (McDonald, 2007, p.187), as with social work per se, is likely to be interpreted according to the context. How might our academic programs accommodate this concept to prepare students for placements in contexts which are sometimes oppositional to that from which they come? Whilst various forms of 'international' social work have been identified which draw upon social work 'professional expertise' (Healy, 2001) the more likely auspices for our student placements in countries in transition to date have been in 'community development' contexts participating in environments and programs in new ways which may fit uncomfortably with their Australian social work. How might we prepare students for 'the development of practices that are relevant in local contexts' to graduate, after a short period of time (seventy days) as a "development practitioner"?(Gray, 2005, p.236).

Pettys et al (2005) promote an intensive and extensive pre-departure program encompassing the geography, politics, economics and social orientation of the placement destination. From our experience we would also recommend that special attention be given to student understanding of gender relations and other social classifications in different contexts. Each group of students on placement in India has indicated that they are quite challenged by these. The most recent reactions were highlighted by the critical incident reports of some students after their visit to an non-government organization (NGO) which provides shelter to trafficked women. Gender also impacts significantly on what tasks male and female students can and cannot undertake in the field. Boyle et al, Tesoriero and Rajaratnam (1999) focus on student preparation for group placements, the group being an important source of support 'during the ongoing stress of engaging intensely with another culture' (p.211). Commenting on international student exchanges between Malaysia and Australia, Martin and Ling (2008) stress the importance of attending to students' physical, psychological and social needs to reduce levels of stress and anxiety and support students to make the necessary adaptations and adjustments to the new culture and learning environment. They also highlight the importance of preparation for the return home to assist with settling back into the home university and culture. They contend that 'all of these activities support cultural adjustment, academic performance, personal development and overall enjoyment of the exchange experience' (p.11).

Pettys et al (2005) identified six methods of preparation and orientation for students engaging in international placements, components of which are:

- special orientation seminars;
- a series of regular orientation sessions prior to departure;
- one-on-one interviews;
- audio-visual materials and reading;
- university language classes; (and)
- region-specific academic classes.

WHAT IS SOCIAL WORK FIELD EDUCATION?

Whereas field work has always had an important place in student assessment for human services programs, "work-integrated- learning" is becoming a curriculum requirement in both generic and vocational courses in many tertiary institutions in Australia. Alongside the human services industry and community needs for multi-skilling and multidisciplinary workers, the recognition of occupationally specific roles and responsibilities is promoted by universities, professional associations, unions and a diversity of vested interest groups. Within this context the professional organization, the Australian Association of Social Work in conjunction with social work practitioners and lecturers stipulate certain characteristics to which student placements in Australia or another country must adhere. In this chapter we consider ICT as a tool, ancillary to the practicum/learning experience, but an integral component in maintaining student access to resources, communication with peers and dialogue with staff at the home university.

Research (Rai, 2004; Skolnik et al, 1999) indicates that field education is an essential part of social work education worldwide. Its primary purpose is to help students to integrate theory and practice. In most countries the standard framework is set by a national professional body situated outside the teaching institutions. Mandatory requirements include supervision by a field instructor and liaison by the School. In summary a successful field education program requires suitable placements, experienced supervisors, adequate time and ongoing interaction between the field and university (Rai, 2004, p. 214).

In Australia field education is regarded as supervised experiential learning, linking and reflecting upon the relationship between theory and practice. A similar concept applies to field education in India where it is defined as "an integral part of the training in Social Work and is intended to develop in the student the skills, attitudes, values and personality characteristics necessary for a professional social worker"(Stella Maris College, par.8). It is a process which is sequential and incremental. An integral and critical component, often omitted from the literature, is the ongoing evaluation, primarily by the field instructor, leading to final assessment, confirmed by the University, which makes the ultimate decision about the satisfactory performance, or otherwise of the student.

Unlike other academic courses which may be fully accessed on-line the factors comprising field education make it highly dependent upon people resources in a diversity of roles. In addition to the field instructor these may include task supervisors, the university field coordinator and the liaison person.

INTERNATIONAL PLACEMENTS

Economic globalization, the changing political climate, the growing use of ICT, demographic shifts and the changing nature of social service agencies (Reisch & Jarman-Rohde, 2000) are factors impacting upon the culture of universities and student profile. In Australia, teaching institutions from secondary schooling upwards are actively marketing their programs internationally. Internationalization of student study plans is also promoted through avenues such as exchange scholarships, international internships and study tours.

What motivates students to opt for international placements? Is it the attraction of exotic places, the desire to travel, an interest in eventually working in countries in transition or the ambition to become involved with large international non government organisations such as the United Nations? Should student motivation be taken into account in placing students far a field? And if so, by what means? Over the past three years alongside the desire to travel and to experience alternate personal growth the major reasons given in their written application to undertake international placements by social work students at RMIT University were to improve their access to future employment in other countries and for learning experience in another culture. Some students hoping to work internationally saw a need for a greater understanding of international/ community development and its relationship with social work. A small number of our students each year, in our experience, require specific individual plans to negotiate field experience in their country of origin.

Our awareness of rising student requests for overseas placements through involvement as field education co-ordinators in two social work programs in Australia has led us to ponder the implications for field education in contexts very different to the origins of living and learning, if one acknowledges that social work is primarily contextually defined.

Literature ranges from simplistic to sophisticated arguments, the majority of articles relating to international placements of social work schools in the United States of America. Boyle et al (1999) see the cultural immersion of students in Mexico accomplished by "staying", "speaking", "visiting" and "attending" (1997, p.204). The major focus of articles is the relationship and implications of international placements to overall social work

curriculum (Tesoriero & Rajaratnam, 2001; Abram, Slosar & Walls, 2005; Pawar, 2000; Johnson, 2004). Mamphiswana and Noyoo (2000) refer to the need to change the Western curriculum they inherited to one more relevant to local social work students. Outlines of different models for providing international placements upon which we have drawn are those documented by Tesoriero and Rajaratnam, Pettys et al (2005), Moore and Collins (2002) and Cornelius and Greif (2005).

Wehbi (2008) categorizes literature about international placements to date in three main areas: 'descriptions of international placement programs, the links between cultural competence and placements and students' experiences upon their return from placement' (p.50). To these we add a fourth dimension which we address later in this chapter. Increased writing has focused upon ICT as an instrument in bridging the distance between students in another country or in isolated local locations.

In reviewing student exchanges Razack (2002) presents several challenges to international placements generally. Whilst acknowledging the significant knowledge gained from a different cultural context the earlier impressions of some students during and upon return from their placement in countries in transition gave support to Razack's view that a 'deeper enquiry into our complicity in maintaining our privileged locations in the north is not usually emphasized' (p.252). Midgley (1997) describes how exchanges were welcomed between industrialized and "developing" nations initially, but with increasing independence in former colonized countries these unilateral exchanges are being questioned. A preferred model is exchanges where there is a genuine partnership and exchange effort with students from both universities participating in the exchange with this supported in university policies and procedures and adequate resource allocation (Martin & Ling, 2008).

ICT AND LOCAL FIELD EDUCATION

An increased number of social work student enrolments, agency concerns regarding rising and repetitive demands for field places, spaces and social worker supervision in the early nineties led to the development of an electronic data base aimed at addressing the conflicts and tensions associated with the then four social work schools in Victoria (Australia) competing for placements, resulting in the establishment of the Combined Schools of Social Work Network (CSSW). Since its origin the Combined Schools of Social Work data base has developed into a comparatively sophisticated system, the starting point for organizing and administering placements for the current six social work schools in Victoria. The system provides an integrated and cost efficient method for dealing with a reasonable proportion of organizations which contribute to the field education component of social work programs.

Principles of the Network are based on core social work values which promote: equal access to quality field placements for all schools; agency rights to privacy (minimizing outside requests for placements) and cooperation between all schools and participating agencies. A strong commitment to these principles is reflected in the importance placed on the processes and active participation of each University's Field Education staff. As with any shared data system complexities arise from the multitude of players contributing and responding to the system. This electronic data base is maintained and sustained by the interactions, dialogue and camaraderie associated to a considerable degree with intermittent face to face interaction. It is certainly through these processes that other significant outcomes have been achieved. Examples of this collaboration include:

- A website with the curriculum and field education profiles of each social work school;

- Regular combined supervisor workshops (beginner and advanced);
- A common student field education assessment framework for state-wide application in conjunction with the national professional association;
- Negotiation with major placement providers regarding equitable distribution of placements; (and)
- Access to placements with other schools overseas partners, including shared pre-departure briefings.

Whilst above we highlight the importance of face-to-face contact to sustain the CSSW system we acknowledge that some of the above functions may be replaced by ICT strategies in the future. An example of this is the development by another Australian University (Charles Sturt University), in conjunction with a network of other major players, of a national, on-line program to train supervisors who take social work and human services students for their practicum. Although initially targeted towards workers in rural and isolated regions, unable to access current face to face supervision training primarily provided in metropolitan centers, one foresees interest from human service practitioners Australia wide who, out of necessity, convenience or preference will choose to acquire supervisory qualifications/ recognition online.

The reduced time "on campus" students now spend at university results in greater dependence upon website/ online access to procedures and pro formas comprising the different stages of field education together with the opportunity for "chat groups" through a distance learning system whilst in the field for extensive periods (one hundred and forty days over two years). Face to face contact with RMIT University via liaison visits and integrative seminars was complemented by the opportunity for students on their first placement to access a web-enabled discussion board.

Approximately two thirds of the students in the class engaged in field education for the first time used this at different stages during their placement. Some students continued to use this as a method of communication with peers after placements finished. This discussion board has now become an integral, albeit fairly informal, component of the field program, a method for sharing and debriefing as well as social networking.

By providing students during international placement access to on-line discussion, we observe that students benefit from sharing issues and concerns. Other outcomes of the discussions as observed by field education staff at Deakin University, a rurally located university in Victoria, Australia, may be input from each other regarding different projects and stimulation and feedback about potentially publishable ideas (Maidment, 2006). As coordinator of international field education for distance mode students at Deakin University (2005-2007), Pattanayak tailored ICT to the needs of the students developing innovative approaches to cater to this population. In lieu of face to face pre-placement workshops, teaching material was electronically forwarded to a group of distance education students followed by three half day teleconference sessions. However, often the practical exercises become a casualty in this process no matter what effort is put in by the field educators to incorporate these in the on-line approaches. ICT inputs are as good as participants adherence to its requirements. As the choice for distance education was governed by factors other than acquiring a qualification, the presence of students for a teleconference itself indicated a high level of commitment to learning. It was also found that ICTs were increasingly used in discussions with potential supervisors and liaison persons internationally to clarify the expectations of students and universities, the curriculum, practice standards and codes of ethics.

The use of the university's electronic Distributed Learning System (DLS) was found to be extremely valuable. The structured direction, which involved specific thematic questions and case studies being posted, provided to the discussions on DLS at the University meant that some students participated more than others. One student who did not contribute to the discussion on-line reported:

I found the discussion extremely useful.... mostly I agreed with the comments/ critiques of others and had little to add, but it has helped me clarify and conceptualize better....therefore I make it a point to review all the postings each week.

The unintended benefits can be far greater than anticipated in this mode of learning.

ICT AND INTERNATIONAL FIELD EDUCATION

What motivates students is a key to understanding the desire for international placements. Globalization, the interconnectedness of communities and societies leading to the blurring of boundaries, and the compression of time and space has meant that there is a greater demand for international placements. Students consider the ability to critically analyze and compare and contrast different elements of theory and practice that is context specific as giving them an edge over others in this highly competitive global marketplace.

It is in this context that a partnership has emerged between an Australian University (RMIT University) and an Institution in India, the Centurion School of Rural Enterprise Management (CSREM) which has been to the mutual benefit of all partners and has been in many cases a test for the ICT technologies in field education. Over the past six years several groups of students from three universities (part of the CSSW network) have been in field placement arrangements in India, initially in a very ad hoc manner. With the passage of time more structure has been provided to the program. Pattanayak's collaboration with the CSSW network, in various capacities, eventuated in placements for students in Orissa, India.

A brief introduction to Orissa may be useful at this point, in endeavoring to understand not only the difficulties in the use of ICT but also the differences between the practice of social work/ community development in the field and the access issues for students to ICT. Orissa, a state on the eastern coast of India is resource rich however 48% of its approximately 38 million population live below the official poverty line. 16% and 22% of its population belongs to the scheduled caste and scheduled tribe categories respectively. These categories are acknowledged by the Constitution of India and have entitlement to positive discrimination because of their historical marginalization. Due to the remoteness of various regions in the state, large pockets of the population (the erstwhile Koraput-Bolangir-Kalahandi districts) have little access to services and are socially excluded.

Where the state has proved to be ineffective in the provision of services, NGO's and private sector agencies have stepped in to fill the gap. It is in this context, that the Centurion group of Institutions (CGI) have come into existence in a remote district of Orissa. Their main objective is to provide opportunities to the excluded populations to gain access to quality education at different levels, extending from primary through to tertiary education. It is with the CGI that RMIT University (Victoria, Australia) has developed a partnership for social work field education. CGI also collaborate with local institutions (state and non-state) in pursuit of their objective. Two such collaborating local NGO's (BREDS and Velugu Association) provide placement experience from Australia. While the two NGO's are actually located in the neighboring state of Andhra Pradesh they share similar demographics.

The experience of total isolation associated with the remoteness of this region has led us to acknowledge the importance of students participating in group placements in Orissa rather than individual field experience. Remoteness also meant that the ICT services provided mainly by the state provider are limited. With the entry into the market of private providers, the situation has improved considerably. The Institutional partner in Orissa, CSREM has made an effort to put in place ICT services to enable students to access their university for academic information and resources, liaison and supervision and also to use e-mail, google talk and skype to communicate with their personal and professional support networks. CSREM has a designated computer laboratory for students on international placements with 24hour Internet connectivity. There is also regular telephone contact with supervisor and liaison person. Where students possess mobile phones, they have been effectively used, especially to seek immediate clarifications. Further, the Institution has put in place audio/ video conferencing facilities for the purposes of teaching, supervision and liaison which will benefit the next group of students. However, these facilities have had differential benefits for students depending on the NGO in which they are placed (primarily due to the distance).

There is another limitation posed to the expectations of students and universities. The practitioners of social work/ community development in the field in Orissa are less dependent on ICT's and draw attention to how they contrast with the aspirations of communities as well as the self reliance that the practitioners are attempting to achieve with these communities. There is a lot of sharing of scarce resources within and between organizations and therefore organizations do not invest heavily in ICT infrastructure. CSREM has stepped in to bridge this gap.

MODELS OF INTERNATIONAL FIELD EDUCATION AND ICT

Experiential learning is an integral part of human service education through structured group interactions and field education. While face-to-face contact is the focus, if not the foundation of human services field education across all human services field education programs, this is being challenged by the increasing preference of students for various means of communication alternate to the traditional telephone, face to face interview and group seminars. The amount, type and means of communication required by the increasing number of students undertaking overseas placements provide visible indicators of this. Tesoriero and Rajaratnam (2001) acknowledge the importance of regular ongoing communication in a variety of ways ancillary to, as well as in support of, the on-site supervision.

The four models of international field education experience identified by Pettys (2005) in a study of twenty-one schools of social work in the United States provides a useful framework for reflecting upon the use of ICT with overseas students from RMIT University between 2005 and 2008. These four models are the:

1.   Independent/ one-time placement model;
2.   Neighbor-country model;
3.   On-site model; (and)
4.   Exchange/ reciprocal model.

Each of these models is considered below.

1. Independent/ One-Time Placement

This model, regarding the placement of an individual student in a host agency is 'usually driven by student interest and/ or experience in a specific geographic region' (Pettys et al, 2005, p.282). In RMIT's program this applies predominantly to students keen to use their placement as grounds for return to their country of origin. Our approval for this is conditional upon the student having strong family connections and supports in that country as well as access to an agency with available professional supervision during placement. Such was the case for a student on placement in South America who had previous travel experience there as well as a command of the local language. The student's communication skills, assessed by

her supervisor as 'excellent, in both spoken and written Spanish' (Final Report, 2006) enabled her to carry out a much needed qualitative evaluation of the non government organization which worked primarily in maternal and child health. Considerable individual briefing was provided pre and post placement. Regardless of the supervision and support provided in-country the expectation of regular communication with the home school has been clearly stated in student feedback.

In the past at RMIT University, we have approved other placements of similar nature arising from a lecturer's connections for the "one-time" learning opportunity in another country (e.g. Zambia, Cambodia). Given the nature of this model students in this category may not be subjected to the same pre-placement procedures or pre-departure briefings.

Accessing and negotiating an appropriate organization for students seeking return to their country of origin may be time consuming for all parties. Planning for the placement in South America was facilitated by one of the student's relatives who worked in human services in that country. A contrast to this is finding an appropriate venue for a student returning to Ethiopia for her final placement. Contacts through International NGOs and informal academic networks were discouraging. The unforeseen opportunity arose whilst one of the field education coordinators was scanning the e-mailed Newsletter of a Global Human Rights Network and found an advertisement for a project worker with a local community organization working with women in Addis Ababa, an area of particular interest to the student. A speedy response came from the Newsletter editor to the request for contact details.

2. Neighbor-Country Model

The "neighbor-country" model which involves links 'with social work programs which were geographically located close to an international border' (Pettys et al, 2005, p.283) refers in the

United States to countries such as Mexico or Canada where the students were often returning as citizens or residents of the neighboring country to do their placement. In Australia this applies to countries in the Asia Pacific region some of which attract a greater student interest than others, being countries in the spotlight owing to political unrest and a high refugee population (e.g. East Timor, Thai Burma border). Factors inhibiting the organization of placements in some of the neighboring countries (Asia Pacific) may relate to the level of safety rating issue by the Foreign Affairs Department/ Government or access to appropriate resources for accommodating and supervising students.

One student on placement in Cambodia relied heavily upon the extended role of her supervisor, a former university staff member; access to telephone and Internet being less unreliable in isolated areas in rural Cambodia where the student was located.

3. On-Site Model

This third model identified by Pettys et al (2005) is based upon an adjunct faculty member in the host country who is delegated to the supervisory and sometimes liaison roles. Our example of this model is coordinated by Pattanayak who has hosted groups of students in India during the past few years. In contrast with the American model which places attention on student screening and selection we have found the pre-departure briefing program a more appropriate method which, on a few occasions has resulted in student withdrawal from the international placement program. An important early link with students has come from Pattanayak's participation each year in one of the pre-departure briefings in Australia. Her continuing relationship with the University staff has helped to address the isolation and limited ICT access of students for certain periods during placement in pairs in rural villages in India. Students were placed in pairs with two different

organizations in isolated rural villages. Telephone liaison was therefore limited to occasions when students returned to the city where Pattanayak resided, and where group and individual supervision was mostly provided.

The ICT methods used for international field education, in addition to printed information packs and additional reading material, in this instance were; telephone/ teleconferencing, Internet access the university library and peer communication via computer and mobile phone. While previously there was greater reliance on teleconferencing, video conferencing, using skype, is planned for the near future.

One student reported that:

The Internet ... has been really important to my placement.... as it's an important source of information to back up field learning and more importantly a link to home. I don't think the previous group of students used Internet or other things as much as I do.

The web has been used as a great source of information in the remote locations where students are on placement as well as a link to the outside world. Information to support various pieces of work students are pursuing as part of their placement is also sourced from the Internet. For example, legislations involved in the formation and functioning of NGO's, case studies of similar programs being undertaken in different parts of the country and the world and the lessons learnt, background material on local issues such as trafficking, to name a few are often quoted by students.

Where students have possessed mobile phones they have been able to contact their supervisors and liaison persons when required besides keeping in touch with families. To date it seems that the use of mobile phones has been under explored and under utilized, especially SMS.

Our findings are consistent with the American experience, of students benefiting from greater learning in more secure environments than in the contexts referred to in the previous two models. This on-site partnership model is the most appropriate structure for addressing the complexities associated with overseas placements. However given the fluid nature of community development contexts, specific learning goals may sometimes only be identified once the student is situated there and engaged in dialogue regarding appropriate or otherwise experience presenting at that time.

Valuable examples of on-site models developed by two other universities in Australia provide placements for students in the Philippines and India. The Philippines on-site field provision is through partnership of another university in Victoria (La Trobe University) with a large non government organization which auspices an international student unit for students from several countries. Philanthropic resources have enabled the university to send a group of students each year to this agency, exposing them to a diversity of services and programs based on a developmental approach in another culture.

A structure for students to acquire intercultural competence, prior to and during placement, in India with a rural non government organization working from a primary health care model situation in South India has been developed by Tesoriero and Rajaratnam. The partnership between one of the universities in South Australia and a large community health complex has extended to joint engagement in research and consultancy with the sharing of expertise 'at national and international levels' (Tesoriero, p.130).

Tesoriero and Rajaratnam (2001) acknowledge the importance of regular ongoing communication in a variety of ways, ancillary to, as well as in support of the on-site supervision. Their model provides guidelines for regular communication. Students are assigned a mentor and a supervisor to whom they are accountable and report regularly in each project. The university provides weekly phone communication for reflection and review of their social work practice and strategies. In addition, students submit and receive feedback through e-mail on a regular analysis of their practice (pp.37-8).

4. Exchange Model

Pettys et. al. (2005) views the fourth model, the "exchange model" as 'the most intensive and demanding on the home university, both in terms of faculty time and university funding' (p.284). RMIT's partnership for student exchange with universities in two neighboring countries, Malaysia and the Philippines provides a particularly viable model for our social work students. Consultation by phone and e-mail, regarding potential placements begins before students depart Australia. The home university is responsible for in-country orientation, placement referral, liaison, access to University resources and ancillary support. A value of this model is that dependence upon communication with the home school is primarily by e-mail and phone. The exchange is reciprocal and in this sense a genuine exchange partnership is entered into. The partnership between the universities has developed beyond the exchanges to include staff exchange and joint research. Visits by staff to these countries, with meetings and briefings with prospective students, have been well received and seen as a sign of the commitment of the universities to work together in mutual partnership.

Like Razack (2002) we have found, in engaging in the exchange model, that 'All students, even those with initial difficulties around culture shock and language differences, reported that their placements were innovative and challenging' (p.260).

Attention to the advantages brought about by increasingly sophisticated ICT risks prioritizing the "medium" above the "message". The questions we pose are two-fold. Firstly regarding the nature of learning that takes place in these contexts. How might it be comparable with learning standards expected of a placement locally? Secondly, should we, and if so how might we understand the effect of student presence upon the communities with which they engage?

Whitmore and Wilson (1997) propose a set of principles for field education partnerships for countries in transition. These include:

- non-intrusive collaboration;
- mutual trust and respect;
- a common analysis of what the problem is;
- a commitment to solidarity;
- equality in the relationships; (and)
- an explicit focus on process and the importance of language.

These principles are demonstrated by the people and institutions responsible for the placements provided in the models in India, Malaysia and the Philippines. The on-site and exchange placement models for Australian students in countries in transition, contextualize students in ways which are distinctly different from placements at home. This is reflected in the formal placement experience as well as overall life experience. Students in India in 2008 acknowledged the great assistance they had from the natural resources specialist who gave them an insight into her role while also discussing the importance of organic farming techniques; and the gender specialist who also accompanied them to the field and explained on site many of the complexities in gender relations which would have otherwise posed a number of questions for the students of the agency both on and off the field. From a more personal perspective certain forms of cultural inclusion, interpreted sometimes as cultural conformity during time away from placement have challenged some students.

INTERNATIONAL PLACEMENT POLICY

Placements carried out through the on-site model and that of the partnership exchange program are considered the more effective frameworks by all parties, with the exception of some instances of the independent/ one-time placement models which "fits", albeit unpredictable. Our field education policy, reviewed annually to take account of any contextual changes offers these models as the major options for students seeking international placements. Overarching this social work specific policy is the RMIT University "global passport" policy regarding international study. In summary the policy for social work field placements in other countries states that placements may be undertaken:

- In conjunction with a university with which we have or are developing a partnership or in a country where we have strong links with staff in an organization (on-site model); or
- A tertiary institution which provides structure for accommodating students holistically (exchange/ partnership model); or
- In the student's country of origin where there are family supports, qualified social work field instructors and student speaks the local language; or
- In a country where student has strong personal reasons for engaging in placement (e.g. previous volunteer/work experience and strong links with the host organization which can provide social work supervision) (independent/ one-time placement model).

Approval is also conditional upon supervision and liaison being available from appropriately qualified local staff (social workers) who have at least two years' experience and are eligible for membership of the professional social work association in the country where the placement is undertaken.

Students planning an overseas placement should be able to articulate what they need to learn on placement in another country in terms of social work knowledge and skills. They must be able to say why this experience in another culture is appropriate in terms of acquiring the required knowledge and skills. Moreover students must be financially capable of funding their travel, accommodation and living expenses whilst on placement overseas. Similarly adequate RMIT University social work/ field education staff resources are essential to negotiate and maintain appropriate contact with all parties during the placements.

Further complexities arise when students may be required to carry out additional course work while on placement. Both access to information for their course work as well as access to discussion and course material is an issue where connectivity is a problem. In 2006, students expressed great frustration at their inability to access both the university discussion board as well as quality information to supplement their learning from the field.

ICT APPLICATION FOR INTERNATIONAL PLACEMENTS

Our experience confirms the need for a well conceptualized policy/ road map for ICT in international placements. However, this may require some resources invested both by the university and other partners. Web based technologies can be further used so as to enable all stakeholders to communicate better.

Clearly some of the steps involved would be that:

- Students have to think through their motivations for an international placement, identify what are the skills/ knowledge and resources they bring to the placement, articulate what they need to learn and fulfill the requirements based on checklists prior to departure: part of this may be to gather adequate information about the placement and various programs that a recipient country may have.

- The information packs to the partnering agencies which need to precede students' placement should be sent on-line by the University well before the student placement.
- Supervision and liaison requirements to be communicated to the agency such that suitable facilities, whether telephone, Internet or designated videoconferencing can be made available when required.
- The use of mobile phones and SMS to be explored further.
- Internet facilities to be made available to students while on placement and web based discussion groups set up on arrival of students, if not prior to arrival.
- Protocol to be established for communication in case of emergencies.

ICT is as beneficial as the system allows it to be. In rural areas often there are power failures and this would mean that there may be interruptions to supervisory/ liaison/ discussion sessions in progress. Efforts are made by the institution to have backup electricity generation systems but this may also take time or fail in some instances for a variety of reasons (for example fuel, missing operator, and such other factors). The Internet facilities in some isolated rural areas in Orissa, India have not stabilized and in many places there are still dial up facilities which may be very slow and may continually disconnect; this is a frustrating experience. Broadband connectivity is proving to be a very useful service provided in some of these locations. The technology available with an agency in a rural area may be obsolete by standards in Australia and therefore students with their knowledge of current technology may not be able to operate them.

In contrast, students on exchange placement in Malaysia and the Philippines benefited from being situated in urban agencies involved in international issues and projects for which they had reasonably sophisticated ICT equipment.

Similarly the university auspicing them enabled students to maintain contact with local university support staff.

Our experience confirms that of Panos (2005) who, through his work with international student placement programs has identified onsite supervision as essential. He promotes the use of videoconferencing for students on placement in remote or isolated locations to provide supervision during placements to complement and support that of the host agency. The use of video-conferencing for supervision of students on international placements was effective in overcoming students' feelings of isolation. Similarly students' abilities to use ICT tools in forming support groups, was identified as a valuable tool for informal communication. However sparse attention has been given in literature to date to the costs associated with ICT. Whilst universities, at least those in Western countries, are placing high priority on learning by alternate flexible modes investment of this nature is often not feasible for local agencies in countries in transition.

ASSOCIATED FACTORS

From our experience with a diversity of overseas placement models key factors can be categorized into organizational and legal, educational and personal.

Organizational and Legal Structure

Clear contracts for all parties need to be negotiated prior to departure, documenting accountability which, especially in countries in transition, extends beyond the education/ learning plan. Where partnerships have been negotiated all involved need an understanding of the nature of the partnership and the students place in this. Issues of accountability, responsibility and duty of care carry a meaning which extends beyond that of placement agencies in the home country. This holds true irrespective of whether or not there is a partnership between the University and host organization. For example what are the implications for supervisors and the accountability of students who may be located with an organization in a rural setting where survival may be dependent upon familiarity with the local culture? Also students sometimes express a curtailment of their liberty when the NGO restricts their movement on their own, but as part of their duty of care, the NGO may consider it a risk to the security of the students to allow the students to venture out on their own. Besides, NGO's have expressed that it is a matter of their reputation as well which is at stake.

Our experience has indicated blurred boundaries regarding responsibility and liability in several instances when students are located in other countries. For example when phoning to arrange an appointment for telephone liaison with a student who had been "driven by interest to a country of her choice" in Europe (an example of the independent/ one-time placement model) we learnt that the student was on vacation in another country. The routine procedure in Australia is to advise the university when taking time out from placement. When the student is overseas should this accountability be formally delegated to the agency? Does the agency assume this responsibility on behalf of the university? Indirectly related to this is the place of "associate" group members. In the past with group placements added complexities have arisen with the unannounced accompaniment or arrival of a friend or partner of one of the group.

Overarching these issues is the question about the extent to which the university should be expected to care for and cater to international students' needs and wants. University policies in Australia must take account of the legislation governing those coming to Australia as international students. For Australian students in other countries the situation may vary according to the institution accommodating them and the socio-political and national security situation of that country. Australian students on recent placement under the exchange model in the Philippines expressed some reticence regarding the "watchful eye" of the local "parent" university. In contrast the observation and experience of their field coordinator during a visit to the country resulted in an appreciation of this "protection" and reassurance of preventive measures regarding two more students soon to begin placements there on exchange. This observation was shared with the next two exchange students to that country, preparing them for this situation and raising their awareness of the benefits in relation to the vulnerability of students as "foreign female" visitors and the risks to which they may be exposed.

Educational

In 2008 students at RMIT University who were planning overseas placements attended five briefings, totaling about fifteen hours, and spanning a period of approximately eight months at these briefings. Former and current lecturers with international development experience and a wealth of wisdom as student teachers and supervisors shared knowledge about core international community development concepts and facilitated a journey of critical reflection upon student motivation, values and aspirations.

All teaching parties have assessed this most recent overseas group placement to India as the smoothest, least problematic and most educationally significant to date. Whilst learning from previous feedback and observation about the need for organized access to ICT and a clearer understanding of the different roles, a major factor contributing to the positive experience – individually and collectively - was the extent and depth of the preplacement briefings, enabling students to develop more realistic expectations of the environment and experience in a totally different culture.

Cross-Cultural Being

The likelihood of less structure and resources in a number of organizations in countries in transition has highlighted the importance of student ability for self-directed learning, an ability to reframe the situation and theoretical understanding. Alongside this is the need to reframe ways of engaging, communicating and relating more holistically, looking at issues rather than individuals. How might students learn to conceptualize collectively rather than analyze individually and 'recognize their own shifting identities' (Razack 2002, p.259).

At the initial stage of placement I didn't quite fully comprehend the significant value of the basic key principles of community development, including the value of community ownership and the ownership of processes and structures, and it quite soon became apparent to me that I needed to further develop my understanding of these principles in order to function appropriately within this organization (Student, India, 2006).

Language

Should students planning overseas placements be required or encouraged to plan from early in their university studies to undertake certain courses such as language electives and international development prior to their departure? To what effect is lack of local language likely to impede practice? Little attention has been given in literature to date to the resource input by NGOs in countries in transition where local agency staff may be required to play the role of interpreter/ support worker for students. Three students on placement in India were provided with an interpreter to accompany them whenever they went into the field. In contrast, as indicated previously, the prior knowledge, experience, skills and language of the student on placement in South America enabled her to carry out a qualitative evaluation of some of the agency services to support a submission for continued funding, a contribution highly valued by the agency. While the lack of knowledge in the local language may prove disadvantageous in certain circumstances, good knowledge of English in students has been found very beneficial to the agencies in India. The structure for the learning is built around how best students can benefit under the circumstances and therefore students have been involved in conceptualising, conducting and documenting research as well as writing project proposals in order to seek funding.

Learning Context

In her article on the dilemmas of international social work (2005) Gray refers to the writing of Tsang and Yan (2001) and Hessle (2004) who suggest that the context-bound nature of social work challenges any claims to a universal authenticity (Gray 2005, p.252). The likelihood of less structure and resources in a number of organizations in countries in transition has highlighted the importance of student ability for self-directed learning, an ability to reframe the situation and theoretical understanding. Alongside this is the need to reframe ways of engaging, communicating and relating more holistically, looking at issues rather than individuals. This extends also to students grappling with the absence of the personal pronoun "I" and an acceptance that they are there primarily to learn, not to do, and if delegated tasks by the agency appreciate their involvement and not judge from a western perspective. Students in Bangladesh grappled with the realization that there is no concept for individuality in that culture. Related to this is the different meaning and relevance of confidentiality and privacy when community development placement experience means "living" in the community immersed on a 24/7 basis.

Theory and Practice Considerations

According to Gray and Fook (2004) 'there are commonalities in theory and practice across widely divergent contexts' (p.262). The "grand metaphor"/ big picture provides an important framework for student learning which involves recognition and valuing of commonalities and differences, a contextually framed social work approach grounded upon social justice and 'valuing dialogical processes within local contexts that does not exclude honoring existing social work knowledge' (Gray 2005, p.233).

Critical Reflection and Assessment

Given the more likely experiential discourse as distinct from outcomes driven placement in certain countries in transition, there is a need for greater diversity of assessment tools to accommodate critical reflection. These include portfolios, written critical issues analysis and reflection at micro, mezo and macro levels. As indicated previously Tesoriero integrates Fook's (1996) approach to reflective practice into the learning process of students at the Rural Unit for Health and Social Affairs (RUHSA) (Tamil Nadu, South India), using her reflective questions for students to question the meaning of their experiences and increase their intercultural sensitivity (Tesoriero, 2006,p. 131).

These will more effectively reflect disciplinary dialogue and exploration of multiple meanings, finding common ground, space and place for exchange of ideas and ideologies with the recognized social work supervision and experienced colleagues; maximizing opportunities to develop relationships with peers, and learning from people with local wisdom.

Heron (2005) found that Canadians returning from overseas needed to '..not only de-brief their international experiences and any encounters with risk that they have had, but also create meaning for themselves out of what they have seen, heard and done' (p. 791).

At this time students may require the most support in making connections between theory and practice. Unfortunately many individual student travel plans post placement and the academic/university calendar in Australia does not easily accommodate these needs.

CONCLUSION

With ICT an integral component of education generally and internationalization of curriculum promoted in various forms for tertiary students, international placements for social work students reflect the benefits of ICT whilst challenging its application. The distinguishing features of social work education are that it is "field" located and that the student is under professional supervision.

Whilst communication amongst key players in social work placements is becoming increasingly dependent upon various modes of technological communication, ICT remains ancillary to and dependent upon certain core characteristics of field education which apply generally, but require more complex planning and greater resourcing for international placements. We refer here to the need for: well conceptualized policy for international placements; pre departure preparation regarding cultural awareness with particular attention to self reflection and realistic expectations; appropriate organizational structures for learning and living in another culture; clear contracts with the professional supervisor/s and other parties engaged with students and an understanding of roles and responsibilities of key players.

Our experience has highlighted the importance of a policy for international field education based on social justice principles, structures in country of destination which can accommodate the student "being" in a very different context and social work curriculum (other courses in addition to pre-placement briefings) which place the student in both global and local paradigms. As with access to effective communication medium

these components are inevitably reliant upon the resources available at the home university.

REFERENCES

Abram, F., Slosar, J., & Walls, R. (2005). Reverse mission. A model for international social work education and transformative intra-national practice. *International Social Work, 48*(2), 161–176. doi:10.1177/0020872805050490

Bowles, W., & Colllingridge, M. (2008). *On-line student supervision training – accessible and co-operative learning in social work* (Unpublished briefing paper). Charles Sturt University, NSW, Australia.

Boyle, D., Nackerud, L., & Kilpatrick, A. (1999). The road less travelled. Cross-cultural, international experiential learning. *International Social Work, 42*(2), 201–214. doi:10.1177/002087289904200208

Combined Schools of Social Work. (2008). *CSSW*. Retrieved January 14, 2009, from http://www.cssw.com.au

Cornelius, L., & Grief, G. (2005). Schools of social work and the nature of their foreign collaborations. *International Social Work, 48*(6), 823–833. doi:10.1177/0020872805057094

Fook, J. (1996). *The reflective researcher*. St. Leonards, NSW: Allen and Unwin.

Gray, M. (2005). Dilemmas of international social work: paradoxical processes in Indigenisation, universalism and imperialism. *International Journal of Social Welfare, 14*, 231–238. doi:10.1111/j.1468-2397.2005.00363.x

Gray, M., & Fook, J. (2004). The quest for a universal social work: Some issues and implications. *Social Work Education, 23*(5), 625–644. doi:10.1080/0261547042000252334

Healy, L. (2001). *International social work: Professional action in an interdependent world.* New York: Oxford University Press.

Heron, B. (2005). Changes and challenges. Preparing social work students for practicum in today's sub-Saharan African context. *International Social Work, 48*(6), 782–793. doi:10.1177/0020872805057088

Ife, J. (1995). *Community development: Creating community alternatives – vision, analysis and practice.* Melbourne, Australia: Longman

Johnson, A. (2004). Increasing internationalization in social work programs. Healy's continuum as a strategic planning guide. *International Social Work, 47*(1), 7–23. doi:10.1177/0020872804036445

Laird, S. (2004). Inter-ethnic conflict: A role for social work in Sub-Saharan Africa. *Social Work Education, 23*(6), 693–709. doi:10.1080/0261547042000294482

Maidment, J. (2006). Using on-line delivery to support students during practicum placements. *Australian Social Work, 59*(1), 47–55. doi:10.1080/03124070500449770

Mamphiswana, D., & Noyoo, N. (2000). Social work education in a changing socio-political and economic dispensation. Perspectives from South Africa. *International Social Work, 43*(1), 21–32.

Martin. J., & Ling, H. K. (2008). International activity through student mobility: Physical, psychological and social adjustment. *International Journal of Learning,* 15(8). Retrieved from http://ijl.cgpublisher.com/product/pub.30/prod.1847

McDonald, C. (2006). *Challenging social work the institutional context of practice.* New York: Palgrave Macmillan.

Midgley, J. O. (1997). *Social welfare in a global context.* Thousand Oaks, CA: Sage.

Moore, S., & Collins, W. (2002). A model for social work field practicum in African American Churches. *Journal of Teaching in Social Work, 22*(3), 171–188. doi:10.1300/J067v22n03_12

Panos, P. (2005). A model for using video-conferencing technology to support international social work field practicum students. *International Social Work, 48*(6), 834–841. doi:10.1177/0020872805057095

Pawar, M. (2000). Social development content in the courses of Australian social work schools. *International Social Work, 43*(3), 277–288. doi:10.1177/002087280004300302

Pettys, G., Panos, P., Cox, S., & Oosthuysen, K. (2005). Four models of international field placement. *International Social Work, 48*(3), 277–288. doi:10.1177/0020872805051705

Rai, G. (2004). International fieldwork experience. A survey of US schools. *International Social Work, 47*(2), 213–226. doi:10.1177/0020872804034138

Razack, N. (2002). A critical examination of international student exchanges. *International Social Work, 45*(2), 251–265.

Reisch, M., & Jarman-Rohde, L. (2000). The future of social work in the United States: Implications for field education. *Journal of Social Work Education, 36*(2), 201–214.

Stella Maris College. Social Work. (2005). *Stella Maris College (autonomous).* Retrieved February 4, 2009, from http://www.stellamariscollege.org/departments/socialwork.asp

Tesoriero, F. (2006). Personal growth towards intercultural competence through an international field education programme. *Australian Social Work, 59*(2), 126–140. doi:10.1080/03124070600651853

Tesoriero, F., & Rajaratnam, A. (2001). Partnership in education. An Australian school of social work and a South Indian primary health care project. *International Social Work*, *44*(1), 31–41. doi:10.1177/002087280104400104

Wehbi, S. (2009). Deconstructing motivations. Challenging international social work placements. *International Social Work*, *52*(1), 48–59. doi:10.1177/0020872808097750

Whitmore, E., & Wilson, M. (1997). Accompanying the process: Social work and international development practice. *International Social Work*, *40*(1), 57–74. doi:10.1177/002087289704000105

ENDNOTE

[1]   The opinions expressed by the author are hers and not those of the organization.

Section 2
Information Communication Technologies and Human Services Delivery

Chapter 10
Developing Information Communication Technologies for the Human Services
Mental Health and Employment

Jennifer Martin
RMIT University, Australia

Elspeth McKay
RMIT University, Australia

ABSTRACT

This chapter introduces a design process for developing useful information communication technologies for the human services. Key to the success of the design process is an in-depth knowledge and understanding of user needs and requirements. The stages involved in the design process are presented in this chapter and include: user and task analysis, persona and scenario development and the establishment of measurable usability goals. A case study illustrates the application of this design process to develop a Web enabled electronic work requirement awareness program (e-WRAP) for people recovering from mental illness seeking employment. The challenge for social workers is to use these new technologies to improve service provision and enhance quality of life without compromising ethical standards of practice; particularly in relation to client confidentiality, privacy and self-determination.

'After the idea, there is plenty of time to learn the technology'. -- James Dyson (1947-), English inventor and businessman, Against the Odds, 1997 in Oxford Dictionary of Quotations (2004, p.294:20).

INTRODUCTION

Information communication technologies today are in abundance. People of all ages, particularly young people communicate through the Internet to access the social networking sites MySpace and Facebook; the online video site YouTube; microblogging sites

DOI: 10.4018/978-1-60566-735-5.ch010

Twitter and Plurk and the virtual world of Second Life. In addition to these are Internet sites such as Wikkipedia, MSN and Google. Most organizations today have a web presence for marketing, attracting users and conducting business. Increasingly organizations in the human services are adopting web technologies to reach user groups to communicate their messages and to increase organizational efficiencies. However the profusion of information on the Internet makes it difficult at times for users to actually locate the information they are seeking. This may be due to diversion sites that can cause considerable frustration, confusion and time delays or an overload of information, with many Internet sources unverified. Access to the Internet can be costly requiring constant updates and virus protection with some media requiring the latest versions of sophisticated software to access them. Available software and the Internet service provider will also affect access and speed.

These new technologies create both challenges and opportunities as designers try to reach their intended user groups using the most appropriate means and messages, delivered in a timely manner. Central to the success of designing useful and usable information communication technologies for the human services is in-depth knowledge and understanding of the target audience, referred to hereafter as "users". The stages involved in the design process are presented including: user and task analysis, persona and scenario development and the establishment of measurable usability goals. This is followed by a case study of mental health and employment illustrating the application of this design process to develop a web enabled Electronic Work Requirement Awareness Program (e-WRAP) designed for people recovering from mental illness seeking employment.

USER ANALYSIS

The main features of user groups are identified by conducting a user analysis. This involves thinking and forming assumptions about what users would like. The next crucial step is to test these assumptions against the "reality" of the users in an endeavor to understand their needs, expectations, knowledge base, experience and preferences. Information is also gained on technologies and software that users have available to them, for example via broadband or dial up, as well as the physical environment where the Internet is accessed. By involving users in the pre-design stage they become active and important partners in the design process. Research techniques that complement each other for conducting a user analysis comprise: contextual interviews, individual interviews, surveys and focus groups (United States Department of Health & Human Services, 2008). The more techniques used the greater the depth of knowledge gained about the needs of users and the less likelihood of design errors. A common mistake to avoid is choosing "flashy" technology over accessibility.

Contextual Interviews

Contextual interviews are similar to participant observation, and involve observing and listening to users while they are engaged with the technologies. These interviews provide information on the physical and social environment as well as the technologies available including means of access, familiarity and level of comfort and support. For instance a person's use will vary according to whether they are on broadband or a modem. Dial up access to the Internet may mean that the users want to use the web quickly so that a telephone line is not tied up for extended periods. Access will vary according to the Internet service provider with many limiting or denying access during peak periods. Insights are gained on whether or not users have anyone who can assist them with the technology and the nature of this support. Contextual interviews are usually informal with the interviewer mindful of not imposing any changes on the environment that is being observed. This is achieved by watching and listening to users and interviewing them by means of questions, probes and reflective statements to gain an understanding of what they are doing, thinking and feeling. The interviewer does not ask users to perform specific tasks or respond to case scenarios.

Individual Interviews

Individual interviews are different to contextual interviews in that they involve collecting information directly from the user and do not include contextual observations. The ultimate goal is to gain deeper understanding and insight into users' ICT needs. Individual interviews allow for a deep understanding of users' attitudes, beliefs, experiences, desires and fears. Individual interviews provide an opportunity to have a detailed one on one discussion where the user has the full attention of the interviewer. This information is usually gained during a 30 minutes to one hour interview that may be conducted in person, on the telephone or by computer aided means such as instant messaging. Information collected during the individual interviews will complement that already gained in the contextual interviews by providing further information as well as confirming or denying observations already made.

Participants are selected on the basis of their embodiment of the main features of the intended user group. An interview protocol, with interview questions designed in neutral language, provides focus and structure with the interviewer mindful of applying this flexibly. The interview style and approach can be adjusted to the personality and communication style of the interviewee, making them feel comfortable and engaged in the interview process.

Interview skills in listening, questioning and follow up probes are useful, particularly those aimed at clarification where the individual interview and contextual interview information differs. For instance, how does the level of comfort with ICT observed in the contextual

interview correspond with the user's individual interview responses? This is also an opportunity to gain feedback on particular ICT applications and content by asking users to rank or rate these. The granting of permission to tape record and transcribe interviews or to have note takers will ensure that as accurate a record as possible of interview responses is obtained.

Individual interviews can assist in refining the questions to be included in online surveys or they can be conducted following online surveys to provide more detailed information about particular users.

Online Surveys

Online surveys are structured interviews with users recording and submitting their responses online. These surveys generally generate a greater number of responses than individual interviews but often they do not have the same depth of information. Individual interviews can inform the survey questions. Online surveys are readily accessible on the Internet and very user friendly. Data collection is relatively easy and efficient as users record their own responses rating and ranking ICT applications and content.

Information can be collected in online surveys during an initial planning phase to learn more about who users are and what they would like. Alternatively they can be conducted after ICT applications have been designed to seek feedback from users as to whether or not these meet their needs and if they have suggestions for improvement. This latter approach is particularly suited to use of new or innovative ICT that users have limited knowledge or experience of. A further possibility is for the survey to remain active for instant feedback at all stages throughout the design, implementation and evaluation process. This allows for ongoing incremental improvements and suggestions while they are fresh in the mind of users. A series of online surveys may be conducted at significant stages of design.

The design team needs to be clear on the purpose of surveying users. Survey distribution may be a pre-existing website for the organization or another site where users go. If multiple postings are made it is important to consider the possibility of multiple responses from the one user and whether or not this poses a problem. It may give a false idea of numbers of users who have responded, yet a frequent user may a have a lot of good ideas. Issues of how the data will be recorded, stored and managed need to be considered carefully with ethical approval obtained where necessary.

Group e-mails through listservs are useful for making direct requests to users to participate in online surveys. A letter of request sent directly to the user, with an embedded hyperlink opening directly to the survey, provides for an easy and immediate response. The more complicated the task the less likelihood of users participating, particularly if it is voluntary. When designing an online survey it is best to keep it short, with 10 or less questions preferred. Questions might include demographic information about users, prior experiences of ICT and what they would like.

Ease of completion is a central consideration with the survey preferably taking 10 minutes or less to complete. Open questions provide rich qualitative data about users' needs and experiences as well as the terminology they use. Closed questions provide aggregate numbers and can be useful when collecting demographic information and for asking users for rankings or ratings of ICT applications, the data analysis being quicker and easier than responses to open ended questions. Time and resources available for compiling and analyzing data will influence the number and type of questions asked. More detailed information can be gained in a further online survey, individual interview or focus group.

Focus Groups

Focus groups are a commonly used research technique, particularly amongst social work research-

ers, educators and practitioners. Information is discussed and shared within the focus group about attitudes, needs, concerns and interests with regard to the design and application of the technologies in relation to the specific context of the user group. This provides a deeper understanding of how users engage with the technology and the problems they face. Information is gained about the culture of the group and shared or diverse viewpoints that can trigger more in-depth discussions. It is also an opportunity to gain information on users' responses to ideas and prototypes.

Focus groups usually comprise of between eight and 12 users, or potential users, for the duration of approximately two hours. During this time a moderated discussion occurs on a range of pre-determined topics or themes. Desired learning outcomes of the focus group are identified and used to structure the discussion by writing a script for the moderator to follow with topics to cover and questions to ask. This script is to be applied flexibly so that the discussion flows smoothly and all participants have an opportunity to contribute to the discussions. This may mean that the moderator changes the order of questions or topics covered but ultimately has covered everything during the time allocated for the focus group. This requires a skilled moderator who is able to keep the discussion focused, deciding when further discussion of a topic is needed and when to move on.

Tape recordings of group sessions and one or more note takers are critical for an accurate recording of the focus group discussions. As the focus of the moderator is managing the discussions and intervening when necessary it is not appropriate for this person to also be a note taker, unless this role is shared with a co-facilitator. In co-facilitation the moderators may take it in turns to chair the group and take notes. Reliance on recordings alone can be problematic, particularly in instances when more than one person is talking at the same time due to background noise and difficulty identifying the speaker. A task analysis provides detailed information on how users achieve their goals and the steps involved.

TASK ANALYSIS

Task analysis is useful in identifying the processes and tasks associated with project design to achieve the desired outcomes (Pruitt & Grundin 2003, p.12). As with user analysis this is influenced by psychological, social and cultural factors, as well as the user's physical environment. Prior knowledge and experience will also influence how tasks are approached. The question of what tasks users need to complete using ICT is considered as well as different levels or types of uses. For example, a tertiary student may be paying a university account, conducting library searches or accessing lecture notes and course materials. The specific steps that students follow in undertaking these tasks are examined. This activity may or may not involve use of ICT. The student may go to the library to conduct their research, rely solely on electronic sources or a mixture of both. A task analysis provides information on how this activity is being conducted and the number of steps involved. How users currently perform tasks is examined with consideration of how efficient this is. If ICT can assist in producing more efficient outcomes this needs to be considered according to how well these match with users' ways of thinking and working as well as contextual factors.

A task analysis provides information on the tasks and activities that the ICT must support and the scope and nature of these. It will inform decisions on the choices of different technologies for different activities that match users' goals, tasks and the steps involved. These steps will be refined to support users achieving their goals in the most efficient and effective manner. Once the user and task analysis have been completed the persona is designed.

PERSONA

The persona is a hypothetical construct that embodies the main features of the population that the project is being designed for. The persona assists in understanding user information needs informing design and accessibility and ultimately suitability. However, it must not become a replacement for active user involvement. User profiles have been used for some time in marketing with the persona introduced in project design by Alan Cooper in the late 1990s. Cooper's (1999) early work focused on goal directed design by creating fictional personas used as a basis for creating activity scenarios. In later years more detailed personas were developed by using interviews and ethnography to gain a clearer picture and understanding of intended user groups across a much wider range of disciplines (Bloomquist, & Arvola, 2002). Lang (2007) stresses the importance of locating the persona within the relevant discipline and the disjuncture that can often unwittingly occur in beliefs and actual practices across disciplines. Where interdisciplinary differences exist these can be managed and resolved by basing decision making on what is best suited to the needs of the persona (McKay & Martin, 2007). Research conducted by Ronkko (2005) in Sweden cautions against tokenistic and inappropriate use of personas to justify design decisions without proper user consultation as well as problems that can occur when power is used inappropriately within the design team.

For personas to be used effectively a strong commitment is required by all members of the project team. The use of abstract representations to guide design have been used extensively, however often designers do not have a shared view of their intended user group and can fall in to the trap of designing for themselves. Cooper (2004) argues that designing for a persona is better than designing for the designer, or for a vaguely defined user group. Hourihan (2002) warns against the project team designing for themselves and losing sight of the intended user group. She comments, 'We thought we were the primary persona. Like a recovering substance abuser, it's a constant challenge for me to refrain – I can always imagine that I'm the user' (p.3). Use of the persona can create a safeguard against this by developing empathy between the designer and the user. It can also prevent "design creep" by providing a constant reference point for all design decisions. "Constant" is not to be confused with "static" as with all human computer interaction it is the dynamic nature of this interaction that is central to its relevance and currency.

Personas superseded the so-called "elastic users" by replacing them with a real identity that becomes an integral part of the project design process. The persona provides a conduit for transmitting a wide range of information about design and use. Whilst Cooper (2004) was not particularly concerned with the persona being representative of the user group, Grundin & Pruitt (2002) argue that representation of the user group is crucial and that this is the main advantage of using a persona. A persona provides a lens that includes the socio-political context and addresses issues around quality of life and difference. By focusing attention on a particular user group, personas assist in identifying different kinds of users as well as those who are not being designed for.

Designing the right persona or set of personas is particular to the main features of the user group and is time and culture specific. Decisions are often made to create maximum effect with others brought up to speed later, or perhaps left behind. Increasingly in the human services decisions are geared to particular user populations with this seen in targeted media campaigns, particularly for young people such as the "safe sex" campaign using text messages on Valentines Day and World Vision's Teenage Affluenza video on YouTube (Ryan 2008).

Personas were used to assist in the development of Microsoft Windows and MSN Explorer. Both of these products were designed to cater for varied and complex user groups across all generations and cultures. When designing Windows two target audiences were identified by using personas and customer segments. The Window's persona team comprised 22 people including technical writers,

graphic designers, usability engineers, product planners and market researchers who developed six personas. A panel of 5,000 users who matched the persona profiles was established and consulted as part of the design team on a regular basis (Pruitt & Grundin, 2003). Like Microsoft, many other organizations including Ford Motor Company, develop and use personas reporting numerous benefits from doing so such as better understanding of users needs, shorter and improved design periods and a superior end product. Similarly, personas aid in educational design for the human services workforce (Martin, McKay, Hawkins & Murthy 2007).

The persona comes to life as a "real person" for whom the project is being designed. Decisions are now being made about a person with a name and identity, albeit hypothetical. Detailed written documentation that succinctly describes the main features of the persona is essential. The level of detail suggested by Freydenson (2002) for a persona includes; 'at least a first and last name, age, goals, background story, a telling quote, e-mail address, job title and a photograph', (p.1). Other features might include: gender, educational background, family, class, health, ability/disability, race, ethnicity and culture, sexuality and spirituality. Cooper (2004) comments, 'All things being equal I will use people of different races, genders, nationalities and colors' (p.3). The persona will change and develop with the project and at times more than one persona may be required, particularly in instances of extreme diversity amongst potential user groups. Freydenson (2002) recommends the development of primary and secondary personas. These personas extend beyond the user to include others such as managers and funding bodies. The main focus is on the primary persona, whilst also being mindful of the needs of secondary personas. Ultimately the primary persona must be satisfied with the system that is delivered, with a common vision and commitment to the persona essential for successful design and implementation. Effective communication is important, particularly with those who may be absent from meetings where the persona is discussed. Creative strategies are required to keep the persona relevant and the focus of activity. It is useful to have something to signify this. This may simply be an empty chair at meetings that represents the presence of the persona in discussions and decision-making.

SCENARIOS

Scenarios are short stories, or narratives, that provide greater detail about users and their particular needs. Depending upon the size and scope of the project, between 10 and 20 of the most common scenarios that depict users and the tasks they need to perform will be written. This keeps the focus on users rather than organizational structures, creating a greater understanding of the content to include in the design and how to best structure this. Scenarios can be created during user analysis. These scenarios can be given to users to follow in usability tests to see if they match their requirements. Three main types are goal based, full scale task and elaborated scenarios (United States Department of Health & Human Services, 2008).

Goal based scenarios include only the activity the user is required to do. An example is a social worker registering a client's name and address on an electronic database. Simple goal based scenarios inform the architecture of the site and content.

Full scale task scenarios support goal based scenarios by including all of the steps involved in achieving a particular goal. This is a technique familiar to workers in the human services using behavior modification programs. Task scenarios can be developed by watching and recording the steps taken by users when performing a task or they can be developed independently by the project team. Most benefits are gained from an approach that is customized to the user group's style of engagement, with the project team adding

improvements and efficiencies that sit comfortably with them.

Elaborated scenarios provide greater detail, allowing for deeper understanding of users' level of comfort and skill in using ICT as well as their motivations and possible fears. This more in-depth understanding assists in developing the required content at an appropriate level. For example an elaborated scenario of the goal based scenario might be this social worker not only required to enter basic registration data but to move from a paper based system of client file notes to an electronic one. An elaborated scenario might be:

A social worker with over twenty years experience uses a computer to access e-mail and write reports. She has been told that a new system will allow for file notes to be sent electronically between agencies. She is not comfortable with the idea of writing personal information about clients on a web site and is particularly concerned about issues of privacy and confidentiality. As a result she has decided that when the new system is introduced she will limit what she puts in her file notes.

An elaborated scenario would include these fears and concerns with strategies developed to address these and avert the possibility of users limiting or modifying the level or type of engagement due to a distrust of the new technologies and how they will be used.

The persona and scenarios are tested, evaluated and further developed by feedback from usability testing with actual, rather than fictitious members of the user group.

USABILITY TESTING

Continuous feedback is obtained by conducting usability tests frequently, particularly early on in the design process. This means problems can be identified early on and are therefore less costly to fix, as well as providing valuable feedback on whether or not the design is achieving its intended outcomes. When conducting usability testing it is important to remember that it is the ICT and its application that is being tested, not the users. Data is collected through observations and user ratings. Five point scales can be used to assess levels of user satisfaction. These tests are generally conducted over a one hour period, with the size of a usability testing group usually between eight to 16 users. This number may vary according to the main characteristics of the user group, with four to six people appropriate for user groups that are fairly homogenous. Smaller groups with varied membership may be used to test particular aspects of a design at different stages of the design process. The staff who have developed the ICT and activities observe and listen carefully, taking notes on user experiences as they follow scenarios to implement the ICT given to them by the project team. This information is used to reflect upon how to improve the design.

It is preferred that usability testing be conducted throughout the design period on a series of proofs and prototypes rather than on a final product only. This requires adequate planning for the allocation of sufficient time and resources. For each round of testing it is important to identify what the specific goals are and to focus on these. For instance, the focus in an early round might be on testing for levels of user comfort, and in a later round on levels of satisfaction. The aim of the test is to determine how well each goal is being met. Typically a usability test is assessing both user performance and preference by collecting data on: usability problems, user performance, task completion, speed, and levels of satisfaction.

Successful, accurate completion of a task in a timely manner is generally considered a more important measurable usability goal than user satisfaction. Results on performance are more reliable than user preference as the latter may be based on levels of comfort, keeping in mind that learning new tasks will generate stress. Low user ratings indicate that the ICT applications need to be improved. However, high ratings do

not necessarily mean that problems do not exist. This could be due to the influence of extraneous factors such as users blaming themselves for difficulties encountered, unwanted personal attention and the particular tendency amongst human services workers to be kind to members the project team.

Ultimately the measure of usability is that the application of the ICT allows users to do their tasks in the same amount of time or less, with similar or improved levels of success and satisfaction. No doubt there will be varied needs and experiences amongst members of the user group with the design tailored to meet as many user needs as possible to successfully complete the required task. Ideally the ICT will improve upon other ways users have achieved their goals or they are not likely to embrace them unless they are compelled to do so. If this is the case, ongoing conflict management strategies will need to be employed while further user and task analysis is conducted (Martin & McKay 2007).

The following case study demonstrates the application of the project design stages of user and task analysis, persona and scenario development, and usability testing for the development of a web based resource to assist people recovering from mental illness gain employment.

CASE STUDY: DESIGN OF ELECTRONIC WORK REQUIREMENT AWARENESS PROGRAM (E-WRAP).

Background

Web based resources available for finding work are primarily listings of positions that can be searched according to type of position, location and pay rate. Templates and examples of resumes are available as well as tips for interview. These sites are targeted at the general population and do not address issues of self-esteem, motivation, concentration, discrimination, stigma and perceptual difficulties associated with recovery from severe mental illness and long term unemployment. The World Wide Web Consortium (W3C) standards for web-design and accessibility do not include design features tailored to meet the needs of people recovering from mental illness (W3C, 2005). Instead, these standards concentrate on the machine-dimension of human computer interaction. As such, they focus on web-access protocol development and browser privacy issues. Despite the Web Access Initiative (WAI) there are no web enabled work searching systems designed for people recovering from mental illness (WAI, 2002). e-WRAP was developed to provide a tailor made web based resource to assist people recovering from mental illness gain employment. Project team members were users, carers, practitioners and academics with expertise in the areas of mental health, psychology, social work and information communication technology. The team's first task was user analysis.

User Analysis

Contextual interviews were conducted with people who were recovering from mental illness by observing and discussing the approaches and strategies they used when looking for work. Useful information was gained on work searching strategies and the varied paper and web resources available. Of particular note was the range of web resources accessed designed for the general population and the lack of sites designed specifically for people recovering from mental illness. Valuable information was also gained on type of Internet access and levels of comfort with accessing and navigating these sites, concentration and frustration when using them, as well as the suitability of the content and design features.

Individual interviews were conducted with users as well as experts in the fields of information communication technology, mental health and vocational rehabilitation and employment. These experts were chosen due to their knowledge and experience with the user group. The individual interviews supplemented the contextual interviews with further information provided on web-based employment services designed to provide open, flexible and distributed access for people who may experience difficulty in returning to work after a long absence. An immediate challenge for the project team was to provide evidence of the need for a more specialized web-mediated work searching system designed specifically for people recovering from mental illness if the project was to proceed.

The project team held many focus group meetings with users and experts. An outcome of these meetings was the need to focus on easily accessible information related to employment as well as support and education concerning mental health and well being. This was in order to enhance the self-confidence of people (all age groups) recovering from mental illness who may have been out of work for many years, or have never experienced paid employment. There was general consensus that the design needed to ensure that navigation was kept simple and that a person could take regular breaks and easily return to the site. It was suggested that in order to return to the Login Screen, the user should only need to press a Close button to finish a session. Re-entry should be made possible again by repeating a simple Login procedure. It was suggested that touch screen technology be used to facilitate easy access to information. This meant that the system should function without a keyboard and mouse. The outcome of much discussion with a user focus group, was that the Home Page should welcome the user through an audio greeting that could be toggled to a textual description as an alternative. Key job seeking options were identified during the focus groups.

Task Analysis

A task analysis enabled identification of the processes and tasks associated with the goal of

Figure 1. e-WRAP prototype log in screen (reproduced in McKay & Martin 2007)

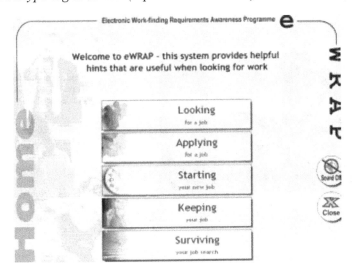

gaining and maintaining suitable employment, as well as promoting and supporting positive mental health and well being. The design was informed by knowledge of the difficulties and frustrations navigating a range of print and electronic work search systems and the absence of any facility designed especially for people recovering from mental illness wanting to re-enter the workforce. Brainstorming assisted in identifying the five key tasks of looking, applying, commencing and keeping work as well as surviving and maintaining motivation and positive self-esteem if unsuccessful. These were developed as the main search menu for site entry and navigation as shown in Figure 1.

Task analysis was used to identify all of the steps involved in each of these activities, informing the development of a persona and scenarios.

Persona

The personal and disciplinary background of members of the project team member led to divergent interests and priorities. A persona proved useful in providing a focus for the project team to develop a more in-depth and shared understanding of what a potential user might look like. A

brainstorming process was used to develop the main features of the persona. A name that could be used for both sexes was originally preferred so as to avoid gender bias in the design. However, it soon became apparent that the persona needed a gender to enable effective communication between team members and to create empathy. Inadvertently team members were referring to the persona as female so this was formalized by naming the persona Jill.

Jill was now the main reference point for all further discussions about the project design and implementation. She came to life not only by name but also in terms of age, gender family, educational background, health and mental health, employment history, housing, socio-economic status and race ethnicity and culture. This was done in a manner that was respectful in the realization that Jill could not possible represent the diversity of people recovering from mental illness who might be looking at returning to work. Figure 2 provides an example of a brief description of a larger persona developed for Jill.

By including several features of disadvantage in the "Jill persona" that are not uncommon to people recovering from mental illness seeking employment, the project team was able to cater

Figure 2. Persona of Jill

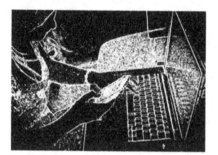

Long-term Unemployed

Jill

Work experience in Bosnia in Travel Agency doing reception and clerical work.

- 26-years-old
- Female
- Single
- Migrated to Australia as a refugee from Bosnia 6 years ago
- No close family in Australia, a few friends
- Lives alone in flat
- Unemployment Benefits
- Has participated in numerous vocational rehabilitation programs
- Comfortable using basic functions on a computer such as e-mail and word processing
- Internet user for basic searches via computers at local library; computer at home without Internet access.
- Diagnosed with schizophrenia six years ago shortly after arriving in Australia. Takes antipsychotic medication daily.

"Everyone has the right to meaningful employment."

Jill spends most of her time looking for work in; newspapers, notice boards at Employment Agencies and searching web based employment sites. She attends a Day Program at a local Community Centre and spends much of her time at home alone. She wants access to "a better quality of life" through paid employment and believes that a regular job will provide her with meaningful activity, an adequate and regular income and social networks.

Key Attributes

- A good organiser
- Hardworking
- Creative
- Concerned about discrimination and stigma of mental illness and racism.

for a wider range of contingency factors in the scenarios developed.

Scenarios

A mapping process assisted in the development of scenarios by identifying Jill's needs, interests and concerns when looking for work and use of ICT. Full scale task scenarios were used to assist Jill achieve particular tasks. For instance, Jill did not have suitable clothes to wear to interviews leading to an additional design feature of information on clothing banks. Elaborated scenarios were written for the five key tasks of "looking, applying, starting, keeping and surviving", identified in the task analysis. A key question was, "What kind of work does Jill want?" with the addition of the search icon "Find My Dream Job" under "Looking For Work." Questions invariably started with "What if?" What if Jill did not want to return to work but simply needed to comply with requirements to keep government benefits?" "What if Jill wants to pursue a career or perhaps she wants a change of career?" Questions were asked around voluntary work vis-à-vis paid employment and the possibility that Jill might need to pursue further education to gain qualifications in the area she wanted to work in. "Was an adequate income a main priority for Jill?" "What was her level of English – written and spoken?" "How had Jill adjusted with issues of resettlement in Australia and possible trauma?" Care was taken to consider all of the possible scenarios that Jill may encounter.

When mentally unwell Jill struggled with motivation, had reduced levels of concentration and an increase in paranoid thoughts and auditory hallucinations contributing to lowered self esteem. Technical aspects were designed so as to be responsive to Jill's mental health and issues of motivation and level of perceptual comfort using e-WRAP. This led to the inclusion of design features that meant Jill could log in and out without losing any data stored as well as addressing issues of privacy. These features were consistent with recommendations made by participants in the focus groups during user analysis. The stigma and discrimination Jill experienced both when seeking employment and in general, as well as already lowered self-esteem, led to the inclusion of design features on dealing with knock backs, general health and well-being, self-care and building self-esteem. Low-cost leisure activities were built into the design in recognition of the loneliness and boredom that Jill experienced, also taking into account the difficulty of managing on a low income. What initially began as an employment focused project broadened into quality of life. Figure 3 shows the menu hierarchy designed for

"Looking for Work".

Touch screen technology was used to design a computer system that was easy to use and tailored to the needs of people recovering from mental illness considering employment. Main features of e-WRAP were design features that were responsive to the difficulties people using the system may experience in relation to motivation, cognition and perception. Pictures, photos, graphics, video streaming and quizzes were used to add variety and make the design interesting, relevant and fun to use. The graphics and images were designed mindful of Jill's mental state.

The instructional designer worked tirelessly to be responsive to the needs identified for Jill to design appropriate screen chattels. For instance, a simple press of each key option was designed to deliver a sub-level menu. The screen chattels were always on display and included: an orientation button (top of screen), audio/text toggle button, page navigation mechanisms: back button (previous screen), a home page button, and the full menu of key job seeking options displayed along the bottom edge of the screen. This framework presented an intuitive/inquisitive approach to information where the user has complete control over where they may wish to go next. In keeping with the 5-star principles of instruction (Merrill 2003) the prototype offered video on demand (Okamoto, Matsui, Inoue & Cristea 2000). These vignettes showed users everyday activities concerning health and safety issues, preparing for an interview, typical job environments, and benefits of socializing at work. Four categories of work were offered; professional, community, health and education, and trades and services. Video On Demand buttons were located beneath each category. The focal point of the prototype was the interactive job selection module with a comprehensive employment knowledge system including job vacancy listings and specific position descriptions (McKay & Martin, 2007).

Figure 3. Looking for work

Reasons for looking	• Have to comply with government requirements • Family pressures • Want a career • Want a regular income • Bored • Lonely
Find my dream	• What I would really love to do? • What I am good at? • What I have you done in the past? • Can I make a career out of this? • Try something new?
What kind of work do I want?	• Don't know • Professional • Technical • Unskilled • Full-time • Part-time
How do I find work?	• Networks • Newspapers • Friends / Family • Internet • Job networks • e-WRAP database
Personality	• Work best on my own • Work best with other people • A quiet workplace • A busy workplace

Usability Testing

A pilot study of e-WRAP was executed over a four month period. Arrangements were made with users to test system components as they were finished progressively. Specific goals were set at each stage of testing to assess; usability problems, user performance in terms of navigation, successful completion of tasks, speed and levels of satisfaction. Preliminary qualitative feedback, including that of several people who were not regular users of computers, was very positive. They found the system easy to use and a helpful resource and were able to relate to the characters in the various Video On Demand vignettes. The prototype was launched at a Mental Health Conference run by the psychiatric disability support sector. This conference attracts a large number of consumers and carers as well as service providers in vocational rehabilitation. A display was set up in the foyer with people able to use e-WRAP at their leisure. Members of the project team were able to observe how people used the navigation system as well as seeking informal and formal feedback. Participants who identified themselves as users, carers, workers, students or academics were asked to complete a short questionnaire on the usefulness and functionality of e-WRAP. Both quantitative and qualitative data was collected on degree of comfort, ease of use, areas for improvement with specific feedback sought on use of video on demand, employer data bases and types of jobs. Respondents were asked what they liked the most about e-WRAP and what they liked the least. Five point rating scales were used to assess levels of satisfaction. Users were asked where they would prefer e-WRAP to be located to ascertain where people would like to access this resource and ultimately whether or not they would use e-WRAP themselves or recommend it to family or friends recovering from mental illness seeking employment.

Observations at the trials and Conference, combined with informal and formal feedback, indicated that users were able to complete tasks with ease and success as well as having high levels of satisfaction. The project team was mindful of the importance of the successful completion of tasks in a timely manner as more significant than reported user satisfaction. Participants acknowledged that whilst there are numerous work search systems available none of these are tailored specifically to the needs of people recovering from mental illness and that e-WRAP is a much needed and welcome resource to assist people recovering from mental illness to achieve their vocational goals. All respondents commented favorably about e-WRAP and supported the idea of developing a live version that included data bases of employers as well as links to all of the other databases indicated in the proto-type.

CONCLUSION

As illustrated in the case scenario of e-WRAP, developing useful and usable Information Communication Technologies for the human services requires in-depth knowledge and understanding of the intended user group. Techniques for user analysis include contextual interviews, individual interviews, online surveys and focus groups. Contextual interviews provide essential information on the intended user group through careful listening and observations of users while they are engaged with the technologies. Individual interviews, online surveys and focus groups allow for more in-depth understanding of users attitudes, beliefs, fears and concerns and the degree to which these are shared amongst members of the user group. Task analysis assists in identifying the processes and tasks associated with project design to achieve the desired outcomes focusing on how users achieve their goals and the steps involved in doing so. Personas aid the design of suitable ICTs by providing a constant reference point for all design decisions on a hypothetical user that embodies the main features of the intended user population. Scenarios based on personas provide greater detail about users' goals and associated tasks, needs and levels of comfort with ICTs. Usability testing throughout all stages of the design process assists in assessing both user performance and preference as data is collected on navigation, successful completion of tasks, speed and levels of satisfaction. This design process facilitates the development and application of information communication technologies that are relevant for the human services. Social workers are encouraged to embrace new technologies to improve service provision and enhance quality of life without compromising ethical standards of practice pertaining to client confidentiality, privacy and self-determination.

REFERENCES

W3C. (2005). *Leading the Web to its full potential.* Retrieved August 19, 2005, from http://www.w3.org

Bloomquist, A., & Arvola, M. (2002). Personas in action: Ethnography in an interaction design team. *Nordic CHI, 12*(23).

Cooper, A. (1999). *The inmates are running the asylum*. UK: Macmillam.

Cooper, A. (2004). *The inmates are running the asylum: Why high tech products drive us crazy and how to restore the sanity* (2nd ed.). UK: Pearson Higher Education.

Freydenson, E. (2002). *Bringing your personas to life in real life*. Retrieved September 9, 2005, from http://boxesandarrows.com/archives/002343.php

Grudin, J., & Pruitt, J. (2002). *Personas, participatory design and product development*. USA: PDC.

Hourihan, M. (2002). *Taking the "you" out of user: My experiencing using personas*. Retrieved September 9, 2005, from http://boxesandarrows.com/archives/002330php

Lang, J. (2007). Crafting a teaching persona. *The Chronicle of Higher Education*, *53*(23), 2.

Martin, J., McKay, E., Hawkins, L., & Murthy, V. (2007). Design-personae: Matching students' learning profiles in Web-based education. In E. McKay (Ed.), *Enhancing learning through human computer interaction*. Hershey, PA: Idea Group Inc.

McKay, E., & Martin, J. (2007). Multidisciplinary collaboration to unravel expert knowledge. In M. Keppell (Ed.), *Instructional design: Case studies in communities of practice*. New York: Information Science Publishing.

Merrill, M. D. (2003). Does your instruction rate 5 stars? In *Proceedings of the eLearning Conference on Design and Development: Instructional Design - Applying first principles of instruction*. Melbourne: Australasian Publications On-Line. Retrieved December 6, 2004, from,http://www.informit.com.au/library/

Okamoto, T., Matsui, T., Inoue, H., & Cristea, A. (2000). A distance-education self-learning support system based on a VOD server. In Kinshuk, C. Jesshope, & T. Okamoto (Eds.), *Proceedings of the International Workshop on Advanced Learning Technologies (IWALT 2000): Advanced Learning Technology: Design and Development Issues* (pp. 71-72). Palmerston North, New Zealand: IEEE Computer Society.

Pruitt, J., & Grudin, J. (2003). *Personas: Practice and theory*. Retrieved January 1, 2008, from http://www.research.microsoft.com/users/jgrudin/publications/personas/Pruitt-Grudin

Ronkko, K. (2005). An empirical study demonstrating how different design constraints, project organization and contexts limited the utility of personas. In *Proceedings of the 38th Conference on System Sciences*, Hawaii.

Ryan, J. (2008). New ways of communicating: How new media is being used to communicate health messages. *Vic Health Letter*, *33*, 16–17.

United States Department of Health & Human Services. (2008). *Your guide to developing useful and usable websites*. Retrieved September 26, 2008, from http://www.usability.gov

WAI. (2002). *Web Access Initiative (WAI): Five primary areas of work*. Retrieved January 3, 2006, from http://www.w3.org/WAI

Chapter 11
Practical Applications of Case Management Software for Practitioners in Health and Human Services

Lesley Cooper
Wilfrid Laurier University, Canada

Dana Fox
Athena Software, Canada

Diane Stanley-Horn
Athena Software, Canada

ABSTRACT

This chapter aims to demonstrate the capabilities and practical applications of a case management software system for not-for-profit organizations. Whilst a variety of software systems are available, for the purposes of this chapter the authors will use/refer to "Penelope," a system designed by Athena, a Kitchener, Ontario software company. Penelope is a sophisticated piece of technology that can collect and analyze information on clients, services, human resources and outcomes. Although a wide range of data can be collected using this software, it cannot make decisions about what to record or how to scrutinize the data. The "what to record" and the "how to analyze and interpret" are management and clinical decisions. Effective use of case management software requires technical, management and analytical skills combined with leadership and imagination. Case management software systems and the information they provide are only as good as the planning and organizational systems in which they are used. The best starting point for practitioners and managers seeking answers to questions about their clients, services, community and policy, and to maximize the capabilities of case management software systems is the development and application of a program logic model unique to the agency in question. A program logic model focuses on the services and programs provided by the agency describing its' inputs, activities, outputs and outcomes. Understanding how to develop and apply their model allows practitioners and managers to perform tasks such as performance monitoring, experimental and quasi experimental approaches program evaluations, and client satisfaction and outcome studies to demon-

DOI: 10.4018/978-1-60566-735-5.ch011

strate the effectiveness of their services to funding bodies, consumer groups, and their boards of directors whilst also providing a tool that can be used to enhance agency performance.

'To err is human but to really foul things up requires a computer'. -- Farmers' Almanac for 1978 'Capsules of Wisdom' in Oxford Dictionary of Quotations (2004, p.670:70).

INTRODUCTION

Case management software programs enable organizations to collect data describing their client population and service provision as well as the outcomes and effectiveness of these services. These programs facilitate agency collection of data about clients and the services provided to them and may be extended to enabling communication, scheduling, billing, clinical notes and evaluation tools. Case management software systems may be purchased as a propriety package or designed in house by organizations to manage their client service data. For the purposes of this chapter, we will confine our comments to the Penelope Case Management Software developed by Athena Software, based in Kitchener, Ontario. This package was designed for health and human service agencies and is based on traditional concepts of case management. In this chapter we will describe Athena's Penelope and use it to demonstrate its' capabilities and practical applications in needs studies, program evaluation, quasi experimental designs demonstrating outcomes and efficacious services.

We will focus on the practical applications of case management software for a variety of reasons. Studies on the not for profit sector reveal that agencies collect data about clients and their programs. This data collection process is traditionally paper based frequently imposing an ever increasing administrative burden with organizations committing time and substantial resources to meet the specific needs of funders rather than those of the organization and its clients. Eakin (2007, p.1) in a

review of accountability and compliance requirements in Canada asserts that *nonprofits are swept up in complex, time consuming and very detailed accountability reporting systems and controls.* Whilst meeting funders' requirements, many not for profit agencies are unable to transform the data into a form suitable for purposes more immediately useful to them. These purposes encompass grant proposal development, program evaluation, fiscal monitoring, project planning, and enhancing their understanding of social problems as well as assisting with day to day management issues. Few organizations employ specialist staff to advise on using and analyzing existing data. Instead of hiring skilled staff to perform these tasks in house, they are likely to use external agencies and consultants at great expense. In this situation, the not-for-profits are at the mercy of the funders' demands and perceptions and the consultant's model of good evaluations. The clear view from the not for profit perspective is that they collect data required by their funders, but are not able to utilize this data for internal purposes because they are overstretched. Not for profits are caught in a dilemma. On one hand they are expected to collect data but on the other, the demands and costs of compliance with funder accountability requirements mean that there is little time or in-house skill to use the data for management and evaluation.

ACCOUNTABILITY REQUIREMENTS

The not for profit sector faces particular challenges from funding bodies which are increasingly requiring greater accountability. This accountability has two components traditional financial accountability and, increasingly, measurement of outcomes. There are rising expectations that services will be targeted at those most in need. These expectations are held by funding bodies including government and community foundations. Quite simply, funding bodies want a return on their investments. To meet these requirements organizations need access to sophisticated information systems that allow ease of data collection and the statistical and analytical capacity to use these systems to best advantage.

The United Way of America (1997) has provided an overview of various accountability demands in the sector over the past 25 to 30 years. Accountability initially focused on fiscal responsibility and documentation of how funds were spent; this focus remains a fundamental concern. A focus on the products or outputs of programs was the next step. These new measures included the number of products delivered (e.g. counseling sessions) and the number of people assisted. Whilst products delivered and people assisted are important and useful statistics, they are crude indicators of quality of service delivery. Over time, funders have focused more on service standard measures that demonstrate and ensure the quality of services and adherence to standards. Some of these standard measures include staff qualifications, staff-client ratios, specific service practices, record keeping and privacy protection. With recent reductions in health and welfare budgets, there has been a shift from looking at standards to addressing whether services were targeted to those most in need. Agencies are increasingly required to provide data that demonstrates services are delivered to those who most need them.

Key Performance Indicators (KPI's) and client satisfaction studies are more recent developments. Key performance indicators were developed by public accounting firms and include ratios of inputs, services, outputs and total costs. Client satisfaction measures have also been developed as part of overall quality assurance measures. These latter measures seek the views of clients on a range of variables including accessibility and customer satisfaction. They provide information to funders about the agency and its operations. Unfortunately

these newer measures do not tell funders about the effectiveness of funded programs and whether clients are better or worse off. The current focus has moved to measurement of program outcomes and benefits for clients. Funders are now seeking quantitative results and evidence from agencies that demonstrate their service effectiveness.

Evidence of changing accountability requirements can be found by "googling" funding guidelines. Several community foundations, as part of their funding application process, ask questions about inputs, activities, outputs, and outcomes (short, medium and long term). Implicit in this request is a program logic approach. They also ask applicants to provide evidence that their proposed intervention is the most effective one to use for the intended beneficiaries. This suggests the importance of measuring outcomes, i.e., a move towards evidence based practice and research. For example, the US Department of Justice, Drug Court Discretionary Grant Program provides funding for non-violent substance abusers with a goal to reduce substance abuse and recidivism of offenders. Agencies funded under this program must provide data to measure the results of their work which includes the percent of participants who re-offend while participating in the drug court program. Specifically this means total number of participants, the number arrested on drug-related charges, the number arrested on non-drug related charges and the number of clients with drug court program violations. The funding body also wants quantitative data on clients who have successfully participated in programs. Compliance with these measures requires good information systems and the analytical skills of staff.

One recently emerging and dramatic pressure on both for profit and not for profit organizations comes from the managed care approach. Here traditional fee for service arrangements are replaced by a system where costs and services are controlled by limiting the amount and type of services provided. The focus is on reducing the costs whilst simultaneously improving quality of care by collecting and using evidence on the effectiveness of clinical interventions. For example, take a person receiving treatment funded by /an insurance company following a car accident. In earlier times, this patient may have been able to receive physiotherapy, massage therapy and chiropractic care simultaneously. This would be a costly arrangement and, as these services were provided concomitantly neither the insurance company nor the therapists themselves would know what particular interventions were successful or to what degree. By taking a managed care approach and monitoring costs and services, insurance companies might now recommend that service providers begin with one therapeutic intervention and only introduce other services after a period of time where the efficacy is demonstrated or where there is a demonstrable need and evidence to provide additional services.

In the managed care environment, providers are expected to have and adhere to explicit practice standards, to review the way their services are utilized and to address quality improvement in their work with clients. This places demands on practice management and is only possible with good electronic information systems. The managed care revolution requires that agencies and practitioners keep accurate patient records, manage their billing, write clear statements about the client's problem and set clear therapeutic goals and outcomes, develop research skills and adhere to standards of practice and established clinical protocols for a variety of clinical problems. There are parallels in the mental health system where Gregoire and Jungers (2007, p.735) expect that counselors need to provide 'a good treatment plan that includes the following elements: a clear statement of the client's problem, specific goals with measurable criteria and time frames for completion of the goals, and a clear statement of the means to be used to achieve these goals'. The elements of a good treatment plan fit with the components of the logic model as described later in this chapter.

ADMINISTRATIVE BURDENS

The process for applying and reporting on funding adds to an agencies administrative burden. In a study of not for profits in Ontario, Eakin (2007) asked agencies to rate the complexity of funding application and reporting processes from simple to complex. A simple application proposal is short with readily accessible information and straightforward program descriptions, whilst a complex proposal has time constraints, requires specific data that is not readily available and specificity on programs and outcomes. In reporting on funding, simple reporting processes require readily available information while extreme reporting requires data that is difficult to obtain, requires exercise of both management and clinical judgment, much additional data and is demanding of staff time. Many not for profit agencies rated the application and reporting process as extreme with few rating them as simple. This reporting process is made more difficult when organizations receive funding from multiple sources thus having numerous reporting requirements. All this takes time and expertise that few agencies are equipped to deal with.

Privacy legislation in Australia (*Privacy Act 1988*) and similar provisions in other countries require compliance with client information management standards which take account of the importance of data security and data quality, provide capacity for individuals to access and correct their personal information whilst emphasizing care in the use of sensitive information. Management information systems such as case management software programs allow organizations to collect and present information to funding bodies whilst maintaining compliance with such legislative demands.

In the health sector, evidence based practice is a standard professional expectation. Evidence based practice is the *conscientious, explicit, and judicious use of current best evidence in making decisions about the care of individual patients* (Sackett, Rosenberg, Gray, Haynes and Richardson 1996, p.71). It brings together integration of clinical expertise and compassionate care of patients with the best available evidence from research. Whilst its utility in health care has been clearly demonstrated, the development of evidence based practice in the human services is in its infancy. There are, nevertheless, promising ways in which this approach can be used for improving knowledge about service and provider users, practitioners, organizations, policy and research (Johnson & Austin 2006). It is expected that evidence based practice and research will be increasingly used in response to greater accountability requirements made by funders leading to specific demands for: outcomes measurement, increasing availability of expertise and resources for evidence based practice, and rising expectations that the not for profit organizations will manage for results.

Managed care is practiced in Canada and the USA and to a lesser extent in other countries. There are, nevertheless, pressures on all not for profit organizations to use aggregated program data to demonstrate their effectiveness. Local foundations are an increasing source of program funding for the not for profit sector. On one hand foundations with tax exemptions are expected to demonstrate results to governments and in turn, foundations demand efficiencies and outcomes from recipient organizations. Governments are result oriented, requiring information from the not for profits sector about their program, progress against objectives and specific results. They now demand that funded programs demonstrate achievement of particular outcomes and outputs as well as effective, efficient and efficacious services. Many organizations are required to achieve these requirements and conduct their own evaluations in order to receive ongoing funding. If not for profits do not have the internal capacity to undertake these evaluations, they may need to hire external consultants, an expensive exercise. Large not for profit organizations receive funding from multiple sources including federal, state, regional or local

organizations with increasingly complex, and possibly overlapping reporting requirements. Unless organizations have, or are able to purchase the analytical and research capacity to separate inputs, activities and outcomes from various programs and transform this data into specific results, their ongoing funding may be jeopardized.

Despite these demands, governments and private funders in the US were generally dissatisfied with the research data that organizations provided to justify grant proposals and support evaluations (Stoeckler 2007, p.111). Funding is not a right or entitlement in the non-government sector. Acceptance of funding means responsibility. Funders expect that services will be directed and targeted to those most in need. It is assumed that there will be fiscal responsibility, accountability for funding and measurement of outcomes. Quality standards are expected, these including use of service protocols, adherence to practice standards, appropriate use of qualified staff, participation in quality assurance, and meeting accreditation standards. Finally governments expect that, wherever possible, practice is based on demonstration of effectiveness. Whilst these are the funding bodies' expectations it does not mean that these bodies will necessarily pay for costs associated with achieving accountability.

In summary, funder demands for greater accountability are outpacing the technical and research capacity of the not for profit sector resulting in many agencies being unable to meet the specific accountability and program evaluation demands of funders. How then can case management software be used to address funders' demands for program monitoring purposes and to develop and address the effectiveness of services? Case management software is a tool providing an organization the capacity to manage, evaluate and monitor programs, research and plan services. The utility of the software is a significant human resource consideration. It may be necessary for agencies to spend money to save money, in other words to weigh up the costs and benefits. The training and development costs could be amortized over time whilst there will be savings with a move from paper based and error prone system to collation and analysis done by the system.

To fully realize the value of software programs, their introduction requires leadership, the organizational readiness to change and the research capacity of staff to maximize the utility of information systems. The introduction of software may also entail a significant diversion of staff from management, administration and service provision to participate in the necessary training.

PENELOPE

Penelope by Athena Software is a feature-rich and flexible case management and client information management solution for mental health and human service providers. The software brings together billing, clinical documentation and outcome management - into a secure and easily implemented web-based package. Penelope is a client-centric system that captures the spectrum of services a client may be receiving, from individual, family and group clinical services to educational and preventive programs. A wealth of demographic, referral, risk and bio-psycho-social information can be collected and custom recovery plans can be built into the system. In addition, the MIS (Management Information System) captures progress notes, signature forms and attachments such as images and external documentation.

At an enterprise level system, Penelope not only accommodates hundreds of concurrent users but facilitates coordination of care through assignment of providers to cases. This provider assignment can encompass different models ranging from primary or multiple providers for a single service, a multi-disciplinary team approach or a single pairing approach for one-to-many services. The integrated scheduler component captures service provision through time and also coordinates service among administrative and clinical staff; an

(optional) integrated billing function accommodates a complex variety of funding and payment scenarios with efficiency and ease. Users, from clinical service providers, to reception, billing staff and management have user-defined authorized access to various aspects of the system and benefit from the specific workflow and reporting features relevant to them. By integrating all components of service provision whilst customizing the user experience the system is extremely efficient and easy to use. With little to no duplicate data entry a wealth of information can be captured. Penelope can be used to report on a wealth of information of interest to the organization as a whole in addition to complete individual case files. Program and funding utilization statistics and client and program outcomes can be related to such service characteristics as length and/or frequency of service, participation in and/or receipt of multiple services, presenting needs/diagnoses, staff and staff caseloads and attributes (qualifications, specializations), demographic variables and more. Such powerful reporting allows organizations to identify strengths and gaps in service, identify and secure recurring and additional funding opportunities and monitor progress towards internal benchmarks. This chapter will focus on this particular aspect of the software.

Core Features

The case file is a central component of the practice information system in all health and human service agencies. In a paper based office, these files hold personal and service information about individual clients and their families. The case file is also a key component in the case management software environment being stored and managed electronically rather than in a file room or cabinet.

In a case management software environment, files are based on individuals participating in, or receiving services from the agency. When an agency accepts a client referral and provides a service, the agency collects, as part of the intake

Figure 1. Individual information

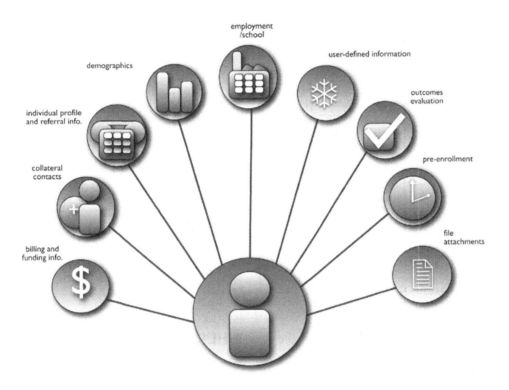

process, information about that individual client. This includes personal identifying and demographic information such as age, address, family size and structure, school information, income and education. The reason for referral is also a critical part of the intake process with details of the referring agency or worker, a critical part of this process being recorded in the data base. In some agencies, information about insurers or account information will also be included. Figure 1 shows the range of information that might be collected about an individual.

Table 1 shows the possible range of information for collection. Whilst user defined variables are not shown in the diagrams these variables comprise data and information unique to the agency and client group, for example in a child protection agency user defined variables may include notifications of child abuse, name and demographic information about those reporting, and reasons for reporting.

This agency may also include information about foster care arrangements, names of carers and respite care arrangements.

Demographic information is supplemented by narrative documents including intake summaries, presenting information, treatment or recovery plans, progress assessment reports, details of incoming and outgoing telephone calls, social history, service provision, intervention and summary statements. The case file provides information about the individual client, case documents, intake summary and referral information and file attachments containing essential information necessary for working effectively with clients as illustrated in Figure 2.

Workers can use the system to schedule activities and appointments, and log information about whether the client has attended their appointments. Although many agencies do not bill clients or insurers, the program incorporates a system that is

Table 1. Range of information for collection

Individual profile	Demographic information	Collateral contact information	Billing / account information
First / last name Date of birth Gender Address Post code Country Phone details Site of service Contact instructions Referral source	Educational attainment Employment status Occupational type Income source Income range New Australian Country of birth Citizenship status	Full name Relationship Organization Address Post code Phone	Total invoiced Total applied receipts Total unapplied receipts Total applied write offs Balance Transaction history Debits Credits
Employment / school information	**Outcomes evaluation information**	**Pre-enrollment information**	**File attachments**
Employer name Work contact Address Phone Email Work comments	Pre / mid / post stage evaluation Surveys completed	Reasons for waiting Waiting for program Waiting for worker Comments Waiting since	Letters Reports Documents of any data type

able to invoice and record payments, track billable services and provide for single and batch invoicing and provide summary financial information.

INFORMATION DOMAINS

Although the Penelope case management information system provides information about individuals and cases that can enable practitioners to manage their case loads effectively and efficiently, the system, more importantly allows aggregation of information into many domains. Put simply information is collected about individual clients at the case level, program and services level and at the activity level. These information domains with examples of associated outcomes are illustrated in Table 2.

Aggregated data allows agencies to use data in a variety of different ways to serve the needs of clients, management of human and financial resources, assessing client satisfaction, program planning and managing funding requirements. Given its simplicity of use the package presents may opportunities for agencies.

WHERE TO START?

Information domains provide a conceptual framework for the collection of standard demographic and user defined information. This is the easy part of the journey. The transition from information collection to management and utilization of this information is more challenging for agencies. The transition from data collection to using data for monitoring and analysis of programs should not be feared by administrators or practitioners. It is helpful to start with some very simple questions and link these ideas to concepts and strategies in the literature.

• What are our questions about our programs? Practitioners have exploratory questions about the services provided and administrators have questions about the use of agency resources to deliver these programs. Both have questions about clients, services to community and policy. These are who, what, how and why questions. They are the questions of interest to the agency and not questions imposed by funders.

Figure 2. Individual and case file information

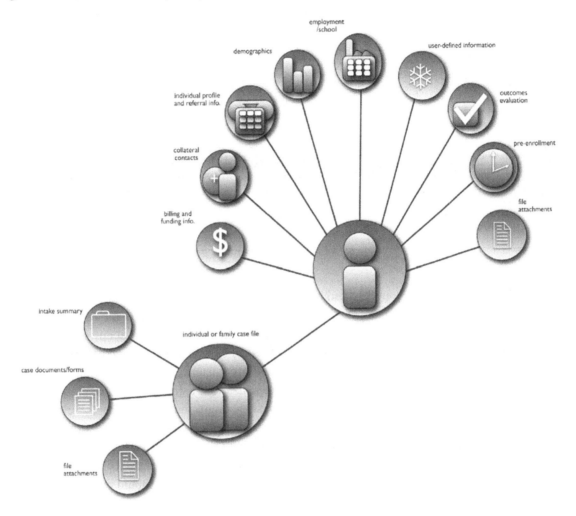

- What questions do we have about our services to clients and community and how do we measure the work we do? At the most simple level these questions relate to performance monitoring. The issues for consideration are what information is collected and how do we interpret the information in the agency.
- What are trying to achieve in our agency? This is a deliberate question about the intentions of programs and services, and expectations about the outcomes we hope to accomplish. These simple questions link to the idea of the program logic model, a map

which is unique to every agency and program. What we are trying to achieve should fit with agency plans, funding submissions and formal evaluations.

- How do we demonstrate the effectiveness of our intervention and use these results to change services? This is a research question. This process can be more complicated and exhaustive when combined with complex analytical and interpretative approaches.

We therefore have four types of questions: exploratory, monitoring and interpretative, in-

Table 2. Information domains

Clinical domain	Service delivery domain	Outcomes evaluations domain
Personal and family information Demographic data Employment data Collateral contact information User defined information Case documentation and notes Clinical activities	Case load statistics Activity status statistics Activity statistics Program specific statistics Presenting issue statistics Case flow statistics	Client self ratings at pre, mid, and post stages of service Percentage change over time Frequency distribution over time Qualitative feedback Client satisfaction results Outcomes reporting by program and funder13
Billing accounting information	**External reporting domain**	**Human resources domain**
Client fees / funder invoices Payments and write offs Subsidy / sliding scale information Program-specific accounting Account aging	Funder specific reporting Program specific reporting Aggregate reporting Population specific reporting	Worker hours – indirect, direct, non-case Activity status by worker Activity types by worker Case load / worker capacity data Worker involvement in specific program Billable hours

tentions and evaluative. Before understanding these questions, it is necessary to understand the concept of the program logic model which assists in understanding these questions.

Logic Model

In simple language, a logic model is a graphic representation used as a guide to convey what agency services are intending to achieve. This guide, unique to every agency provides a mechanism to communicate to funders, researchers and community about services and outcomes. At a more formal level, Frechtling (2007, p.1) defines a logic model as a 'tool that describes the *theory of change* underlying an intervention, product or policy'. This theory of change simply means that when resources and activities are combined in particular ways they will lead to intended outcomes for clients. *If* a particular set of actions are prepared, *then* specific results are expected. These logic models are important aids to assist organizations in applying for grants as they clarify the intended purpose, activities, outputs and outcomes. In addition, these models provide a framework for developing an evaluation study, setting a framework for the information to be

collected and also documenting the intervention and how it worked. Logic models are not fixed as they can be developed at any time during the life cycle of the program and can be modified if the circumstances of the program change. For organizations using a case management software system, logic models provide the elements for data collection enabling compilation of relevant information, and a focus for analysis. Although this chapter will focus on technological aspects of the logic model, it should be remembered that developing logic models is a collaborative endeavor and a dynamic process involving agency staff and other stakeholders. Over time, the logic model used may need revision as practitioners work with the clients and develop new practice knowledge of activities and outcomes.

Logic model components are simple and include inputs, activities, outputs and outcomes. The inputs are resources which are brought to a program including financial, material and human resources. Some programs may have multiple funding sources whilst human resource can include volunteer support, in kind assistance or partnerships with other agencies. Activities are those action steps taken in the program to achieve its stated goals and outputs. Outputs are the results of the program such as products, services and reports produced. Outcomes are the changes to people and situations resulting from the activities and indicate that the aims of the program have been achieved. Documentation of these outcomes provides evidence of the success of the program. Outcomes can be written as short term, medium term and longer term. It is not possible here to address issues in developing program logic models but substantial online resources are available from such organizations as the United Way, Kellogg Foundation as well as print material (Frechtling 2007; Wholey, Hatry & Newcomer 2004).

Although the logic model is a clearly structured approach, its development is a dynamic and iterative process that requires involvement of all staff and takes place over time. McLaughlin and Jordan (2004, p.15) suggest that managers regard the logic model as a process that involves both program participants and other stakeholders associated with the model's implementation. Above all logic modeling is part of long term cultural change. Understanding the program logic model is fundamental in demonstrating outcome measures to funders, preparation of grant application and using data in other forms of inquiry.

The program logic model provides a structure for demonstrating outcomes to funders, a framework for funding applications, and a series of questions for formative and summative program evaluation. As a theory of change is embedded in the logic model, the model with associated outcomes allow for testing of the effectiveness of the change strategy. The particular value of the program logic model lies in program evaluation, a process that includes:

- Development of a conceptual model of the program and identification of key evaluation points
- Development of evaluation questions and definition of measurable outcomes
- Development of an evaluation design
- Collection of data

- Analysis of data
- Provision of information to interested audiences (Frechtling 2007, p.127).

WHAT ARE THE EXPLORATORY QUESTIONS ABOUT OUR PROGRAMS?

This is something that practitioners and administrators do every day although they may not describe this as an investigative, analytical and/or interpretative process. Questions about practice emerge because practitioners and administrators have hypotheses about practice and want confirmation of their intuition. There are many questions that practitioners and management may ask on a day to day basis. Generally, the software program enables practitioners and administrators to use data collected to provide the answers. Listed below are examples of the questions that may be asked.

Questions about services to clients

- How long is our waiting list?
- How quickly do we respond to urgent cases?
- How many hours of service do we provide per client?
- What is the demographic profile of our client group?
- What is the diversity of our client populations?
- How many cases of elder or child abuse have we received?
- What sorts of complaints do we receive from clients about our services?
- How many clients return for further assistance?
- What are the most common problems experienced by our clients?
- What are the health and social risk factors of our clients?
- What sort of health and mental health problems go together?

- What are the most intractable mental health concerns experienced by our clients?

Questions about resources

- How many years of experience do agency staff have?
- What is the range of staff qualifications?
- What is a reasonable workload for staff in a particular service area?
- What is the cost of group work activities and individual therapy?
- How many hours of supervision per year are provided to new and experienced staff?
- What is the cost per person attending training programs?
- Are some staff more effective in working with some clients than with others?

Questions about the agency in the community

- How does our client service profile compare to similar agencies?
- What are the social problems in the neighborhoods served by our agency?
- What are the most urgent unmet needs identified by the clients and community?
- What is the network of referrals and how do we work with these agencies?

Questions about policy

- How does a particular social policy impact on the clients in the agency?
- What are the challenges for clients in accessing health and welfare services such as housing, health services or income support?
- Does the allocation of resources for services match the costs of delivering those services?

The above questions are useful but they need to be linked to a commitment on the part of the agency to engage in measuring and monitoring performance and outcomes. There are several steps in this process including:

- Obtaining and holding the support of managers and stakeholders
- Identifying the questions that the agency wants answered
- Defining the criteria to use in answering those questions
- Understanding the data that needs to be collected
- Determining how that data is to be presented and analyzed.

The steps in beginning this process are elaborated by Wholey (2004) using the concept of evaluability assessment, that is a process undertaken by the agency to determine what evaluations might be useful, explore what evaluations would be feasible and design evaluations.

WHAT ARE THE MONITORING AND INTERPRETATIVE QUESTIONS ABOUT THE WORK WE DO?

Administrators and practitioners also have questions about the quality of their services and programs and rely on quantitative descriptive accounts to track and monitor performance on a regular basis. These questions may relate to resource management, outputs, activities, productivity, service quality, customer satisfaction (Poister 2004). This information can assist agencies to manage for results. Although the data is descriptive, it can also supplement more complex evaluative tools.

Performance monitoring is an important tool in the management and planning of services bringing together collection of data, accountability requirements, theories of social change and performance monitoring measures. The aim of performance monitoring is to track performance in a timely and scheduled manner using a range of measures related to agency programs providing information to managers, stakeholders and policy makers. It can assist agencies to assess how a program is operating and the extent to which program objectives are being achieved in the service delivery. Where objectives are not fully achieved, performance monitoring can assist in rethinking aspects of delivery. Performance monitoring uses client satisfaction measures and can report on cost effectiveness and productivity.

Performance monitoring may be imposed by funders to compare services or deliberately used by agencies as part of their operations. For example; in the Australia health care system, performance monitoring is imposed with hospitals required to measure and report indicators such as patient waiting time for elective surgery or the number of patients who wait longer than 24 hours in emergency. Within a human service agency, similar measures track can what is happening with program outcomes. Measures collected are descriptive and it is not possible to attribute causation. The value of some measures can also be challenged. For example, the size of a case load may not reflect the actual workload of individual practitioners as some cases are complex and other cases have a relatively simple intervention. Similarly, the length of a hospital waiting list may mean that there is a very effective early detection of problems rather than a queue of more serious problems. Once these measures have been developed and there is clarity about their reliability, they can then be used in a variety of different ways by the agency including;

- Use of particular resources used in program areas (e.g. number of support workers needed to care for an older person in their home)
- Output measures (number of cases or clients serviced)

- Productivity measures (cost per investigation of child abuse)
- Service quality especially turnaround time, accessibility, safety, waiting time for diagnostic assessment or time from application for a pension or benefit until a decision is made and provided to the customer
- Outcomes or the extent to which a program is effective
- Cost effectiveness or the ratio of costs to outcomes (cost per discharged consumer)
- Customer satisfaction (for various aspects of service delivery such as therapy, financial assistance, child care or home help) (Poister 2004, pp.99-102).

Much of the information described above can be taken directly from the data management system. The data can be raw numbers, percentages, averages, or indexes which are generally composites representing a particular characteristic. Some performance measures require additional information for collection but this can be part of the intake, assessment and intervention process. This can include questionnaires such as the Health Status Questionnaire, measures of risk factors, social functioning, observations by therapists, follow up data on clients after a set period and surveys. It is important to bear in mind that measures should be specific and oriented to results, understandable, and be reliable, (objective and dependable) and valid (fair and unbiased).

WHAT DO WE INTEND TO ACHIEVE?

Software management programs provide agencies with a tool to record information about their clients and services and then use this information deliberately for a variety of administrative and research purposes. Unfortunately, many social service organizations do not utilize software management programs or management information systems to their full potential if indeed they do possess such programs. Stoecker (2007) notes that not for profits collect a lot of data but do not use much of the data collected. One step in effectively using the tool is to think systematically about programs delivered by the agencies asking what in particular is this program intended to achieve and with what results for the client group. The name given to this approach is the logic model and here agencies specify inputs, activities, outputs and outcomes.

Interpretative Approaches to Outcomes

The program logic model is quantitative in orientation. There are also qualitative evaluative approaches rather than quantitative using interpretative orientations guided by social constructivist theories. Here participants create their own understanding based on past and current experiences alone and in collaboration with others. This interpretative model allows practitioners, to learn as they proceed with the program and modify and adapt according to the clients and issues faced along the way with outcomes developed through the process rather than planned before the program commences. It is particularly relevant in service delivery when the services and problems are complex.

Although interpretive models are qualitative, there is logic to interpretative evaluation with stages that include engagement, discovery, sense making and unfolding (Netting, O'Connor & Fauri 2008, p.136). These stages are not necessarily sequential but more of a spiral progression. The process of engagement and relationship building with diverse groups, discovery and sense making happens simultaneously with a deepening of understanding with the development. Information collected in this process comes from multiple sources including qualitative and quantitative data, narratives from logs or case studies, observations, views of all participants or even the discovery of tensions and ambiguities.

When using interpretative approaches, accountability and the use of information systems pose special challenges. Funders may not like these approaches because outcomes are not clearly quantifiable and therefore hard to evaluate and compare with similarly funded programs. Nevertheless, it is possible to meet funder accountability requirements using information systems. The emergent interpretative models rely on description and documentation of multiple views, relationship building, understanding of complexity, consensus building processes, options and possibilities and the learning process. These can be documented in reflective journals, narratives of critical incidents, day journals, contact logs, methods journals, notes of meetings, and transcripts of significant meetings. These can be supplemented with various forms of quantitative data. Case management software programs can be used to store this data, make and edit notes. They can be stored in the system and retrieved for analysis by exporting them to such programs as NVIVO.

HOW DO WE EVALUATE THE EFFECTIVENESS OF OUR WORK?

There are three ways to demonstrate effectiveness: experimental, quasi experimental designs and evaluations that examine impact. Generally these evaluations are done by large scale organizations rather than the small not for profit. The gold standard for effectiveness studies is experimental randomized studies. These require that participants are randomly assigned to either a treatment group or a non treatment group, called the control group. Generally, these studies are difficult to implement. The outcomes of these groups are then compared to determine the impact of the service or intervention. Quasi experimental designs are similar to experimental designs and are more common because the allocation of subjects to groups is not random. There are several variations of randomized designs including time series based on repeated measures, before and after comparisons and post program comparisons. Finally, effectiveness is evaluated by examining changes in risk or outcomes amongst the client populations. Risk factors that include for example mental health or general health problems are measured to determine the impact of the program.

CASE MANAGEMENT SOFTWARE AND REPORTING

Software programs provide a mechanism for information collection. Penelope software allows tracking of client activity from demographic characteristics of the population and program related perspectives to clinical outcomes. A wide variety of reports can be used to answer basic practice and administrative questions and to allow performance monitoring. Custom surveys can easily be built into the system by users. In addition, the Penelope case management software system includes public domain outcome and evaluation templates that can be used in outcome studies and for inclusion in quasi experimental designs and randomized experimental studies. Examples include Brief Psychiatric Rating Scale, General Satisfaction Survey, Hamilton Anxiety Rating Scale, Global Assessment of Functioning Scale, and Family/Couple Outcomes Survey. Proprietary scales can also be used with this software.

Although this software is both powerful and flexible, the introduction and ongoing management of performance measures, outcome studies and the incorporation of experimental studies does present challenges for organizations. The United Way of America (2000) recognizing that many not for profit organizations were using performance monitoring, required the development of outcome measures as part of funding requirements. They followed up many funded organization with a survey examining the impact of this requirement. Many agencies identified outcome measurement as helpful as it enhanced record keeping and

facilitated success in competing for additional funding and resources. On the other hand they identified lack of access to technical resources to solve problems and inadequate software and staff time to complete these requirements.

Introduction and effective use of case management software systems, such as Penelope will take time. There are some fundamental requirements including the involvement of all staff and stakeholders in the planning, and the support of senior management and the board of directors. Data collection methods, analysis and interpretation of results may need to be supported with additional technical expertise. The system is developed on a trial and error basis with a process of testing, evaluating and making improvements before it meets the needs of management, practitioners and funding bodies. Once established, improvements and modification will also be required. Throughout this process, a range of problems will be presented especially in relation to the quality of agency records. Hatry (2004) identified issues in relation to missing and incomplete data, aggregated data where information is not classified into useful and pertinent categories, quality control for the reasonableness of data and privacy issues.

THE FUTURE

Demonstration of effectiveness using management information systems is here to stay. Software programs to support these initiatives will increasingly be adopted with funder demands and as organizations effectively using such systems will gain competitive funding advantages. Effective software solutions in the human services sector will be ones that address a combination of priorities including cost effectiveness, ease of use, user and system security, decision support and evaluative support. In addition, flexible systems that can accommodate the diverse needs, best practices and specific logic models of human service organizations will have the greatest impact on their success.

There will be an increased public accountability for funding. This will go beyond financial accountability to include service quality and service outcomes. Performance indicators and programs outcomes are likely to be made more public enabling comparisons to be made by the clients they serve. Savvy consumers may elect to attend programs which can demonstrate the best outcomes. This is already occurring in the health sector with use of service indicators such as infection rates of particular hospitals and the community. Scrutiny of performance and outcome measures for funded programs will be undertaken with attention to the relevance, rigor, and interpretation. For example some funding bodies already specify the measures required as part of funding. With this data they are able to make comparisons between the costs and service outcomes. They may use this knowledge to determine future funding. Benchmarking is a process that allows funders to compare performances, outcomes and associated costs for similar services. It allows examination of performance in particular periods of time, outcomes for different target groups, variations of service delivery and performance in similar organizational structures and geographical areas (Pathfinder 2003). Funders may well classify services according to what they interpret as a "good" performance although such a classification system would need to done with some care as different client groups, neighborhoods or populations may exhibit different results.

CONCLUSION

Case management software programs are sophisticated tools with practical capabilities enabling improved management performance and demonstration of outcomes. At a basic level, these software programs facilitate collection of data about clients. Agencies that do not go beyond

data collection are under utilizing the system's capabilities and not getting a return on their investments. With increased accountability requirements from funders, there are expectations that the not for profit sector will need to demonstrate outcomes for clients. This chapter, using Penelope case management software as an illustration has provided practical examples of the way agencies can make the transition from data collection to performance monitoring and demonstration of effectiveness.

REFERENCES

Bureau of Justice Assistance. (2008). *Drug court discretionary grant program*. Retrieved October 31, 2008, from http://www.ojp.usdoj.gov/BJA/grant/drugcourts.html

Commonwealth of Australia. Privacy Act 1988. Canberra: AGPS.

Eakin, L. (2007). *We can't afford to do business this way: A study of the administrative burden resulting from funder accountability and compliance practices*. Toronto, Canada: Wellesley Institute.

Frechtling, J. A. (2007). *Logic modeling methods in program evaluation*. San Francisco: Jossey Bass.

Gregoire, J., & Jungers, C. (2007). *The counseling companion*. Mahwah, NJ: Lawrence Erlbaum.

Hatry, H. H. (2004). Using agency records. In J. S. Wholey, H. P. Hatry, & K. E. Newcomer (Eds.), *Handbook of practical program evaluation*. San Francisco: Jossey Bass.

Johnson, M., & Austin, M. (2006). Evidence-based practice in the social services: Implications for organizational change. *Administration in Social Work, 30*(3), 75–104. doi:10.1300/J147v30n03_06

McLaughlin, J. A., & Jordan, G. B. (2004). Using logic models. In J. S. Wholey, H. P. Hatry, & K. E. Newcomer (Eds.), *Handbook of practical program evaluation.* San Francisco: Jossey Bass.

Netting, F. E., O'Connor, M. K., & Fauri, D. P. (2008). *Comparative approaches to program planning.* Hoboken, NJ: John Wiley.

Pathfinder. (2003). *Guidance on outcomes focused management: Supporting paper: Benchmarking using outcomes information.* Retrieved October 31, 2008, from http://io.ssc.govt.nz/pathfinder/documents/pathfinder-benchmarking.pdf

Poister, T. H. (2004). Performance monitoring. In J. S. Wholey, H. P. Hatry, & K. E. Newcomer (Eds.), *Handbook of practical program evaluation.* San Francisco: Jossey Bass.

Sackett, D. L., Rosenberg, W. M. C., Gray, J. M. J., Haynes, R. B., & Richardson, W. S. (1996). Evidence based medicine: What it is and what it isn't. *BMJ (Clinical Research Ed.), 312,* 71–72.

Stoecker, R. (2007). The research practices and needs of non-profit organizations in an urban center. *Journal of Sociology and Social Welfare, 34*(4), 97–119.

United Way of America. (1997). *Outcome measurement: Showing results in the nonprofit sector.* Retrieved October 31, 2008, from http://www.liveunited.org/Outcomes/Library/ndpaper.cfm

United Way of America. (2000). *Agency experience with outcome measures: Survey findings.* Retrieved October 31, 2008, from http://www.liveunited.org/Outcomes/Resources/What/upload/agencyom.pdf

Wholey, J. S. (2004). Evaluability assessment. In J. S. Wholey, H. P. Hatry, & K. E. Newcomer (Eds.), *Handbook of practical program evaluation.* San Francisco: Jossey Bass.

Wholey, J. S., Hatry, H. P., & Newcomer, K. E. (2004). *Handbook of practical program evaluation.* San Francisco: Jossey Bass.

Chapter 12
The Role of Information and Communications Technologies in Human Rights Monitoring and Advocacy

John Lannon
Leeds Metropolitan University, UK

ABSTRACT

This chapter analyses tools and techniques used to document human rights abuse. It outlines the opportunities and pitfalls associated with the use of information and communication technologies by human rights organizations, and it examines the importance of rigorous documentation to underpin human rights work. Tools developed to help grassroots organizations record usable and actionable information are contrasted with an initiative that actively involves citizens in the reporting of xenophobic attacks. The analysis shows that the tools and systems used to monitor human rights violations are essential to the effective implementation of human rights standards. It also shows that new technologies can empower ordinary citizens to become directly involved in awareness building and debate about human rights abuse.

'Live as if you were to die tomorrow. Learn as if you were to live forever'. -- Mahatma Gandhi (1869-1948), Indian philosopher, internationally esteemed for his doctrine of nonviolent protest.

INTRODUCTION

Human rights are a set of universal claims that exist in order to protect individuals from oppression, discrimination and illegitimate coercion, typically by state actors. They provide the basis upon which the notions of dignity, equality and human security can be upheld and promoted at all levels of society, and they are codified in a widely endorsed set of international undertakings known as the International Bill of Human Rights. This includes the Universal Declaration of Human Rights (UDHR), the International Covenant on Civil and Political Rights (ICCPR), the International Covenant on

DOI: 10.4018/978-1-60566-735-5.ch012

Economic Social and Cultural Rights (ICESCR), and a number of other internationally recognised covenants. These have been given effect to varying degrees at national level in order to provide protection to individuals and to enable them to realise their full potential as human beings.

In a 2003 Harvard University lecture, the former UN High Commissioner for Human Rights Mary Robinson said our challenge today is to give meaning to the values of human rights in our own communities as well as in the global community of nations (Robinson, 2003). Echoing the words of Eleanor Roosevelt who played a vital role in the drafting of the UDHR, she said that without concerned citizen action to uphold human rights at home, we will look in vain for progress in the larger world. In order for the human rights obligations of states to be understood and taken seriously as legal obligations, there is a need for research, analysis and reporting by non-governmental organizations within and on behalf of local communities. Respect for all human rights – including civil, political, economic, social and cultural rights - is primarily the responsibility of national governments. Human rights groups and activists, often with different agendas, work together at local, national and international level to hold them accountable and to bring pressure to bear to address deficiencies in their human rights record.

A number of factors have contributed towards addressing traditional and emerging forms of human rights abuse. These include the emergence of an international human rights regime, growing transnational social movement networks, increasing consciousness and information politics (Brysk, 2002). Globalization creates new opportunities to challenge the state from above and below according to Brysk, but it also creates new human rights problems related to the shrinking of states, the decision-making power of global institutions, the integration of markets, international flows of information and people, and the spread of cultures of intolerance. Information and communication technologies (ICTs) play an important role in all of these. As the various players increasingly leverage and apply new technologies we see significant changes from the traditional distributions of power in the international system (Selian, 2002).

This chapter looks at the role of ICTs in human rights advocacy, and provides an analysis of some of the tools and techniques used to gather, report, analyze and disseminate information on human rights abuses. It outlines the opportunities and challenges associated with the use of ICTs by human rights actors and it examines the importance of rigorous documentation and verifiable information sources to underpin human rights work. This is followed by a case study describing how an initiative that actively involves citizens in the reporting and dissemination of information contributes to awareness raising in relation to a human rights issue. Finally the added value of tools designed specifically to record and analyse human rights data is discussed, and their value in the context of the overall human rights regime is described.

BACKGROUND

ICTs represent the most significant technological breakthrough of the last half century. The costs are declining dramatically, and new applications that improve our human and organizational capabilities are being developed every day. Communications and information flows are becoming more instantaneous, more global and more content-rich as a result of technological innovation and convergence. These have contributed greatly to the enhanced transparency and accessibility of human rights information for citizens, particularly in terms of legal and administrative information, but they have done even more to improve the administrative, organizational and management skills of community and grassroots organizations, and thus 'to tip the scales of power slightly back towards an equilibrium' (Selian, 2002, p.19).

ICTs have transformed the capacity of the worldwide human rights movement to highlight human rights abuse and to advocate for causes and victims of oppression. They make it easier to share and to access information; they facilitate human rights data aggregation and analysis; they offer new tactical approaches to campaigning; and they precipitate real-world activities ranging from local demonstrations to intergovernmental agency lobbying. They also enable global participation, and give local actors and previously invisible groups international visibility.

Accurate and timely information is an indispensable tool for human rights work, and an essential precondition for effective responsive action and the promotion of human rights - whether by organizations, individuals, governments or international institutions (Metzl, 1996). The benefits of ICTs lie not only in the range of their functionality but in the variety and versatility of their application, according to Selian (2002). She says the use of ICTs in human rights work can be broken down broadly into four main realms whose level and quality of interaction (amongst themselves and with one another) has been vastly improved. According to Selian, individuals, non-governmental organizations (NGOs), national governments and supranational institutions have all been empowered insofar as they 'have the means to effectively communicate their stories, agendas, laws and agreements, respectively and with maximum input' (Selian, 2002, p.19).

In particular, human rights NGOs and activists benefit greatly from ICTs as they record and report human rights violations. Organizations and individuals around the world have been making good use of email to report and disseminate details of human rights abuses since the early 1990's. Back then, the development of structures such BurmaNet and the China News Digest created issue-based networks acting on specific human rights violations and informing the world of such abuses (Halpin & Fisher, 1998). Nowadays blogging has become an important tool for grassroots

organizations and activists who want to tell their stories to a global audience. These are assisted by international human rights NGOs like Human Rights Watch who serve as 'alternative wire services for people interested in places and issues rarely covered by mainstream media' (Zuckerman, 2004).

Mobile phones are also becoming more widely used for human rights activism and reporting. They are convenient, relatively reliable, inexpensive, coverage is improving all the time (Currion, 2007), and in most parts of the world their use is much higher than that of computers. With a mobile phone, a witness can report an incident anonymously by sending text messages using pre-paid SIM cards (Verclas, 2007). Mobile phones and digital cameras are also used to shoot footage that can be instrumental in quickly alerting the international community to human rights violations. They can also result in human rights perpetrators being brought to justice; a video recording of Egyptian police brutality that made its way to international bloggers and Youtube helped bring about the arrest and conviction of two police officers in November 2007, for example (BBC News, 2007).

With the widespread dissemination of mobile video there are potential privacy and security implications in exposing the victim as well as the reporter. Nonetheless it is often felt that the benefits of uncovering the abuse outweigh the potential negatives (Verclas, 2007).

Twitter, which is a web-based tool that allows users to create a network of friends and to post a small update from their mobile phone by sending a text message, is another example of how new technologies are being appropriated successfully by the human rights movement. It is ideal for human rights activists as it is free and anonymous, and it enables them to provide live updates and to notify hundreds of contacts simultaneously with one message. One of its most valuable uses therefore is in situations during campaigns and demonstrations where there might be danger of repression, arrests, etc. (Pearson, 2007). This is particularly true in parts of the world where there is limited Internet access, as information can be received as well as updated via a mobile phone.

THE BENEFITS AND PITFALLS OF ICTS FOR HUMAN RIGHTS WORK

ICTs improve the ability of human rights organizations to marshal the facts into a persuasive logical argument (Weyker, 2002). Incident reports gathered over time and linked together using an appropriate information management system can enable an organization to make comparative analyses of patterns of violation in time, space, and social structure (Ball, 1996). The kinds of organizations interested in doing this type of work include grassroots human rights NGOs, United Nations human rights monitoring missions, government human rights bodies and truth commissions. In some cases the focus is on monitoring ongoing conditions; in others it is on studying historical events.

The rise of global communications and media has afforded oppressed groups and individuals better opportunities to pitch their causes to distant audiences (Bob, 2002). With the advent of email and the World Wide Web in the mid 1990's the dissemination of human rights information was no longer restricted to the traditional media and the well-resourced international NGOs like Amnesty International and Human Rights Watch. More recently, a range of online reporting options including message boards, wikis, chat rooms and blogs have enabled activists and reporters to reach a global audience directly within minutes of a human rights violation occurring. Emergent practices of citizen journalism where ordinary people play an active role in the process of collecting, reporting, analyzing and disseminating news and information (Bowman & Willis, 2003) not only get information out quickly and cheaply; they also challenge the traditional approaches to news reporting and

empower oppressed communities.

Citizens in Sri Lanka who have been effectively cut out of mainstream media, for example, have found new ways of expressing themselves, their concerns, their aspirations and their ideas for resolving conflict through a citizen journalism initiative called *Groundviews* (Hattotuwa, 2007). This tri-lingual website (http://www.groundviews. org) features a range of ideas, opinions and analyses on humanitarian issues, media freedom, human rights, peace, democratic governance and constitutional reform. It was set up as a means through which citizens could document their own perspectives on life in conflict zones, call attention to humanitarian emergencies, and give information on security conditions. It also acts as a forum for the type of critical debate that does not take place in mainstream Sri Lankan media today.

The *Groundviews* conversation is still largely in English and is limited to urban areas. It lacks the grammar of age-old diplomacy and sociopolitical norms and is 'raw, visceral, impatient, irreverent, pithy [and] provocative' according to Hattotuwa (2007). Nonetheless in the context of Sri Lanka, where two decades of war have resulted in an ongoing series of struggles to secure human rights, basic human needs and a sustainable peace, citizen journalism initiatives like this play an important role as they have the potential to provide a forum for all citizens to express themselves and their ideas freely.

Another example of how citizens can benefit from ICTs is the Israeli human rights organization B'Tselem's *Shooting Back* project. The project which was launched in January 2007 provides Palestinians with video cameras to capture and expose human rights violations in the Occupied Territories. Most of what has been filmed is Israeli settler violence in the West Bank, done with the complicity of the army and police. Some of it has been aired on Israeli and international television networks and is made available on the Internet, giving global audiences an opportunity to see what is happening to Palestinians on the ground.

As in the case of *Groundviews* in Sri Lanka, *Shooting Back* has empowered Palestinians through citizen journalism and the use of ICTs. The project demonstrates how the video camera is not only a useful tool for documentation and advocacy; it has also become a source of protection for Palestinians (Goodman & Yakobovich, 2007), as settlers often run away when one is produced. Furthermore B'Tselem uses the video evidence to support complaints filed with the army and the police. Palestinian victims of abuse perpetrated by settlers or soldiers are often discouraged from lodging complaints by bureaucratic obstacles but these videos help to promote accountability and to seek legal redress for Palestinian complainants.

Video footage of human rights violations is regularly used in courts, tribunals, legislative bodies and human rights commissions, as well as by the media, transnational organizations and solidarity networks. It is a great way to create public awareness about human rights violations, while also empowering oppressed communities. The Witness archive (http://www.witness.org) is a good example of this in action. It consists of more than 1000 hours of raw footage documenting a vast range of human rights abuses, and features first-hand testimonies, interviews and imagery about rights violations and conflict sites around the world. Witness donates video cameras to human rights organizations and trains and supports their workers to integrate video into human rights campaigns. They also have an online video community for human rights called The Hub (http://hub.witness.org) where anyone can upload, watch and share videos about human rights, as well as take action to help end human rights abuses. According to Gillian Caldwell, executive director of Witness, quoted in Weaver (2005), these tools bestow the power to document events on the local people who experience them – as opposed to journalists visiting from other regions or countries. This goes a long way towards opening the eyes of the world to human rights violations and to promoting public engagement and policy change.

It also serves as a launch pad for campaigns that people around the world can get involved with, and actions they can take to promote and protect human rights.

ICTs also enhance the ability of NGOs to draw other people into the organising efforts of a group or movement and to create new connections through which to collaborate (Weyker, 2002). The Internet in particular has transformed the capacity of social movements – including human rights movements - to build coalitions and networks and to advocate for causes, principles, and other people (Hick & McNutt, 2002). It opens up opportunities for local organizations by giving them national, regional and even global reach, and it facilitates the convergence of organizations with different goals and strategies (Cammaerts & Van Auden-hove, 2003). Transnational human rights networks can influence state practice through information exchanges, provided domestic human rights activists can keep their cause on the international agenda and supply good quality information to their international allies (Burgerman, 1998).

There are pitfalls, however, in the use of ICTs in human rights work. Firstly the proliferation of voices demanding attention for their human rights concerns can lead to a problem of too much noise interfering with effective action (Weyker, 2002). ICTs enable more groups and individuals in countries where human rights violations are occurring to communicate with the outside world, and since these do not always work through a movement or organizational hierarchy there is a risk that mixed messages may be presented. Even worse is the possibility that false statements are unknowingly or unwisely made, thereby calling into question the credibility of reports from the country in question.

Another pitfall identified by Weyker (2002) is that some places are socially, economically or legally unfavourable for the application of these technologies to human rights work. In some cases the communications infrastructure is inadequate; in others the social organization and capacity to effectively exploit the opportunities presented by new technologies is lacking. Human rights organizations can use the Internet to create their own online content and establish peer-to-peer communications for widespread dissemination of information but they need the expertise and resources to do so in a safe environment. Web 2.0 technologies and applications like social bookmarking, wikis, blogs, tags, and RSS (Real Simple Syndication) have helped enormously however. According to (Krasne, 2005) they are already allowing non-profit supporters to build movements for social, environmental, economic, and political change, and the human rights movement is no exception in this regard.

The main threat to the safety of human rights groups that use the Internet is that governments fearful of the free flow of information purposefully try to control or hinder it. In June 2006, for example, the Chinese government announced it was going to step up control of search engines and blogs to block what it called "illegal and unhealthy" content, and western based Internet companies operating in the Chinese market were not slow to help them do this by allowing their tools to be used for surveillance activities and censorship. But the Chinese authorities are not alone in their implementation of restrictive and punitive measures that deny online freedom of expression and information. In 2004, Reporters without Borders chronicled a long list of regimes opposed to Internet freedom. They reported that in Vietnam, for example, web content is extensively censored and e-mail is monitored in order to track down "subversive" Internet users. In Burma only a few hundred hand-picked people - regime officials, top military figures and heads of export companies - are officially allowed Internet access. And in Tunisia, where press freedom is non-existent and many have looked to the Internet as a source of independent information and a place for debating ideas, the determination to gag the Internet is such that the only Internet service providers allowed to serve the public are those

owned by the president's associates (Reporters Without Borders, 2004).

The practices of Internet surveillance and censorship continue around the world, with governments using the presence of undesirable or critical material as a justification for repressive controls and laws. In November 2008, for example, Reporters Without Borders reported that an Egyptian blogger who was arrested in November 2006 because of articles he posted was still serving a prison sentence for "insulting Islam" and "insulting the president" (Reporters Without Borders, 2008). His "crime" was the fact that he had criticized the authoritarian abuses of President Mubarak, and the practice of separating the sexes in the university in which he was studying law.

Equally worrying is the fact that law enforcement and intelligence agencies around the world have developed new surveillance capabilities and have been given new legal powers to monitor Internet users in response to the threat of terrorism. Some countries have even introduced legislation justifying and encouraging such practices, and this further increases the persecution and suffering of human rights defenders. It also undermines their legitimate work and introduces new vulnerabilities within the human rights movement. The key to dealing with these threats is security; human rights defenders need to secure their work by learning about the technologies they use, and in particular about the concepts of computer and Internet operations (Vitaliev, 2007). This, according to Vitalev, will make them more effective in protecting themselves and in promoting the rights of those they try to defend.

Vitalev (2007) outlines the key elements of information and communications security for human rights defenders and organizations at risk. The first is to secure the physical environment in which they operate, as most security incidents that affect the work and livelihood of human rights defenders are connected with physical violence and intrusion into their workplace. But while good physical access barriers can deter some of those seeking unauthorised access to an organization's information repositories, mainly because of the additional time required to circumvent them (Lannon & Halpin, 2006), they usually don't deter state actors who want to access or destroy human rights information. They can work openly and usually have the staff and specialist tools to gain access (Mobbs, 2002).

The next step for human rights defenders and organizations is to address their digital security by installing anti-virus, spyware and firewall tools. For this the security edition of the NGO-in-a-Box CD (http://security.ngoinabox.org/) provides a range of solutions. Having good passwords and changing these every three to six months is also important, as is the use of screen locking and computer startup passwords.

Two other important issues to consider when working with information according to Vitalev (2007) are how to recover it and how to destroy it. Recoverable backups of documents and other information are critical in order to avoid information loss through human error, carelessness, system malfunction or malicious damage. Human rights organizations must therefore give careful consideration to the type, quantity and frequency of backup for their information. Equally it is important for them to ensure that any data which is no longer wanted is properly deleted. This includes wiping temporary files, Internet browsing histories and so on.

Making information inaccessible to all but the intended party is another key consideration for human rights defenders. It provides protection for the defenders themselves, and it is essential in order to avoid jeopardizing the lives of witnesses and victims (PoKempner, 1997). But governments and other interested parties can intercept electronic communications at publicly accessible Internet nodes, through line tapping or disclosure by Internet Service Providers, or by intercepting the main lines that connect their country to the rest of the world. Encryption has therefore become a

necessary and seamless part of electronic communication for human rights defenders in many parts of the world.

Given the sensitivity of much of what they possess and the threat this information could pose to the authorities, human rights organizations clearly need to be vigilant about their information security. Nonetheless a tool like the Internet that can provide immediate communiqués and cheap dissemination of information to a wide international audience is invaluable. Efforts to censor and control the flows of information in and out of countries do not stop the free flow of information across borders. Even in countries where access to technology is scarce and where freedom of expression and association are limited, the Internet therefore provides human rights defenders with the opportunity to stay in contact with support networks and to disseminate recorded human rights abuses quickly and securely.

HUMAN RIGHTS EDUCATION AND ICTS

In a background note to the World Summit on the Information Society in 2003, the Office of the High Commissioner for Human Rights noted that ICT facilitates 'networking among individuals and organizations involved in human rights education; make it easier to share information on successful programmes and practices; and provide access to the many human rights education resources available on the Internet' (Office of the High Commissioner for Human Rights, 2003). In a broader context, Claude and Hick said that ICTs facilitate human rights education and training by helping people to analyse the world around them, to understand that human rights are a way to improve their lives and the lives of others, and to take action to prevent human rights violations (Claude & Hick, 2000). They differentiate between formal human rights education (HRE) which takes place through schools, colleges and universities, non-formal HRE which is any organised, systematic education activity carried on outside the formal system, and informal HRE. The latter may or may not be organised, and is usually unsystematic education, 'having its impact on the lifelong processes by which every person acquires and accumulates knowledge, skills, attitudes and insights from daily experiences and exposure' (Claude & Hick, 2000, p.231).

Flowers (2000) defined human rights education as all learning that develops the knowledge, skills, and values of human rights. It is a complex process that requires cognitive, emotional and active learning according to Mihr (2004). Nonetheless endorsements for human rights education have been proclaimed in various global and regional legal instruments ever since 1945, when the Charter of the United Nations called for cooperation in promoting and encouraging respect for human rights and fundamental freedoms (Andreopoulos & Claude, 1997). This premise, which was reaffirmed in 1993 in Vienna at the United Nations World Conference on Human Rights, creates responsibilities at the State level in terms of formal education. It also creates responsibilities among social institutions, including NGOs, who deliver non-formal education in human rights.

Online human rights education centers now go beyond the provision of material for formal education and training to address the non-formal HRE needs of a variety of sectors. The Human Rights Education Associates (HREA) library (http://www.hrea.org/erc/Library/), for example, which is one of the most extensive online human rights education libraries available to the public, contains over 2,000 full-text guides, curricula, textbooks and other documents that can be used for both formal and non-formal education relating to human rights. In addition to general resources and formal education material, it provides training material for professional groups such as teachers, law enforcement officials and companies. It also includes a range of non-formal education material for women, NGOs, community leaders and youth.

Human rights education involves analysis through reflection on one's own situation (Lannon & Halpin, 2006). The mere gathering of knowledge is not enough for this; there also needs to be awareness building, everyday examples, experience and reflection (Freire, 1995). A good example of how the Internet and other ICTs can be used to meet this challenge is Pambazuka News, a weekly newsletter and platform for social justice in Africa. In keeping with the need for emotional and active learning, it has also become a tool for advocacy in Africa. As part of the 2005 campaign for the ratification of the protocol on the Rights of Women in Africa, for example, two special issues were produced profiling important aspects of the protocol.

According to Shahjahan Siraj, a former online editor of Banglarights.net (an independent web portal that exposes and challenges discriminations and violations of human rights in Bangladesh), 'global information systems, [the] Internet as well as ICTs have opened up the golden gate for human rights promotion in Bangladesh' (Siraj, 2005). ICTs provide public access to information and build a virtual space for community gathering and grassroots development, particularly in the case of marginalized communities, he says, and websites can change a situation dramatically by encouraging participation in debate about human rights abuse. Siraj believes that if such a resource were available in Bangladesh it would gives continuous objective education and awareness both to the human rights defenders and offenders.

MONITORING AND REPORTING HUMAN RIGHTS VIOLATIONS

The human rights regime depends on information that is reliable, trustworthy and relevant. If it is not objective and truthful, it will be ignored (Weyker, 2002), and if it is not presented in a way that is usable by its recipients it has little value.

Human rights standards are set primarily by the

UN, its sub-bodies and other inter-governmental organizations. They are also set by specialized agencies such as the International Labor Organization (ILO) that are linked to the UN, and by regional bodies such as the Council of Europe and the African Union. Human rights monitoring is undertaken to see if these standards are being met in domestic settings, and it involves the repeated collection and recording of information for later use (Guzman & Verstappen, 2003). It is done by the human rights treaty-based committees of the UN (including the Human Right Committee, the Committee on Economic, Social and Cultural Rights, the Committee on the Elimination of Racial Discrimination, and so on), special rapporteurs and other bodies under the UN Commission on Human Rights, and some other specialist agencies. It is also undertaken by government bodies, including human rights commissions, and by NGOs.

Human rights treaty bodies like the UN Human Rights Committee consider periodic reports submitted by UN member states on their compliance with human rights treaties. International NGOs play an important role in this process by providing reliable and independent information to the Committees through reports that shadow the entire state report or provide commentary on specific articles of a convention. These shadow reports, which are an opportunity for NGOs to voice their human rights concerns and criticisms at an international level, rely on unhindered grassroots NGO activity in a country and the flow of information from them. In the absence of these information flows, the attention of the international community will not be drawn to the situation in a country, even if the level of human rights violations there merits attention.

In writing about how to document and respond to allegations of torture within the international system for the protection of human rights, Giffard (2000) said that some NGOs have adopted excellent methods of reporting, but many less experienced NGOs are either unaware of the importance of the information they provide, or have never had

the opportunity to learn how best to present it. A significant proportion of the information received from such NGOs is wasted, she said, not because the allegations are unfounded, but because important facts are omitted, the allegation is worded in excessively political speech, or it is presented in a language that the recipient does not understand or does not have the resources to have translated. In other cases a lack of familiarity with the functions of the various international bodies and mechanisms means that information is incorrectly sent to an authority that is not empowered or mandated to use it effectively.

NGOs generally work with others to gather details of situation or individual cases; to investigate events linked to suspected human rights violations; to produce records and analysis of investigations carried out; and to report to an international body. ICTs simplify all of these steps in the human rights information chain, but without the application of appropriate norms and standards the mistakes highlighted by Giffard (2000) are likely to be repeated.

Human rights NGOs monitor ongoing violations of human rights as well as the compliance of governments with treaty obligations. They collect data relating to violations from various sources including newspaper articles, official reports and documents, medical records, and testimonies from witnesses and people directly involved. Policy-makers, prosecutors, truth commissions, academics and other actors use the information collected, as do the international NGOs that submit shadow reports to the treaty monitoring bodies.

If an organization is recording or investigating large numbers of human rights cases it must have a systematic way to file information. This requires the design and use of a good information management system (Ball, 1996) which gives the organization a way to organise its information and to accumulate information from a diversity of sources over time. This has implications that go far beyond computing, according to Ball. For example, if an organization conceptualizes a human rights event as a single act committed against a single victim, the organization has already ruled out any analysis of repression directed against villages, trade unions, and other groups. To understand targeted government action, attacks against individual victims should therefore be maintained in such a way that they can be viewed as a single mass event.

Another important aspect of human rights monitoring by NGOs is the use of standard formats and controlled vocabularies (Guzman & Verstappen, 2003). A Geneva-based NGO called HURIDOCS (Human Rights Information and Documentation Services, International, http://www.huridocs.org) has produced standard formats for recording human rights events and exchanging information with others in the human rights regime (Dueck, Guzman, & Verstappen, 2001a). Organizations are encouraged to use these when documenting human rights abuse, firstly to describe what happened and who did what to whom, and secondly to provide an account of the actions taken in response. The first part is based on documenting events and acts (an event is something that happens, and it is made up of a single act or a series of related acts such as an attack on a labour leader and the bombing of his office), the people involved and the nature of their involvement. The individuals or groups involved in an event may be victims (the object of an act) or perpetrators (the ones who commits the act).

The second part of the methodology outlined by Dueck, Guzman & Verstappen (2001a) is to describe the actions taken in response to an event and who did them. It covers the provision of information (including an examination of conflicting reports and assessment of the information's reliability), any intervention relating to the event (assistance provided, medical examination, etc.), details of the person providing the information, and details of any intervening parties.

HURIDOCS have also developed micro-thesauri to enhance the effectiveness of ICT-based applications that use the event standard formats.

This helps with data classification, and gives users coherence and consistency in their data entry (Dueck, Guzman, & Verstappen, 2001b). This contains a HURIDOCS Index Terms list which includes all the terms commonly used in human rights work. It also contains coded typologies for types of act (deliberate killing, harassment, violation of the right to privacy, etc), the rights that apply to an event, the physical identification markings on the victim or perpetrator, and the source providing the information.

The use of standards and codes make it easier to record and retrieve information relating to human rights events, especially in cases where computer-based systems are used to store the information. It is also easier to exchange or communicate information to other organizations if they use the same standards and codes. So while it is commonplace for recordings made by witnesses and others in the field to use free form descriptions of an event, the information becomes more valuable if it is encoded using standard formats.

Human rights organizations are also encouraged to use metadata - which is data describing the content, structure and management of information - to describe their published online information, as this makes it easier for search engines to sort and retrieve it. The most widely used standard for this is Dublin Core (http://dublincore.org/). It is a vocabulary of fifteen elements used in information resource descriptions, the semantics of which have been established through consensus by an international, cross-disciplinary group of professionals from librarianship, computer science, text encoding, the museum community, and other related fields of scholarship. The elements include resource properties such as creator, date, description, format, language and publisher.

The use of metadata can be supplemented by use of the HURIDOCS micro-thesauri to describe the content of a record or web page in a human rights context. A good example of how this can benefit human rights workers is HuriSearch (http://www.hurisearch.org), a human rights web search tool developed by HURIDOCS. HuriSearch incorporates Dublin Core metadata into its indexing, and analyses search results using the HURIDOCS Index Terms so that users can easily identify the most prevalent human rights themes on the Web. At the end of 2008, for example, it has indexed over 511,000 human rights Web resources as relating to "women" and almost 440,000 on "health" – both of which are listed in the Index Terms.

CASE STUDY: CITIZENS REPORTING ONLINE IN SOUTH AFRICA

The importance of citizen journalism as means of documenting human rights violations is typified by the *UnitedForAfrica.co.za* portal. This is an interactive online facility set up in May 2008 within days of an outbreak of xenophopic attacks on foreigners in South Africa. Its objective was to enable ordinary people who witnessed or had information about violent incidents to anonymously submit reports.

Incident reporting on UnitedForAfrica.co.za is done using a web-based form. The web reporting provides incident description, location, date and time, incident category (selected from a predefined list) and the names of people involved. It even provides the option of adding links to uploaded video - for example on Youtube. There is also an SMS facility which people can use to text in reports to an advertised number. Leaflets with the number prominently displayed were produced and distributed around potential trouble hotspots. These leaflets highlighted the objectives of the project which were to have stories told; to mobilize members of the public to assist; to mobilize government to react; to raise money and to inform people how they can assist; and to share opinions on the causes and solutions through ongoing dialogue and debate.

None of the reports received by UnitedForAfrica.co.za were published without first verifying the content. A system of checks was implemented which included conducting online searches to see if other commentary existed on the incident, as well as checking if more than one person reported the incident. The portal managers were also anxious to ensure they were not seen to be sensationalising what was happening; the potential repercussions of publishing for individuals, vulnerable groups and society in general always need to be taken into consideration.

The type of information being reported and published by UnitedForAfrica.co.za is typified by the following incident which occurred at the Atteridgeville township on Saturday June 14th 2008 at approximately 2.00pm:

A Mozambican man has been burned alive by a mob during disturbances near the South African capital Pretoria.

The 30-year-old was stoned then set alight in Atteridgeville township after being accused of an arson attack on a shack the day before, said police.

Three suspects were held for murder and robbery as 2,000 rand ($246 £126) were stolen from the man, police said.

Atteridgeville was the scene of a spate of recent attacks on foreigners, in which 62 people died.

A report on this incident was subsequently published by the BBC News in its entirety, with the following additional background information:

Tens of thousands of people were displaced in the violence - blamed on unemployment and scarce resources. It was the worst bloodshed since the end of apartheid in 1994.

There were reports on Saturday of other clashes at a transit camp near Pretoria housing some 2,000 people who have been driven from their homes. Many were reported to be Somalis. (BBC News, 2008)

When the issue of xenophopic attacks against foreigners flared up initially, the mainstream media used UnitedForAfrica.co.za to get first hand reports. The portal manager regularly got approached by a news site and would find himself mediating between them and someone who was closer to what was happening on the ground. It was helpful for the media in South Africa at the time to get information on attacks very quickly without having to run around from location to location. As a result, the issue was being reported more often and to a wider audience than would otherwise receive it.

Once published on UnitedForAfrica.co.za, reports appear on a map-based view for others to see. The map, which is a "mashup" of the xenophobia incident reports and Google Maps, allows users to click on a location or incident to get more information. Mashups, which are the compounding or "mashing" of two or more pieces of web functionality to create powerful applications, are just one example of how Web 2.0 technologies were used in response to the xenophobia crisis. Another is the Afrigator xenophobia page (http://afrigator.com/) which aggregated blog posts and news articles of the crisis.

In the first day after it went live there were 357 site visits to UnitedForAfrica.co.za; on the second there were 932. The portal was used to provide information on where the incidents were happening. This information proved to be quite valuable; site managers were even linking with NGOs on the ground that were providing assistance, and were using the portal as a central point to bring all the data together and to help the NGOs to prioritise their response.

UnitedForAfrica.co.za was designed by a South African web marketing agency called Quirk who also manage and maintain it. It is built using an infrastructure called *Ushahidi*, which means "testimony" in Swahili. The Ushahidi engine was initially developed to map reports of violence in Kenya after the post-election fallout at the beginning of 2008, and has its roots in the collaboration of Kenyan citizen journalists at that time. It provides a platform that any person or organization can use to set up their own means of collecting and visualizing information and it is available as a free, open source application that others can download, implement and use to create awareness of a crisis in their own region.

The core Ushahidi engine is built on the premise that gathering crisis information from the general public provides new insights into events happening in near real-time. It uses direct citizen reporting rather than depending on experts in the field, and has been tested with people working on issues linked to the environment, health, political crises and human rights. The focus is on crisis situation reporting, not just human rights, but while the use of standard event formats and coding has not been implemented, human rights organizations with the expertise to do so can filter and verify the reports to build a picture of the human rights situation in a crisis.

Since mobile phone ownership rates are quite high now, even among some of the poorest members of society, Ushahidi are working with FrontlineSMS to produce a light version of their incident reporting form that can be loaded on a phone. This is free software that enables computer users to send and receive text messages with large groups of people through mobile phones. It enables two-way communication, which is useful for incident reporting by people in the field.

BEYOND CITIZEN JOURNALISM: USING HUMAN RIGHTS EVENT REPORTING TOOLS

According to Benetech, a Californian non-profit company that develops technology-based tools to assist human rights organizations, there are about 10,000 human rights NGOs throughout the world that collect information in the field. Much of the violation and abuse information gathered by grassroots organizations is currently being lost to confiscation, destruction, or neglect, they claim, and as a result the effectiveness of these NGOs is reduced and it is difficult or impossible for prosecutors, truth commissions and international human rights groups to use the information as evidence to hold the perpetrators of human rights abuses accountable (Benetech, 2008).

In response to this problem, Benetech developed the Martus Human Rights Bulletin System, which is a tool designed to collect, organize and securely store human rights violations information. It enables grassroots NGOs to create a searchable and encrypted database on an off-site server and to store their records on this. The software, which is freely available and open source, is used by organizations around the world to protect sensitive information and to shield the identity of victims or witnesses who provide testimony on human rights abuses.

The Martus Human Rights Bulletin System addresses what Benetech say are the four critical requirements for software to protect the records of grassroots human rights groups. These are that it should be

- usable: as easy to use as email, can run on an inexpensive computer and does not require a constant connection to the Internet;
- secure: records are encrypted, stored securely at a remote site, backed up to multiple locations and protected by a unique password;

- searchable: specific violations and identifying details can be searched by groups or outside researchers granted access to the records; and
- transparent: the software is open source so any group can examine the code and make an informed decision about using it (Benetech, 2008)

Some of the organizations that use Martus to protect their data also use Analyzer, which is a software program developed by the Human Rights Data Analysis Group (HRDAG) to organize human rights information for statistical analysis. Data is coded according to the "who did what to whom" model, and records describing the source of the information, the victim(s), the perpetrator(s) and the acts committed are entered, with relationships created between the different pieces of information. Analyzer can combine data from multiple data collection projects, and in so doing it can provide the sort of large-scale statistical analysis required by truth commissions. The HRDAG has assisted the truth and reconciliation commissions in South Africa, Sierra Leone and East Timor and in all of these its work proved to be instrumental in helping the commissions to make powerful and credible findings.

HURIDOCS have developed an alternative data collection system called WinEvSys for human rights NGOs. This is based on the standard formats and micro-thesauri developed by the same organization, and is implemented using the Microsoft Access database software. Unlike the two-stage data collection/analysis approach of Martus and Analyzer, the WinEvSys system can produce analysis and statistics based on type of violation, perpetrator, victim characteristics, geographic area, time period, and so on.

While the WinEvsys database system uses built-in vocabularies to describe all types of violations and all aspects of a human rights case, thus giving a human rights organization flexibility in its data recording, its use requires more training than Martus. HURIDOCS believe, however, that the training is necessary to ensure that NGOs do not over simplify human rights monitoring and reporting. The data richness supported by WinEvSys is necessary, they say, and leads to successful and reliable routine monitoring instead of waiting until a situation has exploded.

HURIDOCS say that human rights information should be accessible, meaning the right information should reach the right people when and where they need it. It should also be usable, meaning it should be presented in such as way as to facilitate analysis and decision-making, and it should be compatible, in order to increase levels of sharing and improve communication and collaboration (HURIDOCS, 2007). All these contribute to making it actionable, which is the most important characteristic of any information collected by human rights organizations.

WinEvsys has been in use for over a decade, and is currently used by human rights organizations in Bangladesh, Mexico, the Philipines, Zimbabwe and elsewhere. In response to feedback, HURIDOCS have decided to update it while keeping the same controlled vocabularies. The new system, which will be called *OpenEvsys* will be a web-based application capable of being deployed as a standalone application, over a local network or over the Internet. According to HURIDOCS this will help organizations to work together more easily on documentation of human rights violations, and will strengthen collaborations to underpin success at the United Nations Human Rights Council's periodic review of states' human rights practices.

CONCLUDING REMARKS

The gathering, storage, analysis and dissemination of human rights information is greatly enhanced by the use of ICTs and by the development and deployment of ICT-based information systems. Many of the information flows between actors in the human rights regime would not take place without these, and as a result the promotion and protection of human rights would be greatly diminished.

Systems are now being deployed with greater speed to provide solutions that are usable, secure and relevant to the needs of the human rights movement. Individuals are being empowered to report and comment on the human rights situation in their own community as the explosion of mobile phone applications, online video sharing and other tools makes it easy to share information about human rights violations with global audiences. Citizen journalists, connected into the communities they report on, can provide an immediacy of reporting that is not possible with mainstream media. Eye witness accounts of human rights violations can be uploaded and used as irrefutable evidence of what is happening under a repressive regime. And human rights defenders that are at risk of intimidation or attack can keep in touch with their network of supporters, just to tell them they are still alive and free.

From a human rights perspective, the lack of attention to detail and concerns over the veracity of what is reported can reduce the value of the information being gathered. Human rights work depends on reliable evidence and on the efforts of grassroots organizations to gather and record information that will bring perpetrators of abuse to justice. These efforts are strengthened as organizations' access to ICTs improves and their capacity to use technology-based tools is enhanced. Tools that strengthen the information management capabilities of human rights organizations provide new opportunities for the human rights movement. Furthermore, the pooling of information from a number of sources enables international watchdogs and agencies to build a more complete picture of what is happening in any part of the world, and thus set in motion processes leading to censure and accountability for human rights abuse.

Thanks to ICTs, the discourse of human rights is now spreading beyond the elite settings of intergovernmental agencies, academic institutions and international NGOs, to the villages and towns of the oppressed. The online world is increasingly being used to stimulate debate and learning about human rights, sometimes through active citizen participation in the reporting of violations. Access to information enables human rights promotion through reflection and learning, and while much of what is reported may never be used to build a case against the human rights offenders, it sets in motion processes that ultimately lead, through empowerment, to greater protection from abuse, persecution and oppression.

REFERENCES

Andreopoulos, G. J., & Claude, R. P. (Eds.). (1997). *Human rights education for the twenty-first century*. Philadelphia: University of Pennsylvania Press.

Ball, P. (1996). *Who did what to whom? Planning and implementing a large scale human rights data project*. Washington, DC: American Association for the Advancement of Science (AAAS).

Benetech. (2008). *Martus: Human rights bulletin system*. Retrieved November 7, 2008, from http://www.martus.org/dl/martus-overview.pdf

Bob, C. (2002). Globalization and the social construction of human rights campaigns. In A. Brysk (Ed.), *Globalization and human rights*. Berkeley, CA: University of California Press.

Bowman, S., & Willis, C. (2003). *We media: How audiences are shaping the future of news and information*. The Media Center at the American Press Institute.

Brysk, A. (2002). Transnational threats and opportunities. In A. Brysk (Ed.), *Globalization and human rights*. Berkeley, CA: University of California Press.

Burgerman, S. D. (1998). Mobilizing principles: The role of transnational activists in promoting human rights principles. *Human Rights Quarterly, 20*(4), 905–924. doi:10.1353/hrq.1998.0035

Cammaerts, B., & Van Audenhove, L. (2003). *ICT-usage of transnational social movements in the networked society: To organise, to mediate and to influence* (No. ASCoR/TNO-STB). Amsterdam/Delft, The Netherlands.

Claude, R. P., & Hick, S. (2000). Human rights education on the Internet: Its day has come. In S. Hick, E. F. Halpin, & E. Hoskins (Eds.), *Human rights and the Internet* (pp. 225-237). Houndmills, UK: MacMillan Press Ltd.

Currion, P. (2007). *Dial H for humanitarian*. Retrieved November 2, 2008, from http://www.humanitarian.info/2007/11/06/dial-h-for-humanitarian/

Dueck, J., Guzman, M., & Verstappen, B. (2001a). *HURIDOCS events standard formats: A tool for documenting human rights violations* (2nd ed.). Versoix, Switzerland: HURIDOCS.

Dueck, J., Guzman, M., & Verstappen, B. (2001b). *Micro-thesauri: A tool for documenting human rights violations* (2nd ed.). Versoix, Switzerland: HURIDOCS.

Flowers, N. (2000). *The human rights education handbook: Effective Practices for learning, action, and change*. Minneapolis, MN: University of Minnesota.

Freire, P. (1995). *Pedagogy of hope, relieving pedagogy of the oppressed*. New York Continuum.

Giffard, C. (2000). *The torture reporting handbook. How to document and respond to allegations of torture within the international system for the protection of human rights*. UK: Human Rights Centre, University of Essex.

Goodman, A., & Yakobovich, O. (2007). Shooting back: The Israeli human rights group B'Tselem gives Palestinians video cameras to document life under occupation. *Democracy Now!* Retrieved November 2, 2008, from http://www.democracynow.org/2007/12/26/shooting_back_the_israeli_human_rights

Guzman, M., & Verstappen, B. (2003). *Human rights monitoring and documentation series, volume 1: What is monitoring.* Versoix, Switzerland: Human Rights Information and Documentation Systems, International (HURIDOCS).

Halpin, E. F., & Fisher, S. M. (1998). *The use of the Internet for the European Parliament's activities for the protection and promotion of human rights* ([Report]. Luxembourg: European Parliament.]. *No. PE, 167,* 227.

Hattotuwa, S. (2007). The promise of citizen journalism. *openDemocracy News Analysis.* Retrieved October 21, 2008, from http://www.opendemocracy.net/terrorism/articles/srilanka220107

Hick, S., & McNutt, J. (Eds.). (2002). *Advocacy, activism and the Internet.* Chicago, IL: Lyceum Press.

HURIDOCS. (2007). *Harnessing the power of information – the importance of standards.* Retrieved October 20, 2008.

Krasne, A. (2005). *What is Web 2.0 anyway? - Indispensable tools your nonprofit should know about.* Retrieved November 2, 2008, from http://www.techsoup.org/learningcenter/webbuilding/archives/page9344.cfm

Lannon, J., & Halpin, E. F. (2006). Human rights movements and the Internet: From local contexts to global engagement. In M. Gascó-Hernández, F. Equiza-López, & M. Acevedo-Ruiz (Eds.), *Information communication technologies and human development: Opportunities and challenges* (pp. 182-209). Hershey, PA: Idea Group Publishing.

Metzl, J. F. (1996). Information technology and human rights. *Human Rights Quarterly, 18*(4), 705–746. doi:10.1353/hrq.1996.0045

Mihr, A. (2004). *Human rights education: Methods, institutions, culture and evaluation.* Institut für Politkwissenschaft, Otto-von-Guericke- Universität

Mobbs, P. (2002). *Participating with safety briefings no. 1: Introducing information security.* Association for Progressive Communications.

News, B. B. C. (2007). *Digital activists expose abuse.* Retrieved November 2, 2008, from http://news.bbc.co.uk/2/hi/americas/7139218.stm

News, B. B. C. (2008). *S Africa mob burns Mozambican man.* Retrieved October 21, 2008, from http://news.bbc.co.uk/2/hi/africa/7455061.stm

Office of the High Commissioner for Human Rights. (2003). *Background note on the information society and human rights* (No. Document WSIS/PC-3/CONTR/178-E). Geneva, Switzerland: Office of the UN High Commissioner for Human Rights.

Pearson, N. (2007). *Mobile phones in emergencies - pubic and personal.* Retrieved November 6, 2008, from http://www.newtactics.org/en/blog/new-tactics/using-mobile-phones-action#comment-521

PoKempner, D. (1997). *Briefing paper: Encryption in the service of human rights.* Human Rights Watch.

Reporters Without Borders. (2004). *The Internet under surveillance: Obstacles to the free flow of information online.* Reporters Without Borders.

Reporters Without Borders. (2008). *Two years for a blog: That's enough! Reporters Without Borders calls for release of blogger Kareem Amer.* Retrieved November 8, 2008 from http://www.rsf.org/article.php3?id_article=29192

Robinson, M. (2003). Making human rights matter: Eleanor Roosevelt's time has come. *Harvard Human Rights Journal*, 16.

Selian, A. N. (2002). *ICTs in support of human rights, democracy and good governance*. International Telecommunications Union.

Siraj, S. (2005). ICT and human rights promotion in Bangladesh: Democratising force of ICT. *i4d*. *Human Rights and ICTs*, 3(7), 27–29.

Verclas, K. (2007). *Mobile phones in human rights reporting*. Retrieved November 2, 2008, from http://mobileactive.org/mobile-phones-human-rights-reporting

Vitaliev, D. (2007). *Digital security and privacy for human rights defenders*. Front Line Defenders. Retrieved November 7, 2008, from http://www. frontlinedefenders.org/manual/en/esecman/

Weaver, C. (2005). Human rights group arms activists with video cameras. *Voice of America*. Retrieved November 2, 2008, from http://www. voanews.com/english/archive/2005-12/2005-12-09-voa98.cfm

Weyker, S. (2002). The ironies of information technology. In A. Brysk (Ed.), *Globalization and human rights* (pp. 115-132). Berkeley, CA: University of California Press.

Zuckerman, E. (2004). *Blog coaches for human rights*. Retrieved November 2, 2008, from http:// www.worldchanging.com/archives/001439. html

Chapter 13

Social Shaping of Technologies for Community Development
Redeployment of Information Communication Technologies among the Kelabit in Bario of the Kelabit Highlands

Poline Bala
University Malaysia Sarawak, Malaysia

ABSTRACT

Using electronic-Bario (e-Bario) project in the Kelabit Highlands of Sarawak in East Malaysia, this chapter explores how the introduction of information communication technologies (ICT) as developmental tools have been mediated and reconfigured by webs of social relations and the intricate interplay of social, political and cultural conditions specific to different social and technical settings. One crucial factor conditioning the effects of the project has been the Kelabit's own desire for, and expectations of, "development" and "progress." This is a quest which ties in closely with two fundamental Kelabit concepts: doo-ness and iyuk. As a result, the social and economic effects of ICT have unfolded through countless open-ended strategic and everyday decisions made by the Kelabit themselves, who actively consume, apply and make use of objects, ideas and services in the Highlands.

'The new electronic interdependence recreates the world in the image of a global village'. -- Marshall McLuhan, The Gutenberg Galaxy in Daintith, John (ed.) Quotations, Bloomsbury (1996, p.256:1).

INTRODUCTION

Over the last 15 years information and communication technologies (ICT) have been increasingly and optimistically promoted as a means of transforming developing countries into "modern" and knowledge-based societies and to alleviate some of the social and economic problems of developing world, particularly those in rural areas. Yet very little is known about the veracity of these aspirations, much less about the long-term social and economic effects of these technologies upon development in rural areas (Keniston, 2002).

Informed by a social shaping technology (SST) framework, this chapter explores how the introduc-

DOI: 10.4018/978-1-60566-735-5.ch013

tion of information communication technologies was mediated and reconfigured by webs of social relations and the intricate interplay of social, political and cultural conditions specific to the Kelabit Highlands. In this way the chapter seeks to achieve a more critical understanding of the relationship between ICT and society that provide an understanding of the implications of ICT for social and economic development and inform current discussions about the emerging "Information Society."

SOCIAL SHAPING AND CONSEQUENCES OF ICT

The social shaping of technology (SST) approach to technology-society relationships has emerged in the late 1980s as an important framework to explore whether technology can be seen as a main force that shapes society or whether society and social values shape the way in which technology affects our lives. With regards to information communication technologies, the approach builds on two main themes: the design and implementation of ICT artifacts and systems; and the implications of ICT for individuals, organizations and society. Within this broad remit the SST approach could not, and will not deny that technology has an effect on society but at the same time emphasizes organizational, cultural, economic and other factors influencing the process of technological change and innovation (Williams and Edge, 1996; Kling, 2000). In other words, deviating from a technological determinism standpoint, SST embraces the centrality of users, society and social values to shape the way in which information communication technologies (ICT), affect our lives, (Dutton, 2001; Rohracher, 2003; Fischer, 1992).

Taking the lead from the SST framework, this chapter explores the social and economic effects of electronic-Bario (e-Bario), an ICT-based community development project implemented in the Kelabit Highlands of Sarawak. This is in order to

shed some light on the character and significance of ICT in different social and technical settings and at the same time to illuminate the processes of shaping the use and impacts of ICT in Bario. It takes into account the role of the Kelabit's own desire for, and expectations of, "development" and "progress." This is a quest which ties in closely with two fundamental Kelabit concepts: *doo*-ness and *iyuk*. As will be made clear later in the chapter, both notions signify movements and good-ness in terms of social status among the Kelabit. By highlighting their significance, this chapter argues that it is the local cultural logic of *doo*-ness and *iyuk* among the Kelabit which is central to the shaping of technology especially how meanings (symbolically) are "inscribed to technologies" (Rose, 2001, p.69), creating a desire for new technologies, and informing their development and appropriation by users in the Highlands. In short Kelabit notions of *iyuk* and *doo*-ness are central to functional and symbolic encoding of technologies in Bario and are crucial factors conditioning the effects of the project. This is evident by the ways in which the social and economic effects of e-Bario have unfolded through countless open-ended strategic and everyday decisions made by the Kelabit themselves, who actively consume, apply and make use of objects, ideas and services in the Highlands.

BACKGROUND: THE E-BARIO PROJECT

Considered the traditional homeland of the Kelabit, the Kelabit Highlands is situated above the rapids found at the headwaters of the Baram and Limbang in Northeast Sarawak, close to the border between Kalimantan and Malaysia in the Miri Division. Although there is no official boundary to define the area, Thong and Bahrin (1993, p.17) estimate that the Highlands comprise an area of approximately 2,500 square kilometers. With an average altitude of 1000 meters above sea level, it is surrounded by some of the highest peaks and rugged mountains in Central Borneo. This out-of-the-way situation is well noted by Harrison (1959): 'There is one [of] or two places on the map of Borneo and, more widely, on the map of the world – where you can get farther away from a known place ..., from what most people call "the world." There are fewer places where you (or I) are likely to be able to feel more remote, more "cut off" from the great outside...' (p.5). Nowadays, flying into the unofficial capital of the Kelabit Highlands known as Bario, is the only practical way to get there. There is no road, and a land expedition requires a river journey plus an additional weeklong trek across forested mountains (Bala, 2002).

But, who are the Kelabit? Numbering at 5,240 in 2000, the Kelabit are one of the smallest ethnic groups in Malaysia. For the past thirty years many have left the Kelabit Highlands for education and job opportunities. As a result only a thousand still remain in the Highlands while the rest are living in cities like Miri, Kuching and Kuala Lumpur, or even overseas in the U.K., U.S.A., Canada, Holland, Australia and New Zealand. This high level of rural-urban migration has led to a geographically-dispersed community, creating almost a clear distinction between the Kelabit who remain in the Highlands (rural Kelabit) and those who have left to live in urban areas (urban Kelabit).

Ironically, it was because of these two social situations: high levels of rural-urban migration of the Kelabit and the geographical remoteness of the Kelabit Highlands that Bario became a test-bed for the e-Bario project. Initiated by an interdisciplinary team of researchers from Universiti Malaysia Sarawak (UNIMAS), e-Bario explored the use of telephones, computers, Very Small Aperture Terminals (VSATs) and the Internet to improve the lives of marginalized groups in remote areas of Sarawak. Initially funded by International Development Research Centre in Canada, it was later adopted by the Malaysian Government as one of its Demonstrator Application Grant Schemes.

The project was largely initiated in response to Malaysia's approach to adopt ICT as essential developmental tools in generating a knowledge and information-based society (UN, 2000, p.9) - a form of society which Malaysia aims to attain by the year 2010 (Goh Beng Lan, 2002, p.190).

In order to facilitate this mass development program, the Malaysian government has set out specific targets. These include: to become an Information Society by the year 2005, whereby people would have access to information, and information becomes a commodity; and to be a Knowledge-based-Society by 2010, with a Malaysian society that values the culture of life-long learning and the creation of knowledge-based products and services. Known as the National Information Communication Technologies Initiatives, the following is a brief review of the mechanisms by which the government aims to attain these targets:

a)   establishment of a National IT Council;
b)   formulation of a National IT Agenda;
c)   development of the Multimedia Super Corridor;
d)   implementation of Bridging the Digital Divide Program (BDDP);
e)   awarding of the DAGS (Demonstrator Application Grant Scheme).

The design of this multi-faceted strategy and the mechanisms, however, does not include a clear picture of how the rural sector of the nation will be situated within the larger framework. Therefore there exists a huge gap between what are in effect two worlds: the government's aspirations for a future knowledge-based economy, and the realities of rural living.

It was within this perceived hiatus in national development planning that e-Bario was conceived as a pilot project to explore whether provision of equal access to ICT can bring economic, social and cultural benefits to rural communities in Sarawak. This is particularly significant for the state of Sarawak, where 60 per cent of its 2.027

million people live in rural areas. Although Sarawak has been promised a full and equitable allocation within Malaysia's mass development plan, many communities have no access to good roads or to telecommunication services (Harris, 1999). Most rural areas lack both telephone lines and a continuous supply of electricity. Bario, in short, exemplified the disconnected portion of the digital divide, and presented a challenging environment in which to test the usefulness and effectiveness of ICT in rural Malaysia (Harris et al., 2001). Since access to ICT is predicted to promote new social, economic and cultural opportunities in rural areas (Enberg, 1998), e-Bario also provides a useful window to explore the roles that ICT can play in advancing community-based development in developing countries. With this in mind, the villagers in Bario were systematically connected to a range of ICT in September 2000 and have grown to include the following physical and technological components.

1. *Computer Laboratories:* Two computer laboratories were designed and equipped with 16 computers due to demand from students and teachers. The lab was also equipped with 2 printers and a scanner.
2. *Telephonic equipment:* The new technologies were installed within the existing communications network, the telephones were placed at strategic locations or important meeting places in Bario, such as the airport, the shop area, the school and also the clinic.
3. *Very Small Aperture Terminals & Network Configuration:* To provide access to telephone (voice) and Internet networks four Internet ground station technologies known as Very Small Aperture Terminals (VSATs) were installed by Telekom Malaysia Berhad. These were located at the shop area, the clinic, the school, and the airport.
4. *Telecentre:* A permanent telecentre, known as Gatuman Bario (Bario Link), was set up in 2001. It is located at Pasar Bario and has

5 rooms: a room for computing services, a visitor's room with table and chairs for meetings and resting, 2 rooms for administration purposes – one for the e-Bario coordinator and the other for technical assistance - and another for staff to monitor and run the day to day management of the telecentre. The telecentre is equipped with 10 computers, an inkjet printer, a laser printer, a laminating machine, a photocopier and Internet access.

5. *Power Supply:* Since Bario is outside the national grid, the telecentre was initially powered by diesel run generators. This power supply has evolved into a hybrid diesel (80%) – solar panel (20%) power supply, and more recently a solar panel – diesel system.
6. *Training and skills:* An Information Technology (IT) Literacy Programme was introduced by the research team from University Malaysia Sarawak in conjunction with COMServe, a local IT company based in Kuching. Training was identified as an ongoing process, and not a one-time or once only activity. The training included word processing, key-board usage, e-mailing, browsing the web, and the management of technologies including trouble shooting.
6. *Website creation:* Due to web hosting problems this information was incorporated into a web site designed by UNIMAS at www.e-bario.com. The web site contains information on the project, and also on the Kelabit Highlands. It was designed to promote Bario as a tourist destination, and is linked with other web sites developed by or used by Kelabit, such as the Online Kelabit Soceity (OKS).
8. *Storage of information – Bario Digital Library:* An experiment with recording, documenting and disseminating Kelabit songs and dances on CD ROM has been developed under the project. It is called the Bario Digital Library (BDL). The first record

contains nine lakuh songs by women in Bario with digital images of each singer singing the *lakuh*. Each song has been transcribed in Kelabit, with English translation. It is a step towards the creation of an electronic record of Kelabit oral stories.

9. *Management and Administration:* "Management and Administration" is not a physical or technological component of e-Bario, but rather a management system, which has been put in place in order to manage the project in Bario, and also the community telecentre. To achieve this, a project coordinator-cum-manager has been appointed by the Council of Elders, Authority for Village Protection and Development (Malay, *Jawatankuasa Keselamatan, Kebersihan Kampung* (JKKK)) and University Malaysia Sarawak to oversee the workings of the initiative in Bario. In addition to the project coordinator, a technical assistant was also trained and appointed to oversee the technical aspects of the project, such as trouble shooting and managing all the equipment and software.

Technologically, the initiative was a milestone in terms of providing equal access to ICT in the Malaysian context, and was identified as "one of the most notable of Malaysia's Internet development initiatives" by the International Telecommunications Union (ITU, 2003). In the international arena, the initiative has put Bario and the Kelabit on the world map - a remote community connected with up-to date technologies – leading to its selection as one of the Top Seven Intelligent Communities of 2001 by The World Teleport Association in New York.

ASSESSING "EFFECTS": WHAT REALLY HAPPENED IN BARIO?

This technological development nonetheless raises important questions. What of the Kelabit themselves? What meanings do they inscribe to the technologies? How have the new technologies come to be incorporated in existing social practices? That is, how have the technologies have been appropriated and used by the Kelabit in Bario?

To explore these questions in detail the next section will highlight two fundamental Kelabit concepts: *iyuk* and *doo*-ness. An understanding of these two concepts can help us to understand on going Kelabit engagement with e-Bario and in turn can highlight the social processes taking place that shaped meanings and usage of technologies in Bario.

Kelabit *Iyuk* and *doo*-ness

Between August 2005 and September 2006, when engaging the Kelabit with discussions on the impact and effects of ICT in the Highlands, their response was always quick and straightforward. I have been told it is about *iyuk* (movement) and the attainment of *doo*-ness (good-ness and better well being). Traditionally these two notions indicate movements and good-ness in terms of social status among the Kelabit. While *iyuk* broadly refers to the notion of movement and specifically to status mobility, *doo*-ness embodies notions of good-ness, success and better well being, or rather the qualities required to constitute a good person such as knowledge, endurance and perseverance, self discipline, hospitality, generosity, and strength (Bala, 2008).

The attainment of *doo*-ness through means and mechanisms of *iyuk* is the basis of all social status among the Kelabit: it represents an ideal that Kelabit individuals and collectively aim to attain and accumulate. It is the the images and ideals of *doo*-ness, and the interweaving processes between *doo*-ness and *iyuk* that have generated and sustained Kelabit modes of engagement with ideas, institutions and objects from the outside world. These externalities are adopted and co-opted by the Kelabit and given meanings, for example, as a means of providing a range of new options and systems for attaining and expressing social status, prestige and power in the Highlands. It is the dynamics between these that is relevant to the way in which Internet, computer, telephone and Very Small Aperture Terminals (VSATs) were received and adapted by the Kelabit in the Highlands and beyond. This is in spite of, or possibly as a response to the Kelabit insulation from much of the world; for instance, prior to World War II, little was known by outsiders of the Kelabits and their surroundings. They were self-sufficient: producing salt, planting rice and hunting and gathering jungle produce for food as main source of protein.

An ethno-historical analysis can establish how over the years the Kelabit forged connections with the rest of the world through a variety of strategies and traditions to attain *iyuk* and *doo*-ness. A clear example of this is how through the cultural activities of travelling far (*me ngerang mado*), the Kelabit came into the possession of prestige items, such as jars, beads and gongs. These were impossible to obtain locally in Central Borneo. Therefore those items that reached the highlands are considered important visible signs of prestige in the community (Saging, 1977; Talla, 1979; Janowski, 1991). Among these prestige items are the T'ang and Ming Chinese jars, locally known as *belanai ma'un* (ancient jars). These are prized as family heirlooms, particularly the150-pound ceramic jars with red dragon.

By traveling far, a person did not only accumulate prestige items but also knowledge. The experiences gained through traveling are considered knowledge, thus the Kelabit notion: *mado lawe, mula'nuk keli* (Far traveling increases one's understanding). As with other prestige objects, knowledge is a good source of high social standing in the longhouses (long structure built on stilts with common areas and separate family dwellings). This suggests that cultural practices of traveling far are important local practices and strategies for *iyuk* of status among the Kelabit; they are important means to incorporate objects and

ideas from the outside world into Kelabit social system. Hence those who possessed these items are highly regarded in the community.

Kelabit *Iyuk, Doo*-ness and Nation-ness

At the same time as the Kelabit absorb objects, ideas and people into their social system, the Kelabit themselves have been integrated into the wider economic and political terrain. Most pertinent here is the formation of Malaysia in September 1963. Sarawak together with Sabah, Singapore and Malaya have formed a federation. Consequentially, the population on the Malaysian side of Borneo was granted Malaysian citizenship and its privileges. With the granting of this citizenship new forms of economic, political and social systems were introduced.

As noted by Anderson (1983) 'Nation-ness is the most universal legitimate value in the political life of our time' (p.12). This process inevitably did not only change how to attain *iyuk* and *doo*-ness but also the very notions of *iyuk* and *doo*-ness in the Kelabit Highlands. That is, what they constitute among the Kelabit in the contemporary world. Said differently, the Kelabit integration into Malaysia as a nation-state has transformed the meaning of *iyuk* and *doo*-ness within the community; increasingly the notions are linked with the Malaysian government's notion of "development" (Malay, *pembangunan*) which is seen as a means for individuals to attain and enjoy affluent and prestigious lifestyles whilst at the same time enabling the whole collective (in this case the Kelabit society) to command high standards of living and respect from others. This is revealed through Kelabit every-day discussions concerning their contemporary identity and standard of living as a group. These discussions often focus on how to attract and bring more development projects into the Highlands for *doo*-ness: big and small infrastructure, better roads, cars, good medical services and effective communication facilities.

In fact, there is a sense of communal pride in being considered a progressive and successful community. Although complex, there is consequently an overall general desire for "development" as promulgated by the Malaysian government as means for *iyuk* and *doo*-ness among rural and urban Kelabit. Seen in this light, e-Bario is just one of many projects being pursued by the Kelabit to promote "progress" in the Kelabit Highlands, partly as a strategy for gaining *doo*-ness and *iyuk* for the Kelabit as a whole.

It is this Kelabit contemporary desire for progress and development, which partly defined the Kelabit on-going engagement with e-Bario in the Kelabit Highlands. If in the past the Kelabit participated in travelling far in search of Chinese jars, beads and other valuable items as part of their strategies for advancement, in the contemporary world the Kelabit are eager to collaborate with the world of progress and development in order to attain better well being (*doo ulun*) in the Highlands.

In order to understand how exactly ICT as developmental tools have been used, or rather are used to increase the Kelabit's livelihood, the next section will highlight the appropriation of technologies for communication, and as means to position or reposition Kelabit interests and their identity as a group.

As described earlier, many Kelabit have left the Highlands for education and job opportunities. This has led to a highly mobile and geographically-dispersed community. As a result of their widespread diaspora the Kelabit are constantly looking for ways and strategies to ease communication between urban and rural Kelabit. It is out of this need that the Kelabit are using e-Bario as new ways and strategies to foster family relations and community connections. This is especially important for many older men and women in the Highlands who welcome the telephone especially as an improved means of communicating with their children living in the cities. The significance of

this is made clear by Maren Talla who is 78 years old. He said, 'In the days before the telephone, I had to fly to and fro between Bario and Miri when I wanted to speak to my son and daughters, who currently are all living in Kuala Lumpur. It's a lot of money to fly down to Miri and Marudi just to speak with them. But now with the telephone, it is so much easier and cheaper. Although I can't see their faces, at least I can hear their voices. It is very satisfying to my soul when I hear them. I usually stop at the *Pasar* (market) to have something to eat and also to call my children on my way to my sheep ranch. It feels so good to be able to hear their voices on the phone; it makes me sleep well in the night. Listening to their voices on the phone calms me.'

The significance of e-Bario however goes beyond easing communication between rural and urban Kelabit for it also signifies that 'we [the Kelabit] are at par with the rest of the world and people.' Although many do not use the Internet in relation to daily activities such as farming and so forth, the presence of the new technologies in Bario is perceived not purely as a means of obtaining better quality information, connectedness and *iyuk*, but also as a symbol that the Kelabit are *doo* (progressive) in that they are not being left behind by others. These technologies are markers and signifiers that they are on a par with others in embracing worldwide shifts of perspective and influence. This is particularly significant in the context of Kelabit's present day marginal or even displaced position within the broader policies and discourse of the Malaysian state and ethnic framework of development.

To explore the situation in detail, the next part of this section will provide a brief overview of Malaysia's ethnic-oriented national development agenda under Malaysia's New Economic Policy (NEP or DEB for *Dasar Ekonomi Baru* in Malay) which was introduced in 1971 in response to race riots in Kuala Lumpur in 1969.

MALAYSIAN ETHNIC FRAMEWORK OF DEVELOPMENT

The Malaysian Ethnic Framework of Development under New Economic Policy (NEP) signifies a development pattern which is tilted towards distributional objectives, albeit along racial lines (Brosius, 2003; Hilley, 2001; King, 1999; Scott, 1985). Underlying the national quest for rapid economic growth is the desire to accelerate the process of restructuring Malaysian society to correct economic imbalance so as to reduce and eventually eliminate the identification of race and ethnicity with economic function (Second Malaysia Plan 1971-1975 provides a thorough outline of the aims and agendas of the policy). Embedded in the framework, however, is the requirement to identify persons based on their ethnic and religious affiliation for the purpose of resource and wealth distribution. As noted by Chandra (1986, p.33), ethnic and religious categories "carry deep meanings for people" in defining a person's existence and purpose especially in accessing political and economic resources in Malaysia.

What are the implications of the framework for the Kelabit, as one of the smallest ethnic groups in Sarawak? The Kelabit have to come to grips with their assimilation and participation within Malaysia's inter-ethnic disparities with regard access to key economic and political resources.

First of all, the Kelabit "peripheral situation" in relation to particular (Malay) political cultures is aggravated by the Highlands' physical distance from centres of power. Without numbers, constituencies, pressure groups or lobbies, and with their out-of-the-way location (Tsing 1993), there is a concern that the Kelabit are not given a hearing in the context of a national integration discourse, which places, as will be made clear later, the Malay-Muslim *bumiputera* at the top of the hierarchy.

Second, although article 153 (Kedit, 1989) guarantees the Kelabit as Bumiputera (lit. the sons of the soil) certain privileges under the New Economic Policy (NEP), the eminent position of Malay *adat istiadat* (customs and traditions) and Islamic religion has created a sense of hegemony and superiority on the part of the Malays over other groups in Malaysia. Consequentially, the prominence of Malay-ness in national discourse tends to benefit the Malays politically, socially and economically (Shamsul, 1986; Jomo, 1985). In the long run this framework has forced ethnic groups into a competitive relationship with each other, in which one group's advancement can mean the retardation of another group (Despres, 1975; Nagata, 1979).

Putting this differently, the NEP and ethnic framework of development as new and shifting political, economic and social contexts have created new form of *iyuk* competition, in which the Kelabit must engage competitively with other citizens who are not Kelabit for economic and political resources. This entails the Kelabit to compete with other ethnic groups for access to government financial support, government grants, development projects and schemes. All this has introduced a particular concern or desire among the Kelabit for new means to project their identity in relation to others in Malaysia and globally; hence constantly looking for strategies for collective political agency and to advance their social status within Malaysia's economic and political terrain.

It is partly due to this dynamic of economic competition that the Kelabit have appropriated e-Bario as a new means and strategy to strengthen and articulate their *iyuk* and *doo*-ness through what Miller and Slater describe as "dynamics of positioning," (2001:18). Dynamics of positioning is a term used to denote how people engage with the ways in which Internet media position them within networks that transcend their immediate location, placing them within wider flows of cultural, political, and economic resources.

A good example of this is how the Kelabit are currently using and transforming e-Bario as a forum and a stage to position and reposition their aspirations for cultural and political *iyuk* and recognition by others. This is reflected in the words of 80 years-old Balang Radu, who claimed that e-Bario has enabled further progress (*iyuk*) for those living in Bario by providing the means to forge connections with the rest of the world. He stated, 'With these new means of communications, our lives are made much easier, although we live isolated in the headwaters of Baram. We can now liaise with the outside world from our villages, including talking to our children in Kuala Lumpur, Kuching and throughout the world. This is progress (*iyuk*) for us. It has made our life easier and we are connected to the rest of the world in a new way. Therefore we are basically very-very pleased with its arrival. We are now on a par with the rest of the world.'

Balang Radu's remarks demonstrate that the new technologies are being incorporated into the Kelabit ongoing pursuit for mechanisms to position themselves within wider networks of interaction that transcend their isolated position in the Highlands. In this way the Kelabit can *continue* to be integrated within (and be part of) the space of global flow of technologies, skills, communication and information. As described in the beginning of this chapter, Kelabit society has long been connected to the outside world through their geographic mobility, and the dispersal of families. In tandem with their experiences, the Kelabit also see themselves as a part of the wider world of progress. Just as the cultural practices of travelling far, and the adoption of school and church have expanded their horizons, so too the Kelabits' contemporary acceptance of ICT like the telephones, the Internet, Very Small Aperture Terminals (VSATs) and computers in the Highlands is seen as an extension of their existing connections to the rest of the world.

This sense of achievement is important for the Kelabit for the specific reasons I have noted earlier. They are deeply concerned about their communal *doo*-ness or status and collective interests in relation to others, especially within Malaysia's

multiracial setting. As I have suggested, one of the ways in which the Kelabit are engaging with this situation is by positioning themselves on the same level with others in their pursuit of progress and success. By their capacity to attract new ideas and technologies into their environment, and their ability to adopt, incorporate, master and recreate them, the Kelabit portray themselves as a successful and progressive people.

e-Bario in this sense can be perceived as having three-fold significance in Bario: it provides means for *iyuk* by making it easier to communicate with diasporic Kelabit; it serves as a strategy for the image management of Kelabit *doo*-ness, in terms of their prestige and social status both locally and on the larger stage of Malaysia and the expanding world environment. It is a marker of Kelabit success. At the same time, it has become a symbolic compensation and a new resource for their relative smallness in numbers, political marginalization within Malaysia's ethnic framework of development and the geographical isolation of the Highlands from centres of power.

This dynamics of positioning is revealing through the ways e-Bario has been integrated within the local political apparatus to become a versatile platform for the Kelabit to position and reposition their interests in relation to the far wider context of state and national development plans. The Internet, computers and software are becoming useful tools and means to form networks, to acquire new skills in the Kelabit Highlands and to position the Kelabit at the forefront of competition for economic and political resources in Malaysia.

A local person, whom I shall refer to as Robert, who returned to Bario on retirement, illustrates this situation. Besides making a living as a tourist guide, Robert is involved in a number of organizations at village level: as secretary to a political party, and as secretary to the development bureau of the Council for Village Protection and Development. In many ways Robert depends on the computing services provided at the telecentre both for his tourism activities and also for conducting research, gathering information and writing documents and reports, including a concise development proposal for the Kelabit Highlands to be submitted for consideration under the Ninth Malaysia Plan. It was in this context that he stated that the Internet gave him access to a mass of information and enabled him to communicate with relevant people and agencies, such as the policy makers, politicians and government officials: 'The Internet seems to reduce the amount of protocol one has to endure in order to get through to these development conveners.'

Robert's statement indicates that some Kelabit are turning to these technologies as means to strategize their actions in their encounters with ideas, intervention and people from the outside world. This is particularly important as new notions of development which include commercial logging and large-scale, futuristic development plans for the Highlands are currently being introduced and implemented in the Bario. For instance, in 2003, commercial logging as a form of development has been introduced in the Kelabit Highlands. This differing concept of development has begun to shift attention away from socio-economic development among the Kelabit to their legal rights and governance in relation to their land and cultural heritage in the Highlands. This has stimulated individuals and groups to speak up after many years of moving in tandem with state-initiated plans for development. This is because there are significant concerns about the potential impact of logging in the Highlands area. These include the effects on watersheds for wet rice cultivation in the area; the Kelabit dependence on the forest for jungle produce and wild game; and the growing ecotourism in the Kelabit Highlands. Numerous people provide guiding and lodging services for Malaysian and international tourists, many of whom are attracted by the opportunities for long-distance trekking. Seen in this light, demands for land for timber concessions are bound to come into conflict with Highlanders in competition for

the same resources. This is due to the very nature of logging is in complete contradiction to the new types of tourism that the Sarawak Tourism Board and the Kelabit themselves want to attract.

Simultaneously, there is a feeling that the Kelabit are dealing with the limitations of available local institutions and practices for confronting the many problems that commercial logging and road building are generating and will continue to do so. One critical issue is the shifting notion of land ownership, which is seen as a steady alienation of the Kelabit from their heritage land, and if left unaddressed, could become a growing arena for political conflict at the village level.

All these social and political processes are beginning to shape Kelabit modes of engagement with ICT, and their outcomes in the Highlands. The use of the Internet, computers and telephone permits a form of political agency, especially as these new forms of intervention threaten to change the physical and cultural landscape of the Highlands. The new technologies inspire those in Bario to reach out to those that have left the Highlands, but still maintain a strong interest in the affairs of the village.

A good example of this is the use of community websites such as the Online Kelabit Society (OKS). As an online forum, the site features discussions on various issues which currently face the Kelabit. It is an on-line forum, and the discussions that take place within it, which allow for exchanges of ideas between members of the community both within Malaysia and beyond. Some topics or themes are the encroachment of commercial logging and the impact of development in Bario, mapping of Native Customary Land and cultural sites in the Kelabit Highlands, and the documentation of the Kelabit language, which are increasingly being managed via the Internet. A recent example of this is an Internet forum to revive the use of the Kelabit language among the younger generation. The initiative was launched by a Kelabit woman living in Miri, who is very concerned about the declining interest for and usage of the language among migrant Kelabit. As a network conducted on the Internet, the discussion list includes Kelabit who are living in Miri, Kuala Lumpur, Kuching, Bario, Bintulu and Singapore. The main concern is to find ways of documenting "extinct" Kelabit words, terms and phrases, while at the same time promoting the use of the language

All this points to the idea that the Internet has become a new means to maintain solidarity, within an increasingly stratified and occupationally mobile population, and in the face of new types of development intervention described. In fact, the significance of Online Kelabit Society, in reproducing and maintaining solidarity among the Kelabit has been likened to the traditional roles of *ruma'kadang* (the longhouse) by one of its regular users. This is because it provides space for the exchanges of ideas and advice, which are important elements of communal living in a longhouse. This suggests that ICT makes it possible for the Kelabit to form new networks and to reproduce effective organization and actions. At the same time, the presence of ICT facilitates a greater agency and capacity for political engagement to question, assess and debate these developments, and to form links with other agencies which might be useful. The various technologies available at the telecentre, for instance desk tops, associated software and the Internet, are currently being used to strategize the Kelabit position in their encounters with commercial logging activities in the Highlands. Examples of this are the documentation of oral histories and the recording of images relating to cultural and historical sites found in the Highlands, as well as the marking of their Global Positioning System (GPS) points. All these are uploaded into a Geographic Information System (GIS) database at the telecentre, to allow for the construction of a land-use history in the form of a digital map, and spatial and temporal analyses of past land use in the region. These in turn are useful historical and legal documents in negotiations with agencies involved in conservation and logging.

In so many ways, the telecentre nowadays has become more than a venue to provide equal access for new technologies in the Highlands. It has increasingly become a place and forum for the Kelabit to present and manage other "development" issues currently facing them in Bario. This trend was made evident through a recent conversation with the local manager, in which he said that, 'e-Bario is not just about ICT anymore. We are also into introducing and managing the implementation of solar power in Bario and have bought a printing and laminating machine for the Centre. So, now people in Bario can print their photographs very easily. We produce the same quality as the shops in town, but at a cheaper rate for our people.' Furthermore, he continued that 'e-Bario has now become the secretariat for all sorts of events and activities in the Kelabit Highlands. Both the church and Council of Elders use the centre to organize their religious and administrative activities.' At the time I spoke to the manager, the Centre was organizing the World Wildlife Fund "Heart of Borneo" Project's yearly symposium in Bario and also for the annual Kelabit Highlands Food and Cultural Festival. Put simply, ongoing negotiations and explorations are taking place to make e-Bario significant and relevant to the people in the Kelabit Highlands beyond the imagined practical outcomes of the initiative, and far beyond the original intentions of the project proposal.

CONCLUSION

In conclusion, what can we learn from e-Bario especially with regards to ICT for community development and its effect at the grass roots level? Experiences in e-Bario made it clear that the introduction of information communication technologies has been mediated and reconfigured by webs of social relations and the intricate interplay of social, political and cultural conditions specific to the Kelabit Highlands. As a result, the social and economic effects of e-Bario unfolded through countless open-ended strategic and everyday decisions made by the Kelabit themselves, who actively consume, apply and make use of objects, ideas and services in the Highlands. As shown in this chapter, one crucial factor conditioning the effects of the project was the Kelabit's own desire for, and expectations of, "development" and "progress."

All this suggests that real-life situations can change the purpose of technologies, and the ways in which they are used may differ greatly from what had been envisaged at the outset. Placed within local social processes and circumstances, the visions of outside policy-makers for introducing ICT as tools for social and economic development may differ markedly from the actual realities of their use and effectiveness in different political and economic settings. As drivers and developmental tools for the creation of a knowledge-based society in Malaysia, the technologies in Bario have not necessarily heralded a new form of society. Rather, they have been partly integrated with or subordinated to existing practices, internal values and socio-political arrangements in the community. Their continued use and adaptation has also provided for new forums of dialogue and communication, allowing a sense of communal identity to be rekindled. In turn, it is within these social processes that the computers, Internet and telephone have been given meaning, and their application modified and developed within the community's social context and in a wider political and economic terrain.

This social shaping of use, and the simultaneous modification of social and political processes facilitated by or inspired by engagements with ICT suggests that it is in the local circumstances that ICT is engaged with, interpreted, represented and woven into the fabric of daily life of those communities within the area. The technologies should not, therefore, be viewed as separate and independent entities, but rather as objects that

gain effect, meaning and relevance through the ways in which they are adopted and become part of the Kelabit social and political life.

As we can see the Kelabit negotiate what value to attribute to the Internet, computers and telephones, and how to apply these technologies to their own political, social and economic circumstances. All this resonates closely with Norman Long's transformative process of planned development, which he describes as 'constantly reshaped by its own internal organization, cultural and political dynamics and by specific conditions it encounters and itself creates, including the responses and strategies of local groups who may struggle to define and defend their own social spaces, cultural boundaries and positions within the wider power field' (2001, p.72).

The presence and use of ICT in Bario facilitate, inspire and modify existing Kelabit social practices, strategies and actions in their on-going engagement with development. This is particularly apparent in their engagement with commercial logging as a new industry in the area. It is an example of local empowerment, whereby the use of ICT has facilitated greater agency for political engagement in the face of this shifting notion of development. The new technologies are seen to increase the Kelabit's opportunities and abilities to make choices and to translate them into desired actions and outcomes. As a direct result, e-Bario has been recreated as a new platform to manage the interface of development in the Kelabit Highlands. In short, the presence of the Internet and computers as technologies of communication and information shape, color and influence the Kelabit response to their current circumstances.

REFERENCES

Anderson, B. R. (1991). *Imagined communities: Reflections on the origins and spread of nationalism.* London: Verso.

Bala, P. (2002). *Changing borders and identities in the Kelabit Highlands: Anthropological reflections on growing up in a Kelabit village near the international border.* Kuching: Dayak Studies Contemporary Series, No. 1, Kuching, Malaysia: The Institute of East Asian Studies, UNIMAS.

Bala, P. (2008). *Desire for progress: The Kelabit experience with information communication technologies (ICTs) for RURAL DEVELOPMENT in Sarawak, East Malaysia.* Unpublished doctoral dissertation, Cambridge: Christ's College, Cambridge University.

Brosius, P. (2003). The forest and the nation negotiating citizenship in Sarawak, East Malaysia. In M. Rosaldo (Ed.), *Cultural citizenship in Island Southeast Asia. Nation and belonging in the Hinterland* (pp. 77-133). Berkeley, CA: University of California Press.

Chandra, M. (1986). Territorial Integration: A personal view. In *The bonding of a nation: Federalism and territorial integration in Malaysia, Proceedings of the First ISIS Conference on National Integration*, Kuala Lumpur, Malaysia (pp.25-37). Kuala Lumpur, Malaysia: ISIS.

Despres, L. (Ed.). (1975). *Ethnicity and resource competition in plural society.* Paris: Mouton Publishers.

Dutton, W. H. (2001[1996]). *Information and communication technologies visions and realities.* Oxford, UK: Oxford University Press.

Ernberg, J. (1998). Empowering communities in the information society: An international perspective. In *The first mile of connectivity*. Rome, Italy: Food and Agriculture Organisation of the United Nations. Retrieved April 28, 2000, from http://www.fao.org/WAICENT/FAOINFO/SUSTDEV/Cddirect/Cdre0028.html

Fischer, C. S. (1992). *America calling. A social history of the telephone to 1940.* Berkeley, CA: University of California Press.

Goh, B. L. (2002). Rethinking modernity: State, Ethnicity, and class in the forging of a modern urban Malaysia. In C. J. W.-L. Wee (Ed.), *Local cultures and the new Asia. The society, culture and capitalism in Southeast Asia* (pp. 185-215). Singapore: Institute of Southeast Asian Studies.

Harris, R. W. (1999). Rural information technology for Sarawak's development . *Sarawak Development Journal*, *2*(1), 72–84.

Harris, R. W., Bala, P., Songan, P., & Khoo, G. L. (2001). Challenges and opportunities in introducing information and communication technologies to the Kelabit community of north central Borneo. *New Media & Society*, *3*(3), 270–296. doi:10.1177/14614440122226092

Harrisson, T. (1959). *World within: A Borneo story.* Singapore: Oxford University Press.

Hilley, J. (2001). *Malaysia: Mahathirism, hegemony and the new opposition (politics in contemporary Asia)*. New York: Zed Books.

International Telecommunication Union. (2003). *Connecting Malaysia's rural communities to the information age: The E-Bario project.* Retrieved October 22, 2008, from http://www.itu.int/ITU-D/ict_stories/themes/case_studies/e-bario.html

Janowski, M. (1991). *Rice, work and community among the Kelabits in Sarawak, East Malaysia.* Unpublished doctoral dissertation, London: London School of Economics, University of London.

Jomo, K. S. (1985). *Malaysia's new economic policies: Evaluations of the mid-term review of the 4th MP.* Kuala Lumpur, Malaysia: Malaysian Economic Association.

Keniston, K. (2002). IT for the common man. Lessons from India. The second M N Srinivas memorial lecture. In *NIAS Special Publication SP7 – 02*. Bangalore, India: National Institute of Advanced Studies.

King, V. T. (1999). *Anthropology and development in South-east Asia: Theory and practice.* Kuala Lumpur, Malaysia: Oxford University Press.

Kling, R. (2000). Learning about information technologies and social change: The contribution of social informatics. *The Information Society, 16*(3), 217–232. doi:10.1080/01972240050133661

Long, N. (2001). *Development sociology: Actor perspectives.* London: Routledge.

Mackay, H. (1995). Theorising the IT/ society relationship. In N. Heap, R. Thomas, G. Einon, R. Mason, & H. Mackay (Eds.), *Information technology and society: A reader* (pp. 41-53). London: Sage Publications.

Nagata, J. (1979). *Malaysian mosaic perspective from a poly-ethnic society.* Vancouver: University of British Columbia Press.

Rohracher, H. (2003). The role of users in the social shaping of environmental technologies. *Innovation, 16*(2), 177–192.

Rose, D. A. (2001). Reconceptualizing the user(s) of-and in-technological innovation: The case of vaccines in the United States. In R. Coombs, K. Green, A. Richards, & V. Walsh (Eds.), *Technology and the market. Demand, users and innovation* (pp. 68-88). Cheltenham, UK: Edward Elgar Publishing.

Saging, R. (1976). *An ethno-history of the Kelabit tribe of Sarawak. A Brief look at the Kelabit tribe before World War II and after.* Graduation Exercise submitted to the Jabatan Sejarah. University of Malaya, in partial fulfilment of the requirements for the Degree of Bachelor of Arts.

Scott, J. C. (1985). *Weapons of the weak: Everyday forms of peasant resistance.* London: Yale University Press.

Shamsul, A. B. (1986). *From British to Bumiputera rule: Local politics and rural development in Malaysia.* Singapore: Institute of South East Asia Studies.

Talla, Y. (1979). *The Kelabit of the Kelabit Highlands, Sarawak* (Report No. 9). Pulau Pinang, Malaysia: School of Comparative Social Sciences, USM.

Thong, L. B., & Bahrain, T. S. (1993). The Bario exodus: A conception of Sarawak urbanization. *Borneo Review, 4*(2), 112–127.

Tsing, A. L. (1993). *In the realm of the diamond queen: Marginality in an out-of-the-way place.* Princeton, NJ: Princeton University Press.

United Nations, E. C. O. S. O. C. (2000). *Development and international cooperation in the twenty-first century: The role of information technology in the context of a knowledge-based global economy* (A Report of the Secretary-General). New York: United Nations.

Williams, R., & Edge, D. (1996). The social shaping of technology. In W. H. Dutton (Ed.), *Information and communication technologies: Visions and realities* (pp. 53-68). Oxford, UK: Oxford University Press.

Chapter 14
Social Policy and Information Communication Technologies

Paul Henman
The University of Queensland, Australia

ABSTRACT

This chapter examines the contribution of information communication technology (ICT) to the operation of social and public policy. The governmentality analytic is introduced as a way in which to highlight how ICT is used by the state in governing populations. The chapter identifies four ways ICTs relate to social and public policy. First, social policy can be a response to ICT innovation and use. Second, ICT is used to implement and administer social policy. Third, ICT is used to develop and evaluate social policy. Fourth, the use of ICT can shape the very nature and substance of social policy. The chapter illustrates these theoretical and conceptual approaches by examining the extensive and innovative use of ICT in Australia's national income security agency, Centrelink.

'Each individual has a universal responsibility to shape institutions to serve human needs'. -- His Holiness the Dalai Lama

INTRODUCTION

Electronic information and communication technologies are now an indispensable element of the operation of government. Governments utilize ICTs for the delivery of government services, the analysis, development and implementation of public policy, the management of government operations, and the conduct of democratic processes. This chapter specifically examines the relationship between social policy and ICTs. While the focus is on ICT use vis-à-vis social policy, as this is the policy area of human services, the observations are equally relevant to the broader domain of public (or government) policy.

The term "social policy" refers to policies enacted by governments that contribute to individual and collective well being. The term "policy" refers to

DOI: 10.4018/978-1-60566-735-5.ch014

decisions and actions undertaken by government, of which legislation is the most formal manifestation of policy. There is no clear cut definition of what is considered "social policy" in contrast to the more encompassing term "public policy". However, welfare, social security, immigration, education and health are clear examples of social policy as are all human services. Taxation, economic and transportation policy involve aspects of social policy, such as tax benefits, labor market regulation and access to public transport respectively.

Until recently, the role of ICTs in government and more particularly in public policy processes has been poorly studied. ICTs have been given some attention by academics in the discipline of information technology, public administration and political science (e.g. Bellamy and Taylor, 1998; Griffin et al, 2007; Frissen, 1999; Heeks, 1999; Heeks, 2006), but virtually no consideration in public policy and social policy. The major exception is the long-standing concern about privacy and data protection, which has generated considerable debate and policy formation. The relative absence of ICTs from understanding government and public/social policy is largely a result of the view that ICTs are mundane technologies that are simply tools to implement government policy decisions. This also reflects a widely held view that policy making and policy administration are two distinct domains, with ICTs being relegated to the domain of public administration. A second reason for the limited consideration of ICTs in social policy and particularly human services has been the traditionally low tech nature of many human service organizations in which considerable professional discretion is involved and where services are delivered by small-scale, voluntary, non-government organizations.

It has been the advent and rapid development of the internet over the past decade that has generated interest in the role of ICTs in government. In particular, such networked ICTs have been linked with public administration reform agendas

to "modernize government" and to provide more "joined-up", individualized and responsive government service delivery. For example, in the UK the link between government reform and ICTs has been made quite explicit in former Prime Minister Blair's modernization agenda (UK 1999) and in the transformational government agenda through shared service delivery (UK 2005). Definitions of "e-government" (also called "electronic government" or "digital government") by national governments and international governmental organizations similarly make the link between ICTs and transformation of government operations, as the following example from the United Nations illustrates:

We put '**e**' *in front of* '**government**' *to recognize that a public administration is in the process of transforming its internal and external relationships with the use of modern information and communication technology (ICT) ...* **E-government** *is a government that applies ICT to transform its internal and external relations.* **Through the application of ICT to its operations,** *a government does not alter its functions or its obligations to remain useful, legitimate, transparent and accountable. If anything, this application raises society's expectations about the performance of government, in all respects, to a much higher level (UN, 2003, pp. 1-2, emphasis in original).*

Of the entire and very broad range of ICTs, internet technologies have come to define the lens of much recent consideration of the use of ICTs in government. Indeed, national governments are now annually benchmarked on the extent to which they use and develop internet technologies. National comparisons of e-government are regularly published by the United Nations Division of Public Economics and Public Administration (www.unpan.org/DPADM/MajorPublications/UNEGovernmentSurvey/tabid/600/Default.aspx) and the Institute of E-government at the Waseda University in Japan (www.obi.giti.waseda.ac.jp/).

Such surveys compare governments on the way in which they make use of internet technologies drawing on the idea that there are stages of e-government development. The United Nations refers to five stages of e-government:

1. Emerging: A government web presence is established through a few independent official sites. Information is limited, basic and static.
2. Enhanced: Content and information is updated with greater regularity.
3. Interactive: Users can download forms, contact officials, and make appointments and requests.
4. Transactional: Users can actually pay for services or conduct financial transactions online.
5. Seamless: Total integration of e-functions and services across administrative and departmental boundaries (UN DPEPA, 2002, p. 10).

Such stages depict government use of internet technologies as evolving from simple to more complex uses, with the implication that more developed usage is associated with more developed forms of public administration, government service delivery and citizen participation.

While the internet technologies applied first in business (as e-commerce) and then in government (as e-government) has provided the impetus and framework for much thinking about ICTs in public and social policy, it is increasingly being recognized that e-government not only involves internet technologies, but other ICTs, including mainframe computers and computer databases, decision support systems or expert systems, telephone call centers, mobile phone SMSing and smart cards. Indeed, digital information and communication technologies were well entrenched in government operations before the internet was invented, and much government use of internet technologies are built on those earlier digital ICTs (Cortada 2008). Moreover, modern government has always been

intrinsically tied up with information and communication technologies. Well before the invention of the integrated circuit, government bureaucratic action was predicated on statistics, paper forms and filing cabinets, punched cards, the telegraph and telephones (Agar, 2003; Higgs, 2004).

Perri 6 (2004) provides one of best considerations of the various uses of ICTs by government and how this varies according to different organizational and individual actors. He argues that e-government consists of four distinct domains of activity:

1. *e-democracy* involves the use of ICTs by government to receive the views of citizens, businesses and organizations;
2. *e-service provision* involves the "delivery of public services over digital networks and media";
3. *e-management* relates to the use of ICTs for managing the use of resources within government; and
4. e-governance refers to the "digital support for policy formulation and the scrutiny and oversight of the achievement of policy goals" (pp. 15-17).

In each of these domains ICT has some, but a varying, relationship with public policy. In e-governance and e-democracy, ICTs are used for thinking about, developing, analyzing and evaluating policy. ICTs implement policy in e-service provision. In e-management, policy is limited to policies on government administration. These observations demonstrate the various ways in which ICTs can be implicated in social and public policy processes.

THEORY AND CONCEPTUAL FRAMEWORK

Governmentality is the conceptual approach used to analyze the role of ICTs in government, and social policy more particularly. Inspired by the work of French philosopher Michel Foucault in the early 1980s, in the last ten years the governmentality analytic has generated a massive body of work that adopts the approach to provide new insights across a wide range of domains.

Mitchell Dean, a leading governmentality scholar, summarizes the conceptual approach as follows:

[Governmentality] deals with how we think about governing, with the different mentalities of government. ... It is a matter not of the representations of individual mind or consciousness, but of the bodies of knowledge, belief and opinion in which we are immersed (Dean, 1999, p. 16).

To be sure, studies of governmentality are not concerned with the way in which government is thought as an idea, but how that "thought operates within our organized ways of doing things, our *regimes of practices,* and with its ambitions and effects" (1999, pp. 17-18, emphasis in original). Governmentality is therefore an *analytics* of government that examines the inter-relations between the conceptualization and practice of government – how each contributes to and forms the other.

Peter Miller and Nikolas Rose make a similar point, by arguing that governmentality involves both "political rationalities" and "technologies of government" (1990; 2008, pp. 26-52; Rose and Miller, 1992). This characterization understands governmentality as both linguistic and discursive, on the one hand, and material, on the other. "Political rationalities" are the discursive, constructive and justificatory elements of government, whereas "technologies of government" are the means with which such discourses are translated into action, or enacted. According to Miller and Rose:

If political rationalities render reality into the domain of thought "technologies of government" seek to translate thought into the domain of reality, and to establish "in the world of persons and things" spaces and devices for acting upon

those entities of which they dream and scheme. (1990, p. 8)

While this perspective may give the impression that "technologies of government" are subservient to "political rationalities" by implementing the latter, Miller and Rose acknowledge that there is a 'complex interweaving of procedures for representing and intervening' (1990, p. 7).

In the context of this chapter, the governmentality approach helps to highlight the ways in which ICTs are involved in processes of governing – or what Foucault calls the "conduct of conduct" – and can therefore be understood as an expression of contemporary operations of power and rule. Of course, the specific utilization of technologies is extremely diverse. They can be mobilized by totalitarian regimes to help coercively control populations. Alternatively, more open liberal democracies' use of ICTs often facilitate more indirect forms of power, such as the use of mass media to shape public opinion and govern through experts (Miller and Rose, 2008, ch. 8).

Understanding government as involving both expressions of political rationalities and technologies of government provides a way in which to engage with a discussion of ICTs and social policy. Indeed, it should be noted that social (and public) policy is itself both an expression of political rationalities, but also a technology of government (Henman, 2006b; Henman, 2009; Walters, 2000).

The Relationship between ICTs and Social Policy

There are four different ways in which ICTs relate to social policy (and public policy more broadly). First, there are a range of social polices *about* ICTs. Some social policies respond to the social problems that ICTs are perceived to bring, while others seek to utilize ICTs as a specific strategy to address social problems. A long-standing policy concern arising from the use of ICTs – both by government and business – is privacy and data protection. It is the ability of digital ICTs to readily copy and circulate data that intensifies concerns about personal privacy. Over the years governments have developed a range of policy instruments to limit the distribution of personal data held by public and private organizations, and to ensure appropriate technological and organizational practices are in place to avoid unauthorized access to personal data (Bennett & Raab, 2006). The policy concern with privacy is very much tied up with concerns about "dataveillance", that is, surveillance through the use of one's data (Lyon, 1994; 2007) and more recently identity fraud, which is the act of claiming to be someone you are not.

The "digital divide" is another social problem which has said to have arisen as a result of ICTs. The argument is that as digital ICTs – and the internet in particular – have become increasingly essential to the conduct of everyday life (such as banking, education and learning, interacting with government and participating in social networks) those without access to those technologies and/or the ability to use them will become increasingly excluded from mainstream society (Norris, 2001; Servon, 2002). A range of social policies have developed to address this concern, including enhancing education, increasing use of ICTs in schools, encouraging markets for low-cost ICTs and providing public access to ICTs and training in their use.

A second way in which ICTs relate to social policy is that the technologies are used to *implement* and *administer* social policies. ICTs are now an essential part of government operations due to their ability to efficiently store, manage, circulate and calculate data. ICTs provide the means by which government officials are able to readily access the personal data of recipients of human services in order to assess eligibility, register changes of circumstances and record actions taken. In calculating benefit eligibility for social security and taxation benefits, ICTs automate policy. Networked ICTs have become particularly significant as governments have increasingly used non-government organizations to deliver human services. Such "outsourcing" of government operations often involves extensive and regular data reporting requirements, which networked ICTs support. Through data-matching exercises, governments use ICTs to assess compliance with social policies to ensure only those individuals and organizations entitled to receive particular benefits, services and payments do so.

Apart from implementing social policy, ICTs are thirdly used in the social policy process for policy analysis, evaluation and development. Administering policy generates immense amounts of data which ICTs can store. Such data holdings are often combined with additional data which are then analyzed to understand the impact, distribution and effectiveness of social policy. Governments increasingly use highly complex computer models to assist policy developers identify the likely impact of proposed policies on different sectors of society. Models are now commonplace in economic forecasting, population change, taxation and social security, retirement incomes projections and climate change (Henman, 2002). Insights gained from using ICTs in analyzing policy domains provide the basis for refining and reforming social policy.

Finally, ICTs *shape* social policies. It is the way in which ICTs operate that can contribute to new forms of social policy. It has been long argued that computers embody a quantitative, calculative and formally-defined form of operation (Henman, 1995; Roszak, 1988; Weizenbaum, 1984) which has shaped social policies to become more focused on quantitative elements of social problems and reduce professional discretion in human service delivery (Alexander, 1990; Garson, 1989; Henman, 1997; Henman, 1999). Computers have also come to define what policies are implementable. They can close off some policy options and while opening up more complex options. Data generated, stored and analyzed by ICTs have also given rise to new insights. One example is an emerged understanding of a differentiated citizenry in which different sub-populations experience different sorts of social risks (such as: long-term unemployment, poor health, and compliance or security) to which social policy responds and ICTs help administer (Henman, 2004).

These four ways in which ICTs and social policy inter-relate will be used to examine ICTs in the case study of Australia's national income security organization, Centrelink.

PRACTICE CONTEXT

The practice context for this chapter is Australia's national welfare delivery agency, Centrelink (www.centrelink.gov.au). Australia is a federated state consisting of three tiers of government: a national, federal government; six state and two territory governments; and approximately 700 local governments. Government responsibility for human service policy making and delivery is distributed across the three tiers of government according to constitutional arrangements. States have responsibility for the delivery of hospitals and community health, education, child protection and police. The federal government has responsibility for taxation and social security benefits, and immigration. Disability services, housing policy and indigenous affairs are shared by both State and Federal governments under negotiated agreements. The federal government has the majority of revenue raising powers and the states the responsibility for delivering the majority of services, resulting in what is called a "vertical fiscal imbalance". This has meant that the federal government has increasingly used its funding powers to influence directions in human service policy and services, leading to greater centralization of social policy.

Following most liberal welfare states (Esping-Andersen, 1990), Australia's human service sector operates in a "mixed economy of welfare", involving government, private for-profit, and voluntary

sectors in the delivery of social services, such as housing, disability support, health and education. Increasingly government funding is used to (partially and wholly) finance human services provided by non-government agencies. In education, one-third of Australian school students attend non-government schools (ABS 2007). In health, two-thirds of all hospital beds are provided by government-owned and operated hospitals and one-third by private hospitals (of which some are for-profit and some church-owned, not-for profit) (Duckett, 2007, pp. 136-140). Employment services are now fully privatized, but remained largely government-funded, with providers being relatively evenly split between private, for-profit organizations and not-for-profit organizations. Centrelink operates within this environment, with many of its clients also utilizing welfare services provided by non-government agencies.

Centrelink was created in 1997 by the Federal government as a government-owned "one stop shop" for the delivery of a wide range of Federal Australian government welfare benefits and services. It was created by splitting the former Department of Social Security (DSS) into two agencies: one focusing on policy; and one on service delivery. Operating on a purchaser-provider model, Centrelink is contracted by nine separate federal social policy agencies to deliver the benefits and services on their behalf to approximately 6.5 million (or about 30 per cent of) Australians. The main focus of Centrelink is the payment of government cash benefits, such as unemployment benefits, age pensions and family benefits, rather than the delivery of welfare services. In international parlance, such benefits constitute Australia's social security system. However, it must be noted that Australia is rare among OECD countries in not having a social insurance system. Instead, Australia finances its largely means-tested benefits through general revenue. Another major role of Centrelink is to assess the employment service needs of unemployed persons before referring them to private employment service providers. Reflecting Centrelink's focus on cash payments, the majority of Centrelink's 25,000 staff are non-professional administrators who utilize Centrelink's ICT infrastructure to input claimant data for assessing eligibility to cash benefits (which are then paid automatically) and to answer client queries. Professionally-trained social workers and other welfare workers constitute a tiny proportion of Centrelink's workforce. These professionals are used to assist in making policy decisions in complex client cases, case managing clients who require financial case management, and managing and providing emergency services in the case of natural disasters.

In 2007, Centrelink's service delivery infrastructure was made up of 316 local offices, 25 telephone call centers, and almost 400 smaller, regional service access points, as well as national and state management offices (Centrelink, 2007, p. 11). Supporting this service delivery infrastructure is an extensive computer network, which is described as 'one of the most sophisticated IT environments in the southern hemisphere' (2007, p. 115). This infrastructure includes several massive mainframe computers linked to numerous Local Area Networks (LANs) incorporating PCs and some dumb terminals (which are simply computers used as monitors to present data processed by an external computer), immense data warehousing capacities, and separate parallel computers for data-matching capabilities. Like other national government social security and social insurance agencies which focus on cash benefits, Centrelink (and its predecessor the Department of Social Security) has always been a very big user and early adopter of ICTs in government. Internationally, Centrelink has a reputation as a technological innovator, which has been recognized within Australia by its receipt of a number of national e-government awards (http://www.finance.gov.au/e-government/better-practice-and-collaboration/e-award.html).

Centrelink operations are significantly shaped by the wider social, political and economic environment. As in most OECD countries, the rise of the New Public Management (Osbourne and Gaebler, 1993; Pollitt, 2003) – which argues for public management to operate according to private business models – has resulted in a widespread use of performance indicators and targets, which focus the mind of front-line staff. Within Centrelink, performance targets include the percentage of benefit claims processed within a given period of time, responding to customer advice within a given time frame, or level of customer satisfaction. Meeting such targets has been a challenge in an environment of complex and fast-changing social policy, and has resulted in considerable problems with inaccurate claims processing (Howard, 2006; Whyte, 2005). Neo-liberal political rationalities have also resulted in an emphasis on identifying benefit overpayments and welfare fraud and blaming recipients for benefit errors, and the development of increasingly coercive, punitive, neo-paternalistic workfare policies to reduce what is perceived to be increasing welfare dependency (Mead, 1997; Peck, 2001). As part of the dual objective of improving service delivery and reducing costs, Centrelink has sought to utilize ICTs for self-service and integrate their operations with other (federal) government agencies and non-government welfare organizations.

CASE STUDY: CENTRELINK

How then has Centrelink used ICTs in its role as a national deliverer of welfare services? This section answers this question according to the four ways ICTs are used in social policy as outlined in the Theory section above. As will be evident, the role of ICTs in human services is extremely extensive and varied, and also has a history of both successes and failures.

First, social policies may be a response to ICTs. In terms of the governmentality framework described in this chapter, this dynamic may be an expression of the way the advent of new ICTs stimulate revised, refined or even new "political rationalities", such as notions of the "digital divide" and its assumption that access to information and ICTs is a necessary component of contemporary society. As a service delivery agency for other government policy agencies, Centrelink itself has a very limited role in making government policy. Of course, Centrelink must implement government policy responses to ICTs, specifically Australia's privacy and data protection laws and national policies regarding accessible government websites. In Australia's national social security system, one significant social policy responding to the emergence of electronic ICTs was initiated by Centrelink's predecessor, the Department of Social Security (DSS).

Introduced in 1995 as a pilot program, the Community Information Network was a policy response seeking to deploy emerging networked ICTs to enhance the living standards of recipients of income support benefits, such as aged and disability pensioners, the unemployed and sole parents. Remarkably, this initiative occurred in the early days of the internet and prefigured the concept of the "digital divide". The then Minister for Social Security, Peter Baldwin, argued that access to information could play an important contribution to enhancing disadvantaged persons' living standards, and that the advent of the internet may exacerbate already present social divisions. The Networks were established by installing personal computers in a number of public and community centre locations within a local region and linking them together in a localized network. Department of Social Security clients in the area were able to use the Networks to communicate with each other and community sector workers through electronic mail and bulletin boards. It was envisaged that clients would be able to use these technologies to do such things as advertise their skills in the hope of being employed, build networks of exchange or swap useful information (Maher & Smith, 1996). The model of this program was later replicated in rural and regional areas, but both programs were ultimately closed down

due to economic considerations, the wide-scale deployment of computers in public libraries and other programs to support access to ICTs for the financially disadvantaged.

Secondly, Centrelink deploys a very large ICT infrastructure to *implement* and *administer* social policies. In terms of the governmentality framework, this use of ICTs is a clear example of the way in which "political rationalities" are made real through "technologies of government". At the core of this ICT infrastructure are mainframe computers that operate separate software systems for managing different categories of payments (namely pensions, allowances and family benefits) which have evolved over time in response to policy and technological changes. Centrelink front-line office staff in both local area offices and call centers are connected to these payment systems through desktop computers connected in Local Area Networks, which are connected to the mainframe computers. The computer system considerably automates the processing of new claims for benefit, updating client information and the electronic payment of benefits into client bank accounts. While human operators enter client data into their desktop, the computer system utilizes the data to calculate eligibility and level of payment a person receives. The system also automates compliance measures, such as checking client data consistency with other Centrelink data. The system also sends out periodic letters to clients requiring response, and if a response is not recorded by human operators as being received by the due date a client's payment is automatically halted. Interestingly, in 1994 the *Social Security Act* was amended to legally authorize the computer to make payment decisions, such as granting and suspending payment (Sutherland, 1994, pp. 172-173 & p. 503).

In recent years, Centrelink has made use of newer ICTs to enhance its operation for both service delivery and efficiency improvements. Developments in on-line computer technology, whereby staff located anywhere within Australia can access client data, has enabled the rise of telephone call centers, operated by Centrelink since the late 1980s. Like many government agencies, Centrelink uses its on-line website to support electronic transactions. Australians are able to electronically alter their client data such as address, telephone, employment level and income. Political and fraud considerations have limited the capacity to make new claims for benefits through the internet. In particular, concerns about the security of personal data transferred across the internet blends with political expectations that income support recipients should be eyeballed to ensure that their claims are legitimate and that the experience is stigmatizing and unpleasant.

While mainframe computers have increasingly automated the assessment of welfare benefit eligibility and the calculation of benefit payment levels, in 2000 Centrelink began development of an expert system or decision support system for family related payments called EDGE. By directly modeling legislation, the expert system technology was viewed as a way in which to enhance the accuracy and consistency of Centrelink's benefit decision-making. However, after slow processing times and costly ongoing maintenance, the system was cancelled in 2004 (Henman, 2009, ch 5).

In the last decade social policies have increasingly embodied a politics of neo-paternalism, whereby those viewed as "failed citizens" are managed in greater detail than the wider population (Peck, 2001; Handler, 2004). An essential aspect of implementing and administering such policies is the use of ICTs for client compliance and surveillance. An example of this is the introduction of a magnetic strip financial debit card in 2008, called a BasicsCard. The card is issued to certain recipients who have a proportion of the welfare payments forcibly quarantined as a result of certain forms of non-compliance, and can only spend that money on essentials (food, clothing, health care and hygiene products). Card holders are only able to use the card in stores that have agreements with Centrelink. While the magnetic strip card clearly operates as a form of surveillance, it also eliminates the onerous paper record keeping by welfare benefit recipients and shop owners under the administrative system it replaced.

ICTs are also used for checking client compliance and detecting welfare fraud, that is, for administering welfare policy more broadly. Since 1988, Centrelink has used high-speed computer systems to match data from Centrelink and other external government agencies (such as taxation, immigration, police) to identify inconsistencies that might suggest overpayment of welfare benefits or even welfare fraud (Cahill, 1994; Clarke, 1995). In 2002, Centrelink trialed the use of telephone voice recognition technologies as an additional way in which to confirm the identity of clients and to manage caller demand. The technology has been subsequently installed across the organization. Privacy is essential to Centrelink's trustworthiness and legal responsibilities, and this technology is a way in which to enhance automatic services and manage service demand, while upholding Centrelink's privacy responsibilities.

Another recent development in social policy, to which ICTs have contributed, is the conduct of targeted benefits and services. Instead of traditional, universal approaches to social policy, targeted approaches seek to segment the recipient population into different categories and provide varied services and/or benefits to each sub-population (Elmer, 2004; Henman, 2004). Targeted approaches to policy and service delivery are seen as more effectively utilizing state resources and providing a more personalized service delivery. ICTs are important in managing such approaches because targeted policies are necessarily more complex than universal approaches, but they also have their downsides (Henman, 2005). One example of Centrelink's use of ICTs for implementing targeted social policy is the Job Seekers Classification Index (JSCI). In use since 1998, the JSCI is used by Centrelink in an initial interview with an unemployed person to rank and classify that person into one of six groups according to their predicted chances of becoming long-term unemployed. The classification is used to identify the predicted level of employment assistance that person requires and the corresponding level of funding the government provides to the client's private employment service agency (McDonald et al, 2003).

ICTs are also central components in implementing a targeted approach to client compliance such that those clients profiled as greater risk of being overpaid receive greater levels of scrutiny (Henman, 2004; Henman & Marston, 2008). Centrelink has also considered targeted reporting mechanisms for unemployed persons. Currently, all unemployment recipients are required to physically report to Centrelink each fortnight, but ICTs enable Centrelink to potentially segment the unemployed population according to levels of "trustworthiness" and differentiate their reporting requirements.

In addition to using ICTs for the implementation of social policy, ICTs are used *in* the social policy process, for example, for policy development and analysis. As with the use of ICTs to implement policy, this use of ICTs can be understood as the development and mobilization of "technologies of government" for the purposes of achieving "political rationalities". Given that Centrelink as a service delivery agency is not responsible for policy development, analysis or evaluation, its use of ICTs in this area is limited. However, the two major policy agencies for which Centrelink provides services—Australia's Federal Department of Families, Housing, Community Services and Indigenous Affairs (FaHCSIA) and the Department of Education, Employment and Workplace Relations (DEEWR)—make extensive use of ICTs for policy analysis, development and evaluation.

Computer modeling is a major use of ICTs in policy development. Australia's social policy departments make use of a number of highly developed computer modeling tools. Due to the complex nature of social security laws and their

interaction with similarly complex taxation laws, computer modeling is an essential component in policy development. It helps policy makers identify the likely consequences of policy proposals. Since the late 1980s a computer modeling tool has been in use in Australia for assisting in the development of social security policy. It indicates the financial effects of a proposed policy on an individual *type* of family. It can also show how the Australian population as a whole will be affected by a proposed policy. In doing so, it identifies winners and losers under a given policy, and the size of the population affected. Consequently, the model also identifies the overall financial and political cost/benefit to government. More recently, FaHCSIA has made use of EDGE, the failed expert system mentioned earlier, for policy development. While EDGE was deemed unsuitable for policy administration, it also has a policy development tool built on the fact that its rule base replicates legislation. By adjusting the rule base to reflect proposed policy change, the policy modeling tool of EDGE can identify possible conflicts in legislation and impacts on hypothetical clients. With these computer modeling tools policy options can be considered, their effects determined and policies refined to achieve the desired fiscal, social and political outcomes. However, by embedding policy in complex computer modeling, their use institutes problems for political and policy accountability and the capacity for citizens to engage in the public debate (Henman 2002).

Statistics generated by ICT is a second key use of technology for the purposes of policy analysis, development and evaluation. Given that policy making is fundamentally based on information, the use of ICTs to generate, store, circulate and analyze largely quantitative data is an important feature of ICT use in government. Centrelink's client administrative data provide an important resource for policy analysis and development. Since 2004, a representative sample of Centrelink client data has been collated to form a longitudinal dataset for policy research by government policy makers and academics. Administrative data is also often supplemented by other national data sets and specialized data collections, which are ultimately managed and analyzed using ICTs. For example, the use of computers to analyze data on periods of unemployment directly led to the development of the previously-mentioned Job Seekers Classification Index and the associated policy to differentiate employment services according to client profiles.

Finally, ICTs *shape* social policies. While it is not widely recognized, the advent and widespread deployment of ICTs in government can shape the nature of social and public policies (Henman, 2006a; Henman, 2009). In terms of the governmentality framework, this use of ICTs is a clear example of the way in which "technologies of government" give rise to new "political rationalities". The analysis of statistics is one area in which this occurs. The analysis of statistics can give rise to new knowledge and insights about the client population. For example, it provides the basis for breaking up the client population into different segments according to different levels of need or risk, which is then manifested in social policy and service delivery responses. The use of the JSCI illustrates how this occurs. Statistics are analyzed to reveal different patterns of unemployment associated with different personal characteristics. This leads policy makers to consider differentiating policy responses that better matches services to the predicted levels of need of unemployed persons. Such policies are viewed as providing a more effective and personalized response to social problems (such as long-term unemployment), but they also individualize our understanding of the causes of these problems. By linking periods of unemployment to personal characteristics, the social elements that contribute to unemployment (such as racial discrimination, poor economic environment) can often get overlooked.

The increasingly *networked* nature of advanced ICTs has also contributed to a recasting of social policy (and public administration). Networked ICTs support the exchange of data between government agencies and beyond. As a consequence, social policies are increasingly being made in one policy domain that requires the input of client data from another policy domain. With the assistance of networked data interchange, benefits or services provided in one domain can be made conditional on client circumstances in another domain. In Centrelink an example of this is the Maternity Immunisation Allowance, a universal payment to parents of children who are fully immunized at 18 months of age. This policy initiative relies on data from the Australian Health Insurance Commission, and in particular, the Australian Childhood Immunisation Register, a database of childhood immunization activity. Indeed, the impetus for the creation of the Register was to support the introduction of the Maternity Immunisation Allowance and similar conditional payments to general medical practitioners. Other conditional policies implemented by Centrelink include making a parent's income support payments conditional on their child not truanting from school, or the absence of child abuse in the household, although the extent to which these policies are reliant on networked ICTs is unclear. While such conditional policies result from political objectives, the rapid emergence and growth of such policies can not be easily disentangled from the networked information infrastructure that makes such policies readily feasible. As with targeted policy, such conditional policies also involve an individualization of social problems. By making receipt of benefits conditional on a person's behavior or activity in another domain, such conditional policies place the sole burden on the individual to resolve the social problem (such as childhood immunization and school truancy).

The use of ICTs in implementing social and public policy raises questions about the emerging nature of the contemporary forms of government and citizenship. In particular, the increasing automation of social policy has led some to argue that

ICTs are helping to install a virtual state, whereby citizens become more marginal to its operations (Frissen 1999). Along similar lines, Bovens and Zouridis (2002) argue that the evolution of IT systems to progressively automate administrative processes has involved an associated evolution of public sector agencies. They argue that original *street level bureaucracies*, in which front-line public servants make administrative decisions within the legislative framework and with the support of ICT, have transformed to *screen-level bureaucracies*, in which ICT leads the activity of government officials whose administrative discretion is reduced as it becomes codified. This is then argued to be replaced by *system-level bureaucracies*, in which front-line government officials become superseded by an integrated and all-encompassing, automated IT system. Bovens and Zouridis see system-level bureaucracies generating significant constitutional challenges arising from the complete automation of policy and the displacement of street-level bureaucrats by automated and codified organisational operations. While this author does not fully embrace these somewhat dystopia analyses, they do raise considerable insights about the contribution of ICTs in subtle reconfigurations of social and public policy, governmental power and the nature of citizenship.

CONCLUSION

It has been argued in this chapter that ICTs play an important role in the development and delivery of social policy. The governmentality framework has provided a way in which to understand ICTs as a component in governmental practices. Such an approach firstly highlights that ICTs can be understood as a mechanism in governing individuals and populations. While such "technologies of government" are often understood as implementing "political rationalities" as expressed through public and social policies, it was also demonstrated

that "technologies of government" can give rise to new "political rationalities". This theoretical framework was deployed in examining the use of ICTs in Australia's national welfare delivery agency, Centrelink, where the widespread and varied nature of ICT use is clear.

While ICTs are often seen as instrumental, in that they implement the dreams and ambitions of those who seek to govern, this chapter has sought to stimulate a critical approach to ICTs as a mechanism of governing that has power effects. Indeed, it was demonstrated that ICTs have been an important component in the reconfiguration of social policies. Increasingly, universal social policies are being individualized through targeted and conditional policies. Such developments are neither unambiguously good nor ill, but provide significant positive and negative elements. On the positive side, such policies enable governments to maximize the effectiveness of their policies and their resource investments by focusing more directly on those populations that are seen to need more direct and intensive intervention. On the negative side, such policies tend to neglect the social dimensions underlying social problems, and may lay the blame and responsibility for addressing them on the individual. Moreover, targeted policies necessarily involve inequality of treatment, which itself can improve policy outcomes, but may also exacerbate social divisions. Targeted policies also imply targeted forms of surveillance. The use of ICTs in social and public policy also raises questions about the nature of contemporary government and citizenship. Some authors provide dystopian images of systemic control and surveillance by the state. Such accounts may well be too extreme, but they can point to significant transformations in government and citizenship which might otherwise be too subtle to detect.

The main message of this chapter is that ICTs are central to the practice of contemporary politics and power in a manner that simultaneously alleviates and adds to social problems.

REFERENCES

Agar, J. (2003). *The government machine.* Cambridge, MA: MIT Press.

Alexander, C. J. (1990). Putting the byte on Canadian social welfare agencies. *Computers & Society, 20*(3), 13–19. doi:10.1145/97351.97365

Australian Bureau of Statistics (ABS). (2007). *Schools, Australia* (Cat. No. 4221.0). Canberra, Australia: ABS.

Bellamy, C., & Taylor, J. A. (1998). *Governing in the information age.* Buckingham, UK: Open University Press.

Bennett, C., & Raab, C. (2006). *The governance of privacy: Policy instruments in global perspective* (2nd ed.). Cambridge, MA: MIT Press.

Bovens, M., & Zouridis, S. (2002). From street-level to system-level bureaucracies. *Public Administration Review, 62*(2), 174–184. doi:10.1111/0033-3352.00168

Cahill, L. (1994). Data-matching in the social security system. *Social Security Journal, June,* 98-108.

Centrelink. (2007). *Annual report 2006-07.* Canberra, Australia.

Clarke, R. (1995). Computer matching by government agencies: The failure of cost/benefit analysis as a control mechanism. *Information Infrastructure and Policy, 4*(1).

Cortada, J. W. (2008). *The digital hand, vol 3: How computers changed the work of American public sector industries.* New York: Oxford University Press.

Dean, M. (1999). *Governmentality.* London: Sage.

Duckett, S. J. (2007). *The Australian health care system* (3rd ed.). Melbourne, Australia: Oxford University Press.

Elmer, G. (2004). *Profiling machines.* Cambridge, MA: MIT Press.

Esping-Andersen, G. (1990). *The three worlds of welfare capitalism.* Cambridge, UK: Polity.

Frissen, P. H. A. (1999). *Politics, governance and technology.* Cheltenham, UK: Edward Elgar.

Garson, B. (1989). *The electronic sweatshop.* Harmondsworth, UK: Penguin.

Griffin, D., Trevorrow, P., & Halpin, E. (Eds.). (2007). *Developments in e-government.* Amsterdam: IOS Press.

Handler, J. (2004). *Social citizenship and workfare in the United States and Western Europe.* Cambridge, UK: Cambridge University Press.

Heeks, R. (Ed.). (1999). *Reinventing government in the information age.* London: Routledge.

Heeks, R. (2006). *Implementing and managing egovernment.* London: Sage.

Henman, P. (1995). The role of computers in texturing the micro-social environment. *The Australian and New Zealand Journal of Sociology, 31*(1), 49–63. doi:10.1177/144078339503100104

Henman, P. (1997). Computer technology - a political player in social policy processes. *Journal of Social Policy, 26*(3), 323–340. doi:10.1017/S0047279497005035

Henman, P. (1999). The bane and benefits of computers in Australia's Department of Social Security. *The International Journal of Sociology and Social Policy, 19*(1/2), 101–129. doi:10.1108/01443339910788686

Henman, P. (2002). Computer modeling and the politics of greenhouse gas policy in Australia. *Social Science Computer Review, 20*(2), 161–173. doi:10.1177/089443930202000206

Henman, P. (2004). Targeted!: Population segmentation, electronic surveillance and governing the unemployed in Australia. *International Sociology, 19*(2), 173–191. doi:10.1177/0268580904042899

Henman, P. (2005). E-government, targeting and data profiling: Policy and ethical issues of differential treatment. *Journal of E-Government, 2*(1), 79–98. doi:10.1300/J399v02n01_05

Henman, P. (2006a). Segmentation and conditionality: Technological reconfigurations in social policy and social citizenship. In G. Marston & C. McDonald (Eds.), *Analysing social policy: A governmental approach* (pp. 205-222). Cheltenham, UK: Edward Elgar.

Henman, P. (2006b). Welfare reform as governance reform: The prospects of a governmentality perspective. In P. Henman & M. Fenger (Eds.), *Administering welfare reform* (pp. 19-41). Bristol, UK: Policy Press.

Henman, P. (2009). *Governing electronically: E-government and the reconfiguration of public administration, policy and power.* Basingstoke, UK: Palgrave Macmillan.

Henman, P., & Marston, G. (2008). The social division of welfare surveillance. *Journal of Social Policy, 37*(2), 187–205. doi:10.1017/S0047279407001705

Higgs, E. (2004). *The information state in England.* Basingstoke, UK: Palgrave Macmillan.

Howard, C. (2006). The new governance of Australian welfare: Street-level contingencies. In P. Henman & M. Fenger (Eds.), *Administering welfare reform* (pp. 137-160). Bristol, UK: Policy Press.

Lyon, D. (1994). *The electronic eye.* Minneapolis, MN: University of Minnesota Press.

Lyon, D. (2007). *Surveillance studies.* Cambridge, UK: Polity.

Maher, J., & Smith, B. (1996). *Future social provision: The department of social security community research project* (Policy Research Paper No. 69). Department of Social Security. Retrieved from http://www.facs.gov.au/internet/facsinternet.nsf/via/research_dss/$file/policyresearchpaperno69.pdf

McDonald, C., Marston, G., & Buckley, A. (2003). Risk technology in Australia: The role of the job seeker classification instrument in employment services. *Critical Social Policy, 23*(4), 498–526. doi:10.1177/02610183030234004

Mead, L. M. (Ed.). (1997). *The new paternalism.* Washington, DC: Brookings Institution Press.

Miller, P., & Rose, N. (1990). Governing economic life. *Economy and Society, 19*(1), 1–31. doi:10.1080/03085149000000001

Miller, P., & Rose, N. (2008). *Governing the present.* Cambridge, UK: Polity.

Nations, U. Division for Public Economics and Public Administration (UN DPEPA). (2002). *Benchmarking e-government: A global perspective.* New York: UN DPEPA. Retrieved from http://unpan1.un.org/intradoc/groups/public/documents/UN/UNPAN021547.pdf

Norris, P. (2001). *Digital divide?* Cambridge, UK: Cambridge University Press.

Osborne, D., & Gaebler, T. (1993). *Reinventing government.* New York: Penguin.

6P. (2004). *E-governance.* Basingstoke, UK: Palgrave Macmillan.

Peck, J. (2001). *Workfare states.* New York: Guilford Press.

Pollitt, C. (2003). *The essential public manager.* Maidenhead, UK: Open University Press.

Rose, N., & Miller, P. (1992). Political power beyond the state: Problematics of government. *The British Journal of Sociology, 43*, 173–205. doi:10.2307/591464

Roszak, T. (1988). *The cult of information.* London: Paladin.

Servon, L. J. (2002). *Bridging the digital divide.* Malden, MA: Blackwell.

Sutherland, P. (1994). *Annotations to the Social Security Act 1991* (2nd ed.). Sydney, Australia: Federation Press, and Welfare Rights & Legal Centre.

United Kingdom (UK). Cabinet Office. (1999). *Modernising government* (Cm 4310). London: TSO.

United Kingdom (UK). Cabinet Office. (2005). *Transformational government: Enabled by technology* (Cm 6683). London: HM Government.

Walters, W. (2000). *Unemployment and government.* Cambridge, UK: Cambridge University Press.

Weizenbaum, J. (1984). *Computer power and human reason.* London: Penguin.

Whyte, R. (2005). *Australia's artful dodger: Centrelink exposed.* Wollongong, Australia: Welfare Watchdog.

Chapter 15
Knowledge Sharing Online
For Health Promotion and Community Education: e–Mavenism

Hyunjung Kim
State University of New York at Buffalo, USA

Michael A. Stefanone
State University of New York at Buffalo USA

ABSTRACT

The aim of this chapter is to explore the utility of online knowledge sharing for the health and human services. Experiences in marketing are used as a basis for the development of three broad and interrelated theoretical concepts—the diffusion of innovations, viral marketing, and online word of mouth advertising—as well as several other influential factors to explain online knowledge sharing. Three major elements that stimulate online knowledge sharing are distilled from these theoretical perspectives including internal factors such as altruism, online social network size, and topic salience. This chapter uses these elements to propose a model of e-Mavenism which explains the cognitive processes that lead to online knowledge sharing behavior. Based on the e-Mavenism model, several strategies are suggested for online health promotion and community education.

Tzu Hungs: Is there one word which can serve as the guiding principle throughout life?

Confucius: It is the word altruism. Do not do to others what you do not want them to do to you.

-- Confucius (K'ung Fu tzu 551-479 BC) replying to Tzu Hungs's question in *Oxford Dictionary of Quotations* (2004, p.238:6).

DOI: 10.4018/978-1-60566-735-5.ch015

INTRODUCTION

The rapid growth of the World Wide Web has seen users adopt various types of Internet-based Information Communication Technologies (ICT) such as e-mail, social networking sites, and virtual communities to support social relationships and facilitate information seeking behavior. Using a diverse set of interactive online media, people communicate and share information with each other and often recommend products and services. Ultimately the interactive, mediated exchanges of information and knowledge among people form the basis of online knowledge sharing. This chapter is divided into four sections. The first section outlines how knowledge sharing online is performed and includes examples from four major online media organizations. These organizations were chosen because of the real world context they offer. Readers are encouraged to incorporate their own past experiences with these organizations and consider how they engage in online knowledge sharing. The second section demonstrates successful applications of knowledge sharing drawn from the field of marketing, and highlights the potential for the application of this knowledge to health and human services education. The third section presents the theoretical concepts based on diffusion of innovations research including electronic word of mouth (e-WOM) and viral marketing. Although the research reviewed in this chapter is derived from marketing studies, it provides a useful theoretical framework for understanding online knowledge sharing for health promotion and community education. Specific factors that contribute to stimulating online knowledge sharing are presented. The last section proposes e-Mavenism as a model for online knowledge sharing for health promotion and community education.

KNOWLEDGE SHARING ONLINE

Various types of online ICT tools facilitate knowledge sharing. Those most closely associated with knowledge sharing are interactive and often interpersonal media such as e-mail, blogs (weblogs), virtual communities, and online video sharing media. E-mail is the most frequently used online medium and has been evaluated as an interactive tool containing the most powerful potential for knowledge sharing online. For example, Fallows (2008) used national-level survey data (n = 2,251) to investigate Internet use and found that over 60 per cent of Internet users send and receive e-mail daily. It has been estimated that in the United

States alone there are well over 100 million daily e-mail users. (Phelps, Lewis, Mobilio, Perry, & Raman, 2005) This is a testament to how active users are in terms of mediated interpersonal communication and highlights the extent to which people are sharing knowledge and information with each other online. E-mail lowers the costs associated with communication, allows people to share information with others in their social network and affords users the power to easily disseminate persuasive messages. After all, receiving messages from friends about products, services or ideas is the core of word of mouth advertising. Given the popularity of e-mail and the potential for knowledge sharing, it is not surprising that organizations are interested in learning more about the antecedents of this behavior.

Pass-along behavior is the most representative process of knowledge sharing via e-mail and is defined as the forwarding of messages received previously (Phelps et al., 2005). This behavior is the mechanism by which people share vast amounts of knowledge and information via e-mail and can also be understood as a form of online knowledge sharing. Furthermore, knowledge sharing via e-mail among peers is persuasive. Phelps et al. (2005) found that e-mail users viewed messages forwarded by their peers as more credible than commercial messages in mass media. This is a product of the personal connection and sense of trust between senders and receivers which is absent in traditional mass media advertising.

"Blogs" are a contemporary version of traditional personal journals and are very popular. People have a long history of appropriating technology to fulfill specific goals. With regard to Internet-based communication technologies, these goals have typically been interpersonal in nature. It is not surprising, then, that blogs have also been widely adopted by users for interpersonal ends. Herring, Scheidt, Bonus, and Wright (2004) examined a random sample of blogs and classified more than 70 per cent as personal journals, in which users posted content generally

231

about their day-to-day lives, often focusing on personal thoughts and feelings. Just as interactive online social networking sites (SNSs) like Myspace.com and Facebook.com, blogs facilitate communication and information sharing among peers. Communication and knowledge sharing via blogs is typically conducted in the form of text-based posts, and recently other innovative media content is being incorporated including video clips (Herschel & Yermish, 2008).

During the process of knowledge sharing via blogs, two stages of asynchronous information exchange are repeated. Bloggers first present their own beliefs, ideas, or references to other information and share this with a network of peers. Feedback in the form of comments from other bloggers is then posted in response to initial posts. In this way, users are able to maintain mediated conversations (albeit asynchronous). Stefanone and Jang (2008) suggest that the broadcast nature of journal-style blogs actually functions to reduce the communication costs associated with communicating with a group of friends and family, regardless of age.

An important factor affecting the proliferation of blogs is ease of use. This is due to the wide variety of software applications and hosting sites available to users. These tools allow anyone with access to a computer and the Internet to create and maintain blogs because little technical knowledge (e.g., HTML) is required (Stefanone & Jang, 2008). Convenient features like trackback, linking and comment posting encourage people to provide feedback both on original posts and previous comments, ultimately promoting interactive communication. This knowledge sharing via blogs is also being adopted as a tool for online marketing distribution for business purposes (Wood, Behling, & Haugen, 2006).

Virtual communities are 'social aggregations that emerge from the Net when enough people carry on those public discussions long enough, with sufficient levels of emotion, to form webs of personal relationships in cyberspace' (Rhein-

gold, 1993, p.6). Even though virtual community members typically do not have any connection offline, they engage in interpersonal communication in these online communities and share their knowledge and experiences together (Hoffman & Novak, 1996; Kozinets, 1999; White & Dorman, 2001). For example, virtual community members share praise and complain about products and services.

Online video sharing tools are the most recent and emerging tool for knowledge sharing and include sites like Youtube.com and Metacafe.com (Herschel, & Yermish, 2008). These sites are comprised of videos created by ordinary people and have been evaluated as 'the most successful of the social network product/services' (Marcus, & Perez, 2007, p.927). Rainie (2008) used national survey data to explore online video sharing and found that over 48 per cent of Internet users visit video sharing sites like Youtube, with the popularity of video sharing having grown by more than 45 per cent in the past year. Online video sharing contributes to information and knowledge transfers (Herschel & Yermish, 2008) and facilitates the construction and maintenance of culture (Marcus, & Perez, 2007). The practice of video sharing is clearly a popular and influential development for resource exchange online, and like blogs, is easy to use. Videos are simply recommended to others by simply embedding URLs in e-mail messages.

APPLICATIONS IN MARKETING

In the field of marketing, online information and knowledge sharing is seen to possess remarkable potential. As described earlier many consumers, and potential consumers, have conversations via online ICTs like e-mail and blogs, and marketers believe that these virtual conversations can be used as an effective channel for conveying promotional information for products and services (Datta, Chowdhury, & Chakraborty, 2005; Gremler, Gwinner, & Brown, 2001). Carl (2006) and Walker

(2004) refer to individuals who actively share and recommend product and service information as "magic" people. By frequently sharing information, these people effectively increase awareness and knowledge across their social networks and do so voluntarily.

Traditionally the sharing of marketing-related information among consumers has been considered one of the most influential marketing methods (Datta et al., 2005). Interpersonal communication and knowledge sharing among consumers has powerful effects on the formation of consumer attitudes and behaviors toward products and services and especially toward new ones. Compared with traditional advertising and "personal selling," the promotion strategy performed by consumer knowledge sharing is considered to be much more effective (Gruen, Osmonbekov, & Czaplewski, 2006). Seventy-nine per cent of Internet users report using e-mail to communicate with their immediate and extended family (Rainie, Fox, Horrigan, Lenhart, & Spooner, 2000), suggesting that the interpersonal nature of the Internet encourages consumer knowledge sharing in virtual environments (Datta et al., 2005).

The marketing field already has documented many successful cases exploiting online knowledge sharing. One of the earliest organizations to apply interactive knowledge sharing via online media was Hotmail (Subramani & Rajagopalan, 2003). Initially Hotmail subscribers numbered less than a million with the number of users increasing eight fold after only eight months because of peer-to-peer information sharing (Constant, Sproull, & Kiesler, 1996; Subramani & Rajagopalan, 2003). Online knowledge sharing strategies have also been applied in journalism. Online daily newspapers worldwide encourage their readers to send content of interest to others by including prompts stating, 'send this story to a friend'. This functionality allows readers to easily distribute these URLs through their personal networks. Delta Airlines and Google use an increasingly multimedia approach for dissemination by leveraging online

videos to share knowledge about their products and services with their consumers (Herschel & Yermish, 2008; Webdriven, 2007). For example, Delta offers videos containing travel tips and Google created videos explaining how to enhance the functionality of their search engine (Herschel & Yermish, 2008, Vascelloaro, 2007).

The potential of online knowledge sharing is not limited to marketing. According to Carl's (2006) analysis, the most frequent online discussion topic in virtual communities focused on "life and living" (24.8 per cent) which includes family, education, food and dining and romantic relationships while the conversation frequency regarding marketing-related issues and products and services represents only about 12 per cent. In addition, it has been suggested that practitioners and educators promoting pro-social issues in the fields of health and human services must consider knowledge sharing online because of its popularity (Carl, 2006; White, & Dorman, 2001). However, little research has investigated the effectiveness of online knowledge sharing as a tool for health promotion and community education.

ONLINE KNOWLEDGE SHARING AND SOCIAL SUPPORT

Early research findings on online knowledge sharing suggest that it performs a secondary function of promoting social support online (White & Dorman, 2001). Social support is defined as the interactions amongst people that support and satisfy their social needs (Kaplan, Cassel, & Gore, 1977). People use ICTs to maintain social support peer groups through which they share knowledge and information with each other. The result is a better quality of life for group members and the social support resources available assists with difficult decision making (White & Dorman, 2001). Thus, for many people, online communities enhance their quality of life.

One of the most compelling examples of benefits accrued from online group membership is social support offered in the context of health-related issues. White and Dorman (2001) maintain that the most common online social support groups focus on health-related issues and are characterized by extensive knowledge sharing via virtual communities, particularly by using group e-mail. White and Dorman (2001) also report that online community members feel an obligation and responsibility to share their valuable knowledge with others, with this stimulating knowledge transfer in these online virtual communities (Burrows, Nettleton, Pleace, Loader, & Muncer, 2000; Mitra, 1997).

White and Dorman (2001) suggest that educators must acknowledge motivations and patterns of people's knowledge sharing behavior and understand how to apply online social support processes for educational purposes. Additionally, Estabrook, Witt and Rainie (2007) highlight the importance of health and other educational information sharing among online users. They suggest that people use online information as their primary information source (58 per cent) to solve health and education problems as opposed to other mass media sources like news papers, television and radio. Online information sources were viewed as being of a high quality. Similarly, Estabrook et al. (2007) found that the Internet has become the primary information source for health and well being information and that this information is reliable; with 93 per cent of Internet users commenting that they were satisfied getting health-related educational information online.

Based on the popularity of the Internet as an information source, it is useful for human services workers to develop their understanding of how knowledge is shared online. More specifically, Phelps et al. (2005) propose the need to understand why people are motivated to share pro-social knowledge with others, and what other critical factors could influence knowledge sharing and community education online. They also suggest that educators can benefit from collaborating with

experts in commercial marketing to maximize the likelihood of success.

Today, it is difficult to find a productive balance between efforts in the commercial realm of marketing and the more altruistic efforts of health promotion and community education. As described earlier, the body of research on knowledge sharing in marketing industry is comparatively advanced in both theoretical and practical aspects, while the application of online knowledge sharing in pro-social domains like health promotion and community education is at an embryonic stage. The following discussion applies some of the main theoretical principles for online knowledge sharing used in marketing and applies these to health promotion and community education.

THEORETICAL FRAMEWORK FOR ONLINE KNOWLEDGE SHARING

Three major theoretical concepts with empirical foundations in the field of marketing are particularly relevant to online knowledge sharing in the human services. These are:

1. Diffusion of innovation (knowledge);
2. Online word of mouth (e-WOM); and
3. Viral marketing

Diffusion of Innovation is 'The process by which an innovation is communicated through certain channels over time among the members of a social system' (Rogers, 1995, p.5). Even though Diffusion of Innovation was initially created to explain the adoption of technology, it has also been used for knowledge and news dissemination. It is useful for knowledge diffusion to be acknowledged by social educators because of its influence on power and culture (Herie & Martin, 2002).

Originally word of mouth (WOM) referrals in offline contexts like face-to-face communication were defined as 'the informal communication directed at other consumers about ownership, or characteristics of particular goods and services and/or their sellers' (Westbrook, 1987, p.261). Simply, WOM referrals are verbal communication between people and include influential communication about product/services among actual and potential consumers, referred to as WOM advertising (Datta et al., 2005). From a marketing perspective, WOM referrals are efficient and effective persuasion methods, compared with traditional advertising media such as television or radio advertising. Research by Herr, Kardes & Kim, 1991, demonstrates that consumers have influential power for constructing positive attitudes and decision making processes towards products and services.

Online Word of Mouth (e-WOM) is 'any positive or negative statement made by potential, actual or former customers about a product or company which is made available to a multitude of people and institutions via the Internet' (Hennig-Thurau, Gwinner, Walsh & Gremler, 2004, p.39). The most distinctive traits of e-WOM are that information and knowledge transfer occurs in online contexts both synchronously and asynchronously over 24 hours a day and 7 days a week while the traditional WOM is usually performed in synchronic face to face settings (White & Dorman, 2001). Additionally, e-WOM allows people to have much more communication and knowledge sharing with anonymous people in virtual contexts as well as their close friends or family (Hennig-Thurau et al., 2004).

e-WOM is growing rapidly via various types of interpersonal media (Brown, Broderick, & Lee, 2007). The most representative examples of online media spurring e-WOM are social networking sites (SNSs) such as Facebook.com or Myspace.com. Applied in marketing these online media facilitate the exchange of views, personal opinions and information about products, services and brands. This knowledge exchange and sharing critically affects purchasing decisions (Brown et al., 2007). Furthermore, the popularity and strong influence

of online peer review and recommendations fuels the marketing industry to invest in websites for consumer and peer reviews and feedback. These sites include BizRate.com and Epinion.com (Smith, Menon, & Sivakumar, 2005).

Viral Marketing is a "marketing technique that seeks to exploit pre-existing social networks to produce exponential increases in brand awareness, through processes similar to the spread of an epidemic" (Datta et al., 2005, p. 72). In other words, viral marketing is a marketing strategy encouraging people's positive knowledge about products and brands to be distributed to others like a virus (Datta et al., 2005). While some researchers insist that viral marketing is just another type of WOM activity (Phelps et al., 2005), the most critical difference between viral marketing and WOM is the dependence on information from commercial sources. While WOM is totally independent of traditional commercial influence, viral marketing is a business strategy using natural WOM communication to achieve corporate goals (Carl, 2006).

FACTORS INFLUENCING ONLINE KNOWLEDGE SHARING

Online WOM can be conducted with anyone, even with strangers regardless of any physical proximity or boundary (Datta et al., 2005). Compared to traditional media and face to face communication, online media allows people to communicate and share information with others outside their usual networks. Constant et al. (1996) argue that people cannot always access appropriate and valuable information from their close ties. Online knowledge sharing via ICT media affords people access to valuable knowledge from potentially global networks.

The unbounded nature of online knowledge sharing is beneficial to health promotion and community education. If social educators disseminate their educational material via online ICT media, it will reach a significantly broader audience as opposed to offline education. White and Dorman (2001) describe how online knowledge sharing is beneficial for those who cannot access offline educational material because of health-related issues. Additionally, health promotion and community education leveraging online knowledge sharing can assist many people who might otherwise not seek information due to possible embarrassment or social stigma.

Interpersonal ICT media such as weblogs and user-generated content do not require users to pay for their use (Marcus & Perez, 2007), and it leads online users to interact and share knowledge with each other via online ICT media without any financial worries. The cost-effectiveness of online knowledge sharing is also a positive factor for education with offline health promotion and community education requiring a significant amount of financial resources for physical space and other facilities.

Online ICT media offer faster and easier knowledge sharing than offline sources. Online social networks make possible more knowledge dissemination with less effort. Group e-mail or the forwarding of e-mails, are examples of efficient modes of knowledge sharing. If social educators use online knowledge sharing strategies effectively, they will be able to disseminate their information to many more people with far less effort. The following case study of e-Mavenism presents a model for online knowledge sharing for health promotion and community education.

CASE STUDY: E-MAVENISM

With the growth of online interactive ICTs, online users who easily and efficiently search online information have more virtual connections (or social network contacts) and consequently are more likely to become more knowledgeable in terms of general information (Belch, Krentler,

& Willis-Flurry, 2005). In addition, users who have many online sources have the tendency to share their knowledge and information with other people. Online knowledge sharing is encouraged by the tendency for information sharing among users.

The psychological tendency to share knowledge with others via virtual interactive ICT media is termed "e-Mavenism." e-Mavenism is a concept adapted from marketing research which has identified the concept of "Market mavens." Market mavens are people who are knowledgeable in general marketing information and eagerly disseminate their knowledge and information with others in their social networks (Walsh, Gwinner, & Swanson, 2004). We propose that the term "e-Mavenism" is effective for explaining the tendency to distribute and share valuable information with others based on a set of common characteristics in an online context.

First, online users exhibiting e-Mavenism and market mavens have a common trait; they are knowledgeable in terms of general information. Phelps et al. (2005) defines mavens as people who disseminate pass-along e-mail frequently. Secondly, e-Mavenism and market mavens do not create content such as opinion leadership, but are simply information distributors (Walsh, et al., 2004). Thirdly, they commonly disseminate their own information and knowledge to other people based on a sense of perceived responsibility and altruism to others. Phelps et al. (2005) use the term "viral maven" in a similar manner to our use of e-Mavenism here.

If educators and professionals in health-related education are to stimulate educational information sharing via online media, they need to understand the cognitive processes that lead to online information distributing behavior. The cognitive model of e-Mavenism presented in Figure 1 is a useful framework for application in the human services.

e-Mavenism is comprised of three constructs including; internal motivation (altruism, obliga-

Figure 1. Cognitive model of e-Mavenism

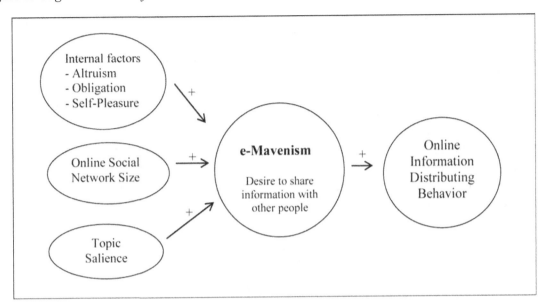

tion and self-pleasure), online social network size, and topic salience.

Internal motivations: Three motivational factors—altruism, obligation and self-pleasure—influence knowledge sharing behavior and e-Mavenism. Altruism, the desire to help and support other people, is consistently reported as the primary motivation of knowledge sharing behavior even though researchers have proposed different motivational factors such as anxiety reduction, self enhancement, vengeance and advice seeking (Datta et al., 2005; Herschel & Yermish, 2008; Walsh, et al., 2004). In addition, there is evidence that a sense of obligation to share information with other people, and the feeling of pleasure by informing others encourages knowledge sharing (Goldsmith, Clark, & Goldsmith, 2006).

Online social network size: As explained earlier, e-Mavenism is conducted by knowledgeable people who have many information sources and the number and diversity of online social network contacts has a positive relationship with knowledge levels (Constant et al, 1996). Online social networks are comprised of more diverse ties because of the number of weak ties including relative strangers (Stefanone, Lackaff & Rosen, 2008). Unlike offline social networks, online weak ties function as bridges for online expertise information sources (Datta et al., 2005; Granovetter, 1973) and increase the diversity of information sources (Constant et. al., 1996). Consequently, information from online weak ties makes online users more generally knowledgeable, which promotes e-Mavenism. Therefore, online network size is a predictor of e-Mavenism.

Topic Salience: The concept of topic salience is closely related to diffusion of innovations, especially in the context of knowledge and news. According to Inoue and Kawakami (2004), people estimate the degree of salience for information in the initial stage of new knowledge diffusion, and decide whether or not to diffuse the new information to others depending on the salience of topic. In the other words, the degree of topic salience is a predictor of knowledge diffusion and knowledge sharing. New information with a high degree of salience is diffused and shared by people much more rapidly and widely than a less salient topic (Rogers & Seidel, 2002).

FUTURE TRENDS

To stimulate motivation health promoters and educators need to attract the interest of online users by appealing to their altruism, feelings of obligation, or the pleasure they obtain by sharing relevant messages. It is expected that the pro-social nature of health related education messages will facilitate this as online users can experience a sense of obligation and altruism simply by sharing health promotion and community education messages. Messages could be promoted well through weak tie online relationships as these are often preferred when people are seeking information and do not have any particular loyalty about an inquiry (Carl, 2006). The salient points of health promotion and community education messages need to be identified and stressed, such as potential risks or benefits, when messages are created for them to be distributed rapidly and widely.

CONCLUSION

As outlined in the e-Mavenism model, online knowledge sharing behaviors are induced by three predictors; internal factors, social network size, and topic salience. Relative to the internal factors, online users have a greater desire to share information with other online users when they feel more obliged to share information and expect the message to be helpful to other online users (altruism). Information is shared more readily with other online users when they are predisposed to achieving self-pleasure for sharing this knowledge with others. Based on these three internal factors, it is suggested that educators and professionals in health-related education should foster a greater sense of obligation, altruism and self-pleasure associated with sharing educational messages by emphasizing the good cause of health promotion and community education. It is further proposed that health promoters and community educators

target weak tie online relationships to distribute their messages. Ultimately whatever the message, it must be perceived as salient by online users in order to maximize their desire to disseminate it throughout their networks.

REFERENCES

Belch, M. A., Krentler, K. A., & Willis-Flurry, L. A. (2005). Teen Internet mavens: Influence in family decision making. *Journal of Business Research*, *58*, 569–575. doi:10.1016/j.jbusres.2003.08.005

Brown, J. J., Broderick, A. J., & Lee, N. (2007). Word of mouth communication within online communities: Conceptualizing the online social network. *Journal of Interactive Marketing*, *21*(3), 2–20. doi:10.1002/dir.20082

Burrows, R., Nettleton, S., Pleace, N., Loader, B., & Muncer, S. (2000). Virtual community care? Social policy and the emergence of computer mediated social support. *Information Communication and Society*, *3*, 95–121. doi:10.1080/136911800359446

Carl, W. J. (2006). What's all the buzz about? *Management Communication Quarterly*, *19*, 601–634. doi:10.1177/0893318905284763

Constant, D., Sproull, L., & Kiesler, S. (1996). The kindness of strangers: The usefulness of electronic weak ties for technical advice. *Organization Science*, *7*(2), 119–135. doi:10.1287/orsc.7.2.119

Datta, P. R., Chowdhury, D. N., & Chakraborty, B. R. (2005). Viral marketing: New form of word-of-mouth through Internet. *Business Review (Federal Reserve Bank of Philadelphia)*, *3*(2), 69–75.

Estabrook, L., Witt, E., & Rainie, L. (2007). *Information searches that solve problems. Pew Internet American Life Project*. Retrieved September 1, 2008, from http://www.pewinternet.org/reports.asp

Fallows, D. (2008). *Search engine use. Pew Internet American Life Project*. Retrieved September 12, 2008, from http://www.pewinternet.org/reports.asp

Goldsmith, R. E., Clark, R. A., & Goldsmith, E. B. (2006). Extending the psychological profile of market mavenism. *Journal of Consumer Behaviour*, *5*, 411–419. doi:10.1002/cb.189

Granovetter, M. S. (1973). The strength of weak ties. *American Journal of Sociology*, *78*, 1360–1380. doi:10.1086/225469

Gremler, D. D., Gwinner, K. P., & Brown, S. W. (2001). Generating word-of-mouth communication through customer-employee relationship. *International Journal of Service Industry Management*, *12*(1), 44–59. doi:10.1108/09564230110382763

Gruen, T. W., Osmonbekow, T., & Czaplewski, A. J. (2006). eWOM: The impact of customer-to-customer online know-how exchange on customer value and loyalty. *Journal of Business Research*, *59*, 449–456. doi:10.1016/j.jbusres.2005.10.004

Hennig-Thurau, T., Gwinner, K. P., Walsh, G., & Gremler, D. D. (2004). Electronic word-of mouth via consumer-opinion platforms: What motivates consumers to articulate themselves on the Internet? *Journal of Interactive Marketing*, *18*(1), 38–52. doi:10.1002/dir.10073

Herie, M., & Martin, G. W. (2002). Knowledge diffusion in social work: A new approach to bridging the gap. *Social Work*, *47*(1), 85–95.

Herr, P. M., Kardes, F. R., & Kim, J. (1991). Effects of word-of-mouth and product-attribute information on persuasion: An accessibility-diagnosticity perspective. *The Journal of Consumer Research*, *17*, 454–462. doi:10.1086/208570

Herring, S. C., Scheidt, L. A., Bonus, S., & Wright, E. (2004). *Bridging the gap: A genre analysis of Weblogs*. Paper presented at the meeting of the 37th Hawaii International Conference on System Sciences, Los Alamitos, CA.

Herschel, R. T., & Yermish, I. (2008). Knowledge transfer: Revising video. *International Journal of Knowledge Management*, *4*(2), 62–74.

Hoffman, D. L., & Novak, T. P. (1996). Marketing in hypermedia computer-mediated environments: Conceptual foundations. *Journal of Marketing*, *60*(3), 50–68. doi:10.2307/1251841

Inoue, Y., & Kawakami, Y. (2004). Factors influencing tabloid news diffusion: Comparison with hard news. *Keio Communication Review*, *26*, 37–52.

Kaplan, B. H., Cassel, J. C., & Gore, S. (1977). Social support and health. *Medical Care*, *15*, 47–58. doi:10.1097/00005650-197705001-00006

Kozinets, R. V. (1999). E-tribalized marketing?: The strategic implications of virtual communities of consumption. *European Management Journal*, *17*(3), 252–264. doi:10.1016/S0263-2373(99)00004-3

Marcus, A., & Perez, A. (2007). m-YouTube mobile UI: Video selection based on social influence. *Lecture Notes in Computer Science*, *4552*, 926–932. doi:10.1007/978-3-540-73110-8_102

Mitra, A. (1997). Virtual culture: Identity and communication in cybersociety. *Year of Publication*, 55-79.

Phelps, J. E., Lewis, R., Mobilio, L., Perry, D., & Raman, N. (2005). Viral marketing or electronic word-of-mouth advertising: Examining consumer responses and motivations to pass-along e-mail. *Journal of Advertising Research*, *44*(4), 333–348.

Rainie, L. (2008). *Video sharing Websites. Pew Internet American Life Project*. Retrieved

Rainie, L., Fox, S., Horrigan, J., Lenhart, A., & Spooner, T. (2000). *Tracking life online: How women use the Internet to cultivate relationships with family and friends. Pew Internet and American Life*. Retrieved September 1, 2008, from http://www.pewinternet.org/pdfs/Report1.pdf

Rheingold, H. (1993). *The virtual community: Homesteading on the electronic frontier*. Reading, MA: Addison-Wesley.

Rogers, E. M. (1995). *Diffusion of innovation* (4th ed.). New York: Free Press.

Rogers, E. M., & Seidel, N. (2002). Diffusion of news of the terrorist attacks September 11, 2001. *Prometheus*, *20*(3), 209–219. doi:10.1080/0810902021014326

September 1, 2008, from http://www.pewinternet.org/reports.asp

Smith, D., Menon, S., & Sivakumar, K. (2005). Online peer and editorial recommendations, trust, and choice in virtual markets. *Journal of Interactive Marketing*, *19*(3), 15–37. doi:10.1002/dir.20041

Stefanone, M. A., & Jang, C. Y. (2008). Writing for friends and family: The interpersonal nature of blogs. *Journal of Computer-Mediated Communication*, *13*, 123–140. doi:10.1111/j.1083-6101.2007.00389.x

Stefanone, M. A., Lackaff, D., & Rosen, D. (2008). We're all stars now: Reality television, Web 2.0, and mediated identities. In *Proceedings of the ACM's nineteenth annual Hypertext and Hypermedia* (pp. 107-112).

Subramani, M. R., & Rajagopalan, B. (2003). Knowledge-sharing and influence in online social networks via viral marketing. *Communications of the ACM*, *46*(12), 300–307. doi:10.1145/953460.953514

Vascelloaro, J. (2007). Social networking goes professional. *Wall Street Journal*, pp. D1-D2.

Walker, R. (2004). The hidden (in plain sight) persuaders. *The New York Times Magazine*, p. 69.

Walsh, G., Gwinner, K. P., & Swanson, S. R. (2004). What makes mavens tick? Exploring the motives of market mavens' initiation of information diffusion. *Journal of Consumer Marketing*, *21*(2), 109–122. doi:10.1108/07363760410525678

Webdriven. (2007). *Delta Airlines employees make travel videos*. *Webdriven*. Retrieved September 1, 2008, from http://www.bewebdriven.com/blog/whats-hot/viral-travel- videos-delta-airlines.php

Westbrook, R. A. (1987). Product consumption-based affective responses and post purchase processes. *JMR, Journal of Marketing Research*, *24*(3), 258–270. doi:10.2307/3151636

White, M., & Dorman, S. M. (2001). Receiving social support online: Implications for health education. *Health Education Research*, *16*(6), 693–707. doi:10.1093/her/16.6.693

Wood, W., Behling, R., & Haugen, S. (2006). Blogs and business: Opportunities and headaches. *Issues in Information Systems*, *7*(2), 314.

Afterword

Dennis Perry*

Chief Information Officer, Australian Labor Party National Secretariat

'Prediction is difficult, especially about the future'

A Danish proverb favoured by Niels Bohr

'The best way to predict the future is to invent it'

Alan Kay

When writing about trends it is wise not to get too carried away by the shiny toys that often pass for new technology. Both of the opening quotations offer a more balanced approach to thinking about the future. Bohr, an atomic physicist and Nobel Laureate worked in that strange place where light can be described as a particle or a wave depending on the experiment. Kay, who has gone some way to inventing the future is described as the "father of the personal computer" (Barnes 2007), having described a prototype personal computer in 1969. Other people are credited with having built the "Micral" the first commercial non-kit computer based on the Intel 8008 microprocessor in 1973, but that's another story.

Kay worked at the Xerox Palo Alto Research Center (PARC), that breeding ground for much of the important information and communications technology (ICT) we take for granted today. A colleague of Kay's, Danny Hillis, has his own view of technology: "the stuff that doesn't really work yet" (Kelly 2007). Once it becomes a good, reliable technology it becomes invisible, and the reasons why it doesn't work at the time may be as much social as technical.

In 1992, I had already connected the Premier's Office in Victoria to the Internet for email – no real World Wide Web as we know it then – and with the improbable domain name of vicgov.oz.au. In 1994, the Australian government was still coming to terms with the Internet, and replied to my email with a fax, thanking me for my email! The Department of Finance had received the email, but was email an accepted (legal) form of communication yet for the Federal government? Thankfully, the domain gov.au was established eventually and now applies to government bodies around Australia.

By 1995, I had read and sent email using a commercial service, on a handheld device, whilst travelling in a cab to the airport. Even though it didn't quite work reliably, this convinced me that wireless technology would feature in my future. I had to wait until 2008 for Apple's iPhone 3G to add GPS to Google Maps so that I could tell the cab driver that the cab was heading in the wrong direction. I was also reading my email and checking something on the Web as a matter of course. The handheld device of 1995 was an HP100-LX with a RadioMail PC card. I also read a book, *Prisoner of Zenda*, on the plane, on that device, where the book was downloaded from Project Gutenberg. This experience convinced me that there is much that is good about social cooperation in making information freely available online. It also convinced me that I needed a bigger device to read books on. In 2009, I am still waiting for Amazon's Kindle (or a Sony ebook PRS-700 for that matter) to be released in Australia, so I can read more books on a convenient portable device.

The people best qualified to write about future technology are the gifted science fiction writers, who see that much further into the distance than ICT professionals. Around the same time I was experimenting with mobile email, John C. Dvorak (1994) wrote about "Trends in the PC Desktop Computer Industry". There is no index entry for "Internet" in his book, but to be fair he acknowledges there will be massive growth in wireless communications [mobile phones and pagers]. However, he cautioned that there could be a backlash against increased personal interconnectivity: 'Insecurity is what these devices are about. Dump them' (p.149). Needless to say, the BlackBerry was not too far away and celebrates its 10th anniversary in 2009.

By 1999, Douglas Adams, a science fiction writer, was able to ridicule the attitudes of journalists and BBC presenters who treated the whole "Internet" thing as '… just a silly fad, just like ham radio in the fifties' (p.1). Happily for the BBC, by 2006, Mark Thompson, the BBC's Director-General, was named as the most influential media person in terms of cultural, economic and political influence in the UK. His ranking was in the Guardian's Annual Top 100, ahead of Apple's Steve Jobs, News Limited's Rupert Murdoch, and the co-founders of Google. This ranking, in part, was recognition of his understanding of the importance of new media.

In 1999, Adams was also more optimistic about what he called pervasive wireless communication, and he drew on material about Nokia, and Finnish experiences with mobile phones. The article he drew on appeared in Wired magazine (Silberman 1999). Adams included observations on Finnish mobile phone users texting (SMSing) one another, and cited comments by Risto Linturi, the principal research fellow for the Helsinki Telephone Corporation, who said '… the roaming, spontaneous gatherings of kids in the streets of Helsinki are not just a glimpse of our wireless future, but a resurgence of our collective past: the rediscovery of an ancient unity coded in our senses'. 'We are herd animals', he says. 'These kids are connected to their herd - they always know where it's moving' (p.6).

In the same Wired article, Yrjö Neuvo, who was Nokia's Chief Technology Officer in 1999, when questioned about the future commented, 'If we have really high beams, we can see to 2005, … Every year we'll be getting something fundamentally new. At 2009 we can't see anything - it's completely dark' (p.4).

Nokia, in 1999 was seen as such a progressive company, that many people assumed it was a Japanese company. Meanwhile, in Japan, NTT DoCoMo launched i-mode for mobile phones, a mobile Internet services that lead to a phenomenal growth in their mobile communications market. The record growth gave rise to a mobile phone culture in Japan, including the availability of novels created to be read on mobile phones.

In 2009, if one were to look at trends, it is apparent that more information, and programs, are moving from personal workstations and from an organisation's servers on to the Internet, or into the "Internet cloud" as it is known. Carr (2008) has written about this recently, but Graham (2004) in his essay "The Other Road Ahead" tells how he and his colleagues started building what are known now as Web applications and specifically what is known now as Yahoo Store, in 1995.

Much of the work at PARC took decades to move from being technology to becoming invisible. But now the pace of change seems to be accelerating, perhaps due to rate at which information can be exchanged. Google, which Carr discusses in his book, produces Web applications that stay as beta software for years. Traditionally, during software development a beta application is something that is not quite ready to be used in production. Perpetual beta is possible with Web applications because any errors can be fixed quickly and the changes are there for everyone to use. Google's Gmail has been in beta since it was first introduced in 2005. In contrast, a patch or bug fix for an application running on a workstation has to be downloaded by everyone and installed on his or her own computer.

The biggest collections of personal information are probably not held in government databases, but on social networking sites like Facebook, MySpace, and in mailboxes on Gmail, Yahoo Mail and Hotmail. Do the users of these sites appreciate what they are divulging to the world? Perhaps they do know – and they don't care? Is there a privacy issue – probably, but does it matter? Is privacy being redefined – is your "social identity" important - and how do we protect our reputation in the 21st century? Solove (2007) presents some frightening examples of what has happened to people who have acquired not only their 15 minutes of fame on YouTube, but everlasting fame, or infamy. But people continue to post images on Flickr and videos on YouTube, which cease to be under their control the moment they

are stored on the servers of private companies, most likely in another country.

Perhaps this is just a progression of the herd keeping in touch, first noted a decade ago in Helsinki with mobile phone use. Of course the mobile phone of today is now a Smartphone that can access the Internet and has applications to allow users to access their social networks and keep in touch via "Twitter," which is SMS on steroids.

The extent to which you can be "tracked" has risks and rewards. The GPS software in your Smartphone that allows you to find your way, also allows you to record your location when you update your social networking application; "I'm doing this, and I happen to be here, and here's a photograph by the way". What if the person updating her or his social network with location information is a prominent politician or celebrity? The mobile phone ruined the plot line for writers where the story relied upon a character being unable to use a telephone because the line had been cut. How will security staff feel about trying to protect a person who advertises where he or she is located?

Location awareness can also be used in a passive way to feed you information. As you walk past a cinema, or a restaurant, current films and show times, or a restaurant menu, can be sent to your Smartphone via a Bluetooth connection. Radio frequency identification (RFID) tags or transponders can reveal something about you at a distance. RFID is currently a technology, (i.e., it doesn't always work well) but it has implications for privacy and security.

On a toll way, an RFID tag (e-tag) can automatically deduct the toll fee, which is convenient and not very intrusive. But a passport with an RFID tag will declare your nationality and an RFID tag in your watch will confirm whether in fact it is a genuine Rolex. Again, this sort of technology has risks and rewards, and opportunities for the provision of human services. Imagine the restaurant interrogating RFID tags in your clothes (designer clothes versus no-name brand) as you walk by and deciding which menu to send to you via the Bluetooth connection.

By 2009, a discipline known as ubiquitous computing (ubicomp) has united research into ways of understanding human-human interaction, mediated by computer, that goes beyond the notion of an individual tethered to a personal computer, or just using a mobile phone for sending a "tweet" to Twitter (see http://en.wikipedia.org/wiki/Ubiquitous_computing). Like many ideas that have had a profound impact on ICT, ubicomp comes from work started at two decades ago at PARC (Weiser et. al., 1999). The flows of information from you via a computing device (a Smartphone) to the Web, or from some local device like an RFID tag to you are examples of ubicomp.

Sometimes it will be an active process, where you provide, or seek information, and on other occasions some passive local information will be exchanged. Gordon Bell has attempted to record his life in his "MyLifeBits" project (Thompson 2007). His recorded life includes e-mails and documents that may already be stored digitally, to phone calls and conversations which may need to be digitised. He also wears a Microsoft Sense-Cam that takes photographs passively, and which can be reviewed later. Research is in progress to see how such a technology can help patients with memory problems or acquired brain injury to retain memories of recent events (see: http://research.microsoft.com/en-us/um/cambridge/projects/sensecam/memory.htm).

If there is one major theme that is emerging it is a new spirit of openness and a readiness to share and cooperate on the provision of information, knowledge and perhaps even wisdom. Wikipedia "the free encyclopedia that anyone can edit" is an online resource that is managed by volunteer editors around the world and has been shown to be as accurate as Encyclopedia Britannica when it comes to science articles (Giles 2005). These findings were challenged by Encyclopedia Britan-

nica, but in the rebuttal of 23 March 2006, Nature concluded with:

We note that Britannica has taken issue with less than half the points our reviewers raised. Both encyclopaedias have made corrections to some of the relevant entries since our article was published.

We do not intend to retract our article (see http://www.nature.com/press_releases/Britannica_response.pdf)

If this resource is contentious, what about the prospect of Medpedia, a medical resource with information supplied by medical professionals and medical organisations? Schneider, in *The Patient from Hell* documented how he used his scientific training to work with his doctors to get the best treatment for his type of cancer (Schneider 2005). Imagine a world where access to high quality evidence-based medicine is freely available. Will everyone have the potential to become a patient from hell?

And what of the Personal Genome Project (PGP) launched by George Church in 2006? By 2013 it has been predicted that a person's genome will be able to be sequenced in 15 minutes, for less than \$US1000.00. PGP aims to put the participants' genetic data, along with other medical data, personality trait material and basic physical measurements on a publicly accessible database. The goal is to allow anyone to use the data for medical research (Singer 2009).

One challenge for the social networking sites is to share information between each other. At present they are "walled gardens" holding their members so they can target them with promotional material. Your identity on one site may not authorise you on another site. Walled gardens and idiosyncratic ways of verifying your personal identity go against the zeitgeist, which is a new spirit of openness.

Many years ago Microsoft tried to develop its own content network, Microsoft Network (MSN) as an alternative to content available on the "public" Internet. Similarly, when I first went to work in Canberra there was much discussion within government about using the Government Open Systems Interconnection Profile (GOSIP) in preference to the "open" Internet Protocol (IP) for networking computers. In both cases the public or open solution won out.

The implications of this new openness to the gathering and sharing of information for human services are unknown. However, it can be a frightening prospect to begin a lecture knowing your students may have instant access to vast information databases, while they are being taught, as well as access to their social networking sites. Your lecture may be rated and posted online like a restaurant review, leading to a greatly increased, or greatly reduced, attendance at the next session. And of course, if the lectures are available to download, then perhaps no-one will feel compelled to attend.

The human services educator, service provider and researcher of the future may need to turn this information, which is so readily accessible, into true knowledge and wisdom. Maybe this has always been the goal of good teaching and research.

In concluding, it is interesting to watch how the early days of Barack Obama's presidency are unfolding; already some people are calling his presidency, President 2.0 (or the Internet President). Obama wants to keep his BlackBerry and instructions were issued to federal agencies along the lines of – "if you have a policy of blocking access to social networking sites, please explain why" (Funnell 2009). When these sorts of actions and directives flow from the top down it will give government bodies and educational institutions flexibility to innovate, or at least explain why they are adhering to "older" ways of doing things.

There are valid security and privacy issues to work through which will slow down the introduction of these new approaches to providing training and services. But the "shifthappens" video presentations in the "Did You Know?" series show us that the challenges are many and the changes will happen quicker than we realise (see: http://www.youtube.com/watch?v=jpEnFwiqdx8).

Dennis Perry[1] PhD
CISSP, MACS

REFERENCES

Adams, D. (1999). How to stop worrying and learn to love the Internet. Retrieved February 1, 2009, from http://www.douglasadams.com/dna/19990901-00-a.html

Barnes, S. B. (2007). Alan Kay: Transforming the computer into a communication medium. *IEEE Annals of the History of Computing, April - June.*

Bohr, N. (1992). *The Nobel Prize in physics 1922.* Retrieved February 1, 2009, from

http://nobelprize.org/nobel_prizes/physics/laureates/1922/bohr-bio.html

Carr, N. (2008). *The big switch: Rewiring the world, from Edison to Google.* New York: W.W. Norton & Co.

Did you know? (2009). Retrieved February 1, 2009, from http://shifthappens.wikispaces.com/

Dvorak, J. C. (1994). *Dvorak predicts: An insider's look at the computer industry.* CA: Osbourne McGraw-Hill.

Funnell, A. (2009). *The Internet president. Radio National Future Tense.* Retrieved February 1, 2009, from http://www.abc.net.au/rn/futuretense/stories/2009/2473039.htm

Giles, J. (2005). Internet encyclopaedias go head to head. *Nature, 438,* 900-901.

Goldschlag, D. (2009). *Guest blog: Presidential BlackBerry means mobile revolution. ZDNet Government.* Retrieved February 1, 2009, from http://government.zdnet.com/?p=4311

Graham, P. (2004). *Hackers and painters: Big ideas from the computer age.* Sebastopol, CA: O'Reilly

Kelly, K. (2007). *Everything that doesn't work yet. The Technium.* Retrieved February 1, 2009, from http://www.kk.org/thetechnium/archives/2007/02/everything_that.php

Guardian. (2006). *Top 100.* Retrieved February 1, 2009, from http://media.guardian.co.uk/top100_2006/index/0,,1807827,00.html

Medpedia special preview. (2008) Retrieved February 1, 2009, from http://www.medpedia.com/index.php/Special:Preview

NTT DoCoMo. (2009). *Company overview.* Retrieved February 1, 2009, from http://www.nttdocomo.com/about/company/index.html

Schneider, S. H., with Lane, J. (2005). *The patient from hell.* Cambridge, MA: Da Capo Press.

Silberman, S. (1999). Just say Nokia. *Wired.* Retrieved February 1, 2009, from http://www.wired.com/wired/archive/7.09/nokia.html

Singer, E. (2009). Interpreting the genome. *Technology review, January/February,* 48-53.

Solove, D. J. (2007). *The future of reputation: Gossip, rumor, and privacy on the Internet.* New Haven, CT: Yale University Press.

Thompson, C. (2007). A head for detail. *Fast company.* Retrieved February 1, 2009, from

http://www.fastcompany.com/magazine/110/head-for-detail.html

Weiser, M., Gold, R., &. Brown, J. S. (1999). The origins of ubiquitous computing research at PARC in the late 1980s. *IBM Systems Journal, 38*(4). Retrieved February 1, 2009, from http://www.research.ibm.com/journal/sj/384/weiser.html

ENDNOTE

Dennis Perry is an independent Information and Communication Technology (ICT) Professional. He has worked with government and commercial bodies on applying ICT solutions to problems. He is also the Chief Information Officer, ALP National Secretariat, but any views expressed are his alone.

Compilation of References

6P. (2004). *E-governance.* Basingstoke, UK: Palgrave Macmillan.

Aboelela, S., Larson, E., Bakken, S., Carrasquillo, O., Formicola, A., & Glied, S. (2007). Defining interdisciplinary research: Conclusions from a critical review of the literature. *Health . Research and Educational Trust, 42*(1), 329–346.

Abram, F., Slosar, J., & Walls, R. (2005). Reverse mission. A model for international social work education and transformative intra-national practice. *International Social Work, 48*(2), 161–176. doi:10.1177/0020872805050490

Agar, J. (2003). *The government machine.* Cambridge, MA: MIT Press.

Alexander, C. J. (1990). Putting the byte on Canadian social welfare agencies. *Computers & Society, 20*(3), 13–19. doi:10.1145/97351.97365

Alexander, G. C. (2003). Reaching out to rural schools: University-practitioner linkage through the Internet. *Journal of Technology and Teacher Education, 11*(2), 321–330.

Allan, J., Pease, B., & Briskman, L. (Eds.). (2003). *Critical social work: An introduction to theories and practice.* Crows Nest NSW: Allen & Unwin.

Aminzade, R., & Pescosolido, B. A. (1999). Introduction to the changing landscape of higher education. In B. A. Pescosolido & R. Aminzade (Eds.), *The social worlds of higher education: Handbook for teaching in a new century* (pp. 6-8). Thousand Oaks, CA: Pine Forge Press.

Anderson, B. R. (1991). *Imagined communities: Reflections on the origins and spread of nationalism.* London: Verso.

Anderson, T., & Elloumi, F. (Eds.). (2004). *Theory and practice of online learning* (2nd ed.). Canada: Athabasca University.

Andreopoulos, G. J., & Claude, R. P. (Eds.). (1997). *Human rights education for the twenty-first century.* Philadelphia: University of Pennsylvania Press.

Arbaugh, J. (2000). Virtual classroom characteristics and student satisfaction with Internet-based MBA courses. *Journal of Management Education, 24*(1), 32–54. doi:10.1177/105256290002400104

Argyris, C., & Schon, D. (1974). *Theory in practice.* San Francisco, CA: Jossey-Bass.

Australian Bureau of Statistics (ABS). (2007). *Schools, Australia* (Cat. No. 4221.0). Canberra, Australia: ABS.

Australian Government. (2008, December). *Employment outlook for health and community services.* Retrieved January 2, 2009, from http://www.skillsinfo.gov.au

Bagshaw, D. (2006). Language, power and gendered identities: The reflexive social worker. *Women in Welfare Education, 8,* 1–11.

Bala, P. (2002). *Changing borders and identities in the Kelabit Highlands: Anthropological reflections on growing up in a Kelabit village near the international border.* Kuching: Dayak Studies Contemporary Series, No. 1, Kuching, Malaysia: The Institute of East Asian Studies, UNIMAS.

Bala, P. (2008). *Desire for progress: The Kelabit experience with information communication technologies (ICTs) for RURAL DEVELOPMENT in Sarawak, East Malaysia.* Unpublished doctoral dissertation, Cambridge: Christ's College, Cambridge University.

Ball, P. (1996). *Who did what to whom? Planning and implementing a large scale human rights data project.* Washington, DC: American Association for the Advancement of Science (AAAS).

Barkley, E. F., Cross, K. P., & Major, C. H. (2005). *Collaborative learning techniques: A handbook for college faculty.* San Francisco: Jossey Bass.

Barth, R. (2001). *Learning by heart.* San Francisco: Jossey-Bass.

Bauman, Z. (2001). *Community: Seeking safety in an insecure world.* Cambridge, UK: Polity Press.

Becher, T. (1981). Towards a definition of disciplinary clusters. *Studies in Higher Education, 6*(2), 109–122. doi:10.1080/03075078112331379362

Belch, M. A., Krentler, K. A., & Willis-Flurry, L. A. (2005). Teen Internet mavens: Influence in family decision making. *Journal of Business Research, 58,* 569–575. doi:10.1016/j.jbusres.2003.08.005

Bell, M. (2001). A case study of an online role-play for academic staff. In G. Kennedy, M. Keppell, C. McNaught, & T. Petrovic (Eds.), *Meeting at the Crossroads, Proceedings of the 18th Ascilite* (pp. 63-72). Retrieved September 9, 2008, from http://www.ascilite.org.au/conferences/melbourne01/pdf/papers/bellm.pdf

Bellamy, C., & Taylor, J. A. (1998). *Governing in the information age.* Buckingham, UK: Open University Press.

Benetech. (2008). *Martus: Human rights bulletin system.* Retrieved November 7, 2008, from http://www.martus.org/dl/martus-overview.pdf

Benigno, V., & Trentin, G. (2000). The evaluation of online courses. *Journal of Computer Assisted Learning, 16,* 259–270. doi:10.1046/j.1365-2729.2000.00137.x

Bennett, C., & Raab, C. (2006). *The governance of privacy: Policy instruments in global perspective* (2nd ed.). Cambridge, MA: MIT Press.

Bennett, S., Harper, B., & Hedberg, J. (2002). Designing real life cases to support authentic design activities. *Australian Journal of Educational Technology, 18*(1), 1–12.

Bento, R. F., & Bento, A. M. (2000). Using the Web to extend and support classroom learning. *College Student Journal, 34*(4), 603–608.

Biggs, J. (2005). *Teaching for quality learning at university.* Buckingham, UK: SRHE and Open University Press.

Biggs, J., & Tang, C. (2007). *Teaching for quality learning at university.* Berkshire, England: McGraw Hill.

Biglan, A. (1973). The characteristics of subject matter in different scientific areas. *The Journal of Applied Psychology, 57,* 195–203. doi:10.1037/h0034701

Bird, L. (2001). Virtual Learning in the workplace: The power of 'communities of practice.' In G. Kennedy, M. Keppell, C. McNaught, & T. Petrovic (Eds.), *Meeting at the Crossroads, Proceedings of the 18th ASCILITE* (pp. 93-100). Retrieved September 9, 2008, from http://www.ascilite.org.au/conferences/melbourne01/pdf/papers/birdl.pdf

Bloomquist, A., & Arvola, M. (2002). Personas in action: Ethnography in an interaction design team. *Nordic CHI, 12*(23).

Bob, C. (2002). Globalization and the social construction of human rights campaigns. In A. Brysk (Ed.), *Globalization and human rights.* Berkeley, CA: University of California Press.

Bogo, M., & Vayda, E. (1987). *The practice of field instruction in social work.* Toronto, Canada: University of Toronto Press.

Bouldin, A. S., Holmes, E. R., & Fortenberry, M. L. (2006). "Blogging" about course concepts: Using technology for reflective journaling in a communications class. *American Journal of Pharmaceutical Education, 70*(4), L1 (8 pages).

Bourn, D., & Bootle, K. (2005). Evaluation of a distance learning, post graduate advanced award in social work programme for child and family social work supervisors and mentors. *Social Work Education, 24*(3), 343–362. doi:10.1080/02615470500050644

Bovens, M., & Zouridis, S. (2002). From street-level to system-level bureaucracies. *Public Administration Review, 62*(2), 174–184. doi:10.1111/0033-3352.00168

Bowles, W., & Colllingridge, M. (2008). *On-line student supervision training – accessible and cooperative learning in social work* (Unpublished briefing paper). Charles Sturt University, NSW, Australia.

Bowman, S., & Willis, C. (2003). *We media: How audiences are shaping the future of news and information.* The Media Center at the American Press Institute.

Boyd, D. M., & Ellison, N. B. (2007). Social network sites: Definition, history, and scholarship. *Journal of Computer-Mediated Communication, 13*(1), 11.

Boyle, D., Nackerud, L., & Kilpatrick, A. (1999). The road less travelled. Cross-cultural, international experiential learning. *International Social Work, 42*(2), 201–214. doi:10.1177/002087289904200208

Brahler, J., Peterson, N., & Johnson, E. (1999). Developing online learning materials for higher education: An overview of current issues. *Educational Technology and Society, 2*(2), 1–8.

Bransford, J. D., Brown, A. L., & Cocking, R. R. (1999). *How people learn: Brain, mind, experience and school.* Washington, DC: Committee on Developments in the Science of Learning.

Brook, C., & Oliver, R. (2003). Online learning communities: Investigating a design framework. *Australian Journal of Educational Technology, 19*(2), 139–160.

Brosius, P. (2003). The forest and the nation negotiating citizenship in Sarawak, East Malaysia. In M. Rosaldo (Ed.), *Cultural citizenship in Island Southeast Asia. Nation and belonging in the Hinterland* (pp. 77-133). Berkeley, CA: University of California Press.

Brown, G., & Johnson-Shull, L. (2000). Teaching online: Now we're talking. *The Technology Source.*

Brown, J. J., Broderick, A. J., & Lee, N. (2007). Word of mouth communication within online communities: Conceptualizing the online social network. *Journal of Interactive Marketing, 21*(3), 2–20. doi:10.1002/dir.20082

Brown, J. S., & Duguid, P. (1999). Learning-in theory and in practice. In *The social life of information* (pp. 117-147). Boston, MA: Harvard Business School Press.

Brown, J. S., Collins, A., & Duguid, P. (1989). Situated cognition and the culture of learning. *Educational Researcher, 18*(1), 32-42. Retrieved November 11, 2001 from http://www.astc.org/resource/educator/situat.htm

Brown, R. E. (2001). The process of community-building in distance learning classes. *Journal of Asynchronous Learning Networks, 5*(2).

Bruffee, K. A. (1992). Collaborative learning and the "Conversation of Mankind." In A. S. Goodsell, M. R. Maher, & V. Tinto (Eds.), *Collaborative learning: A sourcebook for higher education.* University Park, PA: National Centre on Postsecondary Teaching.

Brysk, A. (2002). Transnational threats and opportunities. In A. Brysk (Ed.), *Globalization and human rights.* Berkeley, CA: University of California Press.

Burbules, N. C. (2000). Does the Internet constitute a global educational community. In N. C. Burbules & C. A. Torres (Eds.), *Globalization and education: Critical perspectives* (pp. 323-355). New York: Routledge.

Bureau of Justice Assistance. (2008). *Drug court discretionary grant program.* Retrieved October 31, 2008, from http://www.ojp.usdoj.gov/BJA/grant/drugcourts.html

Burgerman, S. D. (1998). Mobilizing principles: The role of transnational activists in promoting human rights principles. *Human Rights Quarterly, 20*(4), 905–924. doi:10.1353/hrq.1998.0035

Burrows, R., Nettleton, S., Pleace, N., Loader, B., & Muncer, S. (2000). Virtual community care? Social policy and the emergence of computer mediated social support. *Information Communication and Society, 3*, 95–121. doi:10.1080/136911800359446

Buscher, M., O'Brien, J., Rodden, T., & Trevor, J. (2001). "He's behind you": The experience of presence in shared virtual environments. In E. F. Churchill, D. N. Snowdon, & A. J. Munro (Eds.), *Collaborative virtual environments: Digital places and spaces for interaction* (pp. 77-98). London: Springer.

Byrnes, R., & Ellis, A. (2006). The prevalence and characteristics of online assessment in Australian universities. *Australasian Journal of Educational Technology, 22*(1), 104–125.

Cahill, L. (1994). Data-matching in the social security system. *Social Security Journal, June*, 98-108.

Calhoun, C. (1999). The changing character of college: Institutional transformation in American higher education. In B. A. Pescosolido & R. Aminzade (Eds.), *The social worlds of higher education: Handbook for teaching in a new century* (pp. 9-31). Thousand Oaks, CA: Pine Forge Press.

Cammaerts, B., & Van Audenhove, L. (2003). *ICT-usage of transnational social movements in the networked society: To organise, to mediate and to influence* (No. ASCoR/TNO-STB). Amsterdam/Delft, The Netherlands.

Campfens, H. (1997). International review of community development: Theory and practice. In H. Campfens (Ed.), *Community development around the world: Practice, theory, research, training.* Toronto, Canada: University of Toronto Press.

Canadian Association of Schools of Social Work Standards of Accreditation. (2008). *CASWE-ACFTS.* Retrieved September 1, 2008, from http://www.cassw-acess.ca/

Carl, W. J. (2006). What's all the buzz about? *Management Communication Quarterly, 19*, 601–634. doi:10.1177/0893318905284763

Carrick Institute. (2007). *Discipline-based initiatives scheme.* Retrieved from http://www.carrickinstitute.edu.au/carrick/go/home/dpi/pid/82

Carswell, L., Thomas, P., Petra, M., Price, B., & Richards, M. (2000). Distance education via the internet: The student experience. *British Journal of Educational Technology, 31*(1), 29–46. doi:10.1111/1467-8535.00133

Cecez-Kecmanovic, D., & Webb, C. (2000). Towards a communicative model of collaborative Web-mediated learning. *Australian Journal of Educational Technology, 16*(1), 73–85.

Centrelink. (2007). *Annual report 2006-07.* Canberra, Australia.

Chalmers, L., & Keown, P. (2006). Communities of practice and professional development. *International Journal of Lifelong Education, 25*(2), 139–156. doi:10.1080/02601370500510793

Chandra, M. (1986). Territorial Integration: A personal view. In *The bonding of a nation: Federalism and territorial integration in Malaysia, Proceedings of the First ISIS Conference on National Integration*, Kuala Lumpur, Malaysia (pp.25-37). Kuala Lumpur, Malaysia: ISIS.

Chang, C.-C. (2003). Towards a distributed Web-based learning community. *Innovations in Education and Teaching International, 40*(1), 27–42. doi:10.1080/1355800032000038831

Chechele, P. J., & Stofle, G. (2003). Individual therapy online via email and Internet relay chat. In S. Goss & K. Anthony (Eds.), *Technology in counselling and psychotherapy: A practitioner's guide* (pp. 39-58). Basingstoke, NY: Palgrave Macmillan.

Chen, C. J. (2006). The design, development and evaluation of a virtual reality based learning environment. *Australasian Journal of Educational Technology, 22*(1), 39–63.

Chester, A., & Gwynne, G. (1998). Online teaching: Encouraging collaboration through anonymity. *Journal of Computer Mediated Communication, 4*(2). Retrieved July 11, 2007, from http://jcmc.indiana.edu/vol4/issue2/chester.html

Childnet International. (2007). *Young people and social networking services: A Childnet International research report.* Retrieved September 25, 2008, from http://www. digizen.org/socialnetworking

Cho, H., Gay, G., Davidson, B., & Ingraffea, A. (2007). Social networks, communication styles and learning performance in a CSCL community. *Computers & Education, 49,* 309–329. doi:10.1016/j.compedu.2005.07.003

Clark, J. (2000). Collaboration tools in online learning environments. *Asynchronous Learning Networks Magazine, 4*(1). Retrieved October 13, 2008, from http://www. aln.org/publications/magazine/v4n1/clark.asp

Clark, R. C. (2003). *Expertise, learning, and instruction: Building expertise* (2nd ed.). MN, USA: International Society for Performance Improvement.

Clarke, R. (1995). Computer matching by government agencies: The failure of cost/benefit analysis as a control mechanism. *Information Infrastructure and Policy, 4*(1).

Claude, R. P., & Hick, S. (2000). Human rights education on the Internet: Its day has come. In S. Hick, E. F. Halpin, & E. Hoskins (Eds.), *Human rights and the Internet* (pp. 225-237). Houndmills, UK: MacMillan Press Ltd.

Clodius, J. (1994). *Concepts of space and place in a virtual community.* Retrieved August 2, 2003, from http:// dragonmud.org/people/jen/space.html

Coates, H. (2005). The value of student engagement for higher education quality assurance. *Quality in Higher Education, 11*(1), 25–36. doi:10.1080/13538320500074915

Coates, H. (2006). *Excellent measures precede measures of excellence.* Paper presented at the Australian Universities Quality Forum, Perth, Australia.

Coiro, J., Knobel, M., Lankshear, C., & Leu, D. (2008). Central issues in new literacies and new literacies research. In J. Coiro, M. Knobel, C. Lankshear, & D. Leu (Eds.), *Handbook of research on new literacies* (pp. 1-21). New York: Lawrence Erlbaum Associates.

College Access Marketing. (n.d.). *Achieving college access goals: The relevance of new media in reaching first-generation and low-income teens.* Retrieved September

30, 2008, from http://www.collegeaccessmarketing.org/ campaignresourcecenter_ektid232.aspx

Combined Schools of Social Work. (2008). *CSSW.* Retrieved January 14, 2009, from http://www.cssw. com.au

Compete. (2008, September 30). *Compete's top 10 sites ranked by: Page views.* Retrieved September 30, 2008, from http://lists.compete.com

ComScore. (2008, August 12). *Social networking explodes worldwide as sites increase their focus on cultural relevance.* Retrieved September 30, 2008, from http:// www.comscore.com/ press/release.asp?press=2396

Conrad, D. (2002). Deep in the hearts of learners: Insights into the nature of online community. *Journal of Distance Education, 17*(1).

Conrad, D. (2005). Building and maintaining community in cohort-based online learning. *Journal of Distance Education, 20*(1), 1–20.

Constant, D., Sproull, L., & Kiesler, S. (1996). The kindness of strangers: The usefulness of electronic weak ties for technical advice. *Organization Science, 7*(2), 119–135. doi:10.1287/orsc.7.2.119

Cooper, A. (1999). *The inmates are running the asylum.* UK: Macmillam.

Cooper, A. (2004). *The inmates are running the asylum: Why high tech products drive us crazy and how to restore the sanity* (2nd ed.). UK: Pearson Higher Education.

Cooper, L. (2001). Teaching controversial issues online. *New Technology in the Human Services, 13*(3-4), 11–21.

Cornelius, L., & Grief, G. (2005). Schools of social work and the nature of their foreign collaborations. *International Social Work, 48*(6), 823–833. doi:10.1177/0020872805057094

Cortada, J. W. (2008). *The digital hand, vol 3: How computers changed the work of American public sector industries.* New York: Oxford University Press.

Currion, P. (2007). *Dial H for humanitarian*. Retrieved November 2, 2008, from http://www.humanitarian. info/2007/11/06/dial-h-for-humanitarian/

Curtis, D., & Lawson, M. (2001). Exploring collaborative online learning. *Journal of Asynchronous Learning Networks, 5*(1), 22–34.

Curtis, R. (2004). Analyzing students' conversations in chat room. *College Teaching, 52*(4), 143–148. doi:10.3200/CTCH.52.4.143-149

D'Antoni, S., & Mugridge, I. (2004). *Virtual universities and transnational education, UNESCO Forum Report, 2007*. Retrieved July 12, 2007, from http://www.unesco.org/iiep/virtualuniversity/forumfiche

D'Cruz, H., Gillingham, P., & Menendez, S. (2005). Reflexivity, its meanings and relevance for social work: A critical review of the literature. *British Journal of Social Work, 37*, 73–90. doi:10.1093/bjsw/bcl001

Datta, P. R., Chowdhury, D. N., & Chakraborty, B. R. (2005). Viral marketing: New form of word-of-mouth through Internet. *Business Review (Federal Reserve Bank of Philadelphia), 3*(2), 69–75.

Davis, M., & Devlin, M. (2007). *Interdisciplinary higher education: Implications for teaching and learning*. Australia: CSHE centre for study in higher education, University of Melbourne. Melbourne

Day, P. R. (1977). *Methods of learning communication skills*. Oxford, UK: Pergamon Press.

Dean, M. (1999). *Governmentality*. London: Sage.

Demetrious, K. (2007). Playing a critical role: Experiential learning resources and analytical media studies in higher education. In *ICT: Providing choices for learners and learning, Proceedings of the ASCILITE*. Retrieved September 9, 2008, from http://www.ascilite.org.au/conferences/singapore07/procs/demetrious.pdf

Department of Education, Science and Training and Australian National Training Authority. (2002). *Employability skills for the future, Commonwealth Department of Education, Science and Training*. Retrieved June 23, 2008 from http://www.dest.gov.au/archive/ty/publications/employability_skills/final_report.pdf

Despres, L. (Ed.). (1975). *Ethnicity and resource competition in plural society*. Paris: Mouton Publishers.

Dewey, J. (1938). *Experience and education*. New York: Collier.

Di Petta, T. (1998). Community on-line: New professional environments for higher education. *New Directions for Teaching and Learning*, (76): 53–66. doi:10.1002/tl.7604

Dominelli, L. (2004). *Social work: Theory and practice for a changing profession*. Cambridge, UK: Polity Press.

Donath, J., & Boyd, D. (2004). Public displays of connection. *BT Technology Journal, 22*(4), 71–82. doi:10.1023/B:BTTJ.0000047585.06264.cc

Douglas, K. (2007a). E-learning as a way to reflexive practice: Online mediation role-plays. *International Journal of Education, 13*, 73–80.

Douglas, K. (2007b). Mediator accreditation: Using online role-plays to teach theoretical issues. *Australasian Dispute Resolution Journal, 18*, 92–100.

Douglas, K., & Ogilvie, A. (2007). Online role-plays, virtual placements and work integrated learning: Exploring the example of mediation communities of practice. In *Proceedings of the Partnerships for World Graduates Conference*.

Dracup, M. (2008). Role-play in blended learning: A case study exploring the impact of story and other elements. *Australasian Journal of Educational Technology, 24*(3), 294–310.

Duckett, S. J. (2007). *The Australian health care system* (3rd ed.). Melbourne, Australia: Oxford University Press.

Dueck, J., Guzman, M., & Verstappen, B. (2001a). *HURIDOCS events standard formats: A tool for documenting human rights violations* (2nd ed.). Versoix, Switzerland: HURIDOCS.

Dueck, J., Guzman, M., & Verstappen, B. (2001b). *Microthesauri: A tool for documenting human rights violations* (2nd ed.). Versoix, Switzerland: HURIDOCS.

Dutton, W. H. (2001[1996]). *Information and communication technologies visions and realities*. Oxford, UK: Oxford University Press.

Eakin, L. (2007). *We can't afford to do business this way: A study of the administrative burden resulting from funder accountability and compliance practices.* Toronto, Canada: Wellesley Institute.

Eberhardt, D. M. (2007). Facing up to Facebook. *About Campus, 12*(4), 18–26. doi:10.1002/abc.219

Ellison, N., Steinfield, C., & Lampe, C. (2007). The benefits of Facebook "friends": Exploring the relationship between college students' use of online social networks and social capital. *Journal of Computer-Mediated Communication, 12*(3), article 1. Retrieved July 30, 2007, from http://jcmc.indiana.edu/vol12/issue4/ellison.html

Elmer, G. (2004). *Profiling machines*. Cambridge, MA: MIT Press.

Ernberg, J. (1998). Empowering communities in the information society: An international perspective. In *The first mile of connectivity*. Rome, Italy: Food and Agriculture Organisation of the United Nations. Retrieved April 28, 2000, from http://www.fao.org/WAICENT/FAOINFO/SUSTDEV/Cddirect/Cdre0028.html

Esping-Andersen, G. (1990). *The three worlds of welfare capitalism*. Cambridge, UK: Polity.

Estabrook, L., Witt, E., & Rainie, L. (2007). *Information searches that solve problems. Pew Internet American Life Project*. Retrieved September 1, 2008, from http://www.pewinternet.org/reports.asp

Fablusi. (2004). *The online role-play simulation platform*. Retrieved July 25, 2007, from http://www.fablusi.com/

Fallows, D. (2008). *Search engine use. Pew Internet American Life Project*. Retrieved September 12, 2008, from http://www.pewinternet.org/reports.asp

Fischer, C. S. (1992). *America calling. A social history of the telephone to 1940*. Berkeley, CA: University of California Press.

Flowers, N. (2000). *The human rights education handbook: Effective Practices for learning, action, and change*. Minneapolis, MN: University of Minnesota.

Fook, J. (1996). *The reflective researcher*. St. Leonards, NSW: Allen and Unwin.

Fook, J. (1999). Critical reflexivity in education and practice. In B. Pease & J. Fook (Eds.), *Transforming social work*. St. Leonards, AU: Allen & Unwin.

Fook, J. (2002). *Critical social work practice*. Thousand Oaks, CA: Sage Publications.

Fook, J. (2002). *Social work: Critical theory and practice*. London: Sage.

Fountain, R. (2005). *Wiki pedagogy. Dossiers pratiques, profetic*. Retrieved October 13, 2008, from http://www.profetic.org/dossiers/dossier_imprimer.php3?id_rubrique=110

Fountain, R. (2005). *Wiki pedagogy. Dossiers technopedagogiques*. Retrieved September 9, 2008, from http://www.profetic.org/dossiers/dossier_imprimer.php3?id_rubrique=110

Frank, F., & Smith, A. (2006). *Community development and partnerships: A handbook for building community partnerships*. Bentley, Western Australia: Curtin University of Technology.

Freire, P. (1972). *Pedagogy of the oppressed*. New York: The Seabury Press.

Freire, P. (1993). *Pedagogy of the oppressed*. New York: Continuum.

Freire, P. (1995). *Pedagogy of hope, relieving pedagogy of the oppressed*. New York Continuum.

Freydenson, E. (2002). *Bringing your personas to life in real life*. Retrieved September 9, 2005, from http://boxesandarrows.com/archives/002343.php

Frissen, P. H. A. (1999). *Politics, governance and technology*. Cheltenham, UK: Edward Elgar.

Fulton, K. (1999). *How teachers' beliefs about teaching and learning are reflected in their use of technology: Case studies from urban middle schools*. Unpublished dissertation, University of Maryland. Retrieved from http://www.learn.umd.edu/fulton/

Garrison, D. R., & Vaughan, N. D. (2008). *Blended learning in higher education: Framework, principles, and guidelines*. San Francisco: John Wiley & Sons.

Garson, B. (1989). *The electronic sweatshop*. Harmondsworth, UK: Penguin.

Gay, G., Sturgill, A., & Martin, W. (1999). Document-centered peer collaborations: An exploration of the educational uses of networked communication technologies. *Journal of Computer-Mediated Communication, 4*(3). Retrieved October 13, 2008, from http://jcmc.indiana.edu/vol4/issue3/gay.html

Gee, J. P. (2004). *What video games have to teach us about learning and literacy*. New York: Palgrave MacMillian.

Gerrard, C. (2001). Promoting excellence in distance education – a TQM led approach. In K. Ho & M. Donnelly (Eds.), *Integrated Management – Proceedings of the 6th International Conference on ISO 9000 and TQM* (pp. 578-583).

Giffard, C. (2000). *The torture reporting handbook. How to document and respond to allegations of torture within the international system for the protection of human rights*. UK: Human Rights Centre, University of Essex.

Goh, B. L. (2002). Rethinking modernity: State, Ethnicity, and class in the forging of a modern urban Malaysia. In C. J. W.-L. Wee (Ed.), *Local cultures and the new Asia. The society, culture and capitalism in Southeast Asia* (pp. 185-215). Singapore: Institute of Southeast Asian Studies.

Goldenberg, J. (1999). Virtual learning communities: A student's perspective. *Journal of Instruction Delivery Systems, 13*(2), 16–20.

Goldsmith, R. E., Clark, R. A., & Goldsmith, E. B. (2006). Extending the psychological profile of market mavenism. *Journal of Consumer Behaviour, 5*, 411–419. doi:10.1002/cb.189

Goodman, A., & Yakobovich, O. (2007). Shooting back: The Israeli human rights group B'Tselem gives Palestinians video cameras to document life under occupation. *Democracy Now!* Retrieved November 2, 2008, from http://www.democracynow.org/2007/12/26/shooting_back_the_israeli_human_rights

Goodyear, P. (2002). Psychological foundations for networked learning. In C. Steeples & C. Jones (Eds.), *Networked learning: Perspectives and issues* (pp. 49-75). London: Springer.

Goss, S., & Anthony, K. (2003). Introduction. In S. Goss & K. Anthony (Eds.), *Technology in counselling and psychotherapy: A practitioner's guide* (pp. 1-12). Basingstoke, NY: Palgrave Macmillan.

Grabe, M., & Grabe, C. (Eds.). (2001). *Integrating technology for meaningful learning* (3rd ed.). Boston, MA: Houghton Mifflin.

Graham, C. R. (2006). Blended learning system: Definition, current trends, and future directions. In C. J. Bonk & C. R. Graham (Eds.), *Handbook of blended learning: Global perspectives, local designs* (pp. 3-21). San Francisco: Pfeiffer.

Granovetter, M. S. (1973). The strength of weak ties. *American Journal of Sociology, 78*(6), 1360–1380. doi:10.1086/225469

Granovetter, M. S. (1973). The strength of weak ties. *American Journal of Sociology, 78*, 1360–1380. doi:10.1086/225469

Gratton, L. (2007). *Hot spots: Why some teams, workplaces, and organizations buzz with energy – and others don't*. San Francisco, CA: Berrett-Koehler Publishers, Inc.

Grauerholz, E., McKenzie, B., & Romeo, M. (1999). Beyond these walls: Teaching within and outside the expanded classroom – boundaries in the 21st century.

In B. A. Pescosolido & R. Aminzade (Eds.), *The social worlds of higher education: Handbook for teaching in a new century* (pp. 582-600). Thousand Oaks, CA: Pine Forge Press.

Gray, M. (2005). Dilemmas of international social work: paradoxical processes in Indigenisation, universalism and imperialism. *International Journal of Social Welfare, 14,* 231–238. doi:10.1111/j.1468-2397.2005.00363.x

Gray, M., & Fook, J. (2004). The quest for a universal social work: Some issues and implications. *Social Work Education, 23*(5), 625–644. doi:10.1080/0261547042000252334

Green, C. S., & Dorn, D. S. (1999). The changing classroom: The meaning of shifts in higher education for teaching and learning. In B. A. Pescosolido & R. Aminzade (Eds.), *The social worlds of higher education: Handbook for teaching in a new century* (pp. 59-83). Thousand Oaks, CA: Pine Forge Press.

Greenhow, C., Walker, J. D., & Kim, S. (2008, March). *Millenial leaners and net-savvy teens?: Examining Internet use among low-income students.* Paper presented at the American Educational Research Association, New York, NY.

Gregoire, J., & Jungers, C. (2007). *The counseling companion.* Mahwah, NJ: Lawrence Erlbaum.

Gremler, D. D., Gwinner, K. P., & Brown, S. W. (2001). Generating word-of-mouth communication through customer-employee relationship. *International Journal of Service Industry Management, 12*(1), 44–59. doi:10.1108/09564230110382763

Griffin, D., Trevorrow, P., & Halpin, E. (Eds.). (2007). *Developments in e-government.* Amsterdam: IOS Press.

Gross, R., & Acquisti, A. (2005). Information revelation and privacy in online social networks. In [Alexandria, VA: ACM.]. *Proceedings of the WPES, 05,* 71–80.

Grudin, J., & Pruitt, J. (2002). *Personas, participatory design and product development.* USA: PDC.

Gruen, T. W., Osmonbekow, T., & Czaplewski, A. J. (2006). eWOM: The impact of customer-to-customer online know-how exchange on customer value and loyalty. *Journal of Business Research, 59,* 449–456. doi:10.1016/j.jbusres.2005.10.004

Guilar, J. D., & Loring, A. (2008). Dialogue and community in online learning: Lessons from Royal Roads University. *Journal of Distance Education, 22*(3), 19–40.

Gustavsson, N., & MacEachron, A. (2008). Creating foster care youth biographies: A role for the Internet. *Journal of Technology in Human Services, 26*(1). doi:10.1300/J017v26n01_03

Guzman, M., & Verstappen, B. (2003). *Human rights monitoring and documentation series, volume 1: What is monitoring.* Versoix, Switzerland: Human Rights Information and Documentation Systems, International (HURIDOCS).

Halpin, E. F., & Fisher, S. M. (1998). *The use of the Internet for the European Parliament's activities for the protection and promotion of human rights* ([Report). Luxembourg: European Parliament.]. *No. PE, 167,* 227.

Handler, J. (2004). *Social citizenship and workfare in the United States and Western Europe.* Cambridge, UK: Cambridge University Press.

Hanson, J. M., & Sinclair, K. E. (2008). Social constructivist teaching methods in Australian universities - reported uptake and perceived learning effects: A survey of lecturers. *Higher Education Research & Development, 27*(3), 169–186. doi:10.1080/07294360802183754

Hargittai, E. (2007). Whose space? Differences among users and non-users of social network sites. *Journal of Computer-Mediated Communication, 13*(1), article 14. Retrieved September 29, 2008, from http://jcmc.indiana.edu/vol13/issue1/hargittai.html

Harris, L. (2007). *Electronic classroom, electronic community: Virtual social networks and student learning.* Unpublished doctoral dissertation, RMIT University, Melbourne.

Harris, R. W. (1999). Rural information technology for Sarawak's development. *Sarawak Development Journal, 2*(1), 72–84.

Harris, R. W., Bala, P., Songan, P., & Khoo, G. L. (2001). Challenges and opportunities in introducing information and communication technologies to the Kelabit community of north central Borneo. *New Media & Society*, *3*(3), 270–296. doi:10.1177/14614440122226092

Harrisson, T. (1959). *World within: A Borneo story*. Singapore: Oxford University Press.

Hass, N. (2006, January 8). In your facebook.com. *New York Times*.

Hatry, H. H. (2004). Using agency records. In J. S. Wholey, H. P. Hatry, & K. E. Newcomer (Eds.), *Handbook of practical program evaluation*. San Francisco: Jossey Bass.

Hattotuwa, S. (2007). The promise of citizen journalism. *openDemocracy News Analysis*. Retrieved October 21, 2008, from http://www.opendemocracy.net/terrorism/articles/srilanka220107

Haythornthwaite, C. (2005). Social networks and Internet connectivity effects. *Information Communication and Society*, *8*(2), 125–147. doi:10.1080/13691180500146185

Healy, K. (2005). *Social work theories in context*. London: Palgrave MacMillan.

Healy, K. (2005). *Social work theories in context: Creating frameworks for practice*. New York: Palgrave Macmillan.

Healy, L. (2001). *International social work: Professional action in an interdependent world*. New York: Oxford University Press.

Heeks, R. (2006). *Implementing and managing egovernment*. London: Sage.

Heeks, R. (Ed.). (1999). *Reinventing government in the information age*. London: Routledge.

Helft, M., & Stone, B. (2007, October 31). Google and friends to gang up on facebook. *New York Times*.

Henman, P. (1995). The role of computers in texturing the micro-social environment. *The Australian and New Zealand Journal of Sociology*, *31*(1), 49–63. doi:10.1177/144078339503100104

Henman, P. (1997). Computer technology - a political player in social policy processes. *Journal of Social Policy*, *26*(3), 323–340. doi:10.1017/S0047279497005035

Henman, P. (1999). The bane and benefits of computers in Australia's Department of Social Security. *The International Journal of Sociology and Social Policy*, *19*(1/2), 101–129. doi:10.1108/01443339910788686

Henman, P. (2002). Computer modeling and the politics of greenhouse gas policy in Australia. *Social Science Computer Review*, *20*(2), 161–173. doi:10.1177/089443930202000206

Henman, P. (2004). Targeted!: Population segmentation, electronic surveillance and governing the unemployed in Australia. *International Sociology*, *19*(2), 173–191. doi:10.1177/0268580904042899

Henman, P. (2005). E-government, targeting and data profiling: Policy and ethical issues of differential treatment. *Journal of E-Government*, *2*(1), 79–98. doi:10.1300/J399v02n01_05

Henman, P. (2006). Segmentation and conditionality: Technological reconfigurations in social policy and social citizenship. In G. Marston & C. McDonald (Eds.), *Analysing social policy: A governmental approach* (pp. 205-222). Cheltenham, UK: Edward Elgar.

Henman, P. (2006). Welfare reform as governance reform: The prospects of a governmentality perspective. In P. Henman & M. Fenger (Eds.), *Administering welfare reform* (pp. 19-41). Bristol, UK: Policy Press.

Henman, P. (2009). *Governing electronically: E-government and the reconfiguration of public administration, policy and power*. Basingstoke, UK: Palgrave Macmillan.

Henman, P., & Marston, G. (2008). The social division of welfare surveillance. *Journal of Social Policy*, *37*(2), 187–205. doi:10.1017/S0047279407001705

Hennig-Thurau, T., Gwinner, K. P., Walsh, G., & Gremler, D. D. (2004). Electronic word- of mouth via consumer-opinion platforms: What motivates consumers to articulate themselves on the Internet? *Journal of Interactive Marketing*, *18*(1), 38–52. doi:10.1002/dir.10073

Herie, M., & Martin, G. W. (2002). Knowledge diffusion in social work: A new approach to bridging the gap. *Social Work, 47*(1), 85–95.

Heron, B. (2005). Changes and challenges. Preparing social work students for practicum in today's sub-Saharan African context. *International Social Work, 48*(6), 782–793. doi:10.1177/0020872805057088

Herr, P. M., Kardes, F. R., & Kim, J. (1991). Effects of word-of-mouth and product-attribute information on persuasion: An accessibility-diagnosticity perspective. *The Journal of Consumer Research, 17*, 454–462. doi:10.1086/208570

Herring, S. C. (2004). Computer-mediated discourse analysis: An approach to researching online behavior. In S. A. Barab, R. Kling, & J. H. Gray (Eds.), *Designing for virtual communities in the service of learning* (pp. 338-376). New York: Cambridge University Press.

Herring, S. C., Scheidt, L. A., Bonus, S., & Wright, E. (2004). *Bridging the gap: A genre analysis of Weblogs.* Paper presented at the meeting of the 37th Hawaii International Conference on System Sciences, Los Alamitos, CA.

Herrington, A., & Herrington, J. (Eds.). (2006). *Authentic learning environments in higher education.* Hershey, PA: Information Science Publications.

Herschel, R. T., & Yermish, I. (2008). Knowledge transfer: Revising video. *International Journal of Knowledge Management, 4*(2), 62–74.

Hewitt, A., & Forte, A. (2006, November). *Crossing boundaries: Identity management student/faculty relationships on the Facebook.* Paper presented at the the Computer-supported Cooperative Work Conference, Banff, Alberta, Canada.

Hick, S. (2004). Reconceptualizing critical social work. In S. Hick, J. Fook, & R. Pozzuto (Eds.), *Social work: A critical turn* (pp. 39-51). Toronto, Ont.: Thompson Educational Publishing.

Hick, S., & McNutt, J. (Eds.). (2002). *Advocacy, activism and the Internet.* Chicago, IL: Lyceum Press.

Higgs, E. (2004). *The information state in England.* Basingstoke, UK: Palgrave Macmillan.

Hill, C. R. (2005). Everything i need to know i learned online. *Library Journal, 130*(3).

Hilley, J. (2001). *Malaysia: Mahathirism, hegemony and the new opposition (politics in contemporary Asia).* New York: Zed Books.

Hiltz, S. R. (1994). *The virtual classroom: Learning without limits via computer networks.* Norwood, NJ: Ablex.

Hiscock, J., & Marriott, P. (2003). A happy partnership: Using an information portal to integrate information literacy skills into an undergraduate foundation course. *Australian Academic and Research Libraries, 34*(1), 32–41.

Ho, C. P., & Burniske, R. W. (2005). The evolution of a hybrid classroom: Introducing online learning to educators in American Samoa. *TechTrends: Linking Research & Practice to Improve Learning, 49*(1), 24–29.

Hoffman, D. L., & Novak, T. P. (1996). Marketing in hypermedia computer-mediated environments: Conceptual foundations. *Journal of Marketing, 60*(3), 50–68. doi:10.2307/1251841

Hourihan, M. (2002). *Taking the "you" out of user: My experiencing using personas.* Retrieved September 9, 2005, from http://boxesandarrows.com/archives/002330php

Howard, C. (2006). The new governance of Australian welfare: Street-level contingencies. In P. Henman & M. Fenger (Eds.), *Administering welfare reform* (pp. 137-160). Bristol, UK: Policy Press.

Hull, G. A., & Nelson, M. E. (2008, March). *Youth-designed social networking: Literacies, identities, and relationships at the intersection of online and offline experience.* Paper presented at the meeting of the American Educational Research Association, New York, NY.

Hull, G., & Nelson, M. E. (2005). Locating the semiotic power of multimodality. *Written Communication, 22*(2), 224–262. doi:10.1177/074108304274170

Huxor, A. (2001). The role of the personal in social workspaces: Reflections on working in Alpha world. In E. F. Churchill, D. N., & A. J. Munro (Eds.), *Collaborative virtual environments: Digital places and spaces for interaction* (pp. 282-296). London: Springer.

Ife, J. (1995). *Community development: Creating community alternatives - vision analysis and practice*. Melbourne, Australia: Longman Publishing Group.

Ife, J., Healy, K., Spratt, T., & Solomon, B. (2004). Current understandings of critical social work. In S. Hick, J. Fook, & R. Pozzuto (Eds.), *Social work: A critical turn* (pp. 3-23). Toronto, Ont.: Thompson Educational Publishing.

Inoue, Y., & Kawakami, Y. (2004). Factors influencing tabloid news diffusion: Comparison with hard news. *Keio Communication Review, 26*, 37–52.

International Society for Technology in Education. (2007). *The ISTE national educational technology standards (NETS-S) and performance indicators for students*. Retrieved September 26, 2008, from http://www.iste.org/Content/NavigationMenu/NETS/ForStudents/2007Standards/NETS_for_Students_2007_Standards.pdf

International Society for Technology in Education. (2008). *The ISTE national educational technology standards (NETS-T) and performance indicators for teachers*. Retrieved September 26, 2008, from http://www.iste.org/Content/NavigationMenu/NETS/ForTeachers/2008Standards/NETS_T_Standards_Final.pdf

International Telecommunication Union. (2003). *Connecting Malaysia's rural communities to the information age: The E-Bario project*. Retrieved October 22, 2008, from http://www.itu.int/ITU-D/ict_stories/themes/case_studies/e-bario.html

Janowski, M. (1991). *Rice, work and community among the Kelabits in Sarawak, East Malaysia*. Unpublished doctoral dissertation, London: London School of Economics, University of London.

Jarvis, P. (1995). *Adult and continuing education: Theory and practice*. London, UK: Routledge.

Jenkins, H. (2006). *Confronting the challenges of participatory culture: Media education for the 21ˢᵗ century* [White paper for the MacArthur Foundation]. Retrieved July 1, 2008, from http://www.digitallearning.macfound.org

Johnson, A. (2004). Increasing internationalization in social work programs. Healy's continuum as a strategic planning guide. *International Social Work, 47*(1), 7–23. doi:10.1177/0020872804036445

Johnson, D. W., & Johnson, F. P. (2009). *Joining together: Group theory and group skills*. Upper Saddle River, NJ: Pearson.

Johnson, D. W., Johnson, R. J., & Stanne, M. B. (2000). Cooperative learning methods: A meta-analysis. Retrieved October 13, 2008 from http://www.co-operation.org/pages/cl-methods.html

Johnson, D. W., Johnson, R. T., & Smith, K. (1991). *Cooperative learning: Increasing college faculty instructional productivity* (ASHE-ERIC Higher Education Report No. 4). Washington, DC: The George Washington University, School of Education and Human Development.

Johnson, D. W., Johnson, R. T., & Smith, K. A. (1991). *Active learning: Cooperation in the classroom*. Edina, MN: Interaction Book Company.

Johnson, D. W., Johnson, R. T., Holubec, E. D., & Roy, P. (1984). *Circles of learning: Cooperation in the classroom*. Alexandria, VA: Association for Supervision and Curriculum Development.

Johnson, D. W., Johnson, R. T., Holubec, E., & Roy, P. (1984). *Circles of learning: Cooperation in the classroom*. Alexandria, VA: Association for Supervision and Curriculum Development.

Johnson, M., & Austin, M. (2006). Evidence-based practice in the social services: Implications for organizational change. *Administration in Social Work, 30*(3), 75–104. doi:10.1300/J147v30n03_06

Johnson, R., & Johnson, D. (1994). An overview of co-operative learning. In J. Thousand, A. Villa, & A. Nevin (Eds.), *Creativity and collaborative learning: A practical guide to empowering students and teachers* (pp. 31-43). Baltimore, MD: Paul H. Brookes Publishing Co.

Jomo, K. S. (1985). *Malaysia's new economic policies: Evaluations of the mid-term review of the 4ᵗʰ MP*. Kuala Lumpur, Malaysia: Malaysian Economic Association.

Jonassen, D. H. (2000). *Computers as mindtools: Engaging critical thinking* (2ⁿᵈ ed.). Columbus, OH: Merrill-Prentice Hall.

Jones, S. (2005). Using IT to augment authentic learning environments. In A. Herrington & J. Herrington (Eds.), *Authentic learning environments in higher education* (pp. 172-181). Hershey, PA: Information Science Publications.

Jones, S. (2006). Using IT to augment authentic learning environments. In A. Herrington & J. Herrington (Eds.), *Authentic learning environments* in higher education (pp 172-181). USA: Information Science Publishing.

Jones, S. (2007). Adding value to on-line role-plays: Virtual situated learning environments'. In *Proceedings of the Annual ASCILITE Conference*, Singapore.

Jones, S. (2007). Adding value to online role-plays: Virtual situated learning environments. In *ICT: Providing choices for learners and learning, Proceedings of the ASCILITE*. Retrieved September 9, 2008, from http://www.ascilite.org.au/conferences/singapore07/procs/jones-s.pdf.

Jones, S., & McCann, J. (2004). Virtual situated learning environments-the business education model for developing countries in a knowledge era. In *Business education and emerging market economies* (pp. 201-216). Amsterdam: Kluwer.

Jones, S., & McCann, J. (2005). Authentic situated learning environments-the flexible learning alternative for peripatetic managers in a global world of flexible workplaces. *Journal of Workplace Learning–E-Learning at the Workplace, 17*(5/6), 359-369.

Jones, S., & Richardson, J. (2002). Designing an IT-augmented student-centred learning environment. In A. Goody, J. Herrington, & M. Northcote (Eds.), *Quality conversations: Research and development in higher education* (p. 25).

Kaplan, B. H., Cassel, J. C., & Gore, S. (1977). Social support and health. *Medical Care, 15*, 47–58. doi:10.1097/00005650-197705001-00006

Keniston, K. (2002). IT for the common man. Lessons from India. The second M N Srinivas memorial lecture. In *NIAS Special Publication SP7 – 02*. Bangalore, India: National Institute of Advanced Studies.

Kennedy, D. M., Webster, L., Benson, R., James, D., & Bailey, N. (2002). My.Monash: Supporting students and staff in teaching, learning and administration. *Australian Journal of Educational Technology, 18*(1), 24–39.

Kim, A. J. (2000). *Community building on the Web*. Berkeley, CA: Peachpit Press.

King, V. T. (1999). *Anthropology and development in South-east Asia: Theory and practice*. Kuala Lumpur, Malaysia: Oxford University Press.

Kirriemuir, J. (2007). *An update of the July "snapshot" of UK higher and further education developments in second life*

Kitsantas, A., & Chow, A. (2007). College students' perceived threat and preference for seeking help in traditional distributed and distance learning environments. *Computers & Education, 48*, 383–395. doi:10.1016/j.compedu.2005.01.008

Kling, R. (2000). Learning about information technologies and social change: The contribution of social informatics. *The Information Society, 16*(3), 217–232. doi:10.1080/01972240050133661

Kolb, D. (1984). *Experiential learning: Experience as a source of learning and development*. London: Prentice Hall.

Kozinets, R. V. (1999). E-tribalized marketing?: The strategic implications of virtual communities of consumption. *European Management Journal, 17*(3), 252–264. doi:10.1016/S0263-2373(99)00004-3

Krasne, A. (2005). *What is Web 2.0 anyway? - Indispensable tools your nonprofit should know about.* Retrieved November 2, 2008, from http://www.techsoup.org/learningcenter/webbuilding/archives/page9344.cfm

Kraut, R., Kiesler, S., Boneva, B., Cummings, J., Helgeson, V., & Crawford, A. (2002). Internet paradox revisited. *The Journal of Social Issues, 58*(1), 49–74. doi:10.1111/1540-4560.00248

Kuiper, E., Volman, M., & Terwel, J. (2005). The Web as an information resource in k–12 education: Strategies for supporting students in searching and processing information. *Review of Educational Research, 75*(3), 285–328. doi:10.3102/00346543075003285

Kurbel, K. (2001). Virtuality on the students' and on the teachers' sides: A multimedia and Internet based international master program. In ECEF Berlin GmbH (Eds.), *Proceedings of the 7th International Conference on Technology Supported Learning and Training* (pp. 133-136). Berlin Germany: Online Educa.

Kushner, D. (2006). Meet the boy wonder behind facebook.com, the hottest Web site the Internet. *Rolling Stone*.

Laird, S. (2004). Inter-ethnic conflict: A role for social work in Sub-Saharan Africa. *Social Work Education, 23*(6), 693–709. doi:10.1080/0261547042000294482

Lam, C. M., Wong, H., & Leung, T. T. F. (2005). An unfinished reflexive journey: Social work students' reflections on their placement experiences. *British Journal of Social Work, 37*, 91–105. doi:10.1093/bjsw/bcl320

Lang, J. (2007). Crafting a teaching persona. *The Chronicle of Higher Education, 53*(23), 2.

Lannon, J., & Halpin, E. F. (2006). Human rights movements and the Internet: From local contexts to global engagement. In M. Gascó-Hernández, F. Equiza-López, & M. Acevedo-Ruiz (Eds.), *Information communication technologies and human development: Opportunities and challenges* (pp. 182-209). Hershey, PA: Idea Group Publishing.

Laurillard, D. (2002). *Rethinking university teaching: A framework for the effective use of learning technologies* (2nd ed.). London: Routledge / Falmer.

Laurillard, D. M. (1994). Multimedia and the changing experience of the learner. In *Proceedings of the Asia Pacific Information Technology in Training and Education Conference and Exhibition* (pp.19-25). Brisbane, CA: Apitite

Lave, J., & Wenger, E. (1991). *Situated learning: Legitimate peripheral participation*. Cambridge, UK: Cambridge University Press.

Lee, E. (2005). The wonderful world of Wikis. *Contra Costa Times*. Retrieved October 13, 2008, from http://www.accessmylibrary.com/coms2/summary_0286-31685346_ITM

Lenhart, A., & Madden, M. (2007, January 3). *Pew Internet project data memo*. Washington, DC: Pew Charitable Trusts. Retrieved September 29, 2008, from http://www.pewinternet.org/pdfs/PIP_SNS_Data_Memo_Jan_2007.pdf

Lenhart, A., Arafeh, S., Smith, A., & McGill, A. R. (2008, April). *Writing, technology, and teens*. Washington, DC: Pew Charitable Trusts. Retrieved September 29, 2008, from http://pewinternet.org/pdfs/PIP_Writing_Report_FINAL3.pdf

Lenhart, A., Madden, M., Macgill, A. R., & Smith, A. (2007, December 19). *Teens and social media*. Washington, DC: Pew Charitable Trusts.

Lewis, C., & Fabos, B. (2005). Instant messaging, literacies, and social identities. *Reading Research Quarterly, 40*(4), 470-501. Retrieved March 28, 2008, from http://www.reading.org/Library/Retrieve.cfm?D=10.1598/RRQ.40.4.5&F=RRQ-40-4-Lewis.pdf

Linden Labs. (2007). Retrieved January 12, from http://secondlife.com/whatis

Lock, J. V. (2002). Laying the groundwork for the development of learning communities within online courses. *Quarterly Review of Distance Education, 3*(4), 395–408.

Long, N. (2001). *Development sociology: Actor perspectives*. London: Routledge.

Lonne, R. (2007). Working together for health, community services and justice to shape local and global workforces. In *Proceedings of the RMIT University 2007 Partnerships for World Graduates Conference*, Melbourne, Australia.

Lyon, D. (1994). *The electronic eye*. Minneapolis, MN: University of Minnesota Press.

Lyon, D. (2007). *Surveillance studies*. Cambridge, UK: Polity.

Mackay, H. (1995). Theorising the IT/ society relationship. In N. Heap, R. Thomas, G. Einon, R. Mason, & H. Mackay (Eds.), *Information technology and society: A reader* (pp. 41-53). London: Sage Publications.

Maher, J., & Smith, B. (1996). *Future social provision: The department of social security community research project* (Policy Research Paper No. 69). Department of Social Security. Retrieved from http://www.facs.gov.au/internet/facsinternet.nsf/via/research_dss/$file/policyresearchpaperno69.pdf

Maidment, J. (2006). Using on-line delivery to support students during practicum placements. *Australian Social Work, 59*(1), 47–55. doi:10.1080/03124070500449770

Mamphiswana, D., & Noyoo, N. (2000). Social work education in a changing socio-political and economic dispensation. Perspectives from South Africa. *International Social Work, 43*(1), 21–32.

Marcus, A., & Perez, A. (2007). m-YouTube mobile UI: Video selection based on social influence. *Lecture Notes in Computer Science, 4552*, 926–932. doi:10.1007/978-3-540-73110-8_102

Martin, J. (2000). Social workers as mediators. *Australian Social Work, 53*, 33–39. doi:10.1080/03124070008415219

Martin, J. (2007). *Conflict management and mediation*. Port Adelaide, Australia: Ginninderra Press.

Martin, J., & Douglas, K. (2007). Social work and family dispute resolution. *Australian Social Work, 60*, 295–307. doi:10.1080/03124070701519660

Martin, J., McKay, E., & Hawkins, L. (2006). The human-computer interaction spiral. In *Proceedings of the2006 Informing Science and IT Education Joint Conference*, Salford - Greater Manchester, UK (pp. 183-197).

Martin, J., McKay, E., Hawkins, L., & Murthy, V. (2007). Design-personae: Matching students' learning profiles in Web-based education. In E. McKay (Ed.), *Enhancing Learning through human computer interaction*. Hershey, PA: Idea Group Inc.

Martin. J., & Ling, H. K. (2008). International activity through student mobility: Physical, psychological and social adjustment. *International Journal of Learning, 15*(8). Retrieved from http://ijl.cgpublisher.com/product/pub.30/prod.1847

Mayer, R. E. (2001). *Multimedia learning*. New York: Cambridge Press.

Mazar, R., & Nolan, J. (2008). Hacking say and reviving Eliza: Lessons from virtual environments. *Innovate, 5*(2).

Mazer, J. P., Murphy, R. E., & Simonds, C. J. (2007). I'll see you on "Facebook:" The effects of computer-mediated teacher self-disclosure on student motivation, affective learning, and classroom climate. *Communication Education, 56*(1), 1–17. doi:10.1080/03634520601009710

Mazzolini, M., & Maddison, S. (2007). When to jump in: The role of instructors in online discussion forums. *Computers & Education, 49*, 193–213. doi:10.1016/j.compedu.2005.06.011

McDonald, C. (2006). *Challenging social work the institutional context of practice*. New York: Palgrave Macmillan.

McDonald, C., Marston, G., & Buckley, A. (2003). Risk technology in Australia: The role of the job seeker classification instrument in employment services. *Critical Social Policy, 23*(4), 498–526. doi:10.1177/02610183030234004

McGrath, A., & Prinz, W. (2001). All that is solid melts into software. In E. F. Churchill, D. N. Snowdon, & A. J. Munro (Eds.), *Collaborative virtual environments: Digital places and spaces for interaction* (pp. 99-114). London: Springer.

McGrath, D. (2003). Developing a community of learners. *Learning & Leading with Technology, 30*(7), 43–45.

McInnis, C., James, R., & Hartley, R. (2000). *Trends in the first year experience in Australian universities* (No. DETYA No. 6546.HERC00A). Melbourne: Department of Education, Training and Youth Affairs.

McKay, E. (2008). *Human-dimensions of human-computer interaction: Balancing the HCI equation.* Amsterdam: IOS Press.

McKay, E., & Martin, J. (2007). Multidisciplinary collaboration to unravel expert knowledge. In M. Keppell, (Ed.), *Instructional design: Case studies in communities of practice.* Hershey, PA: Information Science Publishing.

McKay, E., Axmann, M., Banjanin, N., & Howat, A. (2007). Towards Web-mediated learning reinforcement: Rewards for online mentoring through effective human-computer interaction. In V. Uskov (Ed.), *Proceedings of the 6th IASTED International Conference on Web-Based Education,* Chamonix, France (pp. 210-215). Retrieved January 2, 2009, from http://www.iasted.org/conferences/pastinfo-557.html

McLaughlan, R., & Kirkpatrick, D. (2008). Online role-based learning designs for teaching complex decision making. In L. Lockyer, S. Bennett, S. Agostinho, & B. Harper (Eds.), *Handbook of research on learning design and learning objects: Issues, applications and technologies.* Hershey, PA: Information Science Reference.

McLaughlin, J. A., & Jordan, G. B. (2004). Using logic models. In J. S. Wholey, H. P. Hatry, & K. E. Newcomer (Eds.), *Handbook of practical program evaluation.* San Francisco: Jossey Bass.

McLoughlin, C., & Luca, J. (2000). Cognitive engagement and higher order thinking through computer conferencing: We know why but do we know how? In

A. Herrmann & M. M. Kulski (Eds.), *Flexible futures in tertiary teaching, Proceedings of the 9th Annual Teaching Learning Forum,* Perth, Curtin University of Technology. Retrieved October 13, 2008, from http://lsn.curtin.edu.au/tlf/tlf2000/mcloughlin.html

McPherson, M. A., & Nunes, J. M. (2008). Critical issues for e-learning delivery: What may seem obvious is not always put into practice. *Journal of Computer Assisted Learning, 24,* 433–445. doi:10.1111/j.1365-2729.2008.00281.x

Mead, L. M. (Ed.). (1997). *The new paternalism.* Washington, DC: Brookings Institution Press.

Merrill, M. D. (2003). Does your instruction rate 5 stars? In *Proceedings of the eLearning Conference on Design and Development: Instructional Design - Applying first principles of instruction.* Melbourne: Australasian Publications On-Line. Retrieved December 6, 2004, from, http://www.informit.com.au/library/

Metzl, J. F. (1996). Information technology and human rights. *Human Rights Quarterly, 18*(4), 705–746. doi:10.1353/hrq.1996.0045

Meyer, J., & Vermunt, J. (2000). Dissonant study orchestrations in higher education manifestations and effects. *Higher Education,* 15.

Mezirow, J. (1991). *Transformational dimensions of adult learning.* San Francisco: Josey-Bass.

Midgley, J. O. (1997). *Social welfare in a global context.* Thousand Oaks, CA: Sage.

Mihr, A. (2004). *Human rights education: Methods, institutions, culture and evaluation.* Institut für Politikwissenschaft, Otto-von-Guericke- Universität

Miller, P., & Rose, N. (1990). Governing economic life. *Economy and Society, 19*(1), 1–31. doi:10.1080/03085149000000001

Miller, P., & Rose, N. (2008). *Governing the present.* Cambridge, UK: Polity.

Millis, B. J., & Cottell, P. G., Jr. (1998). *Cooperative learning for higher education faculty.* Phoenix, AZ: The Oryx Press.

Minshull, G. (2004). *Vles: Beyond the fringe and into the mainstream.* Retrieved June 28, 2006, from http://ferl.becta.org.uk/content_files/ferl/pages/news_events/events/Online_events/VLEs%20-%20into%20the%20mainstream.pdf

Misanchik, M., & Anderson, T. (2000). Building community in an online learning environment: Communication, cooperation and collaboration. Retrieved from http://www.mtsu.edu/-itconf/proceed01/19.html

Mitra, A. (1997). Virtual culture: Identity and communication in cybersociety. *Year of Publication,* 55-79.

Mobbs, P. (2002). *Participating with safety briefings no. 1: Introducing information security.* Association for Progressive Communications.

Moore, S., & Collins, W. (2002). A model for social work field practicum in African American Churches. *Journal of Teaching in Social Work, 22*(3), 171–188. doi:10.1300/J067v22n03_12

Mullaly, B. (2007). *The new structural social work.* Toronto, Ont: Oxford University Press.

Nachmias, R., Mioduser, D., Oren, A., & Ram, J. (2000). Web-supported emergent- collaboration in higher education courses. *Journal of Educational Technology & Society, 3*(3), 94–104.

Nagata, J. (1979). *Malaysian mosaic perspective from a poly-ethnic society.* Vancouver: University of British Columbia Press.

Naidu, S., Ip, A., & Linser, R. (2000). Dynamic goal-based role-play simulation on the Web: A case study. *Educational Technology & Society, 3*(3), Retrieved October 13, 2008, from http://www.ifets.info/journals/3_3/b05.html

National School Board Association. (2007, July). *Creating and connecting: Research and guidelines on social – and educational – networking.* Retrieved September 22, 2008, from http://www.nsba.org/SecondaryMenu/TLN/CreatingandConnecting.aspx

Nations, U. Division for Public Economics and Public Administration (UN DPEPA). (2002). *Benchmarking e-government: A global perspective.* New York: UN DPEPA. Retrieved from http://unpan1.un.org/intradoc/groups/public/documents/UN/UNPAN021547.pdf

Nelson, K., Kift, S., & Harper, W. (2005). *'First portal in a storm': A virtual space for transition students.* Paper presented at the Balance, fidelity, mobility: maintaining the momentum? Proceedings of the 22nd ASCILITE conference, Brisbane, CA, USA.

Netting, F. E., O'Connor, M. K., & Fauri, D. P. (2008). *Comparative approaches to program planning.* Hoboken, NJ: John Wiley.

News, B. B. C. (2007). *Digital activists expose abuse.* Retrieved November 2, 2008, from http://news.bbc.co.uk/2/hi/americas/7139218.stm

News, B. B. C. (2008). *S Africa mob burns Mozambican man.* Retrieved October 21, 2008, from http://news.bbc.co.uk/2/hi/africa/7455061.stm

Norris, P. (2001). *Digital divide?* Cambridge, UK: Cambridge University Press.

O'Looney, J. (2005). Social work and the new semantic information revolution. *Administration in Social Work, 29*(4), 5–34. doi:10.1300/J147v29n04_02

O'Reilly, T. (2005). *What is Web2.0: Design patterns and business models for the next generation of software.* Retrieved October 13, 2008, from http://oreillynet.com/lpt/a/6228

Office of the High Commissioner for Human Rights. (2003). *Background note on the information society and human rights* (No. Document WSIS/PC-3/CONTR/178-E). Geneva, Switzerland: Office of the UN High Commissioner for Human Rights.

Ogilvie, A., & Douglas, K. (2007). Online role-plays and the virtual placement: Aiding reflection in work integrated learning. In *ICT: Providing choices for learners and learning, Proceedings of the ASCILITE.* Retrieved September 9, 2008, from http://www.ascilite.org.au/conferences/singapore07/procs/ogilvie.pdf

Okamoto, T., Matsui, T., Inoue, H., & Cristea, A. (2000). A distance-education self- learning support system based on a VOD server. In Kinshuk, C. Jesshope, & T. Okamoto (Eds.), *Proceedings of the International Workshop on Advanced Learning Technologies (IWALT 2000): Advanced Learning Technology: Design and Development Issues* (pp. 71-72). Palmerston North, New Zealand: IEEE Computer Society.

Osborne, D., & Gaebler, T. (1993). *Reinventing government.* New York: Penguin.

Oullette, P. M. (2006). The acquisition of social work interviewing skills in a Web-based and classroom instructional environment: Results of a study. *Journal of Technology in Human Services, 24*(4), 53–75. doi:10.1300/J017v24n04_04

Owston, R., Garrison, D., & Cook, K. (2006). Blended learning at Canadian universities. In C. Bonk & C. Graham (Eds.), *The handbook of blended learning: Global perspectives, local designs* (pp. 338-349). San Francisco: Pfeiffer.

Owyang, J. (2008, January 9). Social network stats: Facebook, MySpace, reunion. Message posted to http://www.web-strategist.com/blog/2008/01/09/social-network-stats-facebook-myspace-reunion-jan-2008

Palloff, R. M., & Pratt, K. (2001). *Lessons from the cyberspace classroom: The realities of online teaching.* San Francisco: Jossey-Bass Inc.

Palloff, R. M., & Pratt, K. (2003). *The virtual student: A profile and guide to working with online learners.* San Francisco: Jossey-Bass Inc.

Panitz, T. (1997). Collaborative versus cooperative learning – a comparison of the two concepts which will help us understand the underlying nature of interactive learning. *Cooperative Learning and College Teaching, 8*(2), 5–14.

Panos, P. (2005). A model for using videoconferencing technology to support international social work field practicum students. *International Social Work, 48*(6), 834–841. doi:10.1177/0020872805057095

Papert, S., & Harel, I. (1991). *Constructionism.* Norwood, NJ: Ablex Publishing Corporation.

Partnership for 21st Century Skills. (2008). *21st century skills, education & competitiveness: A resource and policy guide.* Retrieved September 30, 2008, from http://www.21stcentury skills.org/documents/21st_century_skills_education_and_competitiveness_guide.pdf

Pathfinder. (2003). *Guidance on outcomes focused management: Supporting paper: Benchmarking using outcomes information.* Retrieved October 31, 2008, from http://io.ssc.govt.nz/pathfinder/documents/pathfinder-benchmarking.pdf

Paul, D. (2006). *We were not the savages* (3rd ed.). Halifax, Canada: Fernwood Publishing.

Pawar, M. (2000). Social development content in the courses of Australian social work schools. *International Social Work, 43*(3), 277–288. doi:10.1177/002087280004300302

Pearson, N. (2007). *Mobile phones in emergencies - pubic and personal.* Retrieved November 6, 2008, from http://www.newtactics.org/en/blog/new-tactics/using-mobile-phones-action#comment-521

Peck, J. (2001). *Workfare states.* New York: Guilford Press.

Perkel, D. (2008). Copy and paste literacy? Literacy practices in the production of a MySpace profile. In K. Drotner, H. S. Jensen, & K. C. Schroeder (Eds.), *Informal learning and digital media: Constructions, contexts, consequences* (pp. 203-224). Newcastle, UK: Cambridge Scholars Press.

Pettys, G., Panos, P., Cox, S., & Oosthuysen, K. (2005). Four models of international field placement. *International Social Work, 48*(3), 277–288. doi:10.1177/0020872805051705

Phelps, J. E., Lewis, R., Mobilio, L., Perry, D., & Raman, N. (2005). Viral marketing or electronic word-of-mouth advertising: Examining consumer responses and motivations to pass-along e-mail. *Journal of Advertising Research, 44*(4), 333–348.

Plantz, M. C., Greenway, M. T., & Hendrick, M. (1997). *Outcome measurement: Showing results in the nonprofit sector*. Retrieved October 31, 2008, from http://www.live-united.org/Outcomes/Resources/What/ndpaper.cfm

Poister, T. H. (2004). Performance monitoring. In J. S. Wholey, H. P. Hatry, & K. E. Newcomer (Eds.), *Handbook of practical program evaluation*. San Francisco: Jossey Bass.

PoKempner, D. (1997). *Briefing paper: Encryption in the service of human rights*. Human Rights Watch.

Pollitt, C. (2003). *The essential public manager*. Maidenhead, UK: Open University Press.

Prasolova-Forland, E., & Divitini, M. (2002, September 9-12). *Supporting learning communities with collaborative virtual environments: Different spatial metaphors*. Paper presented at the IEEE International Conference on Advanced Learning Technologies (ICALT 2002), Kazan, Russia.

Prosser, M., Ramsden, P., Trigwell, K., & Waterhouse, F. (2003). Dissonance in experience of teaching and its relations to the quality of student learning. *Studies in Higher Education, 28*(1), 37–48. doi:10.1080/03075070309299

Pruitt, J., & Grudin, J. (2003). *Personas: Practice and theory*. Retrieved January 1, 2008, from http://www.research.microsoft.com/users/jgrudin/publications/personas/Pruitt-Grudin

Quantcast. (2008, September 30). *MySpace.com*. Retrieved September 30, 2008, from http://www.quantcast.com/myspace.com

Rai, G. (2004). International fieldwork experience. A survey of US schools. *International Social Work, 47*(2), 213–226. doi:10.1177/0020872804034138

Rainie, L. (2008). *Video sharing Websites. Pew Internet American Life Project*. Retrieved

Rainie, L., Fox, S., Horrigan, J., Lenhart, A., & Spooner, T. (2000). *Tracking life online: How women use the Internet to cultivate relationships with family and friends. Pew Internet and American Life*. Retrieved September 1, 2008, from http://www.pewinternet.org/pdfs/Report1.pdf

Ramsden, P. (2003), *Learning to teach in higher education* (2nd ed.). London: Routledge.

Razack, N. (2002). A critical examination of international student exchanges. *International Social Work, 45*(2), 251–265.

Reeves, T. (1993). Evaluating interactive multimedia. In D. Gayeski (Ed.), *Multimedia for learning: Development, application, evaluation* (pp. 97-112). Englewood Cliffs, NJ: Educational Technology Publications.

Reeves, T., Herrington, J., & Oliver, R. (2002). Authentic activities and online learning. In A. Goody, J. Herrington, & M. Northcote (Eds.), *Quality Conversations: Research and Development in Higher Education*.

Reisch, M., & Jarman-Rohde, L. (2000). The future of social work in the United States: Implications for field education. *Journal of Social Work Education, 36*(2), 201–214.

Reporters Without Borders. (2004). *The Internet under surveillance: Obstacles to the free flow of information online*. Reporters Without Borders.

Reporters Without Borders. (2008). *Two years for a blog: That's enough! Reporters Without Borders calls for release of blogger Kareem Amer*. Retrieved November 8, 2008 from http://www.rsf.org/article.php3?id_article=29192

Resnick, M. (1996). Distributed constructionism. In D. Edelson & E. A. Domeshek (Eds.), *ICLS '96: Proceedings of the 1996 international conference on learning sciences* (pp. 280-284). Evanston, IL: International Society of the Learning Sciences.

Reynoldson, C., & Vibert, C. (2005). *Creating value in ict-enabled business education*. Paper presented at the Frontiers of e-Business Research 2005, Tampere, Finland.

Rheingold, H. (1993). *The virtual community: Homesteading on the electronic frontier*. New York: Addison-Wesley.

Richardson, S. (2004). *Employers' contribution to training, formal report*. National Centre for Vocational Education Research (NCVER).

Robbins, S. (2007). *Roll your own lms with Facebook.* Retrieved October 15, 2007, from http://ubernoggin.com/archives/75

Robbins, S. (2007). *Sarnoff, Metcalf, and Reed: The secrets to social network growth.* Retrieved October 15, 2007, from http://ubernoggin.com/archives/102

Roberts, A. (2007). Beyond a participation focus. In *ICT: Providing choices for learners and learning, Proceedings of the ASCILITE.* Retrieved September 9, 2008, from http://www.ascilite.org.au/conferences/singapore07/procs/roberts.pdf

Roberts-DeGennaro, M., & Clapp, J. (2005). Assessing the virtual classroom of a graduate social policy course. *Journal of Teaching in Social Work, 25*(1), 69–88. doi:10.1300/J067v25n01_05

Robertson, I. (2008). Learners' attitudes to Wiki technology in problem based, blended learning for vocational teacher education. *Australasian Journal of Educational Technology, 24*(4), 425–441.

Robinson, M. (2003). Making human rights matter: Eleanor Roosevelt's time has come. *Harvard Human Rights Journal, 16.*

Rogers, E. M. (1995). *Diffusion of innovation* (4th ed.). New York: Free Press.

Rogers, E. M., & Seidel, N. (2002). Diffusion of news of the terrorist attacks September 11, 2001. *Prometheus, 20*(3), 209–219. doi:10.1080/0810902021014326

Rogoff, B. (1990). *Apprenticeship in thinking: Cognitive development in social context.* New York: Oxford University Press.

Rohracher, H. (2003). The role of users in the social shaping of environmental technologies. *Innovation, 16*(2), 177–192.

Ronkko, K. (2005). An empirical study demonstrating how different design constraints, project organization and contexts limited the utility of personas. In *Proceedings of the 38th Conference on System Sciences,* Hawaii.

Rose, D. A. (2001). Reconceptualizing the user(s) of-and in-technological innovation: The case of vaccines in the United States. In R. Coombs, K. Green, A. Richards, & V. Walsh (Eds.), *Technology and the market. Demand, users and innovation* (pp. 68-88). Cheltenham, UK: Edward Elgar Publishing.

Rose, N., & Miller, P. (1992). Political power beyond the state: Problematics of government. *The British Journal of Sociology, 43,* 173–205. doi:10.2307/591464

Rosenbloom, S. (2008, May 1). Status: Looking for work on facebook. *New York Times.*

Ross, B., & Gage, K. (2006). Global perspectives on blended learning. In C. Bonk & C. Graham (Eds.), *The handbook of blended learning: Global perspectives, local designs* (pp. 155-167). San Francisco: Pfeiffer.

Roszak, T. (1988). *The cult of information.* London: Paladin.

Rovai, A. P. (2001). Building classroom community at a distance: A case study. *Educational Technology Research and Development, 49*(4), 33–48. doi:10.1007/BF02504946

Rowan, D. (2007, July 31). Log on and rediscover the generation gap. *The Times* (London).

Rumble, G. (2000). The globalisation of open and flexible learning: Considerations for planners and managers. *Online Journal of Distance Learning Administration, 3*(3). Retrieved January 2, 2009, from http://www.westga.edu/~distance/ojdla/fall33/rumble33.html

Ryan, J. (2008). New ways of communicating: How new media is being used to communicate health messages. *Vic Health Letter, 33,* 16–17.

Sackett, D. L., Rosenberg, W. M. C., Gray, J. M. J., Haynes, R. B., & Richardson, W. S. (1996). Evidence based medicine: What it is and what it isn't. *BMJ (Clinical Research Ed.), 312,* 71–72.

Saging, R. (1976). *An ethno-history of the Kelabit tribe of Sarawak. A Brief look at the Kelabit tribe before World War II and after.* Graduation Exercise submitted to the Jabatan Sejarah. University of Malaya, in partial fulfilment of the requirements for the Degree of Bachelor of Arts.

Salmon, G. (2001). *E-moderating: The key to teaching and learning online*. London: Kogan Page.

Schon, D. (1983). *The reflective practitioner: How professionals think in action*. New York: Basic Books.

Schon, D. (1987). *Educating the reflective practitioner: Toward a new design for teaching and learning in the professions*. San Francisco: Jossey-Bass.

Schwalbe, K. (2006). *Information technology project management*. Canada: Thomson - Course Technology.

Schwier, R. A. (2001). Catalysts, emphases, and elements of virtual learning communities: Implications for research and practice. *The Quarterly Review of Distance Education, 2*(1), 5–18.

Scott, J. C. (1985). *Weapons of the weak: Everyday forms of peasant resistance*. London: Yale University Press.

Selian, A. N. (2002). *ICTs in support of human rights, democracy and good governance*. International Telecommunications Union.

Selim, H. M. (2007). Critical success factors for e-learning acceptance: Confirmatory factor models. *Computers & Education, 49*, 396–413. doi:10.1016/j.compedu.2005.09.004

Sergiovanni, T. J. (1993). *Building community in schools*. San Francisco: Jossey-Bass.

Servon, L. J. (2002). *Bridging the digital divide*. Malden, MA: Blackwell.

Shamsul, A. B. (1986). *From British to Bumiputera rule: Local politics and rural development in Malaysia*. Singapore: Institute of South East Asia Studies.

Shardlow, S. M., & Horwath, J. (2000). Empowering learners through open (distance) programmes: An evaluation of a practice teaching programme. *Social Work Education, 19*(2), 111–123. doi:10.1080/02615470050003502

Sheehy, G. (2008, August). Campaign Hillary: Behind closed doors. *Vanity Fair*, pp. 79-86.

Sherer, P. D., Shea, T. P., & Kristensen, E. (2003). Online communities of practice: A catalyst for faculty development. *Innovative Higher Education, 27*(3), 183–194. doi:10.1023/A:1022355226924

Siebert, D. C., Siebert, C. F., & Spaulding-Givens, J. (2006). Teaching clinical social work skills primarily on line: An evaluation. *Journal of Social Work Education, 42*(2), 325–336.

Siebert, D. C., Siebert, C. F., & Spaulding-Givens, J. (2006). Teaching clinical social work skills primarily online: An evaluation. *Journal of Social Work Education, 42*(2), 325–337.

Siegel, E., Jennings, J. G., Conklin, J., & Napoletano Flynn, S. A. (1998). Distance learning in social work education: Results and implications of a national survey. *Journal of Social Work Education, 34*(1), 71–80.

SimTeach. (2007). *Institutions and organisisations in Second Life*. Retrieved September 18, 2007, from http://www.simteach.com/wiki/index.php?title=Institutions_and_Organizations_in_SL

Siraj, S. (2005). ICT and human rights promotion in Bangladesh: Democratising force of ICT. *i4d . Human Rights and ICTs, 3*(7), 27–29.

SkillsInfo. (2007). *Health and community services employment outlook*. Retrieved January 2, 2009, from http://www.skillsinfo.gov.au/Industries/HealthCommunityServices

Slavin, R. E. (1990). *Cooperative learning: Theory, research and practice*. Boston, MA: Allyn & Bacon.

Smith, D., Menon, S., & Sivakumar, K. (2005). Online peer and editorial recommendations, trust, and choice in virtual markets. *Journal of Interactive Marketing, 19*(3), 15–37. doi:10.1002/dir.20041

Smith, M. K. (2005). Bruce W. Tuckman - forming, storming, norming and performing in groups. *The encyclopaedia of informal education*. Retrieved October 13, 2008, from http://www.infed.org/thinkers/tuckman.htm

Smith, P. R., & Wingerson, N. W. (2006). Is the centrality of relationship in social work education at risk with IVT? *Journal of Technology in Human Services, 24*(2), 23–37. doi:10.1300/J017v24n02_02

Soley, L. C. (1999). Underneath the ivy and the social costs of corporate ties. In B. A. Pescosolido & R. Aminzade (Eds.), *The social worlds of higher education: Handbook for teaching in a new century* (pp. 318-327). Thousand Oaks, CA: Pine Forge Press.

Sonnenwald, D. H., Bergquist, R. E., Maglaughlin, K. L., Kupstas-Soo, E., & Whitton, M. C. (2001). Designing to support collaborative scientific research across distances: The nanoManipulator environment. In E. F. Churchill, D. N. Snowdon, & A. J. Munro (Eds.), *Collaborative virtual environments: Digital places and spaces for interaction* (pp. 202-224). London: Springer.

Soong, B. M. H., Chan, H. C., Chua, B. C., & Loh, K. F. (2001). Critical success factors for on-line course resources. *Computers & Education, 36*(2), 101–120. doi:10.1016/S0360-1315(00)00044-0

Spector, J. M. (2005). Time demands in online instruction. *Distance Education, 26*(1), 5–27. doi:10.1080/01587910500081251

Spencer, D., & Hardy, S. (2008). Deal or no deal: Teaching on-line negotiation to law students. *QUT Law and Justice Journal, 8*(1), 93–117.

Spender, D. (1995). *Nattering on the Net: Women, power, and cyberspace.* Melbourne: Spinifex.

Staughton, D. (2006). How to find and keep the best staff. In *Proceedings of the LIV Small Practice Conference.* Melbourne, Australia: Law Institute of Victoria.

Stefanone, M. A., & Jang, C. Y. (2008). Writing for friends and family: The interpersonal nature of blogs. *Journal of Computer-Mediated Communication, 13*, 123–140. doi:10.1111/j.1083-6101.2007.00389.x

Stefanone, M. A., Lackaff, D., & Rosen, D. (2008). We're all stars now: Reality television, Web 2.0, and mediated identities. In *Proceedings of the ACM's nineteenth annual Hypertext and Hypermedia* (pp. 107-112).

Stein, D. (1998). *Situated learning in adult education. ERIC Digest No 195.* Washington, DC: Office of Educational Research and Improvement (ED). (ERIC Document Reproduction Service No. ED418250)

Stella Maris College. Social Work. (2005). *Stella Maris College (autonomous).* Retrieved February 4, 2009, from http://www.stellamariscollege.org/departments/socialwork.asp

Stocks, J. T., & Freddolino, P. P. (2000). Enhancing computer-mediated teaching through interactivity: The second iteration of a World Wide Web-based graduate social work course. *Research on Social Work Practice, 10*(4), 505–518.

Stoecker, R. (2007). The research practices and needs of non-profit organizations in an urban center. *Journal of Sociology and Social Welfare, 34*(4), 97–119.

Stone, B. (2007, March 3). Social networking's next phase. *New York Times.*

Stone, B. (2008, June 18). At social site, only the businesslike need apply. *New York Times.*

Subramani, M. R., & Rajagopalan, B. (2003). Knowledge-sharing and influence in online social networks via viral marketing. *Communications of the ACM, 46*(12), 300–307. doi:10.1145/953460.953514

Sutherland, P. (1994). *Annotations to the Social Security Act 1991* (2nd ed.). Sydney, Australia: Federation Press, and Welfare Rights & Legal Centre.

Talla, Y. (1979). *The Kelabit of the Kelabit Highlands, Sarawak* (Report No. 9). Pulau Pinang, Malaysia: School of Comparative Social Sciences, USM.

Taylor, C., & White, S. (2000). *Practising reflexivity in health and welfare.* Buckingham, UK: Open University Press.

Tekinarslan, E. (2008). Blogs: A qualitative investigation into an instructor and undergraduate students' experiences. *Australasian Journal of Educational Technology, 24*(4), 402–412.

Tesoriero, F. (2006). Personal growth towards intercultural competence through an international field education programme. *Australian Social Work*, 59(2), 126–140. doi:10.1080/03124070600651853

Tesoriero, F., & Rajaratnam, A. (2001). Partnership in education. An Australian school of social work and a South Indian primary health care project. *International Social Work*, 44(1), 31–41. doi:10.1177/002087280104400104

The University of Melbourne. (2006). *The University of Melbourne teaching and learning plan 2006*. Retrieved July 18, 2006, from http://www.unimelb.edu.au/publications/docs/2006learn_teach.pdf

Thong, L. B., & Bahrain, T. S. (1993). The Bario exodus: A conception of Sarawak urbanization. *Borneo Review*, 4(2), 112–127.

Thurlow, C. (2006). From statistical panic to moral panic: The metadiscursive construction and popular exaggeration of new media language in the print media. *Journal of Computer-Mediated Communication, 11*(3), article 1.

Tinto, V. (1998). Colleges as communities: Taking research on student persistence seriously. *Review of Higher Education, 21*(2), 167–177.

Tinto, V. (2000). Learning better together: The impact of learning communities on student success in higher education. *Journal of Institutional Research, 9*(1), 48–53.

Toennies, F. (1963). *Community and association (gemeinschaft to gesellschaft)*. New York: Harper & Row.

Treleaven, L. (2003). Evaluating a communicative model for Web mediated collaborative learning and design. *Australian Journal of Educational Technology, 19*(1), 100–117.

Trigwell, K., Prosser, M., & Waterhouse, F. (1999). Relations between teachers' approaches to teaching and students' approaches to learning. *Higher Education, 37*, 57–70. doi:10.1023/A:1003548313194

Tsing, A. L. (1993). *In the realm of the diamond queen: Marginality in an out-of-the-way place*. Princeton, NJ: Princeton University Press.

Tuhiwai-Smith, L. *Decolonizing methodologies*. (1999). Dunedin, NZ: University of Otago Press.

Tullar, W. L., & Kaiser, P. R. (2000). The effect of process training on process and outcomes in virtual groups. *Journal of Business Communication, 37*(4), 408–427. doi:10.1177/002194360003700404

Turkle, S. (1997). *Life on the screen: Identity in the age of the Internet*. London: Phoenix.

Turoff, M. (1999). *An end to student segregation: No more separation between distance learning and regular courses*. Retrieved October 13, 2008, from http://web.njit.edu/~turoff/Papers/canadapresent/segregation.htm

United Kingdom (UK). Cabinet Office. (1999). *Modernising government* (Cm 4310). London: TSO.

United Kingdom (UK). Cabinet Office. (2005). *Transformational government: Enabled by technology* (Cm 6683). London: HM Government.

United Nations, E. C. O. S. O. C. (2000). *Development and international cooperation in the twenty-first century: The role of information technology in the context of a knowledge-based global economy* (A Report of the Secretary-General). New York: United Nations.

United States Department of Health & Human Services. (2008). *Your guide to developing useful and usable websites*. Retrieved September 26, 2008, from http://www.usability.gov

United Way of America. (1997). *Outcome measurement: Showing results in the nonprofit sector*. Retrieved October 31, 2008, from http://www.liveunited.org/Outcomes/Library/ndpaper.cfm

United Way of America. (2000). *Agency experience with outcome measures: Survey findings*. Retrieved October 31, 2008, from http://www.liveunited.org/Outcomes/Resources/What/upload/agencyom.pdf

Vascelloaro, J. (2007). Social networking goes professional. *Wall Street Journal*, pp. D1-D2.

Verclas, K. (2007). *Mobile phones in human rights reporting*. Retrieved November 2, 2008, from http://mobileactive.org/mobile-phones-human-rights-reporting

Vince, R. (1998). Behind and beyond Kolb's learning cycle. *Journal of Management Education, 22*(3), 304–319. doi:10.1177/105256299802200304

Vincent, A., & Shepherd, J. (1998). Experiences in teaching Middle East politics via Internet-based role-play simulations. *Journal of Interactive Media in Education, 98*(11), 1–35.

Vitaliev, D. (2007). *Digital security and privacy for human rights defenders.* Front Line Defenders. Retrieved November 7, 2008, from http://www.frontlinedefenders.org/manual/en/esecman/

Volery, T., & Lord, D. (2000). Critical success factors in online education. *International Journal of Educational Management, 14*(5), 216–223. doi:10.1108/09513540010344731

Vygotsky, L. S. (1978). *Mind and society: The development of higher psychological processes.* Cambridge, MA: Harvard University Press.

W3C. (2005). *Leading the Web to its full potential.* Retrieved August 19, 2005, from http://www.w3.org

WAI. (2002). *Web Access Initiative (WAI): Five primary areas of work.* Retrieved January 3, 2006, from http://www.w3.org/WAI

Walker, R. (2004). The hidden (in plain sight) persuaders. *The New York Times Magazine,* p. 69.

Walsh, G., Gwinner, K. P., & Swanson, S. R. (2004). What makes mavens tick? Exploring the motives of market mavens' initiation of information diffusion. *Journal of Consumer Marketing, 21*(2), 109–122. doi:10.1108/07363760410525678

Walters, W. (2000). *Unemployment and government.* Cambridge, UK: Cambridge University Press.

Weaver, C. (2005). Human rights group arms activists with video cameras. *Voice of America.* Retrieved November 2, 2008, from http://www.voanews.com/english/archive/2005-12/2005-12-09-voa98.cfm

Webdriven. (2007). *Delta Airlines employees make travel videos. Webdriven.* Retrieved September 1, 2008, from

http://www.bewebdriven.com/blog/whats-hot/viral-travel-videos-delta-airlines.php

Wehbi, S. (2009). Deconstructing motivations. Challenging international social work placements. *International Social Work, 52*(1), 48–59. doi:10.1177/0020872808097750

Weizenbaum, J. (1984). *Computer power and human reason.* London: Penguin.

Wellman, B., Haase, A. Q., Witte, J., & Hampton, K. (2001, November). Does the Internet increase, decrease, or supplement social capital? Social networks, participation, and community commitment. *The American Behavioral Scientist, 45*(3), 436–456. doi:10.1177/00027640121957286

Wellman, B., Salaff, J., Dimitrova, D., Garton, L., Gulia, M., & Haythornthwaite, C. (1996). Computer networks as social networks: Collaborative work, telework, and virtual community. *Annual Review of Sociology, 22,* 213–238. doi:10.1146/annurev.soc.22.1.213

Wellman, B., Salaff, J., Dimitrova, D., Garton, L., Gulia, M., & Haythornthwaite, C. (1996). Computer networks as social networks: Collaborative work, telework, and virtual community. *Annual Review of Sociology, 22,* 213–238. doi:10.1146/annurev.soc.22.1.213

Wenger, E. (1998). *Communities of practice: Learning, meaning, and identity.* Cambridge, UK: Cambridge University Press.

West, J. (2008). Authentic voices: Utilising audio and video within an online virtual community. *Social Work Education, 27*(6), 665–670. doi:10.1080/02615470802201762

Westbrook, R. A. (1987). Product consumption-based affective responses and post purchase processes. *JMR, Journal of Marketing Research, 24*(3), 258–270. doi:10.2307/3151636

Weyker, S. (2002). The ironies of information technology. In A. Brysk (Ed.), *Globalization and human rights* (pp. 115-132). Berkeley, CA: University of California Press.

White, M., & Dorman, S. M. (2001). Receiving social support online: Implications for health education. *Health Education Research, 16*(6), 693–707. doi:10.1093/her/16.6.693

Whitmore, E., & Wilson, M. (1997). Accompanying the process: Social work and international development practice. *International Social Work, 40*(1), 57–74. doi:10.1177/002087289704000105

Wholey, J. S. (2004). Evaluability assessment. In J. S. Wholey, H. P. Hatry, & K. E. Newcomer (Eds.), *Handbook of practical program evaluation*. San Francisco: Jossey Bass.

Wholey, J. S., Hatry, H. P., & Newcomer, K. E. (2004). *Handbook of practical program evaluation*. San Francisco: Jossey Bass.

Whyte, R. (2005). *Australia's artful dodger: Centrelink exposed*. Wollongong, Australia: Welfare Watchdog.

Wikipedia. (2008, October 1). *List of social networking websites*. Retrieved October 1, 2008, from http://en.wikipedia.org/wiki/List_of_social_networking_websites

Wikipedia: About. (2008, August 30). *Wikipedia, the free encyclopedia*. Retrieved September, 8, 2008, from http://en.wikipedia.org/wiki/Wikipedia:About

Williams, R., & Edge, D. (1996). The social shaping of technology. In W. H. Dutton (Ed.), *Information and communication technologies: Visions and realities* (pp. 53-68). Oxford, UK: Oxford University Press.

Wills, S., & McDougall, A. (2008). Reusability of online role-play as learning objects or learning designs. In L. Lockyer, S. Bennett, S. Agostinho, & B. Harper (Eds.), *Handbook of Research on learning design and learning objects: Issues, applications and technologies*. Hershey, PA: Information Science Reference.

Wilson, B. G. (1995). Metaphors for instruction: Why we talk about learning environments. *Educational Technology, 35*(5), 25–30.

Wolfson, G. K., Magnuson, C. W., & Marsom, G. (2005). Changing the nature of the discourse: Teaching field seminars online. *Journal of Social Work Education, 41*(2), 355–361.

Wood, W., Behling, R., & Haugen, S. (2006). Blogs and business: Opportunities and headaches. *Issues in Information Systems, 7*(2), 314.

World Health Organisation. (1998). *Learning together to work together for health*. Geneva, Switzerland: World Health Organisation.

HURIDOCS. (2007). *Harnessing the power of information – the importance of standards*. Retrieved October 20, 2008.

Young, M., Schrader, P. G., & Zheng, D. (2006). Mmogs as learning environments: An ecological journey into Quest Atlantis and The Sims Online. *Innovate, 2*(4).

Zemsky, R., & Massy, W. F. (2004). *Thwarted innovation: What happened to e-learning and why*. West Chester, PA: The Learning Alliance.

Zhao, C., & Kuh, G. D. (2004). Added value: Learning communities and student engagement. *Research in Higher Education, 45*(2), 115–138. doi:10.1023/B:RIHE.0000015692.88534.de

Zuckerman, E. (2004). *Blog coaches for human rights*. Retrieved November 2, 2008, from http://www.worldchanging.com/archives/001439.html

About the Contributors

Jennifer Martin is an associate professor of social work at RMIT University (Melbourne, Australia). She is currently the coordinator of teaching in mental health and conflict management and mediation at both undergraduate and post graduate levels in the School of Global Studies, Social Science and Planning. She has qualifications in social work and post-secondary education and has participated in training programs on ICT, and has considerable practice experience in these areas. In addition to her research into Web accessibility, human computer interaction, and instructional technologies she has published several articles and conference papers on the design and use of ICT tools to enhance human services education and practice in the *Journal of Computer Assisted Learning*, the *International Journal of E-Learning* and the *Journal of Rehabilitation Research and Development*.

Linette Hawkins is the undergraduate social work field education coordinator at RMIT University (Australia) with research and practice experience is in the flexible delivery of education. She has a Bachelor of Arts, Diploma of Social Studies, and Graduate Diplomas in applied sociology and public policy and a Certificate of Adult Education. She was awarded an RMIT Certificate for Scholarship of Teaching for her work in flexible delivery. Much of her research and writing has been on professional expertise and multidisciplinary collaboration, particularly in community development and field education. This is within local, national and global contexts. Research interests, particularly participatory action research, include flexible delivery of tertiary education, teamwork and multidisciplinary collaboration, standards for practice, professional expertise, field education and human services labor markets.

* * *

Poline Bala is a Senior Lecturer at the Faculty of Social Sciences, University Malaysia Sarawak (UNIMAS). She is also the Deputy Director of Centre of Excellence in Rural Informatics at University Malaysia Sarawak. Her area of interest and research includes examining the impacts of political boundary lines on the formation of cultural, political and economic units at the border regions of Borneo. Most recently her research explores the role of Information Communication Technologies (ICT) on development activities in rural Sarawak. Looking specifically at the e-Bario project which she and a team of researchers initiated in the Kelabit Highlands of Sarawak in 1998, she examines social change that is connected to the use of ICT in Bario of Central Borneo.

Marion Brown, PhD, Assistant Professor, is the Field Education Research Faculty at the Dalhousie School of Social Work in Halifax, Nova Scotia, Canada. Dr. Brown teaches both graduate and undergraduate social work courses both on campus and online and has presented at national and international conferences regarding field education design and delivery across both formats. Within a team of researchers at Dalhousie, Dr. Brown is currently researching the degree to which the accessibility of online social work educational programs is contributing to increased diversity among both the social work student population and the social work practitioner population in the Canadian context.

Sally Burford is a Senior Lecturer in the Faculty of Arts and Design at the University of Canberra. She is the course proponent for the new Master of Information Studies and will convene the new course when it commences in 2009. She brings considerable experience in teaching in the online environment to this new fully online course. Sally managed an online education unit at Flinders University and provided educational design expertise to teaching academics. Her career incorporates 10 years of academic life in the School of Information Studies at Charles Sturt University and a year teaching in Malaysia.

David P. Colachico is a Professor and the Director of Azusa Pacific University's (Azusa, California, USA) Office of Faculty Development. Colachico's previous experience at APU was as a professor in the Department of Teacher Education/Special Education Programs. Colachico earned his doctorate in the area of Curriculum and Instruction from Texas A&M University (College Station, Texas, USA). He has extensive education and training in the field of Special Education as well as K-12 education, and has also served as an educational administrator at the national, state, and local levels. Colachico has been involved in the development and teaching of several courses online for the past ten years. Colachico is the author of several books and articles including "Stress and Children with Disabilities," a chapter in Children and Stress: Understanding and Helping (ACEI, 2001), a book written in reaction to the attack on the World Trade Center on 9/11.

Lesley Cooper is currently Dean of the Faculty of Social Work at Wilfrid Laurier University, Southern Ontario. Canada. Prior to this, she was Head of the School of Social Administration and Social Work at Flinders University in Adelaide. She enjoys teaching, research and writing. Currently, she is working on university and community partnerships. This includes collaboration with the Centre for Family Medicine focusing on interprofessional care for older people with early memory impairment. In conjunction with several agencies she is involved in a bridging program for migrants coming to Canada with professional qualifications in the human services. She is working with Athena Software to develop practical applications of case management software in practicum programs and in the human services.

Kathy Douglas is a lawyer and has worked at RMIT University for a number of years lecturing in law and mediation. She has taught into a variety of different programs servicing the human services sector. She is presently part of the teaching team for the Juris Doctor program at RMIT. She is a mediator with the Department of Justice, Dispute Settlement Centre of Victoria and has conducted mediation training for government and community groups. She has published in a variety of areas including online learning with a focus upon online role-plays.

Dana Fox is currently Director of Business Development with Athena Software, responsible for global sales and business development activities in social services and behavioural health sectors including agencies, funders, government and educational institutions. Dana has researched the needs of over 3000 social service organizations in North America, the United Kingdom, Europe, Caribbean and Asia Pacific. This research documents the evolution of the global social service infrastructure requirements for agencies, funders and government organizations. Dana also lectures on sales performance and business development using Web 3 technology and solution selling skills at the Accelerator Center for Management of Technology and Wilfrid Laurier University. Career highlights include senior marketing management experience in diverse industries: Director, Sales and Customer Service Fuji Graphics Canada; General Manager, VP Sales and Marketing Zenon Environmental Corporation; Regional Manager, Ontario CIBC Finance Inc.; National Sales Manager, Polaroid Canada Ltd.; and Manager, Franchise and Motorsports Events at Uniroyal Goodrich.

Christine Greenhow is a postdoctoral scholar in the Department of Curriculum and Instruction at the University of Minnesota. She earned her doctorate in education from Harvard University. Dr. Greenhow is the recipient of the University of Minnesota's Outstanding Postdoctoral Scholar Award for extraordinary scholarly achievement, 2008-2009. She is the principal investigator on the Youth and Social Media study funded by the Knight Foundation and founding chair of the Social Networks Research Collaborative (www.socialnetresearch.org). Her research explores issues of learning, teaching, literacy, and collaboration in online environments such as social network sites and technology integration in formal and informal learning contexts. Her work has been featured in local, national, and international news media. For more information about her work see: http://www.cgreenhow.org

Lisa Harris is a lecturer in social policy at RMIT University. She has over twenty years experience in the Information Technology industry, development education, community development, social work and social research. For the last seven years she has worked as a consultant to the community and education sectors, providing policy development, staff supervision, process design and facilitation, training, community sector program design, research and analysis. Her current research interests include the significance of community for students studying online, the social and cultural implications of new technologies, the use of research by the community sector to influence social policy and improving the quality of teaching and learning in a University setting.

Paul Henman is senior lecturer in social policy at The University of Queensland, Brisbane, Australia. He holds degrees in computer science and sociology. His main research interest is on the nexus between social policy, public administration, and information technology. He is internationally recognized for his social theoretical examination of e-government. He also maintains an active applied social policy research agenda on the costs of raising children, which have contributed to major policy reform in Australia. His publications include *Administering Welfare Reform: International Transformations in Welfare Governance* (Policy, 2006), which was edited with Menno Fenger, and *Governing Electronically: E-government and the reconfiguration of public administration, policy and power* (Palgrave Macmillan, 2009).

Belinda Johnson is an Associate Lecturer in Social Science at RMIT. She has experience teaching social and political theory in an online environment. Her recent writing addresses online role plays and the pedagogical considerations that arise from this. She is currently part of a research project investigating the potential of developing and undertaking complex role plays online. Her research interests include youth, gender, higher education and technology.

Sandra Jones is the Associate Professor Employment Relations at RMIT. She received an Australian government award for her outstanding contribution to student learning through her innovative design of virtual situated learning environments. She links student globally using these environments to enable students to learn by experience in order to prepare graduates with the employability skills they will need in the increasingly ambiguous global knowledge world of the twenty-first century. She also works extensively with industry to assist the use of these virtual environments as industry training initiatives. She has been awarded a number of Visiting Fellowships to universities in the UK, Canada, USA and within Australia.

Hyunjung Kim is a third year doctoral candidate in the Department of Communication at the State University of New York at Buffalo. Her research interests focus mostly on persuasion strategies in Computer-Mediated-Communication (CMC). Current projects include how online users perceive the referral messages from online friends, and how the strength of social ties and source credibility influence persuasion effect of referral message in CMC.

John Lannon has over 15 years experience working as a software designer/developer, mostly in the telecommunications industry. He now works with the human rights NGO *Aim for human rights* on their human rights impact assessment programme, and is a PhD candidate at Leeds Metropolitan University (UK) where he is studying information management in human rights movements. He has lectured at the Universiy of Limerick (Ireland), and the University of the Witwatersrand and Rhodes University (South Africa). He has also been a human rights activist for over 20 years, and has campaigned on a wide range of issues over that time. He served on the board of the Irish Section of Amnesty International for six years and is a director of several non-profit and charitable organisations, including Soweto Connection which helps communities in South Africa cope with HIV/AIDS.

Elspeth McKay is a Senior Lecturer/Researcher in the School of Business IT at the RMIT University, Australia. Her PhD is in Computer Science and Information Systems, from Deakin University, Geelong, Australia. Elspeth also holds further qualifications in Instructional Design, Computer Education and Business Information Systems. Her work involves developing specialist e-Learning tools implemented through rich internet applications; including: ARPS – an advanced repurposing pilot system, COGNI-WARE – a multi-modal e-Learning framework, GEMS – a global eMuseum System, eWRAP – Electronic work readiness awareness programme, EASY – Educational/academic (skills) screening for the young, offering enhanced accessibility through touch screen technologies. Over the last decade Dr McKay has published extensively in the research fields of HCI and educational technology. In recognition of her contribution to the professional practice of information systems research, she was elected as a Fellow of the Australian Computer Society (ACS).

Supriya Pattanayak has her qualifications from the Tata Institute of Social Sciences, Mumbai (MA), the National Institute of Mental Health and Neuro Sciences, Bangalore (MPhil) and RMIT University, Australia (PhD). She has extensive teaching, research and policy experience and her research interest is in the field of gender and development issues, and social work pedagogy in different contexts. She has experience of working in small and large NGOs, multilateral agencies (UNHCR), bilateral agencies (DFID), federal and state governments and Universities in India and Australia. In her present role as State Representative (Orissa), Department for International Development India (British High Commission), she works collaboratively with various development partners such as National and State Governments, other multilateral (World Bank, UNDP, UNFPA, UNICEF, WHO, WFP) and bilateral (DANIDA) agencies, International NGOs and civil society organisations in pursuance of harmonization of development efforts and achievement of the millennium development goals.

Dennis Perry pioneered information systems for the Victorian State Government and the Australian Labor Party. He worked on the introduction of Freedom of Information in Victoria in 1982 and was responsible for connecting the Premier's Office in Victoria to the Internet. In 1989 Joan Kirner became the first State Premier with an Internet e-mail address. With the change of government in 1992, Dr Perry left the Victorian Government. He started tekniche in 1993 to continue a pattern of innovation in ICT at a national level. The ALP's website, www.alp.org.au was the first political website in the world with a properly registered Internet domain name. His website is http://www.tekniche.com.au.

Beth Robelia is the founder of Kitchen Table Learning a consulting firm in St. Paul, Minnesota. She earned her Ph.D. in Curriculum and Instruction at the University of Minnesota concentrating on STEM education. Her background as a classroom teacher and tutor shapes her research which focuses on experiential and informal learning as well as contexts of learning. She has completed research on how focusing on environmental topics can enhance interest in chemistry. She is currently researching how environmental knowledge is related to behavior and how children's play choices impact STEM skills.

Michael A. Stefanone is a faculty member in the Department of Communication at the State University of New York at Buffalo. His research focuses on the intersection of people, organizations and technology. His current research explores personality differences that influence how people position themselves within social and task networks over time, and how people's social context influences technology adoption and use in the context of Web2.0. He has published in the *International Journal of Human-Computer Interaction, Computer Supported Collaborative Learning, Behavior and Information Technology*, and the *Journal of Computer-Mediated Communication*, among others.

Diane Stanley-Horn is a founder of Athena Software (www.AthenaSoftware.net) with eight years of experience working with human services organizations around the world to implement case management software. Diane is keenly interested in using technology to empower organizations through easing administrative burdens, facilitating the coordination, communication and supervision of service delivery and enhancing an organization's ability to demonstrate the benefits of those services to their clients and communities. Diane received a B.Sc. from Wilfrid Laurier University in 1995, a M.Sc. from the University of Guelph in 1999, and is currently completing a PhD at the University of Guelph, Ontario, Canada as a Natural Sciences and Engineering Research Council of Canada (NSERC) scholar. Diane's experience is rounded by many years of tutoring, volunteer work and University level teaching experience.

Index